Creatures of Empire

Creatures of Empire

HOW DOMESTIC ANIMALS TRANSFORMED EARLY AMERICA

Virginia DeJohn Anderson

OXFORD
UNIVERSITY PRESS
2004

OXFORD
UNIVERSITY PRESS

Oxford   New York
Auckland   Bangkok   Buenos Aires   Cape Town   Chennai
Dar es Salaam   Delhi   Hong Kong   Istanbul   Karachi   Kolkata
Kuala Lumpur   Madrid   Melbourne   Mexico City   Mumbai   Nairobi
São Paulo   Shanghai   Taipei   Tokyo   Toronto

Published by Oxford University Press, Inc.
198 Madison Avenue, New York, New York 10016
www.oup.com

Library of Congress Cataloging-in-Publication Data
Anderson, Virginia DeJohn.
Creatures of Empire : how domestic animals transformed early America / Virginia
DeJohn Anderson.
p. cm.
Includes bibliographical references and index.
ISBN 0-19-515860-1
1. Livestock—United States—History.
2. Livestock—Social aspects—United States—History.
3. Human-animal relationships—United States—History.
4. Indians, Treatment of.
5. United States—Colonial period, ca. 1600–1775.
6. America—Colonization—Social Aspects.
I. Title.

SF51.A655 2004
636'.0973—dc222004043401

Portions of this book were published, in different form, in the following:
"King Philip's Herds: Indians, Colonists, and the Problem of Livestock in Early
        New England," *William and Mary Quarterly,* 3rd ser., 51 (1994): 601–24.
"Animals into the Wilderness: The Development of Livestock Husbandry in the
        Seventeenth-Century Chesapeake," *William and Mary Quarterly,* 3rd ser.,
        59 (2002): 377–408.
"Chickwallop and the Beast: Indian Responses to European Animals in Early New
        England," in Colin G. Calloway and Neal Salisbury, eds., *Reinterpreting New
        England Indians and the Colonial Experience.* Publications of the Colonial
        Society of Massachusetts. Boston, 2003.

Design by planettheo.com

9 8 7 6 5 4 3 2 1
Printed in the United States of America on acid-free paper

for fred

Contents

Acknowledgments

When I began this book, I had no idea what its final shape would be. I have often felt as if I were trying to assemble an exceedingly intricate jigsaw puzzle, with several key pieces missing and no box cover to indicate what the completed picture should look like. Fortunately, like many puzzle-solvers and most authors, I received a great deal of assistance as I toiled away on the project. Some people helped me to decide where a certain piece of evidence might go; others urged me to stand back now and then and try to figure out the dimensions of the whole picture. Still others simply encouraged me to keep at it. I am pleased to be able at last to extend my deepest thanks to all.

I received institutional and financial support at several crucial stages. A fellowship from the Charles Warren Center at Harvard University, supplemented with photocopying funds from the University of Colorado's Graduate Committee on the Arts and Humanities, helped at the outset of the research. I wrote much of the first draft with fellowship support from the American Council of Learned Societies. And I am grateful to Todd Gleeson and Philip DiStefano, Dean of Arts and Sciences and Provost, respectively, of the University of Colorado at Boulder, for the precious gift of time that allowed me to complete the book. The staff at the Interlibrary Loan Office at Norlin Library also provided frequent and timely assistance.

Several scholars have given generously of their time, energy, and expertise to read portions of the manuscript, sometimes more than once, and offer wise advice and useful criticism. Jon Coleman, Vine Deloria, James Drake, Thomas Field, and Marjorie McIntosh approached the work from a variety of perspectives, making valuable suggestions for improvement. So too did the anonymous readers of those parts of the book published in preliminary form in other venues. James Merrell and Daniel Richter not only provided judicious criticism of the manuscript but also, through the example of their own scholarship, set a high standard for the rest of us who seek to understand the complicated history of intercultural encounters in early America. I thank them all for their help, and take responsibility for any errors or shortcomings that remain.

Many friends and colleagues have offered steady encouragement over the years, listening with remarkable patience whenever I rambled on about this project and my frustrations with it. Gloria and Jack Main served as models of scholarly integrity and unstinting friendship; I wish I had finished the book in time for Jack to read it. Peter Boag, Constance Clark, Steven Epstein, Robert Ferry, Julie Greene, Martha and Bob Hanna, Christopher Jedrey, Susan Kent, Scott Miller, Mark and Sharon Pittenger, and Jon Roberts are no less deserving of my deepest gratitude for their advice and moral support. I should also thank the countless graduate and undergraduate students in my classes at the University of Colorado, captive audiences who have at least feigned interest in my work and humored me whenever I told stories about livestock when I should have been talking about something else. In his own inimitable way, Bernard Bailyn has supported this book from its inception, and I hope he agrees that there is some "news" in its pages.

Two people expertly shepherded the work along the path from manuscript to book. Lisa Adams, of the Garamond Agency, helped me to see the potential lurking within a project that often seemed irremediably diffuse. Susan Ferber wielded her editor's pen with masterful precision, saving readers from digressions and infelicities that I would otherwise have inflicted upon them. I also thank Catherine Humphries for her careful production of the completed manuscript. Proofreaders Jamie Kreiner and Jen Simington did an excellent job, as did Pete Brigaitis and Marie Nuchols with their work on the index.

The book has benefited as well from the wise counsel of two scholars and friends. Susan Jones, my colleague at Colorado, drew upon her dual training as veterinarian and historian to guide me through conceptual difficulties and save me from embarrassing errors. Her steady support has been invaluable. I could blame Barbara DeWolfe for making this book take so many years to produce, but instead I will thank her. Her insight—that I ought to examine the Chesapeake colonies as well as New England—was exactly right. To the extent that the book's value derives from its comparative framework, the credit belongs to Barbara.

Although neither of my parents read a word of the book, they contributed to every page. I hope my mother will read it, and deeply regret that my father did not live long enough to do so. My son Samuel, a kindergartner when I began research, has grown into a patient and generous young man whose love and encouragement sustain me more than he knows. Finally, the dedication of this book is but a small payment on the large debt I owe to my husband, Fred. We never followed through on our plan to make vows to "love, honor, and edit" at our wedding. Nevertheless, our life together has fulfilled the promise of those words more than either of us could have known.

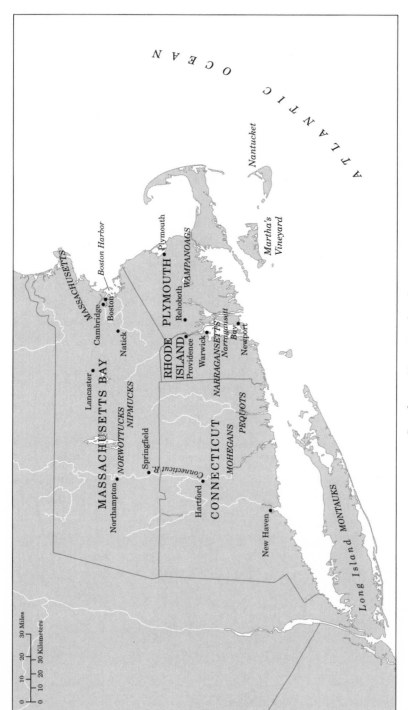

ATLANTIC OCEAN

Nantucket

Martha's Vineyard

MASSACHUSETTS

Boston Harbor

Cambridge ● ● Boston

PLYMOUTH ● Plymouth

Natick ●

Rehoboth ● WAMPANOAGS

Lancaster ●

MASSACHUSETTS BAY

RHODE ISLAND

Providence ●

Warwick ● NARRAGANSETTS

Narragansett Bay

NORWOTTUCKS

NIPMUCKS

Springfield ●

Newport ●

Northampton ● *Connecticut R.*

PEQUOTS

CONNECTICUT

Hartford ●

MOHEGANS

New Haven ●

Long Island MONTAUKS

0   10   20   30 Miles
0   10   20   30 Kilometers

Southern New England

MARYLAND

Delaware
Bay

PATAWOMECKS

Rappahannock R.

Potomac R.

St. Mary's
City

EASTERN
SHORE

RAPPAHANNOCKS

Chesapeake
Bay

POWHATANS

PAMUNKEYS

CHICKAHOMINIES

York R.

ACCOMACKS

VIRGINIA

Jamestown

ATLANTIC
OCEAN

James R.

CHESAPEAKES

| 0 | 10 | 20 | 30 Miles |
| 0 | 10 | 20 | 30 Kilometers |

Tidewater Chesapeake

Seeing Banquo's Ghost

$\mathcal{O}$ne of the oddest historical markers in all of New England can be found in the town of Duxbury, Massachusetts. A simple granite slab, it stands about five feet high and is perhaps two and a half feet wide. It was erected in 1940, shortly after Duxbury citizens observed the tercentenary of their town's founding. Yet the monument does not commemorate Duxbury's beginnings. Nor does it celebrate the achievements of a local notable, note the location of an historic building, or commemorate a battle. The marker instead shows where a fence once stood. Carved into its granite surface are the words: "SITE OF NOOK GATE. HERE A PALISADE WAS ERECTED ACROSS THE NOOK IN 1634. THIS PALISADE WAS A HIGH FENCE TO PREVENT CATTLE FROM STRAYING AND PROBABLY TO KEEP THE INDIANS OUT."

The inscription recalls the familiar proverb about good fences making good neighbors, and yet at the same time it conjures up an unlikely image. The neighbors involved here—Indians, cattle, and (by implication) colonists—are not the typical cast of characters featured in New England histories, let alone on granite monuments. Colonists, of course, appear in force both in histories and on markers, although their fence-building efforts are seldom memorialized. Indians, still scarce on monuments, are at last achieving something like parity in written accounts of New England's past. But cattle? Livestock seldom figure at all in the narrative of colonization, and when they do they usually serve as part of the scenery rather than as historical

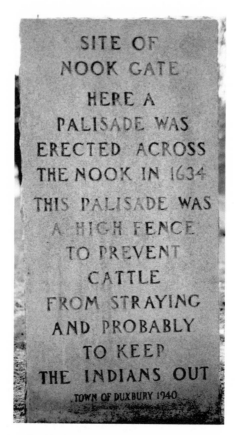

Marker for Nook Gate, Duxbury Massachusetts.
Photograph courtesy of Juan De Zengotita, in author's possession

actors. The Duxbury marker may be the only monument to mention their presence in all of New England.

If only one such memorial had to exist, there would be no better place for it than Duxbury. For all intents and purposes, cattle determined when and where the town would be established. Settlers in nearby Plymouth first broached the subject of creating a new community as early as 1632, once they noticed their proliferating herds overtaxing the local supply of pasture. Several miles up the coast anxious farmers found the open meadows they needed. First a trickle, then a small stream of families made their way with livestock and other belongings to the site of what eventually became Duxbury.[1] The fence that these farmers built in 1634 to protect their animals was most likely a makeshift post-and-rail barricade rather than a sturdy "palisade." It almost certainly failed to keep cattle from straying. During the seventeenth century, New Englanders frequently drove livestock to "nooks" or small peninsulas and tried to confine them by fencing off the narrow entryway. They trusted, often in vain, that the animals would not swim around the barrier.

It is equally unlikely that the fence kept "the Indians out," or was even meant to do so. Colonists in this part of New England, at least during the 1630s, were not in the habit of keeping their distance from Indians. English settlers traded with local Wampanoags, hired their labor, and encountered them often in town and in the woods. Plymouth colonists and Wampanoags had formed a military and diplomatic alliance. While it would be going too far to suggest that the two groups delighted in each other's company, they were not necessarily antagonists. That unfortunate relationship would come soon enough, but discord did not characterize their encounters as early as 1634. Like neighbors everywhere, Indians and colonists were learning how to get along with one another.[2]

The inscription on Duxbury's monument may not be accurate in every particular, but by linking the experiences of Indians, colonists, and cattle it speaks to a larger truth. Historical narratives usually attribute the course of events to the conscious decisions of human actors, yet this is not always the way in which history itself unfolded. Sometimes other kinds of actors were involved, driven by instinct rather than reason. Such was the case in seventeenth-century America, where the lives of Indians and colonists alike were often shaped in unexpected ways by the activities of animals. This book, by incorporating livestock into the history of early America, restores an important element of contingency to the narrative, making it less familiar but no less compelling. It argues that leaving livestock out of the story of early American history is a little like staging *Macbeth* without the scenes in which Banquo's ghost appears. The ghost has no speaking role, but it is nevertheless central to the plot. The same point applies to the part played by livestock in the era of English colonization.

Unlike Banquo's ghost, however, livestock appear in almost every scene. Virtually every body of sources pertaining to seventeenth-century English colonization, from local records to descriptive pamphlets to treaties with Indians, mentions these creatures, often with astonishing frequency. If the sheer number of references in the historical record offered an accurate measure of a topic's significance, one could easily argue that a history of livestock in colonial America is long overdue. But the interpretative challenge of such a project lies in assembling countless documentary fragments into a story that makes a case for the animals' importance, not just their ubiquity. The likely outcome would be less a history of livestock than a history of people with livestock in it.

Creatures of Empire began as an effort to understand why references to livestock appeared so often in documents related to early American history and how paying attention to those references might affect our understanding of the process of colonization. Like the Duxbury memorial, the book introduces three sets of actors: livestock, Indians, and colonists. In contrast to the point of the monument's inscription, however, the book argues that these people and animals shaped the course of colonial history because of their interactions, not their separation from one another. Its story is set not just in New England, but also in the Chesapeake colonies of Virginia and Maryland during the seventeenth century, an era when the most profound encounters occurred and when patterns of behavior emerged that would influence the conduct of generations to come. The regional comparison amplifies the significance of the narrative, for its central findings cannot be characterized as peculiar to only one group of colonists. By following developments in New England and the Chesapeake, the book reveals how a common English background was refracted into distinct colonial experiences that, despite manifest differences, ultimately converged to reach the same bitter end.

This is by no means the first history to posit that animals can play an important role in human affairs. For several decades, environmental historians have taken animals seriously as agents of historical change, particularly in the era of European exploration and expansion. Beginning with the seminal work of Alfred Crosby, numerous studies have accorded livestock an instrumental role in helping Europeans to establish colonies in other parts of the world. Especially in North and South America, the success of those imperial endeavors depended on the migrations of people *and* animals.[3]

Central to many of these narratives is an examination of the ways in which livestock helped to reconfigure New World environments to suit European purposes. By competing with local fauna, clearing away underbrush, and converting native grasses into marketable meat, imported animals assisted in the transformation of forests into farmland. These changes alone sufficed to disrupt the lives of native peoples; by contributing to erosion, altering microclimates, and introducing other ecological shifts, livestock compounded the difficulties that Indians faced after colonization began. Environmental histories thus bring Indians, colonists, and cattle together as participants in a common story, but they do so in a distinctive fashion. Because livestock tend to be discussed in terms of the ecological alterations they produced, the effects of their presence on people are largely indirect, mediated by the environment itself.

This book necessarily incorporates the important findings of such studies, but moves the story in a new direction by exploring direct interactions between humans and livestock. It argues that the animals not only produced changes in the land but also in the hearts and minds and behavior of the peoples who dealt with them. And sooner or later, everyone—Indians and colonists—had to deal with livestock. Despite their status as domesticated creatures, the animals were never wholly under human control. Sometimes they acted in ways that their owners neither predicted nor desired, provoking responses that ran the gamut from apology to aggression. To a remarkable extent, the reactions of Indians and colonists to problems created by livestock became a reliable indicator of the tenor of their relations with one another.

In its insistence that Indian peoples were active participants in the story of colonization, this book draws upon a wealth of recent scholarship that has emphasized precisely this point.[4] Such work places intercultural encounters securely at the center of early American history. Just because the historical record is tipped heavily in favor of the colonists, Indians cannot be relegated to supporting roles. Inspired by their own vision of what a colonized America could be, Indians took the initiative as often as the English did to try to shape the world in which they all lived. If disparities in the documentary record pose one obstacle to a full appreciation of Indians' efforts, an equally formidable problem emerges merely from knowing from the outset how the story will end. No account of Anglo-Indian relations in early America can avoid acknowledging that the English ultimately predominated. Constructing the story to reach that end as directly as possible, however, risks converting a tragedy into a melodrama. Such a narrative strategy ignores the actors' attempts to explore alternatives that did not succeed and fails to ask why events turned out as they did. Perhaps the greatest challenge in composing *Creatures of Empire* lay not in reconstructing what did happen but in imagining what might have been. The conclusion of this book may surprise few readers, but the path it takes to reach that end is anything but direct or predictable.

Since English colonists—unlike livestock and Indians—have always been regarded as key historical actors, it may seem superfluous to reiterate the point here. But colonists have typically been portrayed in their roles as town founders, magistrates, preachers, soldiers, and even parents. Only rarely do they appear as farmers, the role that occupied more of their time and energy than any other. This was the reason why they brought livestock to the New World in the first place, however, and thus it is central to this story. *How* they farmed turns out to be particularly important, for agricultural practices largely determined the circumstances under which Indians, colonists, and cattle encountered one another. Indians farmed too, but did so without domestic animals—a difference that turned out to be far more significant than anyone could have imagined.

Agriculture has never been exclusively an economic activity, but has always reflected cultural assumptions distinctive to particular groups of farmers.[5] Colonial America was no exception in this regard. Although Indians and colonists both farmed, their agricultural activities were embedded in quite different cultural contexts. Indians and colonists did not agree on whether men or women should till the land, how to define property rights, or how humans ought to interact with animals and the natural world in general—all issues that related to agriculture but had broader implications as well. Colonization, by bringing these two sets of assumptions into contact, produced changes in both. Within a few short years, Indians and colonists neither farmed nor thought about animals and farming in quite the same way as they had done before they became neighbors.

Further complicating matters, the English characterized their own livestock-based farming methods as "improvement" and incorporated this notion into their imperial designs. Introducing Indians to civilized ways (which included livestock husbandry) became a principal goal of colonization, and colonial farmers were to help achieve this result through the strength of their example. Such a plan required both the appropriation of land for colonists' farms and the transformation of native villages to make them accord with English models. That transformation failed to occur to the extent that colonists wished, but the appropriation of land proceeded apace. Before long, the expansion of livestock-based agriculture ceased being a model for Indian improvement and instead served almost exclusively as a pretext for conquest, a very different expression of the cultural impact of distinct farming practices.

The significance of the narrative that follows is paradoxically rooted in its preoccupation with details of life so ordinary that they have rarely been considered the stuff of history. Books about colonization in early America more typically dwell on themes of politics, trade, religion, demography, and warfare. Without discounting the importance of these topics (for each has a place here) and with no intention of offering a monocausal explanation for complex events, this book argues that sometimes mundane decisions about how to feed pigs or whether or not to build a fence also could affect the course of history. Three groups comprise the cast of characters. The first is the Algonquian-speaking Indian peoples who lived in the New England and eastern Chesapeake regions. Although this language group in fact comprised dozens of separate bands occupying lands stretching from present-day Nova Scotia to North Carolina, as members of the same linguistic family Algonquian speakers descended from common ancestors and shared cultural characteristics. The other two groups are the English colonists who arrived during the seventeenth century, and the livestock they brought with them to the New World. The book's plot traces their complex interactions as the two immigrant groups attempted to make a place for themselves in America and the Indians tried to retain some hold on the places that had always been theirs. As events turned out, livestock—the one set of characters incapable of making plans—proved fully capable of upsetting the plans of all of the people around them.

Because how people think about animals influences how they interact with them, the book begins with a pair of chapters that explore Indian and English approaches to nonhuman creatures. The comparison reveals that, although the two ways of thinking were not utterly distinct, the differences between them were significant enough to complicate the myriad encounters between Indians and colonists that involved animals. Native understandings of animals fit into a larger set of conceptions about the world that drew no sharp boundary between natural and supernatural realms and did not dictate the subordination of nonhuman creatures. Some animals possessed spiritual power, obliging the humans who hunted or otherwise dealt with them to show respect. Indians thus conceived of their relationship with animals in terms of balance and reciprocity, not domination, let alone ownership. But these ideas about animals, derived in good part from the Indians' experience with wild creatures, ran counter to the views of English settlers whose principal contact was with domesticated beasts. Christian orthodoxy affirmed the colonists' practical experience of dominion over animals that, in the case of livestock, was further reinforced by the animals' legal status as property. For Indians and colonists alike, encounters with new sorts of animals—whether English livestock or New World fauna—tested longstanding habits of thought. That members of both groups initially placed strange creatures into familiar conceptual categories was hardly surprising; whether they would be willing over time to adjust their views to accommodate alternative ways of thinking emerges as one of the main themes of this book.

The three chapters that make up the book's second section move the narrative from the realm of thought to questions of practice. Since England's experience with livestock husbandry was so widespread and stretched so far back in time, inhabitants could not help but see it as normative. Thus when proponents of overseas colonization argued in favor of an agricultural foundation for the new settlements, they implicitly included livestock husbandry as an integral part of the package. In so doing, they formulated plans that encompassed not only the introduction of an English-style agrarian regime but also the imposition of English cultural expectations. Raising livestock was not simply a way to make a living. Ideally animal husbandry inculcated a set of behaviors, all directed toward the efficient exercise of human dominion over lesser creatures, that manifested—at least in their own eyes—the colonists' cultural superiority.

Assumptions about animal husbandry insinuated themselves into England's imperial ideology in subtle ways and influenced much more than agricultural practice itself. Expressing an opinion based on their English experience, colonists asserted that farming with animals was one important hallmark of a civilized society. They claimed that using domestic animals to improve the land helped to legitimize English rights to New World territory. By bringing livestock across the Atlantic, colonists believed that they provided the means to realize America's potential, pursuing a goal that Indians who lacked domestic animals had failed to accomplish. English settlers employed assumptions about the cultural advantages associated with animal husbandry to construct a standard against which to measure the deficiencies they detected in native societies and to prescribe a remedy for their amelioration. Indians who learned how to keep livestock, colonists asserted, would grow in prosperity, advance along the path toward civility, and eventually convert to a Christian faith that considered human dominion over animals to be divinely ordained.

Colonists who extolled the benefits of animal husbandry, whether to defend English claims to New World territory or to exhort Indians to change their ways, made one critical—and, as it turned out, erroneous—assumption. They took it for granted that they would be able to manage their livestock with the same care and attention that they were accustomed to using in England, thereby demonstrating the qualities of stewardship that made animal husbandry a civilized endeavor in the first place. But colonists had no idea how fully their energies would be absorbed in clearing land, planting crops (especially tobacco in the Chesapeake), building houses, and working at all the other tasks necessary to establish new towns and plantations. With scarcely any time or labor to spare for their animals, they had to let livestock take care of themselves. This highly attenuated free-range style of husbandry (which operated year-round in the Chesapeake and seasonally in New England) undermined the colonists' assertions about this aspect of their own civility even as it presented neighboring Indians with a whole set of problems that lacked easy answers.

The colonists' free-range husbandry guaranteed that Indians would encounter livestock at almost every turn, not just in English settlements but also along the shoreline, in the woods, and in their own cornfields. More often than not, those encounters resulted in damage to Indian property, to the offending creatures, or to both. To prevent minor disputes from escalating into major altercations, Indians and colonists spent considerable time and effort trying to figure out what to do with animals no one could really control. The significance of negotiations about livestock, however, extended far beyond the immediate problems they tried to address. The two chapters comprising the final section of the book argue that Indians and colonists used such deliberations to put forth competing visions of what a colonial society should look like. The fates of animals may have been the ostensible reason for negotiation, but the fates of people hung in the balance.

In other times and in other places, Indians and colonists managed to reach mutually acceptable solutions to their problems on a neutral "middle ground" occupied by both groups but controlled by neither.[6] This was not the case in the Chesapeake or New England, two regions where colonists assumed a dominant position fairly quickly. Creative solutions demanded flexibility from both sides, but in the places examined here, Indians proved far more willing than colonists to adjust their ideas and practices to accommodate the changes that livestock introduced to their world. For the most part, colonists restricted their cooperative efforts to showing Indians how to behave like the English. Yet ironically, the more Indians learned how to build fences or make other concessions, the less satisfied the colonists were with the results. Strengthened by demographic advantage, colonists' intransigence only increased over time. By the third quarter of the seventeenth century, changes that Indians had adopted as parts of a broader strategy for survival struck colonists as unwelcome obstacles to English territorial expansion.

Anxiety clearly contributed to the colonists' stance. Concerned about feeding their growing populations and committed to a style of husbandry that required far more space than they had anticipated, colonists could see no alternative but to appropriate Indian land. They often encouraged livestock to initiate the process by letting them move onto Indian territory prior to formal English acquisition. Native objections to these incursions met with little sympathy. As a result, colonists ensured that their animal property would become frequent targets of Indians' retaliation. By the time that simmering tensions reached the boiling point with King Philip's War in New England and Bacon's Rebellion in Virginia, livestock were sure to be implicated as causes, and to suffer as victims, of humans' unresolved differences.

After these deadly conflicts, victorious colonists saw no reason to change their ways and defeated Indians lacked the power to press the point. Colonial farmers exercised greater supervision over livestock only when they could marshal sufficient labor to do so. In the Chesapeake, improvements in animal husbandry awaited the arrival of substantial numbers of African slaves during the eighteenth century. In New England, reliant upon a home-grown rather than an imported labor force, the transition was even longer in coming: not until the nineteenth century did most farmers begin keeping close track of their livestock. By this point there were few Indians left in either region, and fewer still with their own land, to benefit from the new agricultural regimes.

Yet if livestock had been instrumental in dislodging Indians from their lands during the seventeenth century, the creatures also kept colonists on the move. Time and again, English and other European settlers reenacted their predecessors' experience in seeking new territory on which to support proliferating herds. Moving into Indian country and establishing settlements where free-range husbandry once again prevailed, they set the stage for the same sorts of encounters among Indians, colonists, and animals that had occurred many times before in other places. *Creatures of Empire* is thus not so much a tale strictly bounded by time and place as an archetypal story of colonization and westward expansion. Like the first English colonists, subsequent waves of settlers and their American descendants declared that livestock would improve the land and its native inhabitants, but then deployed the animals to displace the Indians. Once the multiplying creatures overran a tract of land, the process began anew. As the advance guard and a primary motive for this relentless expansion, livestock deserve a place in the narrative of American history. In a real sense these creatures, even more than the colonists who brought them, won the race to claim America as their own.

Part One

Thinking
about Animals

Chapter One

Chickwallop
and the Strange Beast

Indians and Animals in Early America

Traveling near the Connecticut River one winter's day, a group of Norwottuck Indians spied a strange beast floundering helplessly in a drift of snow. They advanced cautiously to take a closer look. Although the beast was about the size of a large deer and had horns, it resembled no animal they had ever seen. Surprised by this unexpected discovery, the Norwottucks returned to their village to seek counsel from their sachem, Chickwallop. The sachem wished to see the strange beast for himself and so accompanied the men back to the place where they had found it. The poor animal still lay in the snow. The Indians lifted it to its feet, but when they let go it quickly collapsed under its own weight. Soon, gaunt and shivering, the mysterious creature died of exposure.[1]

This was how Chickwallop, over 30 years later, recalled his first encounter with an animal easily recognizable to any English colonist. It turned out that the unusual creature was only a young cow that had wandered away from Springfield or one of the other new English settlements in the Connecticut Valley. Chickwallop recounted this story in March of 1669, not to remind his listeners of a time when cows were an unusual sight in New England, but to defend himself against charges that he had killed the beast his men had found struggling in the snow. Jeremy Adams, a colonist who lived further south in the town of Hartford, had come forward to claim the cow as his own and to accuse the Norwottuck sachem of shooting it.

What prompted this charge after so many years is not entirely clear, but it may have stemmed from a property deal gone awry. Adams, a man plagued by financial troubles, had recently argued with Chickwallop over the sale of land. Failing to receive satisfaction in that dispute, Adams may have concocted the new charge in the hope that Chickwallop would have to dispose of land to pay a fine for killing the cow. Whatever his reasons, the colonist did not anticipate that the sachem would be able to muster powerful advocates to defend his innocence. Chickwallop took his case to John Pynchon, Springfield's most influential magistrate, who in turn described the circumstances to Connecticut's governor, John Winthrop, Jr. Both officials, convinced that the sachem was telling the truth, made sure that the charge was dropped.[2]

Magistrates did not always give credit to Indian testimony so readily, particularly when it might be used against colonists.[3] In this case, Pynchon and Winthrop also had to trust the accuracy of Chickwallop's memory of an incident that had occurred over 30 years earlier. Embedded in Pynchon's summary of the story, however, are hints as to why he and Winthrop found it plausible. Although the timing of the encounter with the cow was imprecise—"about thirty-three or thirty-four years ago"—the remainder of Chickwallop's account was full of vivid details. The strange beast was first seen "about seven or eight mile eastward" of Springfield in deep snow. Anyone who had lived through the winters of 1635 and 1636 (including Pynchon and Winthrop) could recall the extraordinarily severe weather in both of those seasons. Chickwallop then described the animal, and especially its horns, with such precision that Pynchon confidently identified it as a two- or three-year-old cow. The Springfield magistrate further suggested that he had heard this story before, possibly from sources other than Chickwallop.[4]

While it is important to note that Pynchon and Winthrop found Chickwallop's story to be credible, the account cannot be separated from its context as evidence in a legal dispute. The circumstances of Adams' accusation and the unpredictable effects of memory undoubtedly influenced the retelling. Yet its significance need not depend on a literal recounting of the truth. The story's value instead lies in the way it summons up a vision of Indians encountering English animals for the first time. At some point in his life, whether outside Springfield in 1635 or in another place and at another time,

Chickwallop saw his first cow—an unforgettable experience for someone who thought he knew what sorts of animals belonged in New England's woods. Presented with an occasion in 1669 to describe such an encounter, the sachem could hardly avoid drawing from his own experience to limn a tale that recaptured something of the wonder of finding a mysterious beast. Along with outlining the bare facts of discovery, Chickwallop hinted at the Norwottucks' mingled feelings of surprise, curiosity, concern, and perhaps even fear. The encounter may or may not have occurred precisely as Chickwallop described it, but in either case his story reflects the sensibility of an observer who remembered what it was like to stumble across a strange animal where it ought not to have been.

If there once was a time when Indians could not identify a cow, there had never been a time when Indians did not know about indigenous American animals. Indeed, animals occupied an exceedingly important place in the Indians' world, and not merely as sources of food. Like people everywhere, Indians understood what it meant to be human in some measure by distinguishing themselves from other creatures.[5] Long before English colonists arrived in America, Indians had developed distinctive ideas about animals and patterns of behavior towards them. Deeply embedded in native cultures, these habits of thought and action necessarily influenced the Indians' reception of the strange beasts that the colonists brought with them.

How native peoples would respond to the arrival of livestock proved to be a matter of some concern to colonists, who regarded such creatures as valuable possessions. Indians had little experience with domesticated animals, and it was not clear whether they would immediately recognize livestock as having a different status from the wild beasts with which they were far more familiar. Many encounters between Indians and livestock, like that between Chickwallop and the cow, occurred without colonists being present to identify the animal and explain its relation to an owner. Such circumstances granted Indians considerable freedom, at least at first, to think about livestock according to their own lights and to begin defining a place for them in their world.

The challenge faced by Indians in trying to figure out what to do with these new animals should not be underestimated. Until the colonists began arriving with their livestock by the boatload, Indians had never dealt with a sudden influx of strange creatures. They had seen or heard about European explorers who for decades had appeared now and then along the coast, but the disembarkation of unusual animals added a whole new dimension to these contacts and compounded the effects of colonization once it became clear that Europeans intended to stay. Yet if the situation was novel, Indians did not lack resources for dealing with it. They already understood what animals were and how humans ought to interact with them. What they needed to determine was whether livestock bore a close enough resemblance to American fauna to be considered in the same way.

Although Europeans placed all nonhuman creatures into a generic category of animals, Indians may instead have conceived of animals only as distinct species. Colonists who compiled lists of native vocabulary recorded names for many kinds of animals, but no Indian word for "animal" itself. The closest approximation of a generic term was a word for "beast": *mussane* in the Powhatan language, *penashímwock* in Narragansett, and *puppinashimwog* in Massachusett. These translations, however, may have reflected the English meaning of beast as a four-footed mammal and not any nonhuman creature. The absence of a clear equivalent for animal is striking, since compilers of native lexicons typically recorded words in common use and it seems unlikely that the term never came up in conversation. If this linguistic peculiarity represented a genuine conceptual difference, it suggests that Indians did not conceive of the natural world in terms of a strict human-animal dichotomy but rather as a place characterized by a diversity of living beings.[6]

Indians likewise did not relegate animals to a purely physical existence, as colonists did, but also accorded them spiritual significance. Failing to understand this world view, colonists often mistakenly reported that Indians thought that animals were gods. According to William Strachey, the religious activities of the Powhatans in Virginia included "worshipping bruit beasts." Roger Williams initially made the same assertion about the Narragansetts in Rhode Island. In 1638 he reported that the Narragansetts "have plenty of Gods or divine powers: the Sunn, Moone, Fire, Water, Snow, Earth, the Deere, the Beare etc."[7]

Colonists disagreed on a related point, whether or not Indian gods assumed the forms of animals. Thomas Hariot did not think so, reporting in 1588 that the gods of the Roanoke Indians "are of humane shape, & therefore they represent them by images in the formes of men." Virginia colonists likewise noted that the Powhatans described their chief deity, Okeus, as shaped like a man. In Plymouth Colony, Edward Winslow discovered that Wampanoag Indians would not describe their creator deity, Kiehtan, at all, but merely declared that "[n]ever man saw this Kiehtan; only old men tell them of him." Some New England colonists may also have heard stories about native culture heroes such as Gluskap, or Maushop and his wife Squant, who appeared as giant humans when they created the landscape and worked miracles.[8]

Other English observers reported that Indians indeed believed in deities shaped like animals. William Strachey insisted that a Patawomeck Indian in Virginia told him that the chief god of his people was "a mightie great Hare." On a visit to northern New England in the 1660s, John Josselyn encountered a group of Indians who told him a similar story about a "Beaver, saying that he was their Father." In Massachusetts, Edward Johnson reported that Abbomocho (also known as Hobbomok), a New England Indian deity linked to the underworld, often assumed the shape of an animal. The Englishman claimed to have heard that Abbomocho appeared to people in visions and dreams as a deer, an eagle, a snake, and even (though Johnson's informants may have been enjoying a joke) "sometimes like a white boy."[9]

When Indian religious leaders maintained that they had guardian spirits that took the forms of various animals, colonists were equally disconcerted. One shaman on Martha's Vineyard boasted to a Puritan missionary that his guardian spirits appeared as "Fowls, Fishes, and creeping things." A native religious leader in Rhode Island similarly asserted that his spiritual protectors flew around as crows or hawks, or sometimes slithered across the ground as rattlesnakes. In the guise of such inconspicuous and often disagreeable creatures, these spirits tricked or injured the shamans' enemies.[10]

Indian conceptions of animals, embedded in a cosmology that merged the natural and supernatural worlds, were all but incomprehensible to colonists.[11] Thus they misconstrued the character of native spirit-beings, comparing them to deities on the order of the Christian God, and puzzled over stories of spirits that appeared as animals.[12] None of the English commentators came close to comprehending the distinctive character of native spirituality on its own terms.

Native peoples understood the world to be infused with spiritual power that could assume a multitude of forms. Known among Algonquian peoples as *manit* or *manitou,* this power manifested itself in the appearance, behavior, or simply the rarity of certain kinds of humans, animals, and objects. Possession of *manitou* was not necessarily permanent, but depended upon the favor of powerful guardian spirits who controlled its distribution. Roger Williams glimpsed something of this aspect of native spirituality when he described the Narragansetts' "generall Custome . . . at the apprehension of any Excellency in Men, Women, Birds, Beasts, Fish, &c. to cry out *Manittóo*," but by translating the word as "God," he demonstrated that he misunderstood its meaning.[13]

According to Williams, the Narragansetts in particular identified deer, bears, black foxes, and rabbits as spiritually powerful. The manifestation of *manitou* in these animals was probably linked to their success at eluding hunters. Ascribing *manitou* to black foxes, the Narragansetts noted that hunters "have often seene, but never could take any of them." The Indians also believed that deer had special powers that enabled them to avoid traps and snares. This same quality of elusiveness may have encouraged Narragansetts to "conceive there is some Deitie" in rabbits. Black wolves, both rare and wily, perhaps possessed *manitou* as well, for sachems demanded their unusual pelts as tribute.[14]

Indians detected *manitou* most often in animals that provided food as well as raw materials for tools, clothing, and shelter. Northern native peoples who subsisted primarily by hunting were particularly disposed to perceive spiritual power in their prey. Micmacs, Ojibwas, and Crees, among others, believed that benevolent spirits allowed some game animals to avoid hunters' arrows and traps. Yet even Indians who obtained much of their subsistence through horticulture shared a belief that prey animals might possess *manitou*. Narragansetts who farmed as well as hunted were just as likely as Micmacs or Crees to perceive "divine power" in the deer and bears that they pursued in autumn and winter. The same was true for mixed hunting and farming communities in the Chesapeake region.[15]

Yet not all creatures hunted and consumed by Indians possessed spiritual power. Native peoples rarely detected *manitou* in the game birds or fish that formed an important part of their diet. More to the point, they evidently attributed little if any spiritual significance to whelks and quahogs, although the wampum beads fashioned from these creatures' shells were held sacred. Perceptions of *manitou* were clearly related to animals' utility to humans, but were not wholly defined by it.[16] And in some cases, *manitou* inhered in powerful beings not ordinarily encountered in daily life. Many eastern

Algonquian peoples feared two creatures that scarcely anyone had seen: a giant horned underwater serpent and a sacred thunderbird that occupied the sky world.[17]

The assumption that animals could possess *manitou* literally empowered nonhuman creatures in a manner foreign to the colonists' Christian beliefs. Access to spiritual protection gave animals a special status in native societies. Indians certainly recognized differences between people and animals, but could not regard animals as lesser beings, defined from the moment of Creation as invariably subordinate to humans. Possession of *manitou* could make animals formidable adversaries, especially of people who could not demonstrate a similar quality of "Excellency" as evidence of their own spiritual power. Thus the Indians' beliefs about animals had practical implications for their conduct. Spiritually powerful creatures could not be treated lightly, as if they were merely commodities placed on earth for human benefit.

Colonists displayed as much curiosity about Indian behavior toward animals as they did about native beliefs. Collecting information from a variety of sources—stories or rumors; direct observation of Indians' actions, appearance, or material objects—colonists preserved evidence of how their belief in animals' spiritual power shaped Indians' dealings with all kinds of creatures. Sometimes native conduct bore witness to an awe of certain animals that seemed out of proportion to their physical appearance or to any ostensible threat the creatures might pose. If the true measure of an animal's power lay in the spiritual forces it could summon in its defense, however, caution was the only prudent response.

John Josselyn left a secondhand account of one such incident in Massachusetts. In 1639, Josselyn heard a story about the bizarre reaction of two Indians to the sight of an apparently innocuous creature observed near Cape Ann. A boat manned by the Indians and several English sailors had passed by a rock upon which "a *Sea-Serpent* or *Snake* . . . lay quoiled up like a Cable." The sailors wanted to shoot it, but the Indians "disswaded them, saying, that if he were not kill'd outright, they would be all in danger of their lives." The Indians obviously mistrusted the sailors' marksmanship, and one possible interpretation of their alarm would be that they feared that the wounded animal's thrashing would overturn the boat. But this was almost certainly not the meaning the sailors, or the men who later regaled Josselyn with the story, attached to the incident, since it identified the sailors as foolish and the Indians as wise. The likelier explanation is that the sailors, who did not share the Indians' fear of the animal, regarded their native companions' trepidation as absurd. None of the colonists who witnessed the episode or later recounted it suspected that the Indians' reaction might have had spiritual roots. The Indians quite possibly dreaded wounding an animal with a powerful guardian spirit; they may even have wondered if the creature embodied the elusive giant serpent *manitou*.[18]

The Indians' curious behavior around animals also manifested itself in more prosaic ways. Roger Williams, for instance, was perplexed by the Narragansetts' unusual treatment of crows—birds that English villagers destroyed with abandon because of the way they devoured grain in the fields. American crows behaved no differently, "yet scarce will one *Native* amongst an hundred kil them" to prevent damage to crops. Instead, Narragansett parents stationed their children in "little watch-houses" to keep an eye on planting fields and chase crows away. When Williams inquired into the reason for the Narragansetts' forbearance, he learned that it stemmed from a "tradition, that the Crow brought them at first an *Indian* Graine of Corne in one Eare, and an *Indian* or *French* Beane in another, from the Great God *Kautántouwits* field in the Southwest, from whence they hold came all their Corne and Beanes." Other birds—ducks, geese, swans, cormorants, pigeons—were fair game and Narragansetts killed an "abundance" of them. But the crow's special link to the origins of horticulture earned it protection from hunters. Indians in the Chesapeake region may also have preserved crows: in a late sixteenth-century painting of the village of Secoton in what is now North Carolina, John White depicted a small watch-house on a raised platform situated in the midst of a cornfield.[19]

English observers encountered another aspect of the Indians' special relationship with animals whenever they gazed upon native peoples' bodies. Few aspects of native life fascinated colonists more than the Indians' exotic appearance, which they scrutinized for insight into the Indians' essential natures. Clothing styles and body decoration offered highly visible measures of difference between colonists and natives. Much as their doublets and breeches marked Englishmen as civilized beings, the Indians' fur cloaks and leather leggings—or even more dramatically, their nakedness—betokened

Susquehannock Indian dressed in furs. From the tenth state of the Smith/Hole
map in John Smith, *The Generall Historie of Virginia, New England,
and the Summer Isles,* ... (London, 1624).
Courtesy of The Newberry Library

savagery.[20] Indian attire often appeared virtually indistinguishable from the
animals from which it was fashioned. John Smith judged the Susquehannocks
"the most strange people" in good part because of their peculiar clothing.
"Their attire is the skinnes of Beares, and Woolves," he remarked, and some
men wore bearskin garments in which "the mans necke goes through the
skinnes neck, and the eares of the beare [are] fastned to his shoulders behind,
the nose and teeth hanging downe his breast, and at the end of the nose hung

a Beares Pawe." William Wood reported that, during the wintertime, Massachusetts' native men similarly donned fur "mantles" made of "bear's skins, moose's skins, and beaver skins sewed together, [and] otter skins, and raccoon skins," and kept their arms and hands warm in muffs fashioned from "deep-furred cat skin." Viewed from a distance, Indians draped in such clothing must have presented the English with disconcerting apparitions of beings who resembled animals more than people.[21]

Animal motifs appeared in other sorts of bodily adornment as well. Colonists who got close enough to Indian individuals to examine their flesh in detail expressed amazement at the profusion of animal-shaped decorations imprinted all over their bodies. The faces of Massachusetts Indians, William Wood declared, bore "certain portraitures of beasts, as bears, deers, mooses, wolves, etc.; some of fowls, as of eagles, hawks, etc." These were not produced by "a superficial painting but [by] a certain incision, or else a raising of their skin by a small sharp instrument under which they convey a certain kind of black unchangeable ink which makes the desired form apparent and permanent." Indians in eastern Virginia sported comparable ornamentations. In 1607 George Percy could not help but notice scantily clad native women who tattooed their "bodies, legges, thighes, armes and faces" with images of "Fowles, Fish, or Beasts." John Smith's attention was similarly riveted by the sight of Indian women's bodies "cunningly imbrodered with diverse workes, as beasts, serpentes, artificially wrought into their flesh with blacke spots."[22]

These designs bore some special significance to those who wore them, but few colonists went beyond mere observation to inquire into their meaning. One who did broach the subject was John Lederer, a German physician who lived for a time in Virginia. During the winter of 1669-70, Lederer accompanied a party of adventurers attempting to cross the Blue Ridge Mountains in search of gold. They never completed the journey, but en route Lederer encountered groups of Indians who painted their bodies with all sorts of animal figures. With considerable self-assurance, Lederer expounded on the images' significance. "By the figure of a stag, they imply swiftness," he explained, "by that of a serpent, wrath; of a lion, courage; of a dog, fidelity: by a swan they signifie the English, alluding to their complexion, and flight over the sea."[23] His confident tone notwithstanding, Lederer's explanation almost certainly had little to do with the meanings Indians actually attached to such images. His interpretation instead bore a suspiciously close resemblance to the symbolic associations between virtues and animals found in European heraldry.[24]

Since native peoples could choose from a wide range of representational and abstract designs for body decoration, their preference for animal images was hardly random. These emblems probably did not represent totems, because few Algonquian Indian societies located along the Atlantic coast were organized into clan lineages associated with specific animals.[25] Yet the images surely had spiritual significance, for many of the animals depicted were commonly identified with *manitou* and shamanistic spirits. These spiritual connections may explain why the Indians who wore animal emblems intended them to be permanent. Wood, Percy, and Smith all specified that animal designs in particular were applied as tattoos and not with paint. Indians who chose to display the image of a deer or eagle on their faces or arms expected to do so for life.

Algonquian peoples did not just cloak themselves in fur and inscribe their bodies with figures of various creatures, but also utilized animal materials and images in numerous other ways. Powhatan shamans, for instance, donned ceremonial garb that included a mantle fashioned from feathers and weasel skins and a "crown" made from "a dosen or 16 or more snake skins" stuffed with moss to give them a more lifelike appearance. In both the Chesapeake and New England, Indians exhibited a distinct fondness for using animal parts—and even animals—as ornaments. An astonished William Strachey encountered Powhatan men who sported "a dead ratt tyed by the Taile, and such like Conundrums" as part of their attire. He saw other native people who embellished their pierced ears with the legs of eagles, hawks, and turkeys, or sometimes bear or raccoon claws. Thrusting the claws through their ears, they let the rest of the leg or paw "hang upon the Cheeke to the full view." Even more striking, Strachey reported, was the spectacle of a Powhatan man wearing in his pierced ear "a smale greene and yellow couloured live Snake neere half a yard in length." The wearer allowed the snake to coil around his neck and even "familiarly . . . to kisse his lippes." Massachusetts Indians evidently preferred animal images to real creatures. William Wood, at any rate, mentioned only seeing native peoples with "pendants in their ears, as forms of birds, beasts, and fishes, carved out of bone, shell, and stone."[26]

Animal motifs could be found on many other material objects. Roger Williams saw two-foot-long Narragansett tobacco pipes with "men or beasts carved" on them. Narragansett women ground corn in stone or wooden mortars using pestles topped with animal-shaped effigies. Elsewhere in New

England, native artisans carved amulets in the shape of birds and stone fetishes to look like bears, turtles, or seals. They occasionally etched images representing the thunderbird or serpent *manitous* on rocks. When European goods filtered into native communities, some artisans reshaped them to incorporate animal designs. Thus one Narragansett craftsman took a brass fragment, probably from a kettle, and made a spoon decorated with cutout images of bears.[27]

Similar designs proliferated on material objects in the Chesapeake region. There Indian men also smoked tobacco in pipes with animal-shaped decorations; a favorite motif was a running deer. Native artisans embellished religious structures with images of animals, reinforcing the link between certain creatures and spiritual power. According to John Smith, the temple in which the preeminent chief Powhatan stored his "kind of Treasure" consisted of a framework with four free-standing posts carved with "4 Images as Sentinels, one of a Dragon, another a Beare, the 3 like a Leopard and the fourth like a giantlike man." The juxtaposition of human and animal figures suggested an equivalent symbolic significance, and their deployment at the corners of the temple may have invoked protection from the *manitous* or guardian spirits of the beings they represented. Powhatan himself perhaps entered this building on occasion clad in his special deerskin mantle. Decorated with the figures of a man flanked by a deer and a wolf, all fashioned from small shell beads stitched together, the robe may have displayed these motifs to confer spiritual protection on the wearer.[28]

Chesapeake-area Indians possibly went so far as to employ animal images as a form of written communication. At the turn of the eighteenth century, Robert Beverley reported that Virginia's natives used "a sort of Hieroglyphick, or representation of Birds, Beasts or other things, shewing their different meaning, by the various forms describ'd, and by the different position of the Figures." This may have been a recent innovation adopted to help native people compete with colonists who for nearly a century had monopolized the use of written deeds and other documents for their own advantage. Yet even if it was a fairly new practice, by basing the writing system on animal characters, native inventors invoked an ancient and familiar symbolism.[29]

The endeavor that best expressed the Indians' distinctive approach to animals was hunting with bow and arrow. It was also one activity at which colonists had to concede the Indians' superior skill. John Smith marveled at the stamina of Indian hunters who easily traveled through forest "deserts," often for "some 3 or 4 daies journey without habitation" in search of game. Powhatan hunters also exhibited considerable deftness with their weapons. No stranger to self-promotion, Smith detected the same quality in every Powhatan man who "doth his best to show his dexteritie" at public displays of marksmanship. The stakes, Smith suggested, were high, "for by their excelling in those quallities," Powhatan men "get their wives." Massachusetts Indians did not use target practice as a courting ritual, but according to William Wood they were "good marksmen" nonetheless. Colonists' awe at the Indians' facility with bows and arrows invariably mingled with concern, for the tools of hunting were also weapons of war. Seventeenth-century English soldiers still used bows and arrows, and early colonial arsenals included archery equipment. Seemingly idle comments about Indian skills with these implements were in good part efforts to size up Indians' offensive capabilities.[30]

The Indians' expertise testified to extensive training that began at an early age. John Smith observed that hunting was the "ordinary exercise" of Indian boys "from their infancy." If William Strachey can be believed, Indian mothers in the Chesapeake imposed a rigorous daily regimen of practice on their young sons. Every morning, Strachey reported, a mother would test her son's aim by "throwing Up in the ayre a piece of Mosse or some such light thing" for him to hit with his arrow. If he missed, "he shall not have his Breckfast." The boy's reward for hunger-induced diligence was a public celebration at the time of his first kill. The Pamunkeys of the Chesapeake area, as well as several northern Algonquian peoples, organized feasts to commemorate such occasions. During these festivities the boy's father and his friends, but not the fledgling hunter himself, shared the meat he had provided. As they grew older, Powhatan men often regaled one another at public gatherings with accounts of their hunting prowess acquired through long and painstaking practice.[31]

Beyond physical strength and accurate marksmanship, successful hunting required consummate knowledge of the local terrain and the behavior of prey animals. Native men repeatedly traveled through hunting grounds to familiarize themselves with the landscape. Because of "their continuall ranging," John Smith noted, Virginia's Indians "know all the advantages and places most frequented with Deare" and other game. Over the course of 16 days in 1608, two Powhatan hunters supplied a hundred squirrels a day plus "Turkies, Deare, and other wild beastes" to starving Englishmen who could not fend for themselves. Hunting occupied men mainly during autumn and winter, but preparations extended to the other seasons of the year. Roger Williams noticed that only after Narragansetts had "observed in Spring-time and Summer the haunt of the Deere" did they know the best places to set traps. If the prime locations lay near the village, women and children accompanied the men to help build "little hunting houses of Barks and Rushes" to shelter hunters on subsequent excursions to bait and check traps. Such exercises introduced young boys to their future responsibilities even as they offered Narragansett women a limited role in what was essentially a male occupation.[32]

Skilled hunters, no doubt through a process of trial and error, also acquired an accurate knowledge of prey animals' anatomy. A well-placed shot was as important as a well-timed one. Massachusetts Indians learned "where the very life of every creature lieth," declared William Wood, so that they knew precisely "where to smite him to make him die presently." Native families and communities received little benefit from hunters who wasted precious energy trailing wounded animals through the woods or who lost prey altogether because of a misplaced arrow.[33]

Employing a variety of hunting techniques, Indian men usually worked in groups as they sought elusive animals. Small parties made regular rounds to check traps and snares, or worked together to catch birds in nets or with bows and arrows. Larger groups, sometimes numbering in the hundreds, participated in group drives for deer and other large mammals. In Virginia, native hunters often used fire to direct deer to places from which they could not escape. John Smith saw Indians create a circle of flames around a herd of deer, and then chase them within its bounds, killing "6, 8, 10, or 15 at a hunting." If animals were discovered grazing near a river, some hunters would drive them into the water while others, paddling in canoes, "have Ambuscadoes to kill them."[34]

Successful Powhatan hunters, upon their return from the forest, gathered around special "Altar stones" where they made offerings of "blood, deare suet, and Tobacco" to thank the spirits that had granted them such good fortune.[35] Their actions testified to a belief that their own talents had not wholly determined the productive outcome of the chase. Hunting was not only a display of human prowess but also an opportunity to acknowledge the reciprocal relations linking men and animals. Guided by spiritual protectors, animals offered themselves as gifts to humans in return for evidence of

Timucua Indian hunters observed in Florida wearing deer costumes.
From Theodor de Bry, *America* (Frankfurt, 1590).
Courtesy of Rare Books Division, The New York Public Library,
Astor, Lenox, and Tilden Foundations

gratitude and respect. Rituals like the Powhatan offerings demonstrated proper reverence toward animal *manitous* and ensured that future efforts would meet with success.[36]

Virtually every aspect of their hunting reflected the Indians' understanding of animals as powerful creatures deserving of respect. To catch elusive prey protected by vigilant spirits, hunters in effect adopted the animal's identity by mimicking its appearance and behavior. John Smith observed one Powhatan man don "the skinne of a Deare slit on the one side" before setting out. He thrust his arm through the neck of the deerskin, putting his hand into the head "which is stuffed." The "hornes, head, eies, eares, and every part" were "as arteficially counterfeited as they can devise" to render the hunter's appearance as much like a living deer as possible. The hunter then drew upon his expert knowledge of deer behavior to imitate its actions as he approached his target. If his prey showed any sign of skittishness, the hunter used his hand to turn the stuffed head of his costume "to his best advantage to seeme like a Deare, also gazing and licking himselfe." Only when the animal's suspicion had subsided would the hunter watch for an opportunity to withdraw his hand from the deerskin head, grasp his bow, and unleash an arrow.[37]

John Clayton, an Oxford-educated clergyman who visited Virginia in the mid-1680s, similarly reported hearing about hunters who constructed "artificial sorts of Heads of Boughs of Trees" with the branches simulating antlers. Like the Powhatans' deerskin costumes, these headdresses imitated the appearance of prey. They also served as camouflage, breaking up the outline of the hunter's body to make him less visible in the woods. Wearers of these artificial antlers simulated "the Feeding of the Deer" as they crept forward "by degrees [to] get within Shot." Before embarking on hunting expeditions, however, the men took care to "consecrate" their headdresses "to their Gods," as Clayton put it. The hunters were more likely soliciting the approval of the deer's guardian spirits by means of a propitiatory ritual, acknowledging that success in the hunt depended on forces beyond human control.[38]

Such practices reflected the Indians' understanding of hunting as a process of negotiation with prey animals' spiritual protectors as well as a test of their own skills and physical endurance. The distinctive character of native hunting was further revealed in John Josselyn's description of a moose hunt that he witnessed in northern New England in the 1660s. The Englishman watched in fascination as a party of native hunters moved quickly across the frozen surface of the snow in pursuit of their prey. Hampered by its enormous size, the moose sank through the icy crust, struggled through four-foot drifts, and snagged its antlers in low-lying branches. With every puff of steam launched by labored breathing into the frigid air, the doomed animal signaled its exhaustion. Surrounding the beast, the hunters moved in from all sides to "transpierce him with their Lances." The stricken moose groaned, took a few steps, then collapsed "like a ruined building, making the Earth to quake." At this point the hunters moved in for the kill.[39]

What happened next revealed with particular clarity the ritualized nature of hunting, which required every step to be performed in the correct way and in the proper order. Josselyn's account bears a remarkably close resemblance to the practices of twentieth-century Crees (another Algonquian-speaking people), and the modern example suggests possible symbolic meanings for the seventeenth-century Indians' behavior. Josselyn observed the hunters approach the dying moose and cut its throat. By preventing the animal from suffering a slow and painful death, they avoided offending the animal's guardian spirit and jeopardizing the success of future hunting. Once the moose was dead, the hunters proceeded to skin it. Then the Algonquian women began the heavy work of butchering. They first removed the heart "and from that the bone." Cree men butcher their own game, but like the seventeenth-century Algonquian women, they start by taking out the heart and a thin layer of fat located across the rib cage, to be brought back to camp as "tokens" of the kill. The Algonquian women then removed the moose's left rear foot; among the Crees, the posterior legs of large mammals are considered women's food and are prized for their marrow. Next, the Algonquian women drew out the moose's sinews and cut out its tongue. Cree hunters do likewise, regarding the tongue as a "medicine piece" with sacred connotations. (Josselyn, in another context, described smoked moose tongue as "a dish for a *Sagamor,*" or chief.) Once the Algonquian men prepared a clean surface by using snowshoes to "shovel the snow away to the bare Earth in a circle," the women began the laborious process of cutting away the meat.[40]

Josselyn did not mention how the moose hunters disposed of the animal's bones, but to other seventeenth-century Algonquians, this was an exceedingly important part of the ritual of hunting. Indians in the Hudson Valley, reported Adriaen Van der Donck in 1655, "always burn the beaver bones, and never permit their dogs to gnaw the same" for fear of the consequences. Throwing bones to dogs amounted to a sacrilege that angered prey animals' spiritual protectors, who would retaliate by ensuring that offending hunters were thereafter "unlucky in the chase." In the southern piedmont, the English traveler John Lawson similarly noticed that Indians "carefully preserve the Bones of the Flesh they eat, and burn them" for precisely the same reason. If the hunters "omitted that Custom," they believed that "the Game would leave their Country, and they should not be able to maintain themselves by their Hunting."[41]

All of the rituals of hunting, from the careful preparations beforehand to the proper disposal of bones afterward, cultivated the goodwill of animal spirits who controlled access to prey. These actions, like the Indians' behavior toward animals in general, sought to maintain the delicate balance in relations between humans and other creatures. Native peoples conceived of their connections with animals in terms of mutual support rather than human dominance and shaped their behavior accordingly. In this, as in so many other aspects of Indian culture, the principle of reciprocity structured both thought and conduct.

It was not immediately apparent how livestock would fit into a world where animals possessed powerful spiritual protectors and received respectful treatment from humans. Domestic animals were by definition subservient to people, and colonial owners rarely showed them anything like respect. Figuring out how to deal not only with unusual animals, but also with an unusual status for animals, therefore emerged as significant challenges for native peoples. That Indians could point to few counterparts in their own villages for the colonists' tame creatures did not make facing those challenges any easier.

Nowhere in the New World did colonists see the kinds of domestic creatures they took for granted in England, and they recorded their surprise and consternation in numerous reports sent back home. Confident that his English correspondent would find it as remarkable as he did, Peter Wynne related the curious fact that Virginia's Indians "keep nothing tame about them." William Strachey made a similar observation at somewhat greater length, reporting that native people in Virginia did not "breed Cattell nor bring up tame poultry" in their villages. Although they had lots of turkeys (which Strachey apparently did not regard as tame), these Indians did not "keepe byrds, squirrells, nor tame Partridges, Swan, duck, nor Geese."[42]

Strachey's roster of untamed creatures served less as a set of illustrative examples than as a litany of missed opportunities. English settlers invariably judged the Indians' failure to domesticate New World beasts as evidence of their backwardness. Native peoples in New England had no "Tame Cattle," sniffed John Josselyn, "excepting Lice, and Doggs of a wild breed that they bring up to hunt with." In 1674, Daniel Gookin refuted the theory that America's inhabitants descended from the Tartars of northeastern Asia by pointing out that the ancient Tartars had "kine [cattle], sheep, horses, and camels, and the like tame beasts . . . in great numbers" while the Indians had none. No group of people who enjoyed the benefits of domestic animals, Gookin implied, would have given them up. Rev. William Hubbard reminded the readers of his history of New England that the keeping of domestic animals was "the custom of more civil nations," and thus would not be found among uncivilized Indians. At the turn of the eighteenth century, Virginia's Robert Beverley reiterated what had by then become a commonplace observation: that before the colonists' arrival, the Indians "were without

Boundaries to their Land; and without Property in Cattle," two characteristics that testified to their lack of civility.[43]

The "deficiency" that English observers detected in eastern Algonquian peoples did not apply to all Native American groups. Indians in Mexico had domesticated turkeys, perhaps as early as 3500 BC, and the keeping of these birds eventually spread to ancient Puebloan peoples in what is now the southwestern United States. Inhabitants of the Andes had domesticated llamas and guinea pigs, and the peoples of tropical South America kept Muscovy ducks. Virtually all Native American peoples had dogs. Even so, this list sharply contrasts with Old World inhabitants' roster of domesticated beasts, which included sheep, goats, swine, cattle, horses, and donkeys.[44]

What colonists attributed to backwardness in fact stemmed from circumstances beyond the Indians' control. The Americas simply had very few large animal species capable of being domesticated. Two possibilities—indigenous American horses and camels—became extinct, either through climatic change or overhunting, around 11,000 BC. Various Indian groups grew to depend on bison and caribou, but did so by exploiting the animals' predictable migratory habits rather than by domesticating them. The two large mammals most familiar to eastern Algonquians, deer and bears, were not suitable candidates. In order to be domesticated, animals have to breed in captivity and learn to depend on human caretakers. Domesticable creatures are generally social animals whose group behavior demonstrates a dominance hierarchy. This social structure allows humans to substitute themselves as leaders of the herd and exert control. Candidates for domestication cannot panic and flee at the least provocation or be highly territorial, both of which tendencies disqualified deer. Bears proved unsuitable because of their solitary habits and sheer unpredictability.[45]

Eastern Algonquians did not domesticate local fauna mainly because they could not do so, but also because there was little reason for them to try even with small animals. Indians in Central and South America probably domesticated turkeys and other birds to assure their rising populations of a protein supply in a region lacking large game animals.[46] But at least since around AD 1000 , far less dense Algonquian populations along the eastern seaboard of North America enjoyed a varied diet of wild and cultivated plant foods along with abundant game and fish. With ample protein readily available through hunting, eastern Indians had no incentive to domesticate animals for food, even if likely candidates had been present.[47]

Before the English settlers arrived, eastern Algonquians were familiar with only two kinds of tame beasts: hawks, which they kept around their houses to chase small birds out of cornfields, and dogs.[48] Most colonists, however, asserted that Indian dogs barely qualified as tame creatures. Peter Wynne maintained that Powhatan Indians in Virginia kept "nothing tame about them" even, in his opinion, the "Certeyne kind of Currs" they used for hunting. John Josselyn similarly described New England Indians' dogs as being "of a wild breed." To drive the point home, these men and other colonists suggested that Indian dogs scarcely differed from wolves. Powhatan dogs, according to John Smith, "are like their Wolves, and cannot barke but howle" instead. John Lawson encountered Indian dogs "which are seemingly Wolves, made tame with starving and beating," during his travels in the Carolina piedmont. Going even further, John Josselyn claimed that an "*Indian Dog* is a Creature begotten 'twixt a *Wolf* and a *Fox*" and that the Indians merely found such hybrid animals in the woods, avoiding the effort that actual domestication entailed.[49]

Indian dogs were not in fact wolves, or wolf-fox mixes. Archeological evidence indicates that dogs appeared as a distinct species in North America as much as 11,000 years ago.[50] The colonists' testimony betrayed their preoccupation with the animals' behavior; the dogs did not seem "tame" in any sense that the English understood. They did not sound like English dogs, and failed to act as colonists thought that dogs should. Colonists may further have disparaged Indian dogs simply because of their connection with Indian people. The English tended to ascribe to dogs the status of their owners: the gentleman's hound was a noble beast, but the peddler's companion was nothing more than a filthy cur. The nasty creature that nipped at the heels of English visitors in Indian villages could only be worse.[51]

However unreliable the colonists' comments were about the nature of Indian dogs, their observations accurately indicated the limits of the Indians' experience with domestication. Historically, the process of domesticating animal species (as opposed to taming an individual creature) occurs in stages. Humans first establish loose contact with the desired animals, but exercise no control over their breeding. Next they confine the creatures more closely, to make use of them for food or labor and to monitor their reproduction. Human owners may ultimately engage in selective breeding to enhance certain desirable characteristics of the chosen species, seeking speed or strength in a horse, for instance, or high milk production in dairy cows. Colonial testimony suggested that Indians had reached the first stage of

John White's watercolor of the Indian village of Pomeiooc, near Roanoke
Colony. Indian dog depicted in upper left.
© Copyright The British Museum

domestication with their dogs. They maintained a loose association with the
animals but did not monitor their breeding or even exert much control over
their daily activities. John Smith's comment about the way Indian dogs
howled reinforces this impression. Since only fully domesticated dogs can
bark, Indian dogs probably interbred in the wild with wolves.[52]

Unlike other North American Indians, eastern Algonquians appeared to
make little use of their dogs. Inuit peoples in the Arctic used dogs to find seal
breathing holes in the ice; the Montagnais of Labrador used them in hunting;
Plains Indians trained them to pull heavily laden sleds; Miamis sacrificed
them in religious rites; and Hurons consumed them regularly. But eastern
Algonquians did not eat their dogs (except perhaps in times of famine) and
may not have worked with them. English testimony about hunting, the one
activity that might have involved dogs, was more than a little ambiguous.

Some colonists asserted that Indian hunters indeed brought dogs along with them. Peter Wynne in Virginia, for instance, claimed that the Powhatans employed them while hunting "land fowles." But no colonist, not even John Josselyn in his elaborate account of the moose hunt, actually described Indians hunting with dogs. Colonists may have simply assumed that native hunters used dogs because hunters in England generally did.[53]

Yet native dogs performed other important functions that English observers failed to notice because they took place in or near Indian villages where colonists seldom set foot. Indian dogs earned their keep in part by scavenging, ridding villages of food scraps and reducing the presence of vermin. Carolina Indians did not "starve" their dogs (as John Lawson alleged) so much as leave them to subsist on whatever refuse they could find on their own.[54] Possessing a keen sense of smell, dogs also served as useful scouts on treks through the woods and as sentinels in villages. The first Indians to approach Englishmen near Plymouth were warned by their dog of the colonists' presence and thus made a quick escape. Seventeen years later, during the Pequot War in Connecticut, a howling dog alerted Indians in Mystic Fort to an imminent attack by colonial forces.[55]

The precise nature of Indians' relationships with their dogs is more difficult to discern. It is not clear, for instance, if native dogs belonged to an individual, a family, or an entire village. Whether Indians regarded dogs as pets, kept more for companionship than utility, is also unknown. That eastern Algonquians did place dogs in a special category distinct from other animals, however, seems likely. Narragansetts occasionally used rough drawings of dogs—but apparently not of any other animal—as signature marks on English documents.[56] In addition, burial sites in southern New England dating from AD 800 to 1100 have been found to contain both human and dog remains. Since deceased persons were typically interred with items reflecting their status, occupation, or preference, the dog remains perhaps signified that a favorite animal had been buried with its owner.[57]

The Indians' experience with tame animals, limited though it was, provided a possible framework for understanding the nature of livestock and their connection to the colonists. Like dogs in native villages, cattle and other domesticated beasts lingered around English settlements and were put to use by people in various ways. Unlike wild animals, which Indians generally regarded as the province of men, tame creatures came into contact with both genders. Native women deployed hawks to protect cornfields, and men kept track of dogs. Indians observed similar behavior in colonial settlements, where both men and women tended livestock. Although the analogy between native dogs and English cattle was at best approximate, it nonetheless offered Indians a way to think about livestock and consider how the animals might be incorporated into their world.[58]

Indians often demonstrated considerable flexibility when it came to finding ways to make use of the new things the English brought with them. Yet Indians did not simply accept whatever the colonists offered, or make use of English goods in precisely the same ways that the colonists did. They instead proved highly selective in making choices that reflected their own needs or desires. How livestock might figure in this larger strategy of cultural mixing depended a great deal on how Indians defined them. Regarding livestock as tame creatures similar to dogs was not the only possible option.

Finding an appropriate analogy from the Indians' own experience was important, for it tended to smooth the process of absorbing new goods. It was relatively easy, for instance, for Indians to accept imported copper and glass beads as equivalents of native copper objects and quartz crystals. They had no difficulty fastening shards of glass from broken bottles to the tips of arrows instead of using sharpened pieces of antler or bone. Indian artisans also refashioned various European manufactures to suit native uses and tastes. Craftsmen transformed fragments of brass kettles into spoons and turned pieces of copper pots into bracelets or other ornaments. Substitutions such as these caused little disruption in native culture.[59]

Further evidence of the effort to find parallels, or at least close equivalents, between European and native objects appeared in the names Indians attached to the unfamiliar items. The Narragansetts, Roger Williams reported, had no direct counterpart for English firearms, but seeing "a consimilitude between our Guns and Thunder," they derived a name for the weapons—"*Péskunck*"—from their word for thunder. An amalgam of the Narragansett terms for red earth and kettle produced a word for an English copper kettle (*mishquokuk).* Narragansetts likewise applied their own designation for a boat to a variety of English vessels.[60]

The frequent appearance of imported goods such as beads, iron tools, nails, and mirrors in Indian graves pointed to an equally critical aspect of the process of assimilation.[61] Indians not only assigned familiar names and uses to European products, but on occasion invested those items with ritual meanings comparable to those associated with valuable indigenous objects. As spiritually significant goods, they figured in ceremonies as well as mortuary practices. According to Edward Winslow, the Narragansetts attempted to stave off an epidemic that raged among neighboring peoples by holding a ceremony during which a mix of New World and imported objects, including "kettles, skins, hatchets, beads, [and] knives," were tossed into a large fire as a ritual offering. The Wampanoag shaman who claimed that his guardian spirits occasionally took shape as "Brasse" and "Iron" likewise implied that European metals could be infused with spiritual power. Detecting *manitou* in imported goods in this way allowed Indians to incorporate them into their cosmology, not just their everyday routines.[62]

English livestock, however, were a different matter. Unlike kettles or beads, livestock were animate beings and thus could not be approached as if they were simply another class of trade goods. Although colonists defined domesticated animals as property, Indians did not have an equivalent conceptual category for living chattel. Instead native peoples granted individuals property rights only to animals they had killed. This suggests that Indians did not regard their dogs as private possessions, but rather as creatures available for common use by village men. Lacking the notion that even tame animals could be property, Indians could not have employed such a concept to equate livestock with dogs.[63]

Other compelling reasons further dissuaded Indians from making such a comparison. Insofar as native peoples thought about animals as individual species and not as a generic category, their initial impressions of cattle and horses would have focused on the creatures' distinctive physical and behavioral characteristics. The animals' large size and feeding behavior alone would have discouraged an immediate association with Indian dogs. Most of all, however, the circumstances under which Indians first encountered livestock militated against drawing such an analogy. Domestication, even in the limited form adopted by Indians, is as much a relationship as a condition, signaled by the frequent association of people with certain animals. Yet as the experience of Chickwallop and the Norwottucks illustrated, many Indians often saw their first cow or pig when there were no colonists around to suggest that the animal was something other than a strange kind of wild beast. There was no reason for Indians to imagine that these unusual creatures were domesticated.

That Indians initially associated English livestock with wild rather than tame animals is revealed by the names they assigned to them. From the moment that Europeans first brought livestock to the New World, native peoples searched for analogies to indigenous beasts and then transferred those creatures' names to the immigrant animals. The Nahuas in early sixteenth-century Mexico used their word for deer (*maçatl*) as a name for a Spanish horse; a mare was called *cihuamaçatl,* or female deer. Lacking a Mesoamerican equivalent for sheep, they improvised by using the word *ichcatl*, or cotton. Mayan Indians of the Yucatan Peninsula called a horse a "tapir of Castile." The same process occurred in the English colonies. William Strachey noted that the Powhatans of Virginia used their word for "small bird" *(cawahcheims)* for chicken. According to Roger Williams, the Narragansetts in Rhode Island noticed that an *ockqutchaun*, or woodchuck, was "about the bignesse of a *Pig,* and root[ed] like a *Pig,*" and so they decided to "give this name to all our *Swine.*" The naming of livestock, like the naming of European trade goods, indicated the Indians' determination to think about these animals literally on their own terms.[64]

For Indians truly to think about livestock on their own terms, however, they had to fit cattle, horses, and hogs into a cosmological framework that identified animals as spiritually powerful. Their own dogs, as tame creatures, may have lacked the spiritual protectors associated with forest animals.[65] Yet if livestock resembled wild beasts, they would almost certainly demonstrate *manitou* much as deer and bears did. Perhaps, because of their very strangeness, livestock possessed especially powerful guardian spirits. This concern may have explained the Norwottucks' tentative behavior following their discovery of the cow. They had no way of knowing what sort of spiritual connection the strange beast might have, or what the consequences might be if the Indians did not appease those spirits in the right way.

Other episodes offered more direct evidence of the Indians' anxiety about the potential for offending the spiritual protectors of livestock. One such incident occurred quite early in Virginia. Sometime before 1613, John Smith witnessed what may have been the first encounter between Powhatan Indians and an English boar. The beast stood squarely in their path and, according to Smith, the unsuspecting Indians "were stricken with awfull feare" when the boar "brisled up himself and gnashed his teeth" at them. Smith interpreted their alarm as more than just a reasonable reaction to an unexpected confrontation with a ferocious animal. He instead claimed that the Powhatans thought that the snarling boar was "the God of the Swine, which was offended with them." Although Smith's use of the term "God" betrayed his Christian thinking, the Powhatans had apparently conveyed to him that the nature of their concern was not purely physical.[66]

A similar incident occurred in Massachusetts Bay Colony in 1642. During the summer of that year, rumors of an Indian conspiracy against the colonists swirled throughout New England, prompting magistrates to seek information from native sources in an effort to foil a surprise attack. Three Indians came forward in August to confirm the colonists' worst fears. One of them claimed that his willingness to testify stemmed from an ominous encounter with an English animal. Not long before, this Indian had been "hurt near to death" by an ox-drawn cart. The accident convinced him that the Christian God was angry with him and had sent the "Englishman's cow to kill him, because he had concealed such a conspiracy against the English." Much as guardian spirits infused American fauna with *manitou,* so in the repentant Indian's account had the Christian God empowered this English ox to deal with a human who had caused offense.[67]

If the animal spirits with which Indians were most familiar responded favorably to expressions of respect and acts of reciprocity, so too might the protectors of English livestock. That seemed to be the supposition entertained by native people in a village in the Blue Ridge mountains. When two Englishmen, James Needham and Gabriel Arthur, arrived in a Tomahitan settlement with their Appomattox Indian guide in 1673, they "were very kindly entertained" by the inhabitants. Indeed, the Tomahitans resorted "even to addoration in their cerrimonies of courtesies" toward the visitors. The very first night, the Tomahitans built a "scaffold" upon which their guests could rest, allowing villagers to "stand and gaze at them and not offend them by theire throng." The Indians were no less solicitous of the welfare of the Englishmen's horse. Tied to a stake in the village center, the animal received as much care as the Englishmen did. The following day, the Indians presented the horse (and presumably the human visitors) with a feast that included an "aboundance of corne and all manner of pulse with fish, flesh and beares oyle" in an elaborate ceremony of welcome.[68]

This was not the first time the Tomahitans had seen livestock, for the Englishmen reported that "many swine and cattle" wandered through their village. These animals were either descendants of creatures transported by Spanish adventurers to Florida more than a century earlier or perhaps had strayed more recently from English settlements in eastern Virginia. Needham and Arthur did not observe the Tomahitans treating their cattle and swine with anything like the extraordinary care they bestowed on the horse, which suggests that this might have been the first horse they had ever seen. Impressed by its size, agility, and physical strength—all of which might have indicated that it had a correspondingly powerful guardian spirit—the Tomahitans clearly thought it prudent to accord the animal special respect. When Indians in nearby Carolina first encountered horses they behaved in similar fashion. Regarded as unusually prestigious creatures, horses were not put to work but instead enjoyed a lavish diet and considerable leisure.[69]

Feasts, often arranged by sachems, were important rituals in many Indian societies. Creating ties of obligation between hosts and guests, these occasions reinforced the participants' sense of membership in the community. When the Tomahitans provided the horse with a generous repast, including such special foods as meat and bear's oil, they welcomed it into their community, not as a lowly beast but as an important visitor.[70] Rather than taking their cues from the colonists about how horses ought to be treated, the Tomahitans followed their own code of conduct. Their decision to do so was hardly idiosyncratic, but instead exemplified the Indians' preferred strategy when it came to dealing with the animals introduced by colonists to the New World.

So long as their encounters with livestock were sporadic and took place when few colonists were around, Indians were free to react as they saw fit. That they responded in a culturally consistent way was hardly surprising, for this was typical of their approach to dealing with all sorts of novel circumstances arising from the advent of colonization. Because their own experience with animal domestication was highly attenuated and because they first encountered livestock under conditions that invited comparison with wild animals, Indians generally ascribed to the new beasts the characteristics (and often the names) of familiar forest creatures. Livestock, like various New World animals, might possess *manitou* and call upon guardian spirits for protection. They deserved respect from humans, and could exact revenge if treated inappropriately. Once Indians recovered from the initial shock of meeting up with strange beasts, they could experiment with their usual methods of expressing respect for animals' spiritual power to test their efficacy with livestock.

Indians did not define living animals as property, but they nevertheless believed that animals could supply human needs. Drawing an analogy between livestock and New World fauna implied that English creatures could be hunted so long as the proper rituals were discovered and then followed. The Indians' strategy for integrating livestock into their world thus had the effect of redefining English property as fair game. For colonists, however, livestock differed from wild animals precisely because they were property, a status intrinsic to their identity as domesticated creatures. The Indians could not have known that a distinction that had little or no meaning in their culture would loom so large in the colonists' minds. Yet for English settlers, this was a distinction that made all the difference.

Chapter Two

The Deer with the Red Collar

English Ideas about Animals

𝒪f all the deer that grazed near the small Massachusetts village of Bradford, only one had the ability to get Nathan Webster into trouble. One day early in the spring of 1682, the young buck met up with Webster as it wandered through the yard by Thomas Stickney's house. The deer made no attempt to flee, for it was accustomed to the presence of humans and sensed no danger in Webster's approach. David Wheeler, another villager, had tamed the animal and let it wander freely around the neighborhood to feed on whatever leaves and bark it could find. Most people left the deer alone. Nathan Webster shot it.

Webster, already considered by his neighbors to be an exceedingly disagreeable fellow, did little to improve his reputation by reveling in his malicious prank. When local townsmen complained that he had destroyed someone's property, Webster challenged them to describe the deer's earmark to prove that it had an owner. The deer bore no such mark, but it did wear a red collar around its neck. Webster evidently did not know that, according to English common law, the collar sufficed to demonstrate that the deer indeed belonged to someone, and that he could be held accountable for its destruction just as if he had shot a pig or a cow.[1]

Wild deer were free for the taking in Massachusetts, and Webster could have hunted any of them at will.[2] But in the interest of mischief he played with the distinction between wild and tame animals and targeted a creature distinguished from its wild cousins only by its association with David Wheeler. It is not known where or under what circumstances Wheeler obtained the deer. Perhaps he had found a fawn alone in the woods, or kept one after killing its mother. However he acquired it, by taming the deer he converted it into property. Because that status did not apply to deer in general, as it did to cows or other livestock species, Wheeler had to mark this one animal as his possession. He did not mark its ears, as he might have treated a cow or pig, but the red collar ought to have served as a kind of talisman protecting the buck from appropriation by any other colonist. Although the collar did not in the end save the deer, it at least gave Wheeler grounds to take Webster to court.[3]

Few colonists went to the trouble of taming deer, but none would have disputed Wheeler's right to do so. The assumption that a person could remove a creature from the wild and transform it into property was firmly rooted in a larger set of English beliefs about the character of relations between people and animals. Like all Europeans, English colonists presumed that it was right and proper for humans to exercise dominion over other creatures. Domestication of animal species, even more than the taming of an individual beast, epitomized this relationship of dominance and the assertion of property rights served as its legal corollary.[4] Thus the incident with the deer revealed that Indians were not the only ones to resort to familiar ideas about animals as they figured out how to deal with new beasts. Colonists likewise relied upon customary ways of thinking in their encounters with New World creatures.

As was the case with Indian views of animals, English ideas had developed within a spiritual framework that helped to determine how the colonists would treat the unfamiliar beasts they discovered. The colonists' Christian beliefs dictated specific approaches to animals and encouraged disapproval of native ideas and behavior that did not follow the prescribed models. This propensity to pass judgment on Indians gained added force through historical circumstances. England's first ventures into colonization in the late sixteenth and early seventeenth centuries coincided with a period of significant religious turmoil at home. Keenly aware of the importance of hewing to orthodoxy in thought and action, colonists were especially prone to identify and even emphasize their differences from Indians who fell beyond the Christian pale. Whatever similarities may have existed between their own approaches to animals and those of native peoples remained largely invisible to colonists more interested in distinguishing themselves from the Indians than in finding common ground.

Yet more than anything else, colonists resorted to familiar ideas about animals as a way of imposing order on a strange New World, of making it into a place more like home. An essential part of their strategy was the assertion of dominion over animals, a relationship that the English considered both natural and divinely sanctioned, and all but unknown in America before their arrival. Until they succeeded, the New World would remain a wild place and an uncomfortable home for English settlers. Confident of the necessity as well as the propriety of their endeavor, colonists intended to take possession of America and its fauna, much as David Wheeler staked a claim to his red-collared deer.

Although Christianity with its doctrine of dominion exerted the greatest influence on the colonists' ideas, this religious framework competed with another, even older, set of notions that offered an alternative view of humans' relationships with animals. Seventeenth-century English people were heirs to rich folkloric traditions that identified animals as creatures deserving of special attention, and sometimes even fear or awe. The roots of this folklore ran so deep into the English past that colonists were rarely conscious of its lingering significance. Even those who regarded themselves as the staunchest of Christians carried vestiges of these earlier beliefs with them to the New World. More compatible with the Indians' ideas about animals than were the tenets of Christianity, the diffuse elements of this folkloric tradition nevertheless failed to serve as a effective bridge between cultures. Persistent though its influence was among English people on both sides of the Atlantic, the lore of animals was suspect, more often invoked out of unthinking habit rather than conviction. Any similarities colonists discerned between such beliefs and native ideas about animals would not work to the Indians' advantage.

The origins of England's animal folklore lay in the distant past, in some cases reaching as far back as the teachings of Virgil, Pliny, and other ancients. Certain features bore witness to pre-Christian sources from northern Europe while others survived because they reflected actual observations of animal behavior.[5] No matter what the source, virtually every element of this lore attributed significance to animal behaviors. Folkloric beliefs put people on their guard by teaching that seemingly innocuous animal actions could have good and bad effects on human lives. Offering guidelines to help in interpreting the meaning of animal behavior, folklore supplied tools for coping with an uncertain world.

In perhaps its most popular form, folklore taught people how to predict the weather from observations of animal behavior, a skill of obvious utility to farmers who really did need to make hay while the sun shone. With what was probably a fair rate of accuracy given their country's climate, English people interpreted the sight of low-flying cranes, herons, swallows, and rooks as harbingers of rain. In parts of Northumberland, people called green woodpeckers "rainbirds" in the belief that their appearance forecast precipitation.[6] Ravens that croaked three or four times and then flapped their wings heralded sunshine, as did larks flying high in the sky. When red grouse ventured into farmyards, however, frost or snow was on the way.[7] Birds may have been the favorite sources of weather-knowledge, but were not the only creatures to provide this information. A cat that put its foot over its ear when washing its face, a hedgehog that emerged from the woods, and a chirping cricket all foretold a change in the weather. Farmers could anticipate rain if cattle lay on their right sides or looked toward the south, or if rams skipped about and ate more than usual. If a dog's hair smelled peculiarly strong, or its stomach-rumbles could be heard, rain or snow could be expected.[8]

Birds and other animals were also credited with predicting shifts in human fortunes. If an Essex man saw two crows coming his way, he anticipated good luck. Encounters with ladybugs and—at least in early modern England—black cats were similarly deemed auspicious. Animals appear to have served more frequently, however, as signs of trouble. Barn owls, hares, and mice (if they ran over one's feet) portended bad luck. So too did a dog that howled or dug holes in the earth. Lancashire inhabitants dreaded seeing a magpie; to ward off the bad luck that would surely follow, they raised their hats in salutation to the bird and either made the sign of the cross or crossed their thumbs and spit over them. In the north of England, when rooks forsook a home they foretold the downfall of its resident family. All over the country people could bring bad luck on themselves if they killed certain birds: in Northamptonshire it was robins, in Sussex and Yorkshire swallows, and in Hampshire cuckoos or swallows.[9]

More ominously, animals could be portents of death. Owls, pigeons, and ravens all aroused fears of mortality. A robin entering a house or a stork leaving its roof sent a message of doom. If a swallow landed on someone's shoulder, that person's days were numbered. The sound of a bird tapping at one's window (a sparrow in Wiltshire, a robin in Northamptonshire, a magpie in Ireland) served as a death knell. An invalid could expect a turn for the worse if a dog scraped at the walls of the house.[10]

Ubiquitous though this animal lore was, it is hard to gauge how seriously people took it. Yorkshire villagers may have reflexively warned their neighbors about the dangers of killing swallows with as little genuine concern as people today feel when they caution against crossing paths with a black cat. Seventeenth-century Lancashire men may have laughed as they doffed their caps to passing magpies, if they did it at all. Much of this lore circulated as proverbial statements and highly localized expressions; although the sayings have survived, the contexts in which they were spoken have not.[11] Their very persistence, however—in some cases, to the present day—argues against dismissing these sorts of remarks and the ideas that informed them as meaningless to seventeenth-century English people.

Indeed, one measure of the significance of animal lore was its appearance in the relatively new format of popular printed books. The authors of such works included this material not to lighten serious texts with humorous examples of rustic foolishness but to offer nuggets of information useful to their readers. The agricultural writer John Worlidge, for example, felt no compunctions about including a section on animals as "prognosticks" in a tract that otherwise advocated advanced farming practices. Writers of herbals and emblem books likewise incorporated elements of animal lore into their works.[12] The appearance of this material in print, at a time when reading was a skill possessed mainly by gentlemen, prosperous yeomen, and members of such professions as the church, law, and commerce, indicates that the audience for folkloric notions was not restricted to the lower sorts.[13] John Worlidge specifically addressed his work to the "gentry and yeomanry of England" who he evidently assumed would be interested in the prognosticating prowess of cows and cats and dogs.

The diffuse traditions of animal folklore crossed the Atlantic with little difficulty. English emigrants, steeped in the notion that animals could forecast the weather, never questioned its relevance in a New World setting. Thus colonists prepared for rain when they observed low-flying swallows, heard the cawing of crows, or noticed that their cattle were restless. They enlivened their speech and writing with proverbial phrases that captured the essence of animal lore. Colonists knew what was meant by "fair-weather birds" and reminded one another that hogs could "see the wind." In Massachusetts, Samuel Sewall made regular diary notations around mid-April that "Swallows proclaim the Spring" even though as often as not snow still covered the ground. The notion that birds or other animals could be unwelcome portents likewise survived the ocean crossing. Even so eminent a figure as Harvard president Charles Chauncy worried when a "white peckled Dove Pidgeon" flew against the window of a room shared by Edward Taylor and one of Chauncy's own sons. When the boys opened the window, the bird flew in "& cooed & brissled" at them. President Chauncy, perhaps recalling the dire significance associated with birds tapping against windows and flying into houses, pronounced the event "omenous surely."[14]

Such examples testified to the strength of the impulse to find meaning in the behavior of animals. They bore witness to a prevailing belief that humans were very much a part of nature, and that the fates of all the world's creatures were interconnected. The idea surely came easily to people who regularly encountered animals (not to mention the forces of nature) in their daily lives. Lacking explanations for certain events, whether storms or accidents, people took refuge in the search for correspondences between unusual behavior in animals and unexpected turns in human fortunes. Whether accurate or not, these connections—most of which became clear only in hindsight—offered some comfort in a world where death and disaster often struck without warning and good luck sometimes appeared, like a ladybug, out of nowhere.[15]

Yet the diverse collection of ideas, sayings, and practices that informed the lore of animals coexisted uneasily with Christianity. Many features, such as the association between ravens and bad luck, betrayed pre-Christian roots in belief systems that church officials had no desire to encourage. Some rituals survived by combining pagan and Christian symbolism, as in the practice of making the sign of the cross to ward off a magpie's bad luck. A similar amalgamation characterized a Christmas ritual on the Isle of Man, during which a wren was killed and given a church funeral.[16] A legend that linked a robin to the origins of Christianity likewise merged disparate traditions. During the Crucifixion, so the story went, one brave robin attempted either to remove the nails from the dying Christ's hands and feet or to pluck a spike from the Crown of Thorns (the details vary). A drop of the Savior's blood stained the bird's breast, and its descendants have worn this mark of distinction ever since. Because of the original bird's selfless act, robins deserved protection from harm.[17]

In its basic structure and message, this story of the robin bears a remarkable resemblance to the tale that explained the Narragansetts' special relationship with crows.[18] In each case, a bird's helpful act (relieving the suffering of the dying Christ; bringing the first corn and beans to the Narragansett people) enjoined humans to treat its species with respect. Crows reminded Narragansetts of Kautántouwit's generosity, and robins recalled for English people the sacrifice Christ made on behalf of humanity. Although derived from quite different sources, the persistence of stories like these in both cultures suggested that Indians and the English, despite manifest differences, shared a belief in animal symbolism that was linked to spirituality. Likewise, English people who thought that animals could forecast the weather or influence the direction of human fortunes blurred the distinction between natural and supernatural phenomena, a conceptual division that had even less meaning for Indians.

Possibilities for mutual understanding, however, foundered in good part because of one important difference. While the English assumed that animals could serve as signs, symbols, and portents, they refrained from according nonhuman creatures spiritual power of their own. This relegation of animals to an essentially passive role clashed with the Indians' conception of animal spirits and *manitous,* which intervened in human lives in a far more direct fashion. If there were any parallels the English detected between their own folklore and the Indians' ideas about animal spirits, they were ones that heightened the colonists' desire to differentiate their views from those they attributed to Indians.

Colonists were apt to regard animal spirits as being most similar to the animal familiars that served as witches' diabolic accomplices. Because accused English witches were far more likely than their European counterparts to admit to having animal familiars, this association resonated with particular force among English people on both sides of the Atlantic. Malevolent spirits in England came in all shapes and sizes, appearing as cats, dogs, mice, rats, chickens, toads, rabbits, even ferrets. Witches conversed with their familiars, hatching plans to harm anyone who had offended them. Many people assumed that alleged witches permitted these creatures to suck their blood through special "teats" that investigators claimed to find on witches' bodies as incontrovertible evidence of their guilt.[19] Victims also reported seeing witches consorting with the devil himself, who adopted any number of animal shapes for such encounters. The notion that Satan often disguised himself as an animal became a staple of popular culture in England; ballads and tales recounted his exploits while camouflaged as a black bear, a black dog, or a goat.[20]

The devil assumed the guise of animals in the English colonies as well. One Connecticut boy insisted that Satan materialized before him "in the shape of a fox" and tormented him mercilessly. Other New Englanders claimed to have spied the devil in the form of a white calf, or a "black dog with eyes in his back."[21] Animal familiars likewise assisted New World witches in performing mischief. According to Increase Mather, Bostonians so feared witches' familiars that they would "be in a Sweat, and ready to die away" if a cat walked into the room. Other candidates for suspicion included crows, owls, dogs, and mice. During the notorious witchcraft trials in Salem in 1692, four-year-old Dorcas Good told authorities that her mother's familiars included "three birds, one black, one yellow and that these birds hurt the children and afflicted persons."[22]

Anxiety about witchcraft shaped the colonists' evaluation of Indian comments about animal spirits and *manitous*. The tendency to draw such a parallel reflected a prevalent assumption among colonists that Indians were devil-worshipers anyway. At the start of English colonization in Virginia, John Smith announced that the Powhatans' "chiefe God" was none other than "the Divell," a declaration that set the tone for English opinion on native religion. New England colonial leaders were equally convinced of a diabolical connection. The principal duty of Wampanoag shamans, Plymouth Colony's Edward Winslow asserted, was "calling upon the devil." William Wood believed that Massachusett Indian powwows employed "necromantic charms" to "bring to pass strange things" and heal the sick. Thomas Morton had little doubt that New England Indian shamans consorted with the devil, although his observations of their activities led him to believe they were "but weake witches." Colonists mainly focused on the allegedly nefarious practices of native religious leaders, but their descriptions occasionally introduced animals in ways that echoed accounts of English or colonial witchcraft cases. When a Wampanoag shaman conducted a healing ritual, Edward Winslow reported, he supposedly carried on his shoulder a snake or eagle visible only to him, much as an English witch might be accompanied by a familiar. And just as Satan sometimes appeared to English witches as an animal, Hobbomock—the spirit-being whom Winslow identified as the devil—showed himself to New England Indians in the form of "a deer, a fawn, an eagle, &c. but most ordinarily a snake."[23]

Insofar as associations with witchcraft rather than with more benign aspects of folklore shaped their impressions of native spirituality, colonists were unlikely to perceive similarities between their ways of thinking about animals and those of Indians. The failure of folklore to serve as a cultural bridge, moreover, was virtually foreordained by its increasingly precarious position in English culture. The difficulties in reconciling folkloric beliefs about animals with Christian doctrine were magnified by England's turn to Protestantism in the sixteenth and seventeenth centuries. Religious changes that directed Christians to reject old "superstitions" and divided believers into factions based on fine distinctions in theology and ecclesiology scarcely encouraged English colonists to seize upon animal lore as a serendipitous link to non-Christian Indian spirituality.

England's permanent shift to Protestantism following Elizabeth I's accession in 1558 sparked a campaign against any popular beliefs that might rival true Christianity as preserved in scripture. Clerical authorities and Protestant reformers concentrated their efforts on undermining the authority of the cunning folk, fortune-tellers, and special healers who claimed to have various special powers. Prophecy, alchemy, and astrology joined witchcraft as subjects for attack because they all threatened to supplant theology with magic. Although animal lore never became a specific target in these efforts, a heightened anxiety about Protestant orthodoxy in general exposed the dangers inherent in folkloric beliefs and demanded their eradication.[24]

Certain rituals associated with animal lore invited attack from religious reformers keen on uprooting beliefs and actions that they identified as superstitions—a derogatory label that, not coincidentally, came into increasing use in England during the era of the Protestant Reformation.[25] It scarcely helped matters that some of these practices displayed Catholic as well as pagan influences. This only added to the reasons why Protestant reformers would detest such gestures as making the sign of the cross after spying a magpie or holding a church funeral for a wren. The belief that animal behaviors could predict shifts in human fortunes posed an equally dangerous

threat, luring unsophisticated villagers to conclude that the animals themselves possessed a kind of special, superior knowledge.

The notion that animals might know more than humans contradicted
scripture. According to the Bible, God made animals before He made
humans, but in every way except the timing of their creation, humans took
precedence over other creatures. Only humans were formed in God's own
image. The divine "breath of life" that animated Adam and his descendants
transformed them into "living souls" greater than any animal on earth.
And only humans could hope to achieve eternal salvation. The mere
suggestion that animals might experience immortality was, as one seventeenth-century English preacher put it, an "offensive absurdity." Christ
suffered, died, and rose again for the sake of humankind, not for any other
creatures. God's promise of salvation thus created a permanent divide
between people and animals.[26]

The Lord also decreed that humans, during their time on earth, should
rule over animals. God instructed Adam and Eve and succeeding generations
to "subdue" the land and exercise "dominion over the fish of the sea, and
over the fowl of the air, and over every living thing that moveth upon the
earth." The expulsion from the Garden of Eden brought pain and sorrow to
human lives, and made toil and sweat the price of subduing the earth, but
human dominion over animals remained in force. After the Flood, God
renewed His promise of dominion to Noah and his descendants, announcing
that all living creatures would have "the fear of you and the dread of you."
Thus scripture not only established human uniqueness with regard to other
creatures, but also sanctioned humankind's ascendancy over animals.[27]

Neither of these ideas was uniquely Christian—Aristotle, for instance,
argued for human precedence over animals on the grounds that only people
possessed rational souls—but the rise of Christianity gave them added force.
Over the course of centuries, various religious thinkers blended classical
ideas with scriptural revelation to craft arguments for human superiority.
Early church fathers such as Ambrose and Augustine agreed with Aristotle
that animals' inferiority was grounded in their lack of reason. Writing in the
thirteenth century, Thomas Aquinas reiterated that animals were "without
intellect," adding that their inability to achieve salvation also relegated them
to a lower position in the order of Creation. Eager as many Protestants were
to distance themselves from Catholic teachings, this was one tenet they
wholeheartedly accepted.[28]

The topic of humanity's place within nature likewise engaged early modern European philosophers who concurred on the general point of human superiority even if they differed on specifics. By the seventeenth century, intellectuals concentrated on three attributes that established human uniqueness. One was the capacity for speech, reflecting the assumption that only humans could effectively communicate with each other. Another distinguishing characteristic was the ability to reason. Although animals might display evidence of a rudimentary understanding, this was typically dismissed as mere instinct. Humans alone had a practical intelligence that allowed for imagination, speculation, and deliberation. The third distinctive quality was moral sense. William Perkins, the preeminent English Calvinist theologian, for example, insisted that only "men and Angels" possessed consciences, which permanently distinguished them from soulless animals. In the 1630s, the French philosopher René Descartes emphasized animals' lack of language and reason and their dependence on instinct to conclude that they were little more than machines.[29]

From these multiple intellectual strands emerged a broader conception of the universe as an ordered hierarchy, sometimes called the "Great Chain of Being." God presided at the top in the celestial realm, followed by the angels. Far below angels, and yet far above animals, stood humans. This intermediate position reflected humans' double existence—temporary sojourns on earth succeeded by eternal lives either of salvation or damnation in the hereafter. Next in line were animals confined solely to an earthly existence and arranged in descending ranks determined more by symbolic characteristics than actual physical features. This classification system inspired a popular literary form, the bestiary, combining scientific treatise with morality tale based on miscellaneous oral traditions and written sources. Authors of bestiaries assigned each animal to its proper place, almost always beginning with lions. These creatures owed their preeminence to their status as the "king of beasts," a designation that betrayed the authors' presumptions in favor of monarchy more than any objective consideration of lions' position in the animal world. Tigers and other large felines usually followed, succeeded in turn by various mammals, and then birds, reptiles, and fish. Mythical creatures—unicorns, manticores (part man and part lion, with a scorpion's tail), griffins (half lion, half eagle)—were interspersed with real animals in these compilations, testifying to the eclectic nature of the source material. Like lions and tigers, unicorns and griffins occupied specific places in the universal hierarchy that ordered all of Creation.[30]

Despite the seeming clarity of this view of an ordered universe, there was room for ambiguity. If there were no gaps in the chain of being, for instance, could the division between humans and animals (or humans and angels, for that matter) really be very wide? Once a distinction of any kind was drawn between people and animals, its rationale sooner or later became subject to debate. Did their lack of a conscience dehumanize infants and atheists (defined at the time as people without a moral sense)? What was the status of werewolves and so-called "wild men," whose reported appearances fascinated early modern Europeans precisely because these creatures occupied an uncertain border between man and beast? These questions suggest some of the difficulties faced by intellectuals who sought a coherent justification for complex conceptual categories that defied easy exposition.[31]

Ordinary English people, having had more experience with cattle than with werewolves, rarely pondered these issues at such an abstract level or doubted their intuitive grasp of the differences between humans and animals. Yet these were the same sorts of people who often circulated stories and recited proverbs that undermined the idea of human superiority. Religious reformers were far less concerned about logical contradictions than the threat to scriptural authority. Rooting out folk beliefs in the name of orthodoxy, however, was no easy task. Derived from sources as ancient as those positing human superiority, popular beliefs proved remarkably tenacious. They were part of the fabric of early modern English culture: even the most rigorous Protestants probably grew up watching birds for evidence of rain and worrying about the peculiar behavior of dogs. Translating their religious zeal into an agenda for action, reformers realized that the problem lay not with the existence of animal signs but with their interpretation.

Protestant reformers took direct aim at the assumption that animal signs, along with earthquakes, comets, accidents, and other phenomena, occurred at the whim of fortune and insisted instead that these portents manifested divine intervention in human affairs. They were special providences sent by God as messages to His people. The proper response was for witnesses to such occurrences to search within their hearts for the causes of God's sudden attention. In 1637, for example, when thousands of robins flocked to the Isles of Scilly, where they had never been seen before, William Prynne concluded that the Lord had sent the birds to welcome John Bastwick, banished there because of his Puritanism. By enveloping animal lore along with other forms of popular belief within the capacious blanket of providentialism, religious reformers appropriated them for their own purposes, easing the transition to Protestantism for people committed to the notion that certain animal behaviors had some sort of meaning for humans.[32]

Anxious about the wisdom of their decisions to leave England, colonists were especially vigilant in their search for signs of divine approbation. Almost as soon as they boarded their ships, emigrants scanned sea and sky for portents. The appearance and behavior of animals, as well as dramatic shifts in the weather, offered numerous opportunities for collective introspection. Early one Monday morning during their 1635 voyage to Massachusetts, the Puritan minister Richard Mather and his shipmates gathered on deck to observe the capture of a prodigious porpoise. Mather encouraged his flock to see this "marvelous merry sport" as a sign of the Lord's favor, an entertaining complement to Sunday's formal worship. God was "so good . . . unto us," the minister explained, first to provide "spiritual refreshing to our soules" on the Sabbath and then "delightful recreation to our bodyes, at the taking and opening of this huge and strange fish" the following morning. John Winthrop likewise took note of the arrival of "a wilde pigeon" and "another smalle lande birde" on board the *Arbella* as the ship approached Penobscot Bay. In recording the incident in his journal, Winthrop may have imagined himself a latter-day Noah, who knew the Flood had abated when a dove returned to the Ark bearing an olive leaf in its beak. Perhaps in similar fashion the birds' appearance providentially heralded the imminent, safe end of the *Arbella*'s voyage.[33]

The colonists' keen interest in animal providences may have intensified upon their arrival in the New World. For Winthrop and other Bay Colony leaders preoccupied with creating a godly society, few events were more momentous than the appearance of a snake in the Cambridge meetinghouse in 1648 during the synod called to formalize Congregational worship in New England. No one dared to think that the snake's sudden appearance in the elders' seat during Rev. John Allen's sermon was simply a coincidence. Several men nervously "shifted from it" before Rev. William Thompson stepped on the snake's head while someone else grabbed a pitchfork to kill it. Afterwards John Winthrop had little trouble interpreting the event as a divine providence. "The serpent is the devill" and "the Synode the Representation of the Churches of Christ" in New England, the governor deduced. "The devill had formerly & lately attempted" the "disturbance & dissolution" of the clerical gathering, he went on, but the participants' faith triumphed over Satan's plans "& Chrushed his head."[34]

More prosaic instances of animal providences abounded. In the spring of 1633, Nathaniel Morton reported that "a numerous company of *Flies*" besieged Plymouth colonists, "eat[ing] up the green things" and presaging an "infectious Feaver" that only diminished after the settlers "besought the Lord by Fasting and Prayer." When John Dane of Ipswich went out on a hunting expedition and noticed that his pig had followed him, he interpreted its behavior as a message from God that he should return home. As Dane made his return journey a flock of geese flew overhead. When he managed to shoot "a galant gose in the very nick of time," Dane was convinced that this blessing confirmed his correct interpretation of the earlier providential sign. Other colonists remarked upon unusual animal behaviors but refrained from assigning particular meanings to them. John Hull of Boston, for instance, puzzled over the significance of the "very many bears" that emerged "out of the wilderness" during the autumn of 1663. Five years later, Hull recorded another strange event, this time in Wethersfield, Connecticut, where "a very great swarm of flies, near a mile in breadth and two miles long, thick as bees" passed through town.[35]

Puritans such as Morton, Dane, and Hull may have been especially prone to take note of providences, but the "hotter sort" of Protestants were not alone in imputing religious meaning to unusual animal portents. John Smith, a Protestant though hardly a Puritan, resorted to a providentialist interpretation when a plague of rats descended upon English settlers in Bermuda. The noxious rodents "spread themselves into all parts of the Countrey," Smith reported. Even "fishes have beene taken with rats in their bellies," and no grain field escaped unscathed from the "troupes" of rats that swarmed through them at night. The "great God of heaven," Smith declared, was obviously enraged at officials' mismanagement of the colony and sent the rats as a chastisement. Smith was just as convinced as any strict Calvinist would have been that "the speedy encrease of this vermine" and later their "sudden removall" was a "secret worke of God."[36]

The idea that God might use animals to send messages to His people upheld the principle of hierarchy enshrined in scripture, supplanting the dubious notion that animals might act autonomously as agents of bad luck. In the case of Bermuda, the sharpness of the Lord's rebuke in good part stemmed from His choice of such lowly creatures to deliver it. Providentialism thus became an effective weapon in the Protestant arsenal against popular belief. Reinterpreting animal signs as divine messages also redirected people's responses into more respectable channels. Purely reflexive reactions—making the sign of the cross, or saluting a bird with one's hat—gave way to introspection, a search for God's meaning in the particular animal sign rather than an attempt to ward off the animal's own power.

Even if religious reformers' campaign against folk beliefs fell short of complete success, it nevertheless expanded the compass of Protestantism and discredited views about animals that did not strictly accord with scripture. And although this effort occurred within the framework of English religious history and was mainly aimed at an English audience, its effects reverberated in the colonies. English Protestants inclined to criticize villagers who crossed themselves at the sight of a magpie would hardly be more tolerant of Indians who spoke of powerful animal *manitous.* In one of history's many ironies, religious developments in England encouraged greater disdain for non-Christian ways of viewing the world just at the point when English people encountered the inhabitants of the New World.

The steady advance of Protestant orthodoxy over folk beliefs during the sixteenth and seventeenth centuries sharply diminished the chances that colonists would acknowledge any convergence between their own animal lore and Indian ways of thinking about other creatures. Yet this was not the only potential avenue to cross-cultural understanding when it came to dealing with animals. Whatever their other differences on the subject, Indians and the English could at least agree that animals were good to eat and that hunting was an acceptable means of obtaining meat. Agreement on these basic points, however, did not necessarily signal compatibility. The hierarchical assumptions informing English approaches to hunting bore little relation to Indians' emphasis on reciprocal relations between hunter and prey. As with the definition of animals' spiritual roles, so too with hunting: English perceptions of difference overshadowed recognition of similarities with native peoples.

Eastern Algonquian Indians, like English people, were avid consumers of animal protein. Native inhabitants of New England and the Chesapeake region obtained anywhere from 20 to as much as 90 percent of their calories from meat, fish, and fowl, with amounts varying according to time of the year and proximity to marine resources.[37] The English, in turn, were renowned among early modern Europeans for their meat consumption. At the end of the seventeenth century, Gregory King calculated that English people enjoyed on average over 140 pounds of meat each year—a figure that, to be sure, obscured significant individual variations based on economic status.[38] Both English and Indian consumers particularly relished venison. One English physician maintained that venison was more highly prized in his homeland than anywhere else in Christendom. Likewise in early Rhode Island, Roger Williams translated the Narragansett phrase "I long for Venison" into English, as one of the expressions his native neighbors frequently used.[39]

Much of venison's attraction derived from the difficulty of obtaining it by hunting. An enthusiasm for the chase animated Indian and English hunters alike, all of them eager to experience the satisfaction of making a clean kill. Beyond the level of personal experience, hunting also fulfilled some of the same social functions in England and native America. In both settings, hunting was primarily a male activity, offering regular opportunities for physical exertion and camaraderie. In each culture, hunters followed certain rituals in pursuing deer and dealing with the animals they killed. Like the Indians who studied the movements of deer in order to track them, Englishmen learned how to simulate the sounds of prey animals as a way of luring them within range of weapons. Members of both cultures also knew that hunting honed skills useful in warfare.[40]

These similarities, however, could not obscure the fact that Indian and English hunters held profoundly different views about the nature of their relationship to prey animals. Aware of the power of animal spirits, native hunters treated prey with respect and performed rituals defined by reciprocity. Although not quite a relationship of equals, the connection between Indians and prey was not essentially hierarchical. But notions of domination and subordination were central to the English, who believed that the act of hunting epitomized the divinely sanctioned ascendancy of humankind over animals. As one Englishman asserted in 1642, "man's charter of dominion over the creatures" justified the hunting of any animal deemed worthy of the chase.[41]

English hunters expressed their superiority over prey in various ways, all of which reflected their overarching assumption that animals had been placed on earth for human use. Animals that could be eaten, including deer, rabbits, and wildfowl, thus became prime targets. Nuisance animals—most notably foxes that attacked domestic fowl—were likewise hunted to prevent damage to property. Indians too hunted animals for food and trapped pests like wolves, but they did not follow the English by indulging in the practice that most clearly exemplified the principle of human ascendancy—hunting purely for sport. Convinced that the delights of manly recreation fully justified the sacrifice of animals, English gentlemen made about as powerful an assertion of human dominion as one could imagine. And although many English people disapproved of the wanton exercise of cruelty to animals, there were few formal objections to hunting practices that crossed the line from sport to brutality. The author of *Gentleman's Recreation*, for example, saw nothing wrong with catching a stag with a net, cutting off one of its feet, and releasing it to be chased by bloodhounds. When Queen Elizabeth I grew too old to follow the hounds, she contented herself with using a crossbow to shoot captive deer in an enclosure. Such methods quite explicitly reduced animals to objects for human amusement.[42]

Vivid demonstrations of human dominion especially characterized hunting practices in royal and aristocratic circles. Gentlemen (and sometimes women) aimed arrows or spears at deer, either from stationary platforms or while on horseback. The fates of prey animals now and then depended on royal whim rather than marksmanship. Elizabeth I occasionally bestowed sovereign mercy on a fleeing stag by prohibiting further pursuit, much as she might have pardoned a criminal. In a different vein, her successor James I once allowed a German nobleman to select an individual target from a herd of fallow deer and then had the animal dispatched by huntsmen and hounds while the visitor merely observed the scene. Many a royal or aristocratic hunt culminated in an unmistakable display of dominion with the severed head of a deer presented to the most eminent member of the group and its nose touched to the ground as a sign of submission to the triumphant humans. The contrast with Indian hunting rituals could hardly be starker.[43]

English hunting practices also reinforced the dominion of some people over others. Aristocratic hunters commanded retinues of men whose jobs included controlling the hounds and driving game out of the woods. When the time came to divide up the carcasses of fallen prey, hunters lined up according to rank in a public display of their relative social positions to receive their allotted portions, with the best pieces going to the highest-ranking individuals. If the bag surpassed the needs of the aristocratic table, hunters donated excess meat to suitably grateful underlings, perhaps the local vicar or the village poor. In this as in so many social rituals in early modern England, each participant was reminded of his or her proper place.[44]

Indian men acquired prestige and power through demonstrations of hunting prowess but the activity itself was open to all males. The English, however, conceived of hunting mainly as the perquisite of gentlemen and aristocrats. Ever eager to distinguish themselves from their inferiors, gentlemen vigorously promoted their monopoly over this form of recreation. They found their champion, on this issue at least, in James I, who once asserted that lower class "clowns" ought not to enjoy the privilege of the chase.[45] James wholeheartedly supported Parliament's passage of the Game Act of 1605, one of several measures enacted in the seventeenth century to restrict hunting to the wealthy. The law set stringent property qualifications for hunters that only a minority of Englishmen could meet: an annual income of at least £40 from land or ownership of goods worth a minimum of £200. A yeoman farmer with a lesser estate could not even hunt on his own land, and no tenant could legally pursue game on his landlord's property. Game laws went so far as to prohibit men with insufficient property from owning hunting weapons or hunting dogs.[46]

Besides affirming the importance of social hierarchy, these laws revealed how thoroughly hunting privileges and property rights were entangled with one another. Indian peoples recognized a hunter's right to the animals he killed and native villages asserted a collective sovereignty over hunting territories, but these principles scarcely resembled the intricate web of property rights that characterized hunting in England.[47] Complementing their support of property qualifications, England's upper ranks boldly asserted absolute private rights to hunting lands. The monarch and court favorites claimed royal forests and deer parks as exclusive hunting-grounds, while country gentlemen increasingly enclosed portions of their estates as private reserves for their own hunting pleasure. Lower ranking individuals were not even allowed to shoot deer that wandered off private estates and damaged crops in their fields. These initiatives rested on the presumption that game itself could be regarded as a form of private property restricted to the exclusive use of wealthy people.[48]

Such expansive claims on the part of the gentry did not go uncontested. The noted agricultural writer, Gervase Markham, was hardly the only one to proclaim that hunting was "every honest man's right." Irate commoners tore down fences around private hunting enclosures and carted off the wood to burn in their hearths. Poachers of all ranks defied the game laws. Landless poor folk set traps and snares to supplement meager diets with wild meat. Gangs of gentlemen organized poaching raids to display masculine bravado, settle scores with enemies, or simply acquire venison and rabbit to sell on the black market. Although country gentlemen were better shielded from prosecution by their social rank and wealth, poachers of all sorts faced stiff penalties if caught—fines, imprisonment, or even execution, depending on the kind of prey and the circumstances under which it was hunted.[49]

Gentlemen hunters were sometimes obliged to defend their moral character as well as their property rights. Many English people criticized hunting as a waste of time and money. Staunch Protestants did not universally condemn it, but those who did made sure to couch their opinions in terms of righteous disapproval and not just personal dislike. John Winthrop associated his embrace of Puritanism with a newfound distaste for hunting as an activity that "brings no profite all things considered," although he diluted his message by admitting that he was a poor shot. Rev. Christopher Hooke made his views clear when he informed his London congregation in 1603 that the idle pastime of hunting would not be permitted in heaven.[50]

Whether they approved of it or not, English people generally defined hunting as recreation and not a subsistence activity. This view bore witness to their heavy reliance on domestic animals for most of their meat. English colonists who traveled to the New World found it difficult to see their own experience as the result of historical circumstance and therefore passed judgment on Indians who lacked livestock and thus *did* hunt for subsistence. Predisposed to consider hunting a diversion, colonists tended to regard Indian men, like country gentlemen, as idlers with nothing better to do.

Chesapeake colonists, often gentlemen themselves, were less inclined than New Englanders to be censorious. George Percy merely observed, without complaint, that Indian men in Virginia took "their pleasure in hunting" the local game. John Smith similarly reported that Powhatan men "esteeme" hunting and fishing "a pleasure" as much as English country squires did. But New England colonists, often energized by Puritan self-righteousness, were quick to register disapproval. A brief acquaintance with the Indians of Massachusetts was enough to convince Rev. Francis Higginson that native men "for the most part live idely, they doe nothing but hunt and fish" while their wives "doe all their other worke." Christopher Levett agreed that Indian women were "slaves" whose husbands "will do nothing but kill beasts, fish, etc." As these comments suggest, colonists often embedded their criticism of Indian hunting in a broader set of objections to the ways Indian men and women divided up labor in their villages. Accustomed to social arrangements that assigned agricultural work to men, colonists were dismayed to see Indian women laboring in the fields. This inversion of familiar gender relations intensified the colonists' tendency to dismiss native hunting as recreation and ignore its importance as a subsistence activity.[51]

Had colonists perceived a parallel between native hunters and lower-ranking Englishmen who trapped game in order to put meat on the table, they might have acquired some understanding of a vital part of Indian culture. By likening Indian men to gentlemen of leisure, however, colonists indulged in moral judgments that had little to do with social and economic conditions in native villages. Once the unfavorable comparison had been made, it proved resistant to change and encouraged colonists to make another, equally problematic, assumption. Indians who wasted time with hunting and also failed to domesticate animals obviously needed to learn how to exploit properly the abundant fauna the Lord had placed in the New World for the benefit of humans. It was incumbent on the colonists to show Indians how to do so. Armed with their notions of hierarchy and property rights, English settlers were eager to demonstrate the exercise of dominion in an American setting.

The task that colonists set for themselves was both enormous and unprecedented. None of them had previously attempted to sort out the hierarchical order of an alien environment. None had tried to catalogue an array of strange animals, only some of which resembled creatures that lived in England. Like the Indians who drew upon familiar ideas about animals to interpret their encounters with English livestock, colonists employed their own understanding of animals as creatures subordinate to humans as they surveyed American fauna. Before they could exert dominion over these strange creatures, colonists had to identify them and discover how the Lord intended them to be used. Then colonists could show Indians how they should have been making use of American animals all along.

The extraordinary profusion of New World animals astonished colonists unprepared for such a sight. John Smith, who visited both Virginia and New England, expounded on the "great abundance" of Chesapeake waterfowl and the equally "incredible aboundance" of fish and birds in the northern region. In New England, the "aboundance of Sea-Fish are almost beyond beleeving," Rev. Francis Higginson reported. Thomas Morton claimed that Massachusetts rivers contained so many bass that "wagers have bin layed that one should not throw a stone in the water but that hee should hit a fish." The skies overhead were equally crowded with birds. In Virginia, George Percy observed "an abundance of Fowles of all kindes" flying "as thicke as drops of Hale." They made so much noise that "wee were not able to heare one another speake." There were "millions of millions" of passenger pigeons in New England, John Josselyn announced, so many that they blocked out the sun. William Wood boasted that "I myself have killed twelve score at two shoots." Although the unbridled enthusiasm of these comments may in part be attributed to their appearance in promotional tracts encouraging colonization, they were hardly wholesale fabrications. The Chesapeake and New England regions indeed teemed with wildlife.[52]

Amid such abundance certain familiar English animals, including several species of birds important to folklore, were noticeably absent. With a touch of nostalgia, John Josselyn reported that New England "hath no *Nightingals*, nor *Larks*, nor *Bulfinches*, nor *Sparrows*, nor *Blackbirds*, nor *Magpies*, nor *Jackdawes*, nor *Popinjays*, nor *Rooks*, nor *Pheasants*, nor *Woodcocks*, nor *Quails*, nor *Robins*, nor *Cuckoes*, &c.*" The lack of rats (at least until European ones escaped from ships to infest the New World) offered less cause for regret.[53] Commentators who tried to counterbalance the strangeness of America with reports that some kinds of English animals could be found there often had to admit that Old and New World versions were not quite the same. American turkeys, partridges, geese, ducks, and starlings were bigger; New World hares were smaller. Porcupines resembled hedgehogs, but American squirrels and deer came in several varieties, many of which differed from their English counterparts. William Wood strained the imagination by describing a moose for English readers as "not much unlike red deer." To John Josselyn, the same animal was "a Monster of superfluity." Some colonists thought that foxes were the same on both sides of the Atlantic, but conceded that American ones "doe not stinke, as the Foxes of England" do.[54]

The American woods also harbored creatures with no discernible English equivalents. In describing them, several colonists invoked the lore of wonders, implying that the Lord had created such animals simply to amaze humans. William Wood identified flying squirrels as creatures "more for sight and wonderment than either pleasure or profit." The hummingbird was another marvel. Wood agreed with Thomas Morton that it was "a curious bird to see," to be "admired for shape, coloure, and size." The opossum was even more fascinating. To John Smith it almost resembled a mythical creature, a sort of New World manticore with "a head like a Swine, and a taile like a Rat" and approximating "the bignes of a Cat." Reports of the female opossum's peculiar abdominal pouch and distinctive maternal behavior aroused the curiosity of naturalists on both sides of the Atlantic.[55]

At the same time, bizarre misinformation about other animals circulated in print and by word of mouth, increasing the stock of American prodigies. Porcupines may have borne a close resemblance to English hedgehogs, but in one important respect they differed: according to John Josselyn, porcupines "lay Eggs." He also described an unusual talent displayed by American cormorants. When the birds slept soundly, Josselyn reported, they would "snore like so many Piggs." Perhaps the strangest misconception of all was that American wolves lacked flexible backbones. William Wood declared that "they have no joints from their head to the tail," and pointed out the advantages, at least to humans, of this peculiar anatomy. Because the beasts could not leap or turn around suddenly, they could easily be attacked from behind.[56]

Gathering information about American fauna was a crucial first step toward making sense of an alien environment. The colonists next endeavored to arrange that information within conceptual categories derived from their English experience, for only then could they begin to discern the hierarchical structure intrinsic to America's natural world. The result of their efforts was the compilation of what amounted to New World bestiaries. These accounts not only sought to create order out of the chaos of America's animal life but also ventured to suggest the best uses to which these creatures could be put.

If the authors of these descriptive accounts were somewhat eclectic in their choice of classification schemes, they nevertheless adhered to principles familiar to educated Europeans. As in classical and medieval bestiaries, most New World versions began with mammals, the creatures closest to humans in anatomy and mode of reproduction. Birds generally came next, followed by fish. This organizational scheme represented different habitats of land, air, and water as well as distinctive biological characteristics. Within each division, there was little agreement on proper order beyond a general tendency to list larger animals first. Only William Wood imitated medieval models by beginning with "the kingly lion," although honesty forced him to admit that "I will not say that I ever saw any myself" in Massachusetts. Otherwise, deer or bears appeared first, with such creatures as raccoons, beavers, rabbits, squirrels, and foxes following in descending order. Eagles topped the lists of birds as in medieval bestiaries; thereafter only larger species such as hawks, turkeys, geese, ducks, and pigeons were included. Few compilers bothered to mention reptiles or insects. Incomplete though they might have been, these lists reassured English readers that a natural hierarchy prevailed in America as in the rest of the world, testifying to the universality of the divine order of Creation.[57]

The principle of hierarchy dominated these lists, but utility to humans also shaped their design. By identifying the "most desirable, useful, and beneficial creatures" in America or, more bluntly, categorizing them either as "commodities" or "discommodities," the compilers of these lists revealed their human-centered approach to the natural world.[58] The potential use for these animals exciting the greatest interest, particularly in the early years of settlement, was as food. Colonists took literally God's promise to Noah that "every moving thing that liveth shall be meat for you," rejecting only insects and reptiles. One did not have to be a gentleman or a poacher to dine on venison or rabbit. Colonists likewise tried moose meat, which John Josselyn found "moist and lushious somewhat like Horse flesh," as well as squirrels, raccoons, beavers, and porcupines. Bear was pronounced "excellent, with a better taste then beefe," so long as the animal's "venomous" brain was avoided. Adventurous colonists sampled wildcat, which Thomas Morton and Josselyn compared to lamb. William Wood tasted otter but admitted it was "none of the best meat." English settlers roasted turkeys, geese, ducks, and any number of other wildfowl—even owls and crows. Josselyn identified "birds for the dish" to assist his readers; Wood advised his to abstain from cormorant, "the worst of fowls for meat, tasting rank and fishy." Seafood was so abundant that Francis Higginson complained of being "cloyed" with a surfeit of lobster.[59] Before 1660, Chesapeake settlers relied on wild sources for as much as 40 percent of the meat in their diet.[60] Sorting animals according to their compatibility with English tastes in this way amounted to culinary imperialism, as much an exercise in taking possession of the New World as was making maps and naming territorial landmarks.

Colonists outdid one another in imagining other benefits that could be derived from American fauna. Seal skins would be "good for diverse uses," William Wood advised, and seal oil "very good to burn in lamps." Swans provided feathers for pillows and quills for pens. Colonists' hats could sport bands made of snake skins; their clothes and bedding could be scented with muskrat "stones wrapt in Cotten-wool." The ever-inventive John Josselyn suggested using dogfish skins "to cover Boxes and Instrument Cases," and the rougher skins of stingrays on "Boxes and Hafts of Knives, and Rapier sticks." Vulture skins would be "good to line doublets with," and the tough hides of sea elephants Josselyn judged "excellent" for making straps. He thought seal skins made wonderful gloves. Certain scarlet mussels had "a purple Vein, which being prickt with a Needle yieldeth a perfect purple or scarlet juice" that produced an indelible dye. New World animals might even serve the needs of the rare New Englander with a penchant for sport. Josselyn, a man with scant affection for Puritan killjoys, heartily recommended hunting foxes in wintertime and remarked on the singular enjoyment to be had from hunting and baiting wolves.[61]

True to his training as a physician, Josselyn was indefatigable in his search for medical applications for animals (or at least parts of them). Many of his suggestions reflected his belief in the doctrine of signatures, which posited that the external appearance of certain plants and animals indicated how they might be used to heal human suffering. More often associated with herbal remedies—for instance, treating jaundice with the yellow juice of celandine—the idea also applied to animal-based substances. Thus Josselyn advocated wearing a vulture's skull around the neck to treat a headache, mixing the ashes of dolphin teeth with honey to ease teething pain in infants, using the "bone" near a moose's heart as a cordial, and concocting rattlesnake antivenin by adding the dried and pulverized heart of a snake to wine or beer. Invoking the related theory of isopathy, which proposed treating a diseased part of the body with a substance produced by that same body part in an animal, Josselyn recommended a cocktail of wolf dung and white wine to ease colic.[62]

Less outlandish remedies may actually have offered some relief from pain. The "grease" of all sorts of animals, from bears and raccoons to rattlesnakes and whales, supplied liniment for aches, bruises, sciatica, and broken bones. The fat of pond frogs soothed burns, "leaving no Scar."[63] Some of Josselyn's other suggestions, however, reveal more about the kinds of afflictions suffered by colonists than their chances for a cure. Beaver grease, he declared, would heal "Nerves, Convulsions, Epilepsies, Apoplexies," and as an added bonus, the animal's tail was an aphrodisiac. The ashes of a sea turtle, mixed with oil or bear grease, restored hair to balding pates. Women troubled with "the Mother Fits" (hysteria) might find relief by inhaling fumes produced by burning seal oil or castoreum from beaver glands. As far as Josselyn was concerned, American fauna offered a veritable pharmacopoeia to English settlers.[64]

Authors who compiled these kinds of lists paid less attention to "discommodious" animals that were either nuisances or threats to health and safety. Only a few writers mentioned them, in part to offset suspicions that their accounts of America were too good to be true. For Francis Higginson, the category of noisome animals included mosquitoes and snakes. Josselyn enlarged the roster of "venomous and pestilent Creatures" to encompass mice, bats, wasps, and horseflies. William Wood lumped skunks, ferrets, and foxes together as "beasts of offence" whose "impudence" led them to raid henhouses. As always, the creatures' worth was measured by their utility, or in this case their inconvenience, to humankind.[65]

Observers on the whole preferred to accentuate the benefits provided by New World animals. Advice about how best to exploit American creatures for food and medicine spoke to the most basic needs of colonists and therefore took precedence over other uses. But colonial enterprises, all of which initially depended on borrowed money, faced other pressing requirements beyond mere survival. Thus an interest in figuring out how animals could produce profit was never far from colonists' minds. John Smith focused his attention on fish, which he predicted would likely be the "maine Staple" of the New England economy. One early Virginia colonist similarly estimated that "meerly our fishing for Sturgeon cannot be lesse worth than 1000 li a yeare, leaving hering and codd as possibilityes.[66]

Animals whose meat filled colonists' stomachs also provided skins and furs that could be sold to line their pockets. Assessing the advantages of Roanoke in 1588, Thomas Hariot reckoned that otter and other furs "wil yeelde good profite." Deer hides were "good merchandize," announced Thomas Morton, and beaver pelts, "the best marchantable commodity that can be found," earned ten shillings a pound. Lynx, marten, and fox furs likewise attracted buyers.[67] Exportable commodities like fish and furs excited the greatest interest, but in New England colonists with more modest aspirations could profit from a thriving local market for wildfowl. According to William Wood, nearly every bird had its price: six shillings for a swan, four shillings for a good-sized turkey cock, two shillings for a crane, six to eighteen pence per goose (depending on the color), six pence for a duck, and four pence a partridge.[68]

Like the organizational schemes informing New World bestiaries, the assignment of prices to animals reflected hierarchical assumptions. Shillings and pence served both as quantitative and qualitative measures of animals' value relative to the needs and desires of the humans who took precedence over them. Yet classifying animals not just in terms of their utility but also their market value added a new dimension to the relationship of dominion. Putting a price on animals symbolized the conversion of creatures into commodities. Once New World animals had been identified as useful goods, colonists were faced with the task of figuring out how the bundle of customs and laws that regulated private property in England would apply to American creatures.

That task was complicated by a feature of English common law that made it difficult for people to claim exclusive ownership of wild animals. According to common law, the creatures that ran at liberty in the woods and the fish that swam in rivers and ocean were *ferae naturae*, or "wild in nature," and as such were exempt from any claim to private possession. This designation contributed to the controversy over game laws, which arose over the Crown's contested assumption of a prerogative right to all the game in England. It was not at all clear if the Crown had exclusive right to the New World's animals, if they belonged to Indians, or if colonists could appropriate creatures as they wished.[69]

Common law, however, did recognize the possibility of an individual claiming a limited right to wild animals that had been tamed or otherwise restrained by the exercise of human dominion. This alternative construction of property rights had developed in England over the course of centuries to protect the rights of ownership over domesticated animals. Toward the end of the seventeenth century, the English philosopher John Locke would incorporate this idea into his general theory of property, declaring that anyone who tamed animals "did thereby acquire a propriety in them" defensible in law. Colonists like David Wheeler evidently presumed that the same right extended to colonists who tamed wild animals in the New World. The red collar he fastened on his deer was meant to signify the animal's removal from the state of nature and its new status as property.[70]

However much taming an individual animal established an owner's property rights, colonists were far more interested in domesticating whole species of New World creatures, which promised substantial economic benefits.[71] Although no English settler had ever actually domesticated an animal, few proponents of this project seemed to be deterred by inexperience. Colonists who wrote about American fauna were constantly on the lookout for potentially domesticable species. They achieved success with one lucky pick, converting turkeys from wildfowl to barnyard animals. John Josselyn reported that by the 1670s it had become "very rare to meet with a wild *Turkie* in the Woods" of New England, while colonists kept flocks of them "about their Houses as tame as ours in *England.*"[72]

Colonists did not stop with turkeys but instead entertained notions of domesticating all sorts of creatures. Beavers, with their valuable pelts, offered a particularly tempting target. John Josselyn, for one, assumed that the rodents could be made into farm animals. "They will be tame," he claimed, offering as evidence the improbable story of a beaver "that not long since was kept at *Boston* in the *Massachusetts-Bay,* and would run up and down the streets, returning home without a call." A group of French refugees who settled in Virginia towards the end of the seventeenth century contemplated "a design, of getting into the breed of Buffaloes," fascinated by the fact that the beasts were "much larger than other Cattle, and have the benefit of being natural to the Climate." Certain New Englanders likewise thought that moose could be domesticated. According to William Wood, a few of the region's colonists had "some thoughts of keeping them tame and to accustom them to the yoke," perhaps using them as dairy animals as well. The scheme appeared to make eminent sense, "first, because they are so fruitful, bringing forth three at a time, being likewise very uberous [milk-producing]; secondly, because they will live in winter without fodder."[73]

In concocting these schemes, however, the colonists' reach exceeded their grasp. None of these creatures is well suited to domestication. Josselyn's claims notwithstanding, beavers resist domestication largely because of the difficulty of maintaining enormous tracts of woodland to provide them with food. Although buffalo are related to cattle, they are prone to stress-related disorders when kept in confinement. Modern ranchers thus prefer to experiment with bison-cattle hybrids in order to produce a more tractable beast. The colonists who envisioned domesticated moose may have known that, during the seventeenth century, Swedish farmers occasionally plowed with teams of castrated elk bulls and obtained milk from elk cows. King Karl I even ordered some of his courtiers to ride elk because they could move faster than horses. But the physical power and natural skittishness of moose, their preference for inaccessible forested swamps, and the difficulty of providing them with diets high in bark and woody fiber, all posed formidable obstacles to domestication. Moreover, the beasts were not quite as prolific as William Wood supposed, generally producing two, but only rarely three, offspring at a time.[74]

The impracticality of these plans became clear with time, and there is no evidence that serious attempts to realize them ever materialized. The ideas that inspired such schemes were nevertheless significant insofar as they exposed the colonists' assumption that New World animals were at their disposal. Every new use they could think of for an American creature constituted an implied reproach of Indians who had failed to profit from these animals anywhere near the extent that colonists thought possible. Important as economic gain was to colonists, however, their myriad plans served a larger purpose. As they sorted out which creatures could be eaten, which could be sold, which should be destroyed as vermin, and which might be tamed, colonists rearranged the seeming chaos of New World nature into its proper order.

English colonists brought with them a bundle of disparate ideas to apply to their encounters with New World animals. As events unfolded, some assumptions turned out to have greater salience than others. Notions derived from folklore, which might have supplied a tenuous link to Indian ways of thinking, gave way to an emphasis on orthodox Christian tenets that sharply differentiated humans from other creatures, denied animals any independent spiritual status, and sanctioned human dominion over the natural world. The hierarchical underpinnings of English-style hunting likewise diminished its usefulness as a bridge to Indian culture.

Ideas about hierarchy and human dominion over animals did not persist as mere abstractions, but took concrete form in colonists' plans for remaking the New World in England's image. Efforts to categorize animals according to their uses initiated the process of appropriation. Schemes to domesticate New World creatures aimed to replicate the form of dominion that English settlers knew best. Underlying all of these plans was the firm conviction that animals could be made into private property. Though few such designs ever came to fruition, colonists never abandoned their desire to serve as models of the proper relationship between people and animals. Instead they came to realize that to do so they would need help from home in the form of livestock, domesticated animals already recognized in practice and in law as property. The order of Creation would be demonstrated most effectively not by deer with red collars, but by cattle, swine, and other livestock brought from England.

Part Two

Settling with Animals

Chapter Three

The Company of Cattle

Domestication and Colonization

$\mathcal{A}$s the eighth-born son of the earl of Northumberland, George Percy had scant hope of inheriting a fortune in England. Too many brothers stood in line before him to claim portions of the paternal estate. Percy would have to make his way in the world on the strength of his good name and his own exertions. Following a brief stint as a soldier in the Netherlands, the 26-year-old set his sights on Virginia as the place where he would make his mark. Visions of gold may have fired Percy's imagination as he embarked with the first expedition to the colony in December 1606. If so, he resembled countless other European colonists who found the lure of New World treasure irresistible. Yet whatever fantasies drew him across the Atlantic, once Percy arrived in Virginia a rather more prosaic substance aroused his enthusiasm: grass. "In this Countrye," he exclaimed, "I have seene many great and large Medowes having excellent good pasture for any Cattle."[1]

For all the distance he had traveled, Percy could not help but inspect the area around Chesapeake Bay with eyes accustomed to scanning an English landscape. The coastal meadows, not the forbidding forest, captured his attention because they looked more familiar. Virginia seemed less like a wilderness to him and more like undeveloped land waiting for improvement. It was hardly surprising that Percy would project a vision of grazing livestock onto such a vista. The young gentleman had spent his boyhood in grand country houses; from their windows he could look in almost any direction and see green pastures dotted with cattle and sheep. Without livestock, the view in Virginia seemed strangely incomplete.[2] The absence of domestic animals struck Percy all the more forcefully because the land seemed to have been made just for them.

George Percy was not the only colonist to think about cattle as he appraised the potential of American land. Francis Perkins similarly reckoned that Virginia's woods and meadows were luxuriant enough to support "any kind of live stock, especially pigs and goats, even if there were a million of them." In New England, William Bradford believed that Plymouth Colony's herds could increase a hundredfold without running out of pasture. Lush grasslands that "never had been eaten with Cattle" would easily sustain colonists' animals, reported Rev. Francis Higginson. Prospective Massachusetts settlers learned from William Wood that there was "so much hay ground in the country as the richest voyagers that shall venture thither need not fear want of fodder" no matter how much their herds multiplied. From northern New England to Chesapeake Bay, the east coast of America resembled an earthly paradise for livestock.[3]

The match between New World meadows and Old World domestic animals seemed so perfect that colonists might be forgiven for thinking that they fulfilled a divine plan by bringing livestock to America. The transportation of such creatures certainly promoted the colonists' more worldly designs. Like all European adventurers in the New World, the English were thoroughly accustomed to working with livestock and assumed that successful colonization schemes would necessarily include domestic animals. Colonists expected to rely on cattle, swine, and horses for milk, meat, and muscle power just as much as did English people who stayed at home.

But mere survival could hardly be the primary goal of risky and expensive colonial enterprises. Everyone who participated in these ventures, from Puritan farmers to merchants to scions of some of England's best families, hoped to do somewhat better than that. Their visions of what they intended to accomplish obviously reflected individual economic considerations but also partook of a much broader collective mission: a shared assumption that colonization would confer the blessings of civilization on a savage land. Such a grand agenda ennobled the efforts of all involved, whether they stayed in England and invested money in the Virginia Company or crossed the Atlantic and pulled stumps out of a newly cleared field. This civilizing mission accorded livestock a symbolic role equal to their practical contributions toward the establishment of an English empire.

When George Percy envisioned Chesapeake meadows filled with cattle, he thought less about beef and milk than about the way that peacefully grazing herds served as familiar emblems of civilized life. His imaginative transformation of the landscape silently removed deer, bears, wolves, and other wild beasts and replaced them with English creatures known for docile dependence on their owners. Because domesticated animals' subservience to humans so clearly exemplified the divine order of Creation, their presence in the New World would mark the land as Christian as well as English. Once colonists and their animals had established themselves in America, Indians who had hitherto ignored the divine injunction to exercise dominion over lesser creatures would have appropriate models to follow.

Percy and other colonists who indulged in bucolic fantasies of New World vistas complete with livestock took it for granted that they would manage their animals as vigilantly as English farmers did. They assumed that, like all good husbandmen, they would control virtually every aspect of their animals' lives, from birth to death, keeping order on their farms. In the New World, as in the Old, livestock would remain chattel property, a legal status that reinforced their subordination to human needs. By the power of their example, and using the creatures they knew best, colonists would demonstrate how civilized people lived and prospered in the company of cattle. English animals, no less than English people, would help to build a New World empire.

The English were acutely aware of their tardiness in establishing permanent settlements in America. Only in 1607, with the planting of Jamestown, could they boast of the same accomplishment that Spain had achieved in the Caribbean, Mexico, and Peru almost a century earlier. It scarcely helped England's self-confidence when neither Virginia nor any other English colony yielded the stores of precious metals that fueled Spain's imperial expansion. Since direct comparison with its Catholic rival only emphasized their own nation's shortcomings, English promoters of New World settlement adopted a different tactic. They sought to discredit Spanish colonialism, despite its impressive results, and extol their own country's distinctive approach to empire. The upshot of their efforts was the formulation of an imperial vision that unwittingly assigned livestock an instrumental role in England's overseas expansion.

In making their case against Spain's imperial enterprises, the English emphasized the ruthless tactics of the *conquistadores*. They described Spanish soldiers battling their way into possession of vast, and vastly lucrative, territories with no regard for the fate of indigenous peoples. Like latter-day Roman legions, *conquistadores* subdued native populations through intimidation and unspeakable cruelty. Reiterations of this story gave rise to the notorious "Black Legend" that propagandists constructed for England's benefit. Although a few enthusiasts suggested that England should follow Spain's violent but highly effective example, most English advocates of colonization instead argued in favor of an ideological approach that advertised their nation's moral superiority in the contest for New World possessions.[4]

The English looked to Roman legal theory to justify their imperial ambitions. Central to their thinking was the concept of *res nullius*, which held that "empty things," including land, remained common property until they were put to use. With use came rights: by investing labor in the land, a person could stake a claim to private ownership. Proponents of colonization argued that the discovery of "empty" land conferred similar rights on a nation. They accordingly depicted America as a boundless space open to anyone willing to make good use of it. Exploiting unfortunate native peoples, as did the Spanish, did not constitute good use. But farming, because it required the investment of labor and capital, clearly established legitimate claims. English imperial promoters could not have devised an argument more congenial to English taste and experience. It conformed to England's longstanding agrarian tradition and also enjoyed the stamp of divine approval. Agriculture originated, after all, in the Lord's instruction to Adam and Eve to "replenish the earth, and subdue it." Ever since the beginning of human history, farmers had diligently fulfilled the Lord's wishes. Now it was time for America to shed its wilderness aspect and join other lands under the plow. England's empire would be an agricultural one.[5]

To make their case, advocates of colonization had to demonstrate that the New World was indeed empty and thus such characterizations proliferated in early accounts. Virginia, according to William Strachey, was "vast" and "uninhabited." William Bradford portrayed the land around Plymouth as "vast and unpeopled"; to Robert Cushman it was "a vast and empty chaos." Francis Higginson regarded it a "great pittie" that so much good land near Salem lay "altogether unoccupied" by anyone; elsewhere in Massachusetts, reported William Wood, there were "thousands of acres that yet was never meddled with."[6] A few commentators realized that coastal New England's apparent emptiness was of fairly recent origin, the result of an epidemic that swept through the area and carried off perhaps as many as nine out of ten native people. Yet their inclination to attribute this disaster to divine intervention, whereby the Lord "made roome" for English colonists, exposed the self-justifying quality of these depictions of a vacant New World.[7]

Colonists could not avoid acknowledging the presence of Indians, but still insisted that the land was essentially unoccupied. Even after John Smith counted over 2,700 "fighting men" in the Chesapeake Bay area (suggesting a total native population of four or five times that number) and described the Indians' devotion to farming, he characterized the land as uninhabited by "industrious people" and therefore ripe for English settlement.[8] No amount of contact with native villages could convince English observers that Indians were anything but rootless wanderers, equivalent to the wild animals that shared the wilderness with them. The Indians in Virginia "live and lie up and downe in troupes like heards of Deare in a Forrest," claimed the author of *Nova Britannia.* To William Bradford, New England Indians were "savage and brutish men which range up and down, little otherwise than the wild beasts" in the woods. Robert Cushman agreed that Indians were few in number "and do but run over the grass, as do also the foxes and wild beasts." Such animal analogies carried legal as well as descriptive weight. Wild animals had no rights to the lands over which they roamed, and neither did the Indians. Robert Gray made the point explicitly, observing that Virginia's "Savages have no particular proprietie in any part or parcell of that Country, but only a general recidencie there, as wild beasts have in the forest."[9] Colonists who envisioned cattle grazing where deer and foxes once ranged had little difficulty imagining themselves replacing peripatetic Indians in similar fashion.

The insistence that Indians only lightly touched the land where they dwelled became the mainstay of England's justification for colonization. Without it, colonists could hardly invoke the idea of *res nullius* and defend their appropriation of "empty" territory. As a corollary to this argument, some colonists portrayed Indians as living in the "state of nature" that theoretically preceded the beginnings of civilization. John Locke would eventually incorporate this notion into his treatise on the origin of property rights, proclaiming that "in the beginning all the world was America." The idea certainly played an important role in convincing John Winthrop of the legitimacy of settling Massachusetts. Defending English occupation of "Land which hath beene soe longe possessed by others," Winthrop dwelled on the primitive character of native society, which, he argued, gave Indians only "a Naturall Right" to their lands. Natural rights, Winthrop explained, originated "when men held the earth in common every man sowing and feeding where he pleased," much as the Indians allegedly did. Men acquired civil rights only when they appropriated tracts of land to themselves and used them intensively. This was what the English intended to do, and their actions would establish superior civil rights, overriding the feebler claims of the native inhabitants.[10] Time and again, colonists reserved the concept of civility to themselves. Nowhere in the New World, asserted Robert Johnson, did Indians have the "civill use of any thing." William Bradford likewise found America to be "devoid of all civil inhabitants" and thus an appropriate destination for his company of godly English people.[11]

At best, Indians could lay claim to the small plots they actually cultivated. If, Winthrop asserted, "we leave them sufficient for their use, we may lawfully take the rest" for English farms. Virginia's colonists would not deprive the Indians of their cornfields, declared William Strachey, but only "breake up new growndes" that lay vacant.[12] By making agriculture the sole measure of use, however, colonists denied Indians any claim to the hunting lands essential to their way of life. Woodlands were simply "waste," and thus could be appropriated by anyone who converted them into planting fields. The mental map that colonists superimposed on the New World convinced them that there was plenty of land for Indians and newcomers alike. "The *Indians*," wrote Francis Higginson, "are not able to make use of the one fourth part of the Land," which left an "abundance of ground" for colonists. There was "more then enough for them and us," John Winthrop agreed. One English-man suggested that Virginia's native inhabitants could strengthen their claims to land if they followed the colonists' example and expanded their agricultural activities. Should the Indians "conjoyne their labours with ours," offered Robert Johnson, they "shall enjoy equall priviledges with us."[13]

Some colonists recognized the Indians' agricultural efforts. William Wood went so far as to declare that Indian women in Massachusetts "exceed our

English husbandmen," keeping each plot "so clear with their clamshell hoes as if it were a garden rather than a corn field." Such comments, however, were often meant to disparage Indian men who did not work in the fields as much as to praise Indian farming techniques.[14] Indian horticulture also failed to measure up to English standards because it neither produced substantial surpluses nor effected permanent changes in the landscape. Lacking barns, fences, and extensive tracts devoted to single crops, the cultivated areas of the New World bore little resemblance to an English rural scene. Such impressions convinced colonists that, by establishing English-style farms, they could expose Indians to "a new way of Thrift or husbandry" to improve their lives. The godly farmers of Massachusetts, declared Rev. John White, "shall teach providence and industry" to native peoples plagued by idleness and want.[15]

At first, colonial farms and villages could probably be heard before they could be seen. The sounds of trees crashing to the ground, saws and axes shaping timber into planks and boards, hammers rapping on the beams and clapboard of houses, and men grunting while digging postholes for fences all announced colonists' occupation of another tract of land. By erecting buildings and marking boundaries, they performed the duties they thought necessary to establish legal claims to empty territory. These activities, along with English-style agriculture, "improved" the land in ways that Indian practices did not. Fixed dwellings, permanent planting fields, a sedentary population—these were the signs of English life with which the colonists expected to impress native peoples. The "example of our course of living," Rev. John White confidently predicted, "cannot but in time breed civility" among the Indians.[16]

Once the din of hammers and saws diminished, the lowing of cattle, neighing of horses, and grunting of swine heralded the presence of colonists' towns and plantations. These sounds bore witness to the colonists' identification of another deficiency of Indian agriculture: the lack of livestock. For America truly to reach its potential, colonists insisted, livestock had to be part of the process. Ralph Lane, traveling with the first expedition to Roanoke in 1585, believed that "if Virginia had but Horses and Kine in some reasonable proportion, . . . being inhabited with English, no realme in Christendome were comparable to it." Sir Richard Grenville likewise deemed it essential that Roanoke be provided "with suche cattell & beastes as are fitte and necessary" for without them colonial farms would not thrive. Even after it became clear that tobacco offered the best chance to rescue the struggling Virginia colony, John Pory insisted the colony would only reach "perfection"

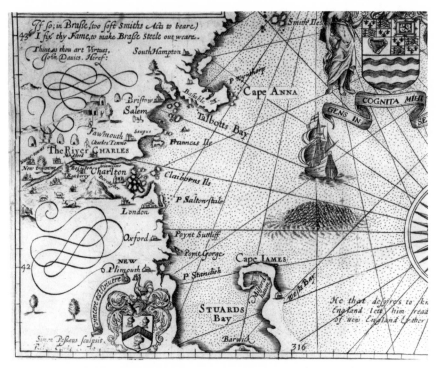

Early map of New England, showing English towns and grazing cows.
Detail from map in John Smith, *New England Observed...*, 1631 ed.
Courtesy of American Antiquarian Society

if it had "the English plough, Vineyards, and Cattle." In New England, Francis Higginson similarly believed that "honest Christians" needed cattle "to make use of this fruitfull Land."[17]

Such claims also reflected the colonists' belief that staking a civil right to land had historically involved a partnership between people and livestock, and would do so again in America. Over time, as "men and theire Cattell encreased," John Winthrop noted, "they appropriated certaine parcells of Grownde by inclosing and peculiar manuerance," making improvements that confirmed private ownership. Here Winthrop drew on the contemporary double meaning of manurance—to occupy and work the land generally, and more specifically to apply dung to enrich the soil—to acknowledge the vital role of livestock. Indians, in good part because they lacked domestic animals, had not made the transition from collective to individual rights. Because they "inclose noe Land, neither have any setled habytation, nor any tame Cattle to improve the Land by," Winthrop continued, Indian claims to their underutilized territory could legitimately be superseded by colonists who arrived with livestock in tow.[18]

The prospective displacement of New World peoples and animals by European immigrants inspired pictures as well as words. Cartographers often decorated early maps of America with drawings of indigenous fauna. Bears, deer, beavers, foxes, turkeys and other birds, sometimes scattered among stands of trees, designated the wild and vacant lands that Europeans intended to occupy. Only rarely were Indian palisades or wigwams included to suggest human habitation. Over time, images of domestic animals began to appear in areas where colonists had either settled or planned to do so. Perhaps the best example, at least for the early English colonies, of what can only be called imaginative imperialism is the printed map that accompanied John Smith's *New England Observed,* published in 1631. Town names materialize along the Massachusetts coast—including London, Oxford, and "Bristow"—where no English towns then existed. The Isles of Shoals became (if only temporarily) "Smith's Iles." The London printer of the map, James Reeve, even named a point on the Maine coast after himself. And along the south shore of the Charles River, where there actually were colonial settlements, the cartographer depicted cows grazing and taking their ease. Like the tiny houses or churches that marked the locations of colonial towns, cows symbolized the parts of America that had become civilized.[19]

For all their emphasis on fixity as the key to civilized living, it is ironic that colonists would dwell so much on the role of conspicuously mobile creatures in establishing English rights to American land. But colonists fully expected to harness their animals' movements to serve the cause of permanence. Ox teams would help to clear fields, pull plows, and drag heavy timber. Cattle and sheep would improve the land with their grazing and, along with swine, feed the growing human populations of colonial settlements. Horses would carry colonists from one thriving village to another. The fences that would keep domestic animals' movements in check symbolized the improvements that established farmers' property rights. And the animals were, after all, private property themselves. Carefully managed and supervised by their owners, helping to reshape the land in England's image, livestock epitomized the many transformations in store for the New World and its native inhabitants.

Colonists born and raised in England never questioned the indispensability of livestock for all sorts of human endeavors. With the exception of the Netherlands, England had the highest ratio of domestic animals per man and per cultivated acre anywhere in Europe. One estimate, dating from 1696, reckoned that there were 4.5 million cattle, 12 million sheep, and 2 million hogs in England and Wales at a point when the human population totaled 5.3 million. Virtually every family with access to farmland owned some sort of creature. The animals' contribution to England's agrarian economy is literally incalculable, for seventeenth-century farmers left few records from which livestock's productivity can be measured. It is no exaggeration to say, however, that without its millions of domestic beasts, England's economy (indeed, its history) would have followed a very different trajectory.[20]

Though concentrated in the countryside, livestock also inhabited England's towns and cities. John Stow recalled that, as a youth in London, he regularly visited a farmer in one of the outer wards to fetch fresh milk for his family. Artisans occasionally supplemented craft work with small-scale livestock husbandry, especially if they had wives and children to help care for the animals. Residents of London and provincial cities alike dodged around errant pigs, fought their ways through alleys clogged with horse-drawn carts, and complained about the stench emanating from piles of dung and the carcasses of dead beasts.[21] Nowhere in England could one avoid the sight, sound, or smell of domestic animals.

Seventeenth-century English people considered livestock an inescapable part of their world, not only because of their ubiquity but also because the beasts seemed to have been around forever. Animal husbandry of a primitive sort commenced in England around 2500 BC when people began following herds of wild cattle, sheep, and swine. Early efforts at management consisted mainly of directing the creatures into well-watered valleys or confining them in stone-walled enclosures. Actual domestication occurred once the animals grew accustomed to human contact and successfully bred in captivity. Their owners could now work with them as well as eat them. Over time, as people gained knowledge of their animals' needs, they began to clear wooded areas to create pastures for cattle and horses, preserving some forests where swine could root for nuts and plants. When the Domesday book was compiled in the eleventh century, surveyors classified areas of woodland according to the numbers of pigs they could support, indicating the close association between one species and its preferred habitat. England's heavy dependence on livestock was firmly rooted by this point, and would persist for nearly another millennium.[22]

By the time English colonists prepared to move to the New World, the landscape of their home country bore witness to centuries of labor by farmers working in partnership with animals. An intricate mosaic of fields, pastures, forests, and farms distinguished one region from another; in some cases, just a few miles separated villages with quite different field arrangements and agricultural economies, reflecting environmental conditions and market opportunities as well as historical patterns of land use. Local variations also testified to farmers' concentration on different kinds of livestock husbandry. To the north and west, the predominant pattern was one of immense open pastures where large numbers of sheep and cattle were driven for communal grazing. Interspersed among the meadows were arable fields where farmers grew wheat and other grains, often working the land in common. To the south and east lay the "wood-pasture" region familiar to most prospective colonists. One eighteenth-century traveler through Norfolk's wood-pasture lands described how "the eye seems ever on the verge of a forest, which is, as it were by enchantment, continually changing into enclosures and hedgerows." In the early seventeenth century, enclosures were as yet piecemeal endeavors, appearing wherever farmers specializing in cattle- and pig-raising divided larger estates into individual family farms and left hedges to serve as natural fences around pastures.[23]

Not only did livestock help to modify the landscape of early modern England, they also shaped the lives of their owners in countless ways. Gervase Markham, one of England's foremost agricultural writers of the period, went so far as to suggest that the ideal husbandman spent far more time each day with his livestock than with his wife and children—as much as 14 of 17 waking hours.[24] Although few people probably measured up to Markham's high standard, most farmers indeed devoted a great deal of time to their livestock. This was especially true for residents of wood-pasture country, where income from livestock production typically exceeded earnings generated by the sale of crops. The authors of the agricultural manuals flowing from the presses in the sixteenth and seventeenth centuries repeatedly emphasized that constant diligence was the essence of good husbandry and the key to prosperity.

When proper supervision of animals faltered, English trespass law stepped in. Controlling livestock was a legal as well as a moral responsibility. Even if his cattle or swine wandered through gaps in a neighbor's fence, the livestock owner would be held liable for resulting damage and could not argue that the neighbor's negligence was a mitigating factor. The onus was on the owner to restrain his animals, not on the neighbor to maintain his fences. Nevertheless, farmers were supposed to inspect their own hedges and fences for breaches that cattle always seemed to find or make. Pigs presented a different challenge. Fed on household scraps and leftover whey from dairy production, they often had free run of the yard. Moreover, wherever woods were available, farmers let swine loose for up to two months in autumn to fatten on mast. Keepers accompanied the creatures to the forest, but did not always keep track of their charges. Strays rooting around in nearby fields or gardens occasionally left a trail of destruction in their wake. To allow swine to forage and yet prevent them from digging, farmers resorted to a variety of physical restraints, mandated in some places by local ordinance. They attached yokes to pigs' necks to hinder them from crawling under fences or through hedges. They bored holes in hogs' snouts and inserted metal rings or pieces of holly, or sometimes "cut asunder the sinews on both sides" of a pig's nose so that "when he would digge, the groine of his nose will fall downe." Widely regarded as the most "troublesome to rule" of all farm animals, swine tested the ingenuity and patience of owners required to keep them under control.[25]

The careful management that characterized good husbandry extended to nearly every aspect of farm animals' lives and farmers' daily routines. Freed from the communal decision making that prevailed in open field regions, wood-pasture farmers more easily adapted their practices in response to family needs and market shifts.[26] They could also experiment with agricultural innovations, such as trying out new diets for their livestock. Some of them sowed pastures with clover, cinquefoil, and sainfoin to provide cattle with more nutritious fodder, cultivating turnips and other root crops for winter feed.[27] Readers of Leonard Mascal's *The Government of Cattell* could follow his advice about fattening animals for slaughter. Mascal assured farmers that feeding swine crabapples and concoctions of barley and peas—and making them drunk "now and then"—produced good lard as well as a reputation for good husbandry.[28]

Well-fed animals in turn produced an abundance of manure, one of the most valuable substances on any farm. Some farmers spread an average of three loads on each acre of arable ground every year. In an era when there were few other ways to increase soil fertility, the judicious application of manure could substantially boost productivity. Thus few other topics so engaged the interest of writers keen on agricultural improvement. Thomas Tusser and Gervase Markham both emphasized the critical importance of enriching fields with manure. In *Systema Agriculturae,* John Worlidge explained at considerable length which animal's dung worked best on which kind of land, and how best to prepare manure before spreading it. Wood-pasture farmers, because their livestock grazed within enclosures, had easiest access to fertilizer; as John Winthrop attested, "inclosing and peculiar maneurance" indeed went hand in hand.[29]

Important as domestic animals were to agricultural productivity, farmers could not afford to let herds exceed the grazing capacity of their lands and also had to pay attention to changing family needs and market demands. Rather than letting nature take its course, husbandmen regularly intervened in their animals' reproductive lives. Their efforts fell far short of selective breeding, in large part because seventeenth-century English farmers had only a rudimentary understanding of breed classifications. As often as not animals were categorized by color, which was sometimes linked to behavioral characteristics. Leonard Mascal, for instance, identified black and red oxen as the hardest workers but disparaged a white ox as the "worst of all colours."[30] Selective breeding was less important to these farmers than maintaining balance between animals and land and increasing the manageability of their herds. The principal method of manipulating reproduction was to castrate all but a few male animals, which limited herd size and also reduced aggressive displays of dominance. The recourse to castration may date from the very beginnings of livestock husbandry as a means of controlling unpredictable creatures. Leonard Mascal assured his readers that one bull would suffice for sixty cows, and one boar for ten sows. Castration of other males produced a double benefit as neutered animals became more tractable and accumulated more body fat, improving the quality of their meat.[31]

Farmers also controlled the timing of their livestock's reproductive activity. The goal was to have grazing animals such as cattle, horses, and sheep born in the late winter or early spring so that the young could be turned into fresh green pastures soon after weaning. To ensure that newborn calves would appear around February, farmers only allowed bulls near cows in late spring. Horses and sheep, which retain the seasonal breeding cycles inherited from wild ancestors, required less monitoring. Supervising the reproduction of any kind of livestock was greatly facilitated by confining animals in enclosures; livestock grazing in open fields could not so easily be prevented from promiscuous breeding. Swine were generally left to their own devices. With a four-month gestational period, year-round fertility, and litters of up to a dozen piglets at a time, their numbers could increase quickly.[32]

Few domestic animals lived out their natural lifespans. Household needs and market demands influenced farmers' decisions about when to dispatch certain creatures. Gervase Markham cautioned that "a Sow can bring up no more Pigs than she hath teats," and so a sensible husbandman would preserve only the right number of piglets. Leonard Mascal similarly recommended that farmers raise only so many calves "as you can conveniently keep" and slaughter or sell the surplus.[33] Animals that farmers could not afford to feed over the winter were slaughtered in autumn. Aging livestock that produced less milk, failed to breed, or lost strength were fattened for meat. A cow could live 15 years, admitted Leonard Mascal, but what good was a "feeble and weary" creature? An ox, though he too could make it to 15 or 16 years of age, "will serve well to labour till he be ten years, not after so good." Keeping animals much beyond the point of their greatest productivity, these writers warned, ran counter to the principles of good husbandry.[34]

The sage advice dispensed by Mascal, Markham, and other agricultural writers reinforced the myriad common-sense decisions that punctuated farmers' daily routines. Livestock were at once a form of capital, a source of income, and a potential liability, and had to be managed in such a way as to maximize economic benefits and minimize costs. Such considerations guided farmers' attempts to extract as much labor as possible from draft animals without overexerting them. Gervase Markham advised plowmen to adjust their expectations of their teams according to the kind of land to be tilled, much as they would calibrate their own efforts to match the difficulty of a task. A team of oxen or horses could plow two or three acres a day on sandy soil, but only an acre or an acre and a half on "stiff" ground. Any farmer who pushed his animals too hard would pay the price sooner or later.[35]

Animal husbandry typically required less labor from human workers than arable farming did. But even farmers who specialized in livestock husbandry also raised crops and needed help to supplement the efforts of their own families. There was a ready supply of temporary laborers in seventeenth-century England, men and women willing to hire themselves out for a brief period or to contract to work for a year in return for food, lodging, and modest wages. Most rural youths spent part of their adolescence working for others. Livestock farmers preferred to hire servants for an entire year, since the labor requirements of animal husbandry followed a regular cycle rather than fluctuating with the seasons. Young women generally performed tasks related to dairying while men cleaned and fed the animals, tilled fields, hauled manure, and maintained hedges and fences. Every farmer sought "trusty and skilfull" men, as Leonard Mascal put it, "to look and often resort unto his cattell" and keep them well and in order.[36]

Livestock husbandry was not just a way to make a living; it was also a way of life. Done properly, it reinforced a set of behaviors that seventeenth-century English people regarded as normative and emblematic of civilized existence. Just rearing livestock was not good enough: as one contemporary noted, the "keping of cowes is of it self a verie idle lyfe and a fitt nursurie for a theif."[37] But farmers who raised crops and animals on well-tended lands personified an English agrarian ideal. They were prudent and well organized, following rigorous daily and seasonal routines dictated by climate, habit, economic goals, and their livestock's needs. They were economical, saving table scraps for hogs and manure for their fields, as well as experimental, adopting new agricultural techniques if they promised significant benefits. By maintaining the hedges, fences, and ditches around their farms, husbandmen preserved the physical markers that testified to civilized use of the land. And as Christians they exemplified divinely sanctioned dominion over animals. They were, in short, everything Indians were not.

Colonists who extolled the benefits that livestock would introduce to the New World likewise identified animal husbandry as a civilized enterprise. But this assumption revealed their predilection to see livestock principally as objects whose behavior was subject to human control and efficiently marshaled to serve their owners' interests. Livestock would bring "perfection" to Virginia only if they were yoked to a plow, confined within fences, or ringed through the nose. This emphasis on animals as tools or as meat on the hoof, however, did not do justice to the complexity of livestock husbandry. Unlike a tract of land, wheat in the barn, or shoes in a craftsman's shop, domestic animals were *living* property—agents as well as objects. The animals could, at times, seem more like members of the family, and obstreperous ones at that, than controllable property.

🐂 🐂 🐂

The number of animals on most enclosed farms in seventeenth-century England—a couple of dozen cows, half as many pigs, maybe a horse or two—was few enough that farmers could identify each beast by its face and sometimes its name, much as they might recognize members of their extended family. Few English farmers actually *lived* with their livestock. Byre houses, which sheltered people and animals under the same roof, were uncommon and generally found only in western counties. But in most regions servants slept in chambers or lofts above stables, and adults spent many of their waking hours among their animals.[38] Daily, often intensely physical, contact with livestock fostered an intimacy that was at best a deeply submerged theme of agricultural manuals but was nevertheless as much a part of livestock husbandry as human mastery. Such closeness could mitigate the exploitative potential of a relationship based legally and theoretically on owners' absolute control. At times, however, it could also undermine the supposedly rigid boundaries between humans and animals.

The degree of intimacy correlated with the nature and frequency of contact. A decade spent working with the same oxen or horses bred a sense of partnership between a farmer and his team. Training draft animals in the first place demanded considerable time and effort. Leonard Mascal's instructions on how to "tame" an ox prescribed extensive physical contact, mixing mastery and mercy in nearly equal doses. He advised husbandmen to wait until an ox was at least three years old; before that age the animal was "too weake and tender" for hard labor. Over a period of several days, as young oxen adjusted to wearing a yoke, farmers should "approach gently . . . and speake them faire, and so accustom them to see and behold their keeper: then rub their heads, and touch their nostrils and mozels, so that they may know and feele the scent of their keeper." Mascal further advised rubbing the animal's belly and legs, opening its mouth and touching its tongue, rubbing its palate with salt. A young ox should first plow light soil, yoked to a gentle veteran that would guide him through his paces. If the ox lay down "in the furrow . . . he ought not suddenly to be corrected and raised againe by violence, but by some gentle means after a little rest" encouraged to rise.

Only an obviously lazy animal deserved punishment. In that case, the farmer should bind its feet so it "cannot rise to feed . . . and so he shall be constrained through hunger and thirst to leave his weary slothfulnesse" and get on with its job. Reduced to its essentials, Mascal's advice resembled the process by which someone might train a servant, an apprentice, or a child, although with fellow humans familiarity need not be established through so much sustained physical contact.[39]

Horses and dairy cattle, touched and spoken to every day, were often given names that signaled familiarity and even affection. Farmers used these names to *address* their livestock and not just to identify them. The names bestowed on working ox pairs, for instance, were meant to sound distinct so each animal would know when it was being commanded to do something. Colonists too named their New World cattle, oxen, and horses. One Virginian owned dairy cows called Litefoot, Primrose, Brindle, and Hart; another had a mare called Noby. Robert Parr of Maryland bequeathed his cows "old begger, Cherry, Coll, . . . Nansey, Pye [and] Youwngbegger" to his two heirs. Daniel Clark of Ipswich, Massachusetts, plowed with his oxen "stare & burnette" while in nearby Wenham, Roger Haskell yoked up "black & Butter." No one in England or the colonies bothered to name pigs, goats, or sheep, mainly because they were considered lesser creatures and their contact with owners was more intermittent.[40]

Yet even nameless swine and sheep occasionally required attention. In an era without professional veterinarians, farmers helped animals give birth, soothed their injuries, and nursed their illnesses. "Ye must often oversee and visit your troups of cattell against any infirmity that may dayly hap," warned Mascal, or risk losing valuable beasts. The most frequently consulted sections of published agricultural tracts may have been the lengthy descriptions of livestock maladies, accompanied by equally detailed advice on remedies. Suffice it to say that administering many of the potions and salves prescribed in these accounts brought farmers into exceedingly close contact with sick animals.[41]

Farmers who stroked, dosed, trained, and spoke to livestock often developed sentimental ties with their animals that seemed to match in emotional intensity their connections to relatives and friends. At the very least, a gentle cow milked twice a day for years, or an ox toiling patiently in good weather and bad, season after season, might receive the kind of affection more typically bestowed on dogs or other pets. English colonists, even dour New Englanders, now and then exhibited such feelings. Distressed by the disappearance of a favorite heifer in the autumn of 1662, Obadiah Wood of Ipswich, Massachusetts, visited his neighbors to ask if anyone had seen it. When one man inquired how the cow might be identified, Wood explained that "if you Com neare And hold out your hand to her, the heffer will Com to you, for I used to give her 'BisCake'," much as one might offer a treat to a child. Thomas Minor's diary notations similarly hint, in more subtle fashion, at the emotional ties that sometimes linked man and beast. Late winter and early spring were the times when the Connecticut farmer's cows began to give birth to calves. One cow named Browne gave Minor particular concern, and he tracked her condition in his diary. On 19 February 1656, she produced a calf in what seemed to have been a difficult delivery. Nine days later, Minor noted that at last she "begin to mend." Her recovery, however, was brief; on 16 April, "Browne died." Minor typically took note of when livestock were slaughtered or killed by wolves, as might be expected of a farmer keeping track of his economic investment in animals. But over the more than three decades covered by Minor's diary, Browne was the only cow that, in death, was mentioned by name.[42]

Cruelty to animals, of course, could be as much a part of livestock husbandry as affection. To a certain extent, mistreatment of animals was embedded in popular culture. English people in this period amused themselves by watching bear- and bull-baiting sessions and betting on cockfights in which the winner was the sole survivor. County fairs sometimes included contests featuring participants who bit the heads off live birds. Children skinned live frogs, tortured cats, and poked needles through the heads of hens to see how long they would survive. Hurting livestock was typically not a form of entertainment so much as a symptom of frustration, fatigue, or indifference. Farmers might beat recalcitrant animals, feed them short rations, let wounds fester, ignore illnesses. Few formal sanctions restrained either negligence or outright brutality. Informal interventions in the form of complaints by concerned neighbors or passersby may have kept the worst excesses in check, or simply out of sight. Such protests as did occur often focused as much (or more) on the effects of cruel behavior on human character as on the welfare of animal victims. People who hurt livestock displayed an unseemly lack of self-control that might predispose them to erupt violently in other ways. A dual concern for perpetrators and their victims prompted Puritan Massachusetts to outlaw "any Tyranny or Cruelty towards any Bruit Creatures, which are usually kept for the use of Man." Yet there is no evidence that any Bay colonist was ever prosecuted for violations that almost certainly occurred. Sustained interest in the welfare of animals would not come for another century, and significant legal protection even later than that.[43]

Seventeenth-century husbandmen may have lacked a modern sensibility regarding animal rights, but economic incentives probably made deliberate cruelty towards livestock the exception, not the rule. Many farmers conceived of their relationship with their "Bruit Creatures" in terms of responsibility or stewardship as well as power. When Leonard Mascal entitled his agricultural tract *The Government of Cattell*, he made sure that his readers understood that the kind of government he had in mind was closer to benevolent despotism than tyranny. No one questioned farmers' authority, but they "ought to show themselves conductors and guiders of cattel, and not as masters" of their animals.[44] Some commentators argued that this approach best represented the Lord's intent when He entrusted Adam and his descendants with dominion over the beasts. John Calvin even weighed in on the subject. When God made beasts subject to humankind, the Protestant reformer insisted, "he did it with the condition that we should handle them gently." Like fellow human beings, an English preacher instructed, livestock should be treated considerately during the week and allowed to observe the Sabbath as a day of rest.[45]

The idea of stewardship reinforced the belief that livestock husbandry ought to tame its practitioners, suppressing base impulses and making them better people. By emphasizing that livestock were living creatures, not just tools to be used and discarded, this way of thinking also left room for farmers to develop affection toward the animals entrusted to their care. But by assigning livestock a status approaching that of servants or even children, as beings to be ruled with a kind but steady hand, the concept of stewardship muddled the theoretically distinct categories of human and animal. Domestication created a special niche for certain animals, suspended somewhere between people and wild beasts. Its usefulness to humankind was quite obvious, its dangers less so.

Nothing revealed the ambiguity of livestock's status as living property more vividly than the accusations that flew during reported outbreaks of witchcraft. When horses collapsed, pigs had fits, cows ceased giving milk, calves began "a-roaring," and chickens dropped dead, English people on both sides of the Atlantic started looking for the devil's minions. Leonard Mascal realized that any number of natural maladies could afflict horses, but also knew when something else was afoot. If a farmer's horse became "vehemently" ill, stopped eating, foamed at the mouth, or ran about as if it were mad, "he be bewitched." Livestock scarcely ever figured as witches' familiars; dogs and, especially, cats were the domestic animals most frequently mentioned in that capacity. But cows, horses, sheep, and swine made particularly tempting targets for *maleficium* on at least two counts. First, they were valuable property. Many accused witches were comparatively poor, and since injuries to animals often occurred after the accused had been denied charity, it was easy for afflicted neighbors to suspect that envy had fueled such malevolence. Second, as living forms of property, livestock served as proxies for their owners in ways that no inanimate possession could. Drying up a cow's milk, for instance, could readily be seen as a none-too-subtle attack against a nursing mother, hinting at a complex set of functional and symbolic associations linking female gender roles in humans and animals. As if to emphasize the uncertain boundary between people and livestock, the fits and roaring of bewitched creatures reportedly mimicked the sufferings and sounds of human victims.[46]

Bewitched livestock could hardly be held responsible for their erratic behavior, but the case was far less clear for domestic animals that engaged in unacceptable activities apparently of their own volition. Oxen that refused to plow were deemed lazy; cattle or horses that ignored their masters' commands were malicious or "unruly," a term also used to describe recalcitrant children or servants. Any creature prone to destroy fences became known as a "common pale-breaker," an epithet that echoed the labels of "common thief" or "common scold" assigned to human malefactors. Such animals often received treatment that amounted to punishment, suggesting that they were being held accountable for their misdeeds. In Maryland, uncontrollable horses that leaped fences and romped through colonists' fields were taken up and (if too small to be good breeding stock) castrated to calm them down. Townsmen in Hempstead on Long Island banished from the common dairy herd all calves that nursed from cows other than their mothers because they stole milk from another livestock owner.[47]

Dogs may have been the worst animal offenders. In England and the colonies, it was permissible to destroy dogs that disturbed or killed livestock. As early as 1635, Salem townsmen passed a local ordinance prescribing punishment for dogs that attacked poultry. Dogs were also held accountable if they killed swine or sheep, attacked horses or cattle, spoiled catches of fish, or entered meetinghouses during religious services. A 1692 law gave Bostonians free rein to kill any dog they saw "sezing upon cowes and catle." They did not first have to inform the dog's owner, and if the owner complained, "the selectmen will beare them out in there so acting." At times, however, summary justice at the hands of a casual witness gave way to more elaborate procedures. In 1648, Massachusetts's assembly enacted a measure familiar to residents in the English countryside: a law that prescribed hanging as the penalty for dogs that harassed sheep. If the owner refused to hang his own dog, the constable would do it for him. Seventeenth-century inhabitants of Wethersfield, Connecticut, probably performed these ritual executions near where Hang Dog Lane runs today.[48]

Unlike human criminals, these dogs received death sentences without benefit of trial. In contrast to France and other western European countries, England and its colonies lacked a legal tradition of trying animals accused of serious crimes. Yet judicial proceedings would only have compounded the effect produced by stringing up dogs. By inflicting a form of punishment eerily reminiscent of the grisly scenes at Tyburn, this punishment blurred what was supposed to be a fundamental distinction between people and animals. If, in theory, humans alone possessed a capacity for moral reasoning, how could a dog be held liable for its actions? Did anyone think that hanging one dog deterred others from attacking sheep? How could oxen even be accused of laziness, or horses of willfulness, or calves of the theft of milk, if they were nothing more than brute beasts acting purely on instinct?[49]

Abstract categories of difference constructed by intellectuals dissolved in the din and disorder of village and farmyard. It was no accident that the animals most often regarded as possessing rudimentary moral understanding were domesticated. If oxen could be trained to pull a plow, dogs taught to herd sheep, and heifers made to nibble "BisCake" from an owner's hand, they obviously had some capacity to learn, or at least to respond to a system of rewards and punishments. When Leonard Mascal advised owners of lazy oxen to tie their animals' feet so they could not feed, he assumed that oxen could figure out why they were being fettered and reform their behavior.[50] If animals could choose to behave properly, it followed that they could also choose to do wrong. Missed commands became disobedience, undesirable actions a defiance of authority. Domestic animals could be punished because they deserved it.[51]

Their owners deserved punishment, too. Animals' misbehavior advertised their owners' failure to maintain control. The community was compelled to step in, not only to provide restitution for an aggrieved party but also to remind delinquent owners of their responsibilities. Unruly dogs might not be deterred by the sight of a hound dangling from a gibbet, but masters of rambunctious dogs might pay closer attention to their animals' conduct. Authorities often coupled punishments for misbehaving animals with penalties (usually fines) for their owners, in the belief that man and beast shared culpability.[52] Yet by identifying human and animal offenders as partners in crime, measures intended to restore the proper hierarchical relationship between people and animals could have the opposite effect of suggesting how little difference there could be between the two.

No act, however, threatened to erase the boundary between people and animals quite so thoroughly as bestiality. A practice almost certainly limited to societies with domesticated creatures, it aroused a horror disproportionate to its probable frequency. From the Middle Ages on, it was considered an offense too appalling even to name. Sexual relations with animals took the intimacy inherent in small-scale livestock husbandry a step too far. It confused categories that contemporaries regarded as distinct and reduced man to the level of beast as no other act could. In accordance with Old Testament injunction, English courts prosecuted bestiality as a capital crime beginning in the sixteenth century. Implicated animals were also slain, not so much because they were held responsible for their actions as because they had been defiled by the forbidden congress. English colonists eventually transferred a horror of bestiality and equally severe legal penalties, along with the practice itself, to the New World.[53]

More than just an economic endeavor, livestock husbandry entangled people and animals in an elaborate web of functional and sentimental relations based on reciprocal dependency. Domestic animals fulfilled a number of human needs, some acceptable, some not. At the same time, owners' care and attention contributed to the animals' well-being. Human dominion over livestock was absolute in theory but tempered in practice. On most farms, ownership translated into some semblance of stewardship. Confident that domestic beasts tamed the people who possessed them, English colonists assumed that the creatures would naturally promote their civilizing mission in the New World. Even before prospective emigrants had a chance to read the many paeans to American pastures, they made plans to bring livestock with them.

All Europeans, not just the English, enlisted livestock as partners in colonization. Christopher Columbus first transported horses, cattle, swine, sheep, and goats to Caribbean islands on his second voyage in 1493. Wherever Spanish *conquistadores* went thereafter, European domestic animals followed. These included not only the horses that carried Spanish soldiers into battle, but also the cattle, sheep, swine, and goats that fed them. Rapidly proliferating livestock populations supplied breeding stock for each step of the Spanish imperial advance. Hernán Cortés looked to Hispaniola for livestock to bring to Mexico, and Mexican swine later accompanied Francisco Pizarro and his men to Peru. Hernando de Soto acquired Cuban pigs for his expedition to Florida. Together the Spanish and their domestic animals made for a motley, but highly effective, invasion force.[54]

Other European explorers followed suit. Portuguese colonists brought cattle and swine to Brazil in the 1530s. Pigs adapted well to the tropical environment, cattle less so. Portuguese ships deposited cattle on Sable Island in the north Atlantic in the 1540s to provision fishermen on their seasonal voyages to the Grand Banks and nearby waters. Before long any passing European ship appropriated what it needed from the island's multiplying herds. In 1604, Samuel de Champlain reported French expeditions making free use of Sable Island's cattle.[55] The French also transported animals from home to mainland Canada. France's first successful New World colony at Port Royal in Acadia soon had a burgeoning pig population. Quebec had swine at least as early as 1609. Cattle arrived there sometime after 1618 and within five years were so numerous that colonists made regular expeditions to riverside meadows at Cape Tourmente, several miles away, to cut hay and carry it back by boat.[56] And as might be expected for a colony founded by the European country most dependent on livestock, the Dutch West India Company furnished New Netherland with ample supplies of cattle, hogs, horses, and sheep.[57]

The English followed what had become established procedure in equipping their New World colonies with livestock. Like other European settlers, they tried to procure animals as near as possible to their destinations, since it was easier and cheaper than transporting beasts and fodder all the way across the Atlantic. The first expedition to Roanoke in 1585 traveled by way of Hispaniola, where Sir Richard Grenville purchased animals. Two years later, John White and his company of men, women, and children en route to Roanoke likewise planned an island detour to acquire livestock.[58]

By the seventeenth century, officials of joint-stock companies regarded buying livestock as one of many start-up costs of establishing new colonies. Even the underfunded Newfoundland Company arranged to purchase goats, pigs, and poultry.[59] The larger and better capitalized Virginia Company intended from the start to provide its colonists with a regular supply of animals. Two years after the first ships landed at Jamestown, the settlement had, by one resident's count, "6 mares and a horse, 5 or 600 swine, as many hens and chickens; some goates, [and] some sheep." An expedition sent to relieve the struggling colony in 1611 brought not only a new governor, Sir Thomas Dale, but an "extraordinary supply of one hundred Kine, and two hundred Swine" that may have received a heartier welcome from starving settlers than Dale did. In 1619, the Company treasurer, Sir Edwin Sandys, calculated that future shipments of cattle should include "20 young Heifers" for every hundred men. The Company planned in 1620 to send 200 more cattle, 400 Welsh goats, 20 mares, and "80 Asses from Fraunce." Company officials subsequently negotiated with an Irish merchant to transport "fayr and lardge Cattle and of our English breed" to Virginia. At a projected price of £10 per cow (the merchant wanted £12), the expense of supplying Virginia with livestock quickly mounted.[60]

Such high costs may have deterred the Plymouth Company from furnishing its colony with domestic animals, at least at first. The *Mayflower* brought plenty of colonists but no livestock in 1620, surely exacerbating the "starving time" of the Pilgrims' first year and making it far more difficult for them to cultivate the land. Only in 1623 did Emmanuel Altham at last report seeing "six goats, about fifty hogs and pigs, also divers hens" in Plymouth. Another year passed before Edward Winslow returned to England to procure "three heifers and a bull, the first beginning of any cattle of that kind" in the colony. Horses did not arrive until 1625, sheep perhaps not until the 1640s. Plymouth's slow growth and limited economic development cannot wholly be attributed to the initial shortage of livestock, but this surely deepened the Pilgrims' troubles.[61]

The Massachusetts Bay Company avoided making the same mistake. A year before the first fleet of ships set sail, company officials estimated that

"20 cowes & bulls" and "10 mares & horses" would be required for every hundred men. When the 11 vessels of the Winthrop Fleet gathered at the Isle of Wight in the spring of 1630 to prepare for the Atlantic crossing, the ratio of animal to human passengers was higher than the projected estimate: 240 cows and about 60 horses accompanied 700 emigrants. John Winthrop recorded in his journal the arrival of thousands more people and animals during the 1630s.[62] Emigrant families supplemented Company herds with their own livestock. Francis Higginson advised prospective emigrants to "bring mares, kine, and sheep as many as they can," avoiding pregnant animals "for they are in more danger to perish at sea." Before joining the Winthrop Fleet in 1630, Robert Parke arranged for his son to "b[u]y for me Six Coues [cows] and three mayers and a horse" to take aboard. Benjamin Cooper, who died en route to Boston in 1637, had brought eight bullocks with him. Capital investment in livestock, by both the Company and individual emigrants, amounted to a substantial sum. Edward Johnson estimated the expense of transporting "the Swine, Goates, Sheepe, Neate [cattle] and Horse" that accompanied the initial wave of colonists to be "twelve thousand pound beside the price they cost" to purchase.[63]

No colonist who left an account of the transatlantic crossing mentioned what it was like to spend eight to ten weeks in close quarters aboard ship with dozens of restive animals. Absorbed by their own anxieties, emigrants who described their voyages dwelled instead on the miseries of seasickness, the terror induced by tempests, and the relief occasioned by good weather.[64] But the animals' passage could hardly have been less traumatic. Confined to dark, fetid stalls below decks, livestock struggled to keep their footing as ships rose and sank with ocean swells. During storms, their terrified bellows and squeals added to the cacophony produced by lashing rains, howling winds, creaking timbers, and human shrieks and stammered prayers. A distressingly large number of animals perished at sea. Thomas Dudley, who sailed to Massachusetts in 1630, recalled that "half of our cows and almost all our mares and goats" died during the crossing. All the human passengers on the *Handmaid* arrived safely at Plymouth in October 1630, but ten of 28 cows did not. Forty heifers out of 61 died on the *James*'s 1632 voyage from London to Massachusetts; a year later, 40 sheep succumbed on another New England-bound ship.[65] The prospect of losing so many animals during long voyages encouraged colonists to seek closer sources of supply than distant England. Ships bound for the Chesapeake sometimes procured livestock in the West Indies. Vessels headed for New England typically tracked across the North Atlantic and rarely took so extensive a detour. Another alternative, Francis Higginson suggested, was for colonists to purchase livestock in Ireland, which lay "in the way" and trimmed a few days off the animals' voyages.[66]

Weak, dehydrated, and unsteady on their feet, surviving livestock reached destinations that further tested their diminished strength. New England and the Chesapeake may have lain on roughly the same latitudes as southern Europe and North Africa, but their climates were anything but Mediterranean. Colonists, assuming that world climates remained consistent along latitudes, anticipated the sort of warm weather that would nurture grapes, oranges, olives, and other exotic crops.[67] To make matters worse, English colonization occurred in the midst of a "little ice age," lasting from about 1350 to 1850, that brought unusually cold weather to eastern North America. John Smith reported an "extreame" frost in Virginia during the winter of 1607–08. The next year, a violent storm with "extreame wind, raine, frost, and snowe" forced Smith and a party of soldiers "to keepe Christmas" in an Indian village because they could not make it back to Jamestown. New England winters were even fiercer. Richard Garrard was shipwrecked en route to Plymouth in December 1630 and froze to death, despite the ministrations of Indians who tried to save him. Three of Garrard's companions died as well, their flesh "mortified with the frost." Massachusetts magistrates decided in 1634 that "by reason of the great snowes & frostes" they would not "keepe Courtes in the 3: winter months."[68] Livestock shivered along with their owners. In late December 1630, John Winthrop lamented that "manye of our Cowes & goates were forced to be still abroad" in freezing weather. The "greatest parte" of the cattle brought to Connecticut in 1636 died from exposure. John Winter, the manager of a trading post on Richmond Island off Maine's coast, fought a losing battle with the elements as he tried to keep pigs and goats from freezing. In Virginia, many livestock succumbed to cold during the harsh winter of 1675. Although cattle and swine are surprisingly resilient species, the onslaught of bitter American winters was often more than the hardiest constitutions could bear.[69]

Drought, especially in the southern colonies, posed an equally dangerous hazard for man and beast. Settlement at both Roanoke and Jamestown commenced during periods of extreme drought, which may have led to the disappearance of the North Carolina colony and almost certainly contributed to the hardships of early Virginia. Colonists and cattle alike sickened after drinking the unusually brackish water from the lower James River. Food crops for settlers and forage for animals withered in the heat and dryness, adding hunger to thirst.[70] Physiological stress produced by the trauma of transatlantic voyages and adjustment to unexpected New World conditions made weakened animals especially vulnerable to disease. Although colonists were too preoccupied with their own maladies to record the state of their animals' health with any precision or regularity, livestock—particularly in the Chesapeake—were plagued by cattle ticks, kidney worms, and a host of other unwelcome parasites.[71]

Colonists did complain incessantly about losing livestock to predators, a problem English husbandmen no longer encountered. Wolves, which had disappeared in England by about 1500, roamed freely in New World forests and joined bears in availing themselves of a new kind of prey. A frustrated John Winter reported from Maine in the 1630s that wolves and bears killed so many pigs that the others grew "fearfull to stay any way of[f] in the woods" where they normally foraged. John Winthrop took to carrying a gun wherever he went as protection against the wolves that "came dayly about the house, & killed swine & Calves" at will. The anonymous author of an "Essay on the Ordering of Towns" proposed that New Englanders join forces to "suppress" the "Swampes and such Rubbish waest grownds" around their communities where "ravenous unsatiable" wolves congregated.[72] Chesapeake colonists raised their own litany of complaints about losing livestock to wolves. In neither region did colonists suspect that the problem may in part have been of their own making. Wolf and bear populations may have surged as a result of the colonists' introduction of a new food supply. Adult cattle and horses—and even pigs, according to Roger Williams—could hold their own against wolves, but younger animals made tempting targets. Colonial officials responded to farmers' complaints by offering bounties to anyone who would help rid the land of the despised predators. Renewing these acts became a regular feature of legislative agendas throughout the seventeenth century, indicating that decades of effort failed to make colonial settlements completely safe for livestock.[73]

In the Chesapeake, at least at first, the colonists themselves turned out to be equally voracious predators. Starving Jamestown settlers, unwilling or unable to produce their own food and unsuccessful in their attempts to seize enough from the Indians, declared open season on what was supposed to have been Virginia's breeding stock. By the end of the calamitous winter of 1609-10, John Smith reported, "our commanders and officers" had eaten up "our hogs, hens, goats, sheep, horse, or what lived," leaving only "some small proportions (sometimes)" for everybody else. Desperate colonists even resorted to cannibalism and eating the flesh from exhumed corpses. Matters had only slightly improved when Sir Thomas Gates arrived in May 1610 to take over as deputy governor, followed by the governor himself, Lord De la Warr, in June. Gates and his successor, Sir Thomas Dale, concluded that only martial law could salvage the failing colony. They devised a legal code that, among its many stern provisions, included a measure to protect what few domestic animals remained. It became a capital crime to kill "any Bull, Cow, Calfe, Mare, Horse, Colt, Goate, Swine, Cocke, Henne, Chicken, Dogge, Turkie, or any tame Cattel, or Poultry, of what condition soever" without permission, whether the animal was privately owned or company property.[74]

For years regular infusions of imported animals augmented livestock numbers, much as colonists themselves relied on immigration to increase their population. Animals' reproductive rates were not at first sufficient to achieve significant growth. John Smith's boast that "3 sowes in one yeare increased [to] 60 and od pigges" was precisely the sort of wild exaggeration that fed unrealistic expectations. Those three sows more likely produced nine, or at most 18 to 20 surviving piglets if they farrowed twice that year. Ralph Hamor's rosy account of Virginia's livestock "plentifully increasing and thriving" in 1615 similarly reflected wishful thinking on the part of someone eager to cast a faltering commercial enterprise in the best possible light, for domestic animal populations had not yet become self-sustaining. But high hopes were not easily dashed, as the heirs of Abraham Peirsey discovered to their dismay. Peirsey had borrowed two cows from Samuel Argall in 1621, and 17 years later a Virginia jury calculated that those cows must have produced 50 offspring, which Peirsey's heirs now owed to Argall's descendants. If not utterly impossible, such an extraordinary rate of increase and survival was highly unlikely.[75]

In Virginia, supply ships tried to keep pace with colonists' needs. But even as late as 1619, Company officials had to coerce colonists into prudent management of their herds with a stern prohibition against the slaughter of breeding cattle. A census made the following year recorded just over 300 head of cattle, about the same number of "tame" swine (excluding hogs running wild in the woods), more than 200 goats, and 11 horses, which suggests considerable attrition among livestock despite over a decade of importation and reproduction. Edward Waterhouse almost certainly stretched the truth when he counted nearly 1,500 cattle in Virginia in 1622, about one beast for every colonist and a five-fold increase in just two years. Other sources suggest that the supply of animals from England dwindled as the Virginia Company's financial position worsened. Fewer than 200 head of cattle total may have arrived in the last four years of Company rule.[76]

Virginia's livestock population suffered two major setbacks in 1622-23. First, untold numbers of animals were killed in the Powhatan Indians' surprise attack on the colony in March 1622. Then, a mysterious "generall death of men and Cattle" followed the next winter. One distressed survivor lamented that "he that had 40 hoggs about his house hath one or two: and a hundredth henns hath now 3 or 4." As for "tame Cattle," there were "no more to be had." Another census of animals conducted less than two years later counted just 365 cattle, 518 swine, 215 goats, and one horse; this differed little from the totals of five years earlier.[77]

After the Virginia Company went bankrupt in 1624, the flow of imports sharply declined, forcing colonists to rely much more heavily on natural increase to build their herds. The House of Burgesses reiterated familiar prohibitions against the slaughter of breeding animals that colonists evidently heeded. Slowly but surely, Virginia's livestock multiplied. According to one estimate, in 1649 there were 20,000 head of cattle, 200 horses, 50 asses, 3,000 sheep, 5,000 goats, "innumerable" swine, and poultry "without number." The figures may have been inflated, but they did not misrepresent the general upward trend. By the early 1630s, it was commonly assumed that Virginia had cattle to spare. The founders of Maryland carried instructions from the King requiring Virginia to supply the new colony with livestock. Planters balked at this command, not because they lacked the animals but because they opposed the establishment of a Catholic refuge on their borders. Virginians showed far less reluctance, however, when it came to exporting surplus livestock at a profit to Barbados and New England. The colony's livestock population had at last become self-sustaining, long before its human population did.[78]

New England's livestock, like its colonists, began reproducing themselves much more quickly. William Wood scolded Massachusetts's detractors in 1634 with the rejoinder that no place "where for four thousand souls there are fifteen hundred head of cattle, besides four thousand goats and swine innumerable" could truly be considered impoverished. New England's dependence on imported animals, obtained mostly from England and Virginia, lasted perhaps 20 years. Many beasts arrived in company with their emigrating owners, as part of the capital brought to set up farms. John Winthrop reassured an English correspondent in 1634 that "the yearly access of new Commers . . . have supplied all our wants, for Cattle," and the steady migration of people and livestock had another six or seven years to run. At the same time, Bay colonists' demand for animals drove the price of a cow up to an exorbitant £20, inducing nearby Plymouth settlers to part with some of their livestock at a handsome profit.[79]

Certainly by the 1650s, New England's livestock population was growing on its own. Edward Johnson calculated that the Bay Colony at that point had 12,000 cattle and 3,000 sheep. His tally of people and animals in each town sustained the impression that livestock had become ubiquitous. The ratio of cattle to households in Charlestown, Dorchester, Roxbury, and Watertown was nearly three to one. In newer towns like Newbury, Concord, and Sudbury, it reached six to one. These figures roughly correspond to modern estimates derived from tax lists and probate inventories, and do not include swine, sheep, goats, or horses. Livestock also filled Connecticut and Rhode Island towns, and even wolf-plagued frontier settlements in Maine, by mid-century.[80] With domestic supplies assured, colonists sought outlets for surplus animals. Market opportunities beckoned in New Netherland and especially the West Indies, and New Englanders wasted little time in taking advantage of them.[81]

Sooner or later, livestock proliferated in every New World settlement to which they had been introduced.[82] Animals adapted remarkably well to a variety of climates and terrains, surviving in spite of new predators and parasites. Colonial livestock may not have bred as quickly or steadily as animals sheltered on English or Dutch farms, but over time their numbers swelled nonetheless. By 1650, English animals of all sorts outnumbered English colonists. Already in scattered parts of eastern Massachusetts and along the river valleys of Tidewater Virginia it was becoming easier to spot a cow or a pig than to catch a glimpse of a deer.

George Percy, who arrived in Virginia in 1607 imagining good fortune for himself and great changes for the land, left for England five years later after a brief but ignominious career as a brutal soldier and the inept governor of a faltering colonial outpost. He had acquired a substantial landed estate, but did not remain in the colony long enough to cultivate his fields or fill his meadows with grazing cattle. At the time of Percy's return voyage in 1612, more persistent Virginia colonists had abandoned elusive dreams of gold and replaced them with visions of farms producing some kind of lucrative crop on broad acres cleared of trees and Indians. No one as yet gave much thought to tobacco.

Everyone assumed that colonial farms, whether they appeared in the Chesapeake or New England, needed livestock. More prolific than the people who brought them, domestic animals became potent symbols of English expansion into the "vacant" lands of America. Thousands of cattle and hogs roaming through meadows and woods fulfilled the early promise of tiny cows sketched onto maps and fanciful population figures tucked into progress reports penned by anxious settlers. Yet colonists intended their animals to represent not just English habitation, but English civility. They anticipated reweaving in all its intricacy the complex web of functional and sentimental relationships that bound humans and domestic creatures together. Colonial farmers would provide Indians with powerful models of how civilized people improved animals, the land, and themselves. These assumptions, however, failed to account for the very different conditions under which livestock husbandry would be pursued in America. The New World proved far more congenial to the multiplication of livestock than to their management.

Chapter Four

The Wild Gangs
of the Chesapeake

Livestock Husbandry in the South

$\mathcal{F}$ifty years after its founding, the Virginia colony still struggled with two problems that had plagued it from the start. One persistent nuisance was wolves, whose numbers appeared to grow relentlessly along with their appetite for livestock. Tense relations with the Indians constituted another, more serious area of concern. In 1656 the House of Burgesses conceived of a plan to solve both problems at once. The lawmakers decided to enlist Indian cooperation in the campaign against wolves and in the quest for peace. They proposed that every time a group of Indians brought eight wolves' heads to county officials, the hunters' "King or Great Man" would receive a cow as a reward. The intended impact on the wolf population was clear enough, but how this peculiar bounty would improve relations between Indians and colonists was not self-evident. Thus the burgesses offered a brief explanation for this part of their strategy. Giving a cow to Indians, they asserted, "will be a step to civilizing them and to making them Christians" and those transformations, in turn, would promote peace.[1]

This statement summed up a welter of assumptions about domestic animals and livestock husbandry. The burgesses' choice of a cow, rather than any other species of livestock, indicated the nature of the changes they hoped to produce. "Civilizing" the Indians clearly meant making them more like the

English. Horses would not do the job because they encouraged mobility, which colonists regarded as the bane of native society, and could also be used for warfare. Swine, sheep, and goats held too low a status in the barnyard hierarchy and were too self-sufficient. As valuable and versatile creatures requiring careful management, however, cows were ideal instruments for introducing Indians to English ways. The burgesses apparently envisioned Indian families putting down roots in villages encircled by enclosed pastures, native women milking docile cows, and men and boys carting dung to enrich worn-out cornfields and cutting hay to nourish growing herds. In effect domesticated by their own cows, Indians would more easily imbibe the Christian principles that underscored a new way of life.[2]

Cows further served the cause of peace, the burgesses reasoned, because they gave native leaders "something to hazard & loose besides their lives" in the event of conflict. Once Indians had property at stake they would presumably forswear violence out of self-interest. This pronouncement betrayed the burgesses' own predilections by implying that civilized people valued possessions at least as much as their lives. The legislators conspicuously ignored the fact that European rulers (let alone Virginia's colonists) seldom, if ever, abstained from warfare for fear of losing their estates. Likewise they conveniently overlooked Indian claims to land, natural resources, housing, and other goods when portraying native peoples as propertyless. By bestowing cows on native "kings" rather than on the actual wolf hunters, the burgesses also assumed that Indian leaders could prevent impetuous warriors from attacking the English simply by reminding them that the sachem's cattle were now at stake. Possession of such a rare commodity would surely bolster sachems' prestige among their own people.[3]

Virginians' confidence in the civilizing power of cattle bore little relation to their own experience as livestock keepers in America. Long before 1656, Chesapeake colonists abandoned any pretense of conscientious husbandry. Devoting most of their labor to the all-important tobacco crop, colonists paid little attention to livestock and avoided making extensive improvements to the land. Few planters demonstrated proper stewardship over the animals under their care, a dereliction that European visitors to the early Chesapeake were quick to criticize. Freed from many of the constraints imposed by English-style husbandry, livestock changed too. Tractable cattle and horses turned pugnacious; unruly swine grew fiercer and roamed the woods in formidable "wild gangs." Such creatures hardly served as emblems of civility.

Retaining one critical feature of their English experience, however, Chesapeake colonists persisted in identifying their animals as private property. Indeed, the abandonment of so many familiar habits of husbandry made relations of property all the more important. It was as property, colonists believed, that domestic animals most effectively transformed people. Virginia's burgesses never doubted that ownership of livestock would convince Indians to choose civilization, Christianity, and peace over savagery, paganism, and war. Yet Chesapeake colonists discovered, much to their consternation, that possession of animal property carried greater weight than ever before in defining their own civility. This realization proved all the more disconcerting when colonists learned that lackadaisical husbandry practices loosened their hold over the very creatures that helped to identify them as a superior people. These unforeseen circumstances only increased the anxiety of colonists intent on presenting themselves to the Indians, and to the world at large, as exemplars of civilization in a savage New World.

No one would ever have mistaken an average seventeenth-century Chesapeake plantation for an English farm. On approach, visitors might have had difficulty even seeing the plantation for the trees. Colonists only cleared as much land as they could immediately use, saving the rest for a later time or another generation. A half acre for a house lot and garden, an acre for an orchard, six or so acres for corn, and maybe another six or seven for tobacco was as much as a small family with a servant or two could manage at first. These modest clearings lay within sight of dense woods and tangled thickets, with countless tree stumps bearing silent witness to the plantation's recent condition.[4]

Beyond the small, ramshackle dwellings that housed planters and their families, one looked in vain for any of the outbuildings typically found on an English yeoman's farm. Seventeenth-century Chesapeake farmers built few barns, cowsheds, stables, pigsties, or dairies. Each plantation had at least one tobacco house where, after the harvest, workers hung tobacco stalks to cure on scaffolds before the leaves could be prepared for shipment to England. Instead of hedges or stone walls, a few rudimentary "worm" fences surrounded orchards and fields. Made from split rails arranged in a zigzag pattern that required no digging of postholes, these fences were notable more for their ease of construction than their durability.[5] None of these fences encircled pastures full of cattle or sheep. In fact, other than a couple of chickens scratching in the yard and perhaps a wandering pig or two, scarcely any livestock would be visible at all. For all the thousands of farm animals reportedly in the Chesapeake by midcentury, few appeared to live on anyone's farm.

Everything from the dilapidated buildings and crude living conditions to the curious absence of animals on these plantations reflected the colonists' devotion to tobacco. With the economic survival of Virginia and Maryland, not to mention their own prosperity, hanging in the balance, English settlers concentrated their efforts on producing the one crop with a guaranteed market. Planters scrambled for land and laborers, seeking an advantage over their competitors and temporarily forgoing expenditures that would improve their quality of life. They also reconfigured animal husbandry to fit with tobacco's demands. Even before tobacco reigned supreme, Virginia's leaders had relegated livestock to a supporting role in the colony's development. "Corne and Cattell we passe over," sniffed company treasurer Sir Edwin Sandys in 1620, "being only for sustenance of the People." That attitude gained support as tobacco cultivation spread. Few planters wanted to assign the scarce and expensive servants they had to import from England to care for livestock when they could be hoeing tobacco. English husbandry practices, dependent upon a ready supply of workers, would have to give way to a less laborious livestock regime.[6]

One key feature of the new Chesapeake regime was a different mix of livestock than would be found on most English farms. Virtually every species of European farm animal came to Virginia and Maryland, but not all of them adapted well to the new environment or new methods of management. Sheep, for instance, were hard to find on Tidewater plantations during most of the seventeenth century because the "humility of their nature," as one Marylander put it, made them easy prey for wolves. Since colonial sheep foraged through thickets rather than grazing in smooth pastures, their fleeces were "torn off their Backs by Briers, and Bushes," the wool lost. Mutton was likewise a scarce commodity. Sheep flourished only in the eighteenth century after more land had been cleared and predators eliminated.[7]

The gradual disappearance of goats may have involved a deliberate campaign on the colonists' part. Brought by the hundreds to early

Jamestown, probably for milk rather than meat, few goats could be found in the region by midcentury. Their penchant for chewing the bark off apple trees may have been their downfall. Unwilling to devote their energies to growing barley for beer, planters relied on orchards for cider to drink in its stead and would brook no threat to one of the few pleasures in their lives.[8]

Oxen were also a rare sight on most Chesapeake farms. Following Indian practice, colonists hoed tobacco and corn instead of using plows and oxen. A census from 1620 reported that one out of three "horned cattle" in Virginia was an ox, but the animals mainly helped with hauling logs and other heavy loads rather than cultivation. As of 1615, according to one witness, there were all of "three or foure Ploughes" at work in Virginia. Even at midcentury, there were only about 150 plows to be found in a colony with an English population approaching 12,000. Similarly in seventeenth-century Maryland, just one in twenty planters owned a plow and presumably the oxen to pull it. Durand of Dauphiné, a visiting Frenchman, observed that as late as in 1686, Virginians still "do not know what it is to work the land with cattle."[9]

They did not work the land with horses either, even though the animals could easily have pulled plows through the sandy, stone-free soil of the Tidewater region. So long as planting fields were littered with stumps, no draft animal could do an efficient job. Thus horses, like oxen, remained scarce in the Chesapeake at least during the first half of the seventeenth century. One account reported just 200 of the animals in Virginia as late as 1649. The dearth of horses magnified the colonists' isolation. Plantations lay widely dispersed along rivers and creeks, which made shipping tobacco easier but required planters to resort to canoes to visit one another. A desire to improve transportation may have inspired the House of Burgesses to prohibit the export of horses until 1668. Only then did their numbers in Virginia and Maryland reach a high enough level that *importing* horses was soon forbidden.[10]

Cattle proliferated in the Chesapeake but performed fewer functions in the colonial setting than in England. Perhaps the most glaring difference was the neglect of dairying. Planters keen on maximizing tobacco production mostly imported male servants—six men for every woman early in the century and still two or three males for every female in the 1690s—leaving few women available for what was regarded as a female occupation. John Lewger, reporting to Lord Baltimore in January 1639 on Maryland's progress, explicitly used the gender imbalance as an excuse when he declared that "the dairy will require a woman" and no suitable candidate could be found.[11] Part of the problem also lay with Chesapeake cattle. English cows might supply as much as two gallons of milk a day, but Chesapeake cows, ill-nourished on poor-quality natural forage and sensitive to summertime heat, barely produced a quart or two. Low in butterfat, the milk yielded inferior butter and cheese that spoiled quickly in warm summer temperatures. Even in winter, Virginians avoided milking their cows, for according to John Clayton, they somehow had "a Notion that it would kill them." Most observers found the local butter edible enough, but the cheese, described by one Maryland governor as "so Ranke and soe full of Eyes," tempted few consumers.[12]

Chesapeake cattle and hogs were used almost exclusively for meat. Here, at least, English settlers had the advantage over their compatriots at home, even though roast beef was reputedly England's national symbol. Only about half of the English population could afford to eat meat, usually bacon rather than beef, more than once or twice a week. These fortunate inhabitants indulged to an extent that amazed Continental visitors, consuming on average nearly 150 pounds annually per person.[13] Despite frontier conditions, many Chesapeake colonists may have come close to, or even exceeded, that amount. The early preponderance of game in the colonists' diet gave way by midcentury to meat from livestock. Average annual consumption ranged from 45 to 200 pounds, depending on age, gender, and economic status. Even servants expected meat in their rations and complained to county courts if their masters failed to provide it. Some planters came to understand that meat was necessary as well as desirable, providing essential nutrients to ward off pellagra and other diseases linked to a heavily corn-based diet.[14]

Instead of replicating English patterns of livestock ownership, Chesapeake colonists concentrated on raising the animals that required the least amount of attention. Limiting their use of oxen, horses, and dairy cattle, and all but abandoning vulnerable sheep and troublesome goats, colonists focused on hogs and beef cattle. Yet important as these animals were to the colonists' survival, they received minimal supervision. Chesapeake colonists were simply unwilling to divert valuable labor from tobacco to care for cattle and hogs with anything like the diligence associated with good husbandry.

Officials of the Virginia Company too easily assumed that English husbandry would prevail in early Jamestown. In 1609 they reminded Deputy Governor Thomas Gates to "give order that yor Catle be kept in heards waited and attended on by some small watch" much as they might be managed in an English village. Jamestown and other settlements did appoint cowkeepers, but they spent more time keeping an eye out for wolves and Indians than keeping track of wandering cattle.[15] With manpower in short supply, Gates and other colonial authorities tried using physical barriers to assist, or even substitute for, human keepers. In 1611, Gates ordered colonists to build a palisade to protect hogs, and over the next two decades Virginians erected a six-mile-long fence between the James and York rivers. Colonists subsequently boasted that they had created an enclosed range as large as the English county of Kent. Inhabitants in Rochdale Hundred, up the James River, fenced in a tract of 20 circuit miles. Colonists also deposited livestock on offshore islands that had been emptied of wolves, such as the "Ile of Hogges" so designated by 1609. Marylanders fortified Palmer's Island and by 1638 stocked it with 13 head of cattle. The following year, Father Andrew White advised Lord Baltimore to have his agents "choose some large Iland for a breede of Swine" and "a heard of goates and yong calfes" where they could "grow upp into great flocks without any farther cost att all." Once livestock had been confined to islands or enclosed in enormous ranges they could presumably fend for themselves.[16]

A few colonists initially expected to keep animals penned on their plantations. John Lewger planned to "build sties and necessary penns" for his swine, grow corn for them, and regularly "lead them out to their places of feeding" on his Maryland farm. Authorities requested that colonists in particular pen their hogs to prevent them from rooting around in planting fields. In 1640 Virginia's assembly for this very reason ordered colonists to pen hogs at night and hire keepers for them during the day. The inhabitants of St. Mary's City in Maryland likewise urged the province's council in 1685 to require owners to lock up their swine.[17] Toward the end of the century, some planters penned cattle at night, or temporarily confined calves as a way to lure dairy cows back to the plantation.[18]

For the most part, however, the disadvantages of penning livestock far outweighed the benefits. Building fences and sheds was fairly easy, but feeding animals confined within them was not. Modern beef cattle eat about 2 percent of their weight in hay each day, or about 20 pounds for a 1,000-pound cow, and drink as much as 12 gallons of water. Adult swine consume five or six pounds of food daily. A working horse needs a daily ration of 20 pounds or so of fodder, and since horses digest hay less efficiently than cattle, they require oats or another supplemental grain. Early Chesapeake farmers, already hard-pressed to tend their corn and tobacco fields, could not clear and plant another few acres just for their livestock or spare the labor to gather hay or build barns in which to keep it. And they could not afford to buy what they could not produce themselves. In 1690 one Marylander charged as much as 100 pounds of tobacco a month to feed six penned hogs. Purchased winter feed could amount to 10 or 15 percent of the value of the animals that ate it. Faced with such trouble and expense, colonists avoided building pens and ignored the laws requiring them to do so.[19]

It was far easier to let livestock find their own food, and so Chesapeake colonists abandoned English methods in favor of free-range husbandry. By 1643, their innovation gained legal sanction in Virginia. That year the House of Burgesses required colonists to fence in their crops, not their animals, a decision that effectively gave livestock the run of the land. In 1646, legislators further ruled that a "sufficient" fence had to be four and a half feet high and "substantiall close downe to the bottome" to thwart both leaping cattle and rooting swine. Only an aggrieved farmer who had such a fence and kept it in good repair could sue the owner of trespassing animals for damage. These policies reversed common English practice that, by the seventeenth century, placed a much greater burden on livestock owners to control their animals. Virginia's assembly even passed a measure that protected livestock owners from charges of trespass. So long as he notified his neighbors, every planter had the right to "seake or fetch his owne cattle and hoggs from off any mans land." Maryland's legislature enacted similar laws, requiring five-foot-high fences to discourage horses as well as cattle.[20]

A necessary response to labor scarcity, free-range husbandry in turn produced other adaptations. Planters who did not pen their livestock did not have dung available for fertilizer. After three or four years sowed with tobacco, followed by a year or two in corn, planting fields sharply declined in fertility. But colonists with exhausted land "never manure it to bring it to heart again," complained one English observer accustomed to better management. Instead they cleared new fields and let the old ones lie fallow for up to 20 years. Only near the end of the seventeenth century did some planters adopt a field rotation system, working a quarter of their acreage, letting cattle graze on another quarter, and leaving the remaining half in woodland. After four years, they rearranged fences to confine cattle on the exhausted cropland and tilled the former pasture. Only cornfields received this treatment; when tobacco lands were manured, "Smoakers say they can plainly taste the fulsomness of the Dung."[21]

For most of the seventeenth century, Chesapeake land not only lacked careful manuring but much of it was not even cleared. Visitors expecting to behold an open landscape of cultivated fields were sadly disappointed to see a great deal of dense woodland instead. Noting that "not the hundredth Part of the Country is yet clear'd from the Wood," three royal officials who toured eastern Virginia in 1697 reproached colonists for laziness.[22] Some of this wooded land probably included overgrown fallow fields, but other tracts were left uncleared by design. As long as planters let livestock run at large, they had to set aside lands where the animals could forage. Because woodlands did not provide optimal grazing, farmers substituted quantity for quality. Just one free-ranging cow needed as much as five acres of pinewoods to sustain itself in summer and 15 acres in winter; in deciduous forest, the winter requirements were higher. Even poorer planters, with perhaps ten cows and as many swine, needed access to 150 or more acres of woods to support their animals, depending on the composition of the forest. Wealthier planters, with herds six or seven times larger, required correspondingly larger tracts. The forest remained standing, in short, because it had to.[23]

Colonists aimed for the right mix of lands on their plantations. As John Clayton noted, planters sought to ensure that they had "enough to plant, and for their Stocks and Herds of Cattle to range and feed in." By the 1680s, a ratio of about twice as much forest to cleared land sufficed. That was how Ralph Wormeley managed Rosegill, his grand plantation along the Rappahannock River. Two-thirds of his 6,000 acres remained forested for numerous livestock that, at the time of Wormeley's death in 1701, included 439 head of cattle, 86 sheep, an unknown number of horses, and too many pigs to count.[24] Less wealthy planters, with much smaller holdings, depended on free access to lands not yet granted to private owners, which many people regarded as a vast commons open to all. Dick Willan of Maryland, whose cattle and hogs ran at large on the aptly named "Pork Hall neck," could vouch for the importance of public range. When Willan heard rumors that Pork Hall neck was about to be granted to someone, he protested to authorities that "if any body did seate that land it would ruin him in his stock."[25] His anxious response testified not only to colonists' urgent need for adequate grazing lands but also to the ease with which tensions flared if some men were accommodated at the expense of others.

The dispersal of free-ranging livestock, whether on private or public property, temporarily reduced another kind of stress. The animals' impact on the environment remained limited so long as their population density in any one location stayed low. Over time, however, rising numbers of livestock gradually altered the woodlands that supported them. Cattle set loose in pine forests foraged selectively on grasses and the undergrowth of oaks and other hardwoods. Pigs went after acorns and seeds on the forest floor, but also killed smaller trees by gnawing on their roots. Where animals tended to congregate, near clearings and streams, they compacted the soil and crushed ground covers, encouraging erosion. Environmental changes were at first minor, but livestock nonetheless initiated a set of alterations that reduced the land's capacity to sustain them.[26] This development, in turn, encouraged livestock to range further afield and their owners to appropriate more land for them.

By the 1670s, a seemingly relentless flood of English settlers lined the shores of Chesapeake Bay, pushed up the James, Rappahannock, and Potomac Rivers, and occupied the narrow peninsula of the Eastern Shore. Prospective planters were constantly on the lookout for good land near water transportation and plenty of forest for their livestock. They acquired as many acres as possible so they could abandon old fields for new and find fresh grazing for animals on their estates. Good neighbors, or at least close ones, were a secondary consideration. The demands of tobacco and livestock conspired to keep colonists spread out along rivers, a quarter of a mile or more apart. With such dispersed settlement, marketplaces were slow to appear, churches to gather, and towns to form.[27] Protecting the interests of free-range animals hardly accounted for all of these developments, but the colonists' style of husbandry certainly contributed to them. If cows were supposed to promote civilization, the character of colonial Chesapeake society suggests that they failed at their task.

Had they been able to examine their own behavior objectively, Chesapeake colonists would surely have been stunned to see how far they had drifted from English practices. For all their presumptions of civility, they acted more like native farmers than English husbandmen. They lived in small clusters scattered along waterways, as Indians did, instead of settling in large towns. They grew native crops of corn and tobacco using native-style hoes, not English plows. Like Indian farmers, they let exhausted fields lie fallow for decades and cleared new plots, putting little effort into enclosing land and none into its "manurance." Although colonial women could hardly disassemble their houses and carry them on their backs, as native women customarily did, the colonists' material goods evoked a sense of sparseness and impermanence usually reserved for descriptions of Indian villages. And the livestock that carried such symbolic weight no longer performed the multiple tasks associated with English husbandry. Colonists, like Indians, used animals almost exclusively for meat, and like native hunters' prey, English livestock could most often be found in the woods.

Enough English characteristics remained, of course, to distinguish colonists from Indians and preserve the colonists' image of themselves as a civilized people. English settlers eschewed seasonal mobility and remained on their hardscrabble plantations year-round. They typically, though not invariably, sent men instead of women to labor in the fields.[28] They spoke English, obeyed English laws and (from a distance) an English king. Even if they did not always have churches in which to do so, they worshiped the Christian God. And they recognized and defended individual property rights that contrasted with the Indians' preference for collective ownership. Colonists extended those property rights to the animals they brought from England. Their exercise of dominion over those animals, however, grew exceptionally fragile under their new husbandry regime. Just as English settlers had begun to resemble Indians in certain ways, English animals at times appeared to be going wild.

In the seventeenth-century Chesapeake, animals left to their own devices altered in appearance and behavior. The colonists barely seemed to notice, but European visitors to the region were shocked and criticized the animals' negligent owners. Because livestock spent more time away from plantations than on them, colonists found it difficult even to keep track of how many animals they owned. Some beasts went off to forage and never came back to the plantation at all. If this was dominion over animals, it was dominion of a most peculiar sort.

Rev. Alexander Whitaker, minister of Henrico in Virginia, was among the first to disparage the colonists' deficient husbandry practices. Writing in 1613, when the survival of Virginia's livestock remained uncertain, the minister argued that they would do fine "if they might bee provided for." But this was precisely what colonists were unable or unwilling to do. Instead they expected livestock to fend for themselves, finding whatever sustenance they could in the woods and meadows. This was as true in 1611, when cattle "lived without other feeding than the grasse they found," as in 1688, when John Clayton saw Virginian cattle "pined and starved" because they could find "little or no Grass in winter." In springtime, hungry cattle ventured into swamps "where they perish," mired in the mud. Like Clayton, Durand of Dauphiné found much to criticize. Because "nothing was given them to drink," Virginian hogs invaded peach orchards and "kept drunk on the fruit." Colonists did "not know what it is to save hay" as winter fodder. After a severe snowstorm, the Frenchman was appalled to see cattle forced to "eat the bark of the trees because the grass was covered." It was little short of a miracle that cattle ever wandered back to their home plantations; they obviously did so "rather by instinct than by any care the planters take of them." Even one of Virginia's native sons, Robert Beverley, writing at the turn of the eighteenth century, felt compelled to upbraid his neighbors for "exceeding Ill-husbandry" towards their cattle and for making their hogs "find their own Support in the Woods."[29]

Distressed by what he saw in Virginia, John Clayton bemoaned the fact that negligent planters behaved in ways that "one would think *English* Men should not be guilty of." Turning his attention to a colonial "Lady," he tried to convince her to sow winter wheat so that "she might turn thereon her weak Cattle" in spring. Clayton likewise advised her to "carefully gather her *Indian* Corn-tops, and Blades, and all her Straw" for winter fodder and to plant sainfoin, a nutritious forage crop grown by many English livestock farmers. In the end, the unnamed lady planted the wheat and saved straw and cornstalks, but ignored the sainfoin.[30] Other critics acknowledged that while some planters did provide food for livestock, it was hardly enough to make a difference. "All that they give their Cattel in winter is only the husks of their *Indian* corn, unless it be some of them that have a little wheat-straw," complained Thomas Glover. Even these coarse rations were doled out to livestock in meager portions, barely sufficient "to keep them alive," in Glover's view. Durand of Dauphiné noted that planters provided "little more care to their horses than to their cattle." After a hard ride, colonists unsaddled their mounts, fed them a little corn, and then drove the animals "all covered with sweat . . . out into the woods, where they eat what they can find" or, as often as not, went hungry.[31]

Colonists also failed to provide shelter for their animals, no matter what the season or the weather. After a severe January snowstorm, Durand of

Dauphiné admonished planters for having "no mercy upon their cattle." He "saw the poor beasts of a morning all covered with snow and trembling with the cold," although he nevertheless had to admit that "I saw no dead cattle." Hogs, too, ran "where they list," rain or shine, summer or winter. Even chickens were left to roost in trees year round. John Clayton proposed that colonists who were too lazy to build winter shelter for livestock could put the animals in empty tobacco barns. For the most part this suggestion, like so many others offered by the censorious Englishman, fell on deaf ears.[32]

Poorly treated Chesapeake animals conspicuously lacked the robust appearance of well-tended English livestock. Notwithstanding a few early reports that colonial animals "doe become much bigger of body then the breed from whence they came," the creatures struck most observers, particularly after midcentury, as being noticeably smaller than English beasts.[33] If colonists only took care of their cattle, they "might be much larger than they are," Thomas Glover declared. Robert Beverley agreed that colonists' neglect of livestock "stint[ed] their Growth; so that they seldom or never grow so large as they would do, if they were well manag'd." By the 1690s, Maryland legislators voiced concern about "the small stature of Stallions" in their colony.[34] Full-grown Chesapeake hogs may have weighed as little as 100 pounds, steers perhaps 500 pounds. Horses less than 14 hands high (56 inches) at the shoulder abounded in the Maryland woods. Chesapeake livestock literally did not measure up to English standards.[35]

Uncontrolled breeding and insufficient diet helped to produce this result. Natural forage, richer in bulk than nutrients, supplied inadequate protein to ensure proper growth. Even today wild ponies living on native grasses on the Chesapeake island of Assateague rarely exceed 13 hands (52 inches) at the shoulder, and will only grow larger if captured as foals and fed an enriched diet. Over time, proliferating colonial herds may have overgrazed woodlands, compounding the problem of dietary insufficiency.[36]

For the most part, observers struck by the reduced size of livestock attributed this unfortunate development to planters' negligence rather than to any intrinsic deficiencies in the Chesapeake environment. To do otherwise was to question the suitability of the New World for English people and their animals, a dangerous line of thought. English settlement was supposed to bring improvement for America's land and native peoples, not degeneration in English transplants. Blaming colonists for the physiological changes in their livestock, however, preserved the illusion of English control. What mismanagement had wrought, good husbandry could reverse.[37]

Yet the decision to let livestock run at large effectively prevented colonists from practicing good husbandry. Colonists often had trouble even finding their animals. Planters and their servants periodically embarked on lengthy expeditions into the woods to search for missing creatures. One Marylander admitted to spending three days looking for errant hogs. Another hired Indians to try and find his pigs. In 1634, an utterly frustrated Virginian named James Knott despaired of ever finding his ox and three heifers, all of which had run "wyld in the woods . . . ever since they were calfes." Rev. Hugh Jones reported that even in the 1720s some planters could "spend the morning in ranging several miles in the woods to find and catch their horses" just so they could ride them a couple of miles to church or, fittingly, to a horse race.[38]

Not all reconnaissance missions ended happily. Animals often injured themselves in woods and swamps. One Virginian, all too familiar with the perils faced by wandering cattle, saw fit to name one of his cows "brooken leggs." Another colonist, Robert Hutchinson, lost his mare Noby when she hurt herself running through the tangled woods. Hutchinson's neighbor, George Gynne, reported seeing the horse fall as she looked back for her colt while jumping over a fallen tree. Gynne and a companion "went to stretch her Neck" but they "could doe noe good" because the mare's spine had snapped. John Clayton insisted that "several Persons lose ten, twenty or thirty Head of Cattle in a Year" through injury or straying into marshes. Although Clayton probably exaggerated, he drew attention to the fact that loss as well as injury was an unavoidable part of free-range husbandry. Livestock owners regularly plastered courthouse doors with notices of lost animals that had ambled off into the woods and swamps and not returned. They included detailed descriptions in hopes that the beasts might turn up on someone else's property. Among Henry Edwards's missing cattle were a "Browne Cow with a starr in her fforehead beinge old" and a "Heffer three yeare old blackish browne" that had strayed from his plantation in Virginia's Accomack County. Many of these errant beasts were gone for good.[39]

Under the circumstances, it is hardly surprising that colonists sometimes lost track of how many animals they actually possessed. Livestock not only grazed and died in the woods, but also gave birth there. In 1643, Robert Smith admitted to Maryland's Provincial Court that he "hath some hogs in the woods but how many he knoweth not." When Robert Cole made a record of his

Reproduction of early-seventeenth-century shilling from Bermuda
(then known as Sommer Island), with image of a wild hog.
Reproduced from the original held by the Department of Special
Collections of the University Libraries of Notre Dame

property in 1662 prior to sailing to England, he admitted that the "number of my hoggs is uncertaine butt of them that come home I thinke there is twenty nine of them and four young piggs." A decade later, Luke Gardiner, as guardian of the deceased Cole's estate, rendered a similarly vague account of livestock holdings, noting that the number of "horses mares & Colts in the woods" was "uncertaine." By the end of the century, this haphazard style of accounting had become routine. Robert Beverley acknowledged that in Virginia "when an Inventory of any considerable Man's Estate is taken by the Executors, the Hogs are left out, and not listed in the Appraisement," presumably because no one knew their number or whereabouts.[40]

The colonists' dominion over their animals was further undermined by a natural process that none of them anticipated. Livestock that absconded for good eventually went feral, and these creatures soon populated the woods in alarming numbers. As early as 1620, census takers in Virginia declined to enumerate the "Swine of the fforest," and colonists in future years would have had even greater difficulty counting feral creatures. "Wild Gangs" of feral cattle, horses, and hogs roamed the forest and occasionally ventured onto plantations. These animals presented colonial planters with a challenge that no seventeenth-century English farmer had to face.[41]

Chesapeake livestock in general appeared scrawny and unkempt, but feral creatures tended to be even smaller and thinner. They were also decidedly shaggier, with horses and cattle sporting thick coats and feral pigs developing a dense coat of curly underfur. Over time, other morphological changes occurred. Wild cattle grew longer horns. Feral swine had flatter skulls and formidable tusks, as well as longer legs and snouts. It might take a few generations for these physical differences to become fully visible, but the span of a pig generation is all of two or three years. The same was roughly true for wild cattle; for wild horses the timing might be three to four years. Certainly by midcentury, and probably somewhat earlier, distinctively different versions of domestic livestock had infiltrated the Chesapeake woods.[42]

For the most part, these creatures avoided settled areas. John Clayton attributed the elusiveness of wild cattle to their "great Acuteness of Smelling," which alerted them to the approach of humans. Wild horses were "so swift, that 'tis difficult to catch them," reported Robert Beverley. When any were captured, he noted, "they are so sullen, that they can't be tam'd." Beverley likened wild hogs to bears and wildcats in their propensity to "fly from the Face of Man."[43]

Encounters between colonists and feral livestock nevertheless did happen, and people learned that the animals were not only "sullen" but downright aggressive. During the breeding season, wild stallions and bulls fought with other males in their herds for dominance. Feral cows with calves and wild sows with piglets roamed the woods in gangs, and the wary mothers instinctively took the offensive against anyone who came near their young. At times, feral males approached plantations seeking new mates. In 1650, angry livestock owners in Maryland complained about "theire tame Cattell carried away and spoiled by Wild Bulls" and insisted that the provincial government do something about the problem. Interbreeding between wild stallions and plantation mares, Marylanders argued, "doth both Lessen & spoyle the whole breed and Streyne of all horses." When they were not occupied with finding mates, the animals galloped through fields and meadows, inflicting "grievious and intollerable" damage on crops and fences.[44]

The ungovernable behavior of feral livestock differed in degree but not in kind from the conduct of supposedly tame animals. Chesapeake livestock had a bad reputation that followed them wherever they went. Dutch settlers at New Amstel on the Delaware River, for instance, found that the cattle they obtained from Virginia were "accustomed, for the most part, to run wild and are hard to be managed."[45] Such comments carried more than a whiff of censure, directed not only at the rambunctious animals but at their obviously negligent former owners. So much of what European farmers took for granted about livestock husbandry, from the need to feed and shelter animals to the responsibility for keeping track of their whereabouts, had vanished from Tidewater plantations. Living much of the time in the forest, Chesapeake livestock appeared to have become part of the forest. Other than the fact of their Old World origins, it seemed that little remained to distinguish them from American fauna.

Yet one important distinction did remain, and it was a distinction that made all the difference. Even the scrawniest pig, sprouting wiry fur and flashing sharp tusks, gnawing on the same acorns that attracted squirrels and porcupines, was—unlike the squirrels and porcupines—someone's property. Planters may have relinquished the care and feeding of their animals to nature, but they refused wholly to abandon their livestock to the woods. Failing at the practical exercise of dominion over their animals, colonists steadfastly retained the principled assertion of dominion through legal possession. It was no wonder that Virginia's House of Burgesses invoked property rights in 1656 when they linked cattle ownership to civility. The insistence that domestic animals were property was one of the few vestiges of English-style husbandry that remained in the Chesapeake to help identify colonial farming as civilized. It was all the more disconcerting, therefore, when colonists discovered that claims to animal property were harder to maintain in the Chesapeake than they had been in England. The compromises that planters made in diverting labor from livestock to tobacco ended up loosening owners' grip over the creatures that were supposed to help make the colonies more like England.

Colonists themselves were largely responsible for this state of affairs. Certain unscrupulous settlers were quick to take advantage of the lax supervision of livestock and prey on the property of others. Although Durand of Dauphiné at one point blithely asserted that the "only robbers the planters fear . . . are the wolves," colonists frequently suspected another kind of predator.[46] Theft of livestock emerged as a persistent problem almost from the start of English settlement in the Chesapeake. Following the 1622 Powhatan uprising, starving colonists appropriated virtually any animal they could lay their hands on. Dismayed by such wanton misbehavior, Governor Francis Wyatt and his council proclaimed that anyone convicted of stealing any "Beasts or Birds of Domesticall or tame nature" worth more than 12 pence would be put to death. Stealing creatures of lesser value earned the offender a whipping. Lest anyone complain that "in England the vallue of some of these tame things is farre lesse" than it was in Virginia, and thus merited a lesser charge than felony, Wyatt countered that "here they are of farr higher rates, by reason of theire scarscitie, and therefore wilbe found punishable with no lesse than Death."[47]

The problem of scarcity, but not the incidence of thievery, diminished over time. As livestock populations rebounded, a first offense for hog stealing ceased to be prosecuted as a felony. After 1647, convicted first-time hog thieves in Virginia paid for their misdeed not with their lives but with 2,000 pounds of tobacco. The result was a veritable epidemic of this particular crime. The legislatures of both Virginia and Maryland passed more laws against pilfering hogs than stealing any other animal. They regularly renewed such measures, often with escalating penalties ranging from fines to corporal punishment, yet hog stealing remained "a generall crime usually comitted and seldom or never detected or prosecuted."[48]

Even under the best of circumstances, enforcement of these laws was difficult. It was not enough just to report that one's hogs were missing; a plaintiff also needed a culprit, a witness if possible, and evidence—which, given its edibility, was usually hard to find. This may explain why formal prosecutions relating to missing livestock were relatively rare in the Chesapeake compared to rates of indictment for similar offenses in England. More often than not, trials degenerated into rancorous exchanges of charges and countercharges. In 1658 in Maryland, for example, accusations of hog stealing flew back and forth among revelers during a night of "merry drinking & dancing" but could not be adjudicated for lack of evidence. Kent County residents John and Jane Salter and William Price landed in court when their neighbors began losing hogs "very strangly of a suden" and "pork [was] offten seene" in the Salters' house even though they "had no hogs of theire owne to kill." Thomas Baker came under suspicion in Charles County for telling John Wood that "hee was sory thear was no meat in the hows but it shoold not bee so long" before there was some. Sure enough, Baker soon appeared with a dead hog. This testimony actually emerged in a case in which *Baker* was the plaintiff, charging his neighbors with theft and defamation for calling him a common hog stealer.[49]

If some accused thieves resented the damage to their reputations, others flaunted their behavior as if daring anyone to bring charges. Several men who wound up in court had set their dogs on someone else's hogs, effectively advertising their mischief to all within earshot. One of the least subtle thieves in Accomack County, Virginia, was John Pettijohn, whose *modus operandi* involved throwing corn at others' swine to lure them away and then turning his dogs loose on the hapless creatures. When one of his dogs grabbed a pig in April 1680, Pettijohn snatched the prize away, smacked it on the head with an ax, "stuck him and opened his belly and pulled forth his gutts," and then dragged the carcass "to the roote of a tree and threw junks of wood on him" to hide the evidence. Pettijohn might have gotten away with this escapade if he had not gone to John Cole's house later that day and boasted that he had killed one of Christopher Tompson's hogs.[50]

Cattle and horses disappeared too, seized by any number of "evil minded people." Marylanders stole cattle from the proprietor's herds and from each other with equal nonchalance. Officials in Virginia suspected that debtors who moved to the frontier (and away from their creditors) stocked their new farms with stolen cattle. In 1658, the House of Burgesses decreed that prospective emigrants had to give notice of their plans to leave, satisfy all debts, and have four neighbors certify that they actually owned the cattle they intended to take with them. Residents of Cecil County, Maryland, similarly attributed an upsurge in cattle rustling to the founding of Pennsylvania, accusing "diverse wicked persons inhabiting in Delaware precincts" of driving off Maryland livestock and seeking refuge in the new colony. Marylanders petitioned their proprietor, who was then dealing with the Penn family over boundaries, to make restitution of stolen livestock part of the negotiations.[51]

Although Virginia legislators made servitude one of the punishments for hog stealing, assuming that indigent young men were the likeliest malefactors, servants and debtors had no monopoly on larceny. More than a few men at the upper ranks of society succumbed to the same temptation. In 1617, Virginia's governor Samuel Argall was suspected of diverting cattle and other company property to his own use. Dr. John Potts, who served as acting governor of the colony in 1628, was later convicted of having "gotten into a greate stock of cattell" by nefarious means. Later on in Maryland, some men appointed as rangers to round up wild horses were suspected of a similar offense.[52]

The planters' lackadaisical style of husbandry aggravated the perception that livestock were all but free for the taking. So long as animals wandered far from their home plantations, mixed indiscriminately with livestock from other farms, and showed little evidence of human care and attention, it was hard to tell the difference between stray animals and abandoned ones. Roughly following English common law, the Virginia legislature ruled in 1656 that anyone who happened upon a stray animal had to report within a month to the county court and state where the beast had been found and what it looked like so that its owner might know where to retrieve it. In England, an unclaimed animal was forfeit to the crown or the crown's grantee; in Virginia, the finder could keep the creature if no owner came forward within a year and a day. Behind these apparent similarities, however, lay an important difference. Most English livestock were either confined or supervised, making a stray animal an anomaly. But "stray" animals were the rule in the Chesapeake, rendering their appropriation by dishonest colonists hard to stop or even detect.[53]

Matters were further complicated by the mixture of free-range animals, missing strays, and feral livestock in the Chesapeake woods. Thieves wasted little time turning these circumstances to their advantage. The abundance of wild pigs, for instance, gave accused hog thieves like William Price and John and Jane Salter a perfect alibi. Yes, they had killed a hog, they admitted to a Maryland court on New Year's day in 1656, but it was not from William Eliot's herd. The creature in question, they insisted, was a "wild small hog." Because the pig's ears were gone—eaten by dogs, so the defendants claimed—there was little evidence to prove the charge of theft. All that remained was a "thick fatt singed peece of meat" and both sides in the case ended up arguing over whether or not a wild hog could really have had that much fat.[54]

In the Chesapeake, as in England, livestock owners could protect their rights to mobile property by marking their animals. A few seventeenth-century planters branded cattle on the horn, but most colonists preferred to clip animals' ears.[55] Virtually every family had its own earmark, involving some combination of slits, holes, half-circles, forks, "fleur-de-lis," or crop-ping. They registered their marks at the county court, where the information was recorded to help in identifying strays. Colonists regarded earmarks as a form of personal property to be handed down through the generations. In 1658 when Thomas Gerard neglected to register his earmark and William Evans then used it himself, an angry Gerard took the case to Maryland's Provincial Court. Gerard protested that his mark was "of a long standing, although not heretofore recorded" and had been "injuriously taken" from him. Since Evans had not yet used it, Gerard argued, the earmark ought to be restored to its rightful, if negligent, owner. Far from finding this a frivolous proceeding, Maryland's governor not only heard the case but, in an unusual move, polled the councillors for their individual opinions. Four of the five officials sided with Evans, noting his compliance with the law. The governor, however, found merit in Gerard's emotional plea and asked Evans to relinquish his claim. Evans did so, and a chastened Gerard promptly recorded the mark in his own name.[56]

Earmarks offered livestock owners useful, but hardly fail-safe, protection against theft. Planters could challenge anyone they suspected of pilfering and then butchering one of their creatures to produce the animal's ears in court. If the ears bore the plaintiff's mark, he had all the proof he needed; if not, the defendant might go free. But few malefactors were foolish enough to supply the evidence necessary for their own conviction, resorting instead to "Cutting and mangling" the ears of filched animals to disguise the mark. They could even dispose of the ears altogether, although this ploy only landed them in deeper trouble if they were caught. When Thomas Hebden failed to produce the ears of two hogs that he had allegedly stolen and butchered, his excuse that the ears "were at home" did not wash with magistrates who fined him a thousand pounds of tobacco. William Price likewise received little sympathy from justices in Kent County, Maryland, when he explained that his dog ate the ears of the hog in question. Aggrieved livestock owners may have considered the cropped ears and branded foreheads of convicted hog thieves to be unusually fitting punishments, marking them like the livestock they had stolen.[57]

Before they could assert even imperfect control by marking their animals, planters had to find the creatures. Combing the woods for piglets, calves, and foals became a rite of spring that might consume days, even weeks. Cattle, horses, and swine all tended to graze within a defined home range, but if forage and water were in short supply, they could wander as much as ten to twenty miles from home. Owners followed trails of broken branches, trampled underbrush, and animal droppings to discover their creatures' favorite haunts. They took advantage of certain animals' innate sociability to track them down, exploiting one of the characteristics that had made the creatures good candidates for domestication in the first place.[58] Swine, for instance, tended to gather in groups of sows with their young, making them somewhat easier to locate. Robert Beverley recorded the common wisdom that planters ought to look for their pigs "when they are young, to mark them; for if there be any markt in a Gang of Hogs, they determine the Property of the rest." Working from this assumption, three Marylanders scoured the woods in 1650 "to looke for Sowes that had pigs," marking any piglets they found with their own marked sows. A 1671 Maryland law confirmed this general understanding by casting suspicion on anyone carrying off unmarked pigs, unless they had been found on the person's plantation or had been "in Company with his owne Hoggs."[59]

These marking expeditions, besides establishing property rights, served another critically important function by introducing a young creature to its owner. Unless owners maintained some sort of association with their livestock, encouraging the animals to feel comfortable around people, the creatures would cease to be domesticated in any meaningful sense. Planters began to imprint young livestock with this necessary human connection when they found and marked them. Frightened calves and piglets, squirming with the pain of ear cutting, could be soothed by gentle stroking before being returned to their mothers. Earmarking thus created more than just a legal bond between livestock and their owners; it also started a process of socialization.[60]

Planters may also have used this opportunity to geld young male animals, a method of "physiological taming" that rendered the creatures less aggressive. It also helped planters distinguish their free-ranging steers from wild bulls, and may even have reduced the chances that livestock would go feral. Robert Cole of Maryland evidently engaged in the practice, for in 1662 his herd of 35 cattle included only one bull. In Maryland more generally, the ratio of bulls to cows was one to seven, high enough to permit herds to grow while still keeping the number of troublesome animals in check.[61]

Once planters established this initial contact with young livestock, they periodically reinforced it by setting out a small amount of corn or husks to lure the animals back to the plantation. Visitors mistook this for regular feeding and invariably accused colonists of starving their beasts. In 1680, the visiting Dutchman Jasper Danckaerts charged Maryland farmers with "wretchedness, if not cruelty" toward livestock. But planters never meant for such rations to sustain their animals: that was what the woods were for. These offerings instead trained livestock to return home regularly, making them available for the planter's use. Even John Clayton, perhaps the most resolute critic of Chesapeake husbandry, had to admit that the Virginians' habit of putting a little corn out for their cattle morning and evening had the advantage of making them "linger about the Houses for more." By the late seventeenth century, some planters used food to lure swine into pens or empty tobacco barns where they could be fattened for slaughter. Pregnant cows and farrowing swine that came back to the plantation sometimes ended up in pens until they gave birth, which simplified the planter's task of marking newborn animals.[62]

Clipping animals' ears and setting out corn offered rather limited solutions to the problem of keeping track of livestock, and these measures certainly struck many observers as poor substitutes for conscientious stewardship. The incidence of theft further suggested that in the seventeenth-century Chesapeake security of animal property was an idea honored more in the breach than the observance. Yet despite the challenges posed by free-range husbandry, the colonists were determined to uphold the principle of individual legal possession, insisting that their creatures belonged in a separate category from New World beasts.

🐄 🐄 🐄

Enforcing that distinction, however, created a host of problems. Livestock that loitered near certain plantations, or sported earmarks or branded horns, obviously belonged to someone. But were wild cattle, hogs, and horses property too, simply because they belonged to the same species as domestic animals? If so, whose property were they? Far from being a trivial issue, determining the status of wild livestock cut to the heart of the colonial enterprise in thoroughly unexpected ways.

Colonists could not afford to make fine distinctions between one kind of cow and another if the creatures were going to be unambiguous symbols of civility. This was especially true in a setting where the colonists' "tame" cattle roamed as freely as feral beasts. Planters hardly wanted Indians, who were supposed to see cows both as property and as emblems of English superiority, to conclude that only some cattle fulfilled those roles. Neither did colonial officials care to make it easier for thieving colonists to defend themselves by claiming that some livestock were indeed free for the taking. The very notion that familiar English animals, always before considered property, could lose that designation was also deeply upsetting. Few planters seem to have been bothered by the need to care for their animals in new ways, but changing the way they *thought* about livestock was another matter. Surprised by the appearance of a parallel population of wild livestock cohabiting the Chesapeake woods alongside their still-domesticated cousins, colonists were forced to address two related questions. How had some livestock come to be wild? Did these renegade creatures still belong to someone?

However much they may have discussed the matter over back fences, in taverns, or while trudging through the woods looking for wayward beasts, colonists rarely recorded their opinions about why livestock went wild. But those few colonists who did try to explain what happened agreed wholeheartedly on the answer. Livestock went wild, neither because of some natural process nor because free-range husbandry set them loose, but because people drove them to it. This opinion surfaced quite clearly on two separate occasions, once in Maryland in the 1650s and again in Virginia in the 1670s. As they addressed problems created by wild cattle, planters found that they could only blame themselves.

The petition sent by 17 Kent County inhabitants to Maryland's governor and council in November 1650 fairly seethed with its authors' exasperation. For upwards of five years, wild cattle had run amok in the county. Time and again, wild bulls lured tame cows away from plantations to join their harems. No one knew how many wild cattle there were or who owned them and no one was trying to bring them back under control. The petitioners, unwilling to take the initiative in solving the problem because it involved property and not just pests, placed it squarely in the magistrates' hands. They "humbly" asked the Provincial Court to "appoint some speedy course to bee taken for the getting upp of the said Wild Cattell," ending their depredations once and for all.[63]

Acknowledging the seriousness of the problem, the court easily identified its cause. The "first occasion of the running Wild of the Cattell" in Kent County, the magistrates agreed, occurred during "the late troubles happening in this Province." Everyone in Maryland knew what they meant. Those "troubles" began in the 1640s as the effects of the English Civil War reverberated in the colony. Protestant settlers schemed to take advantage of English events by overthrowing the proprietorship of the Catholic Lord Baltimore. When one Protestant rebel, Richard Ingle, invaded the capital of St. Mary's City in 1645, Governor Leonard Calvert fled to Virginia. For two years, chaos reigned. Colonists abandoned their farms. Rebels looted and burned their neighbors' estates. Maryland's English population plummeted from over 500 in 1644 to less than 200 by the time Calvert returned in 1646. And during this upheaval livestock, like people, took to their heels.[64]

Nothing short of a rebellion among men, therefore, drove cattle to abandon their wonted tameness. And as with the human uprising, the magistrates called for the suppression of this new revolt, recruiting citizen posses to help with the job. Only men who could "clayme any Interest in the said Wild Cattell" and prove it could participate in the roundups. Incorrigible wild bulls, like the ringleaders of a mob, would be killed if they refused to submit, but all other animals would be taken alive. The captured beasts, as well as the meat from any that had to be killed for safety's sake, would be distributed solely to colonists who could certify "what Cattell every of them had which ranne wild amongst the said Cattell and when." The Provincial Court arranged for a representative to make sure that the proprietor's interests were likewise protected. Requiring proof of ownership was a tall order when so many animals had absconded from their home plantations as much as a half a decade earlier. Yet to magistrates and inhabitants alike this was a necessary measure. Order would not be fully restored until the animals were returned to their proper masters and the creatures' inherent status as chattel had been reaffirmed.[65]

Some 20 years later, two irate Virginians similarly announced that people were at fault when cattle went wild. Thomas Tracker and John Lecatt, who owned a piece of marsh between Curratuck and Nandua creeks that had become a favorite haunt of wild cattle, wanted to get the unruly beasts out of there. So the two men fenced off their property and in September 1672 posted a notice that they had done so on the Accomack County courthouse door. This was no hastily scrawled message, but rather a thoroughgoing diatribe against unnamed "ill disposed persons" whom the men held responsible for the wild cattle's existence. The beasts had "beene driven from their former gentlenes," the two Virginians asserted, by "unlawfull shootinge, huntinge, & worryeinge with doggs" perpetrated by unsavory local characters. Tracker and Lecatt expressed concern that their new fence would be crushed by rampaging animals "forced to seeke such their wonted shelters by the violence & rapine of such greedy pursuers, *whose wills are sufficient to determine any cattle whatsoever to bee wild.*"[66]

If those people who drove cattle to distraction thought that their actions turned other men's property into free goods, they were wrong. Disruptive though the animals might be, they remained someone's property and taking them still constituted theft. Thus Tracker and Lecatt knew that they could not simply kill any beast that broke through their fence. The point of their notice was to give neighbors fair warning to "recover any such their cattle" that might be nearby and to announce that "Wee must be constrained . . . for the securinge of our owne Interests in good and quiet order to destroy all such returninge wilde cattle" that subsequently encroached on their land. Only as a last resort would the men dispatch unclaimed animals forfeited by their delinquent owners.[67]

Convinced that going wild resulted from human interference, colonists refused to entertain the possibility that the animals' behavior could have been instinctual. In their view, livestock were not so much independent actors as passive objects of human manipulation. This way of thinking reassured colonists unhappy with the turn of events, for it implied that going wild was a reversible process. Nothing had really altered the animals' essential nature as domesticated creatures. Rescued from their wild state, livestock could be restored to their "former gentlenes." And even in their wild state, they remained property.

The desire to classify all Chesapeake livestock as chattel, whether wild or not, accorded far better with English assumptions than with Chesapeake conditions. It cast doubt on the legitimacy of killing wild livestock even if every attempt had been made to find out to whom the creatures belonged. Moreover, efforts to assign owners to unclaimed errant beasts generated disagreements and exposed fissures within Chesapeake society that threatened to widen as time went on. But ignoring the problem would not make it go away.

So long as it remained in business, the joint-stock company that founded Virginia presumed ownership of unclaimed wild livestock on the grounds that it had originally paid to bring their forebears from England. When one prospective settler inquired about stocking his plantation with swine, for instance, the Company allowed him take a hundred of its "Hoggs out of the fforest" so long as he repaid the loan in seven years with the same number of beasts. Only one bold group of colonists launched a formal challenge to the Company's assertion of its rights in this regard. In June 1622, Capt. John Martin and several other malcontents sent a petition to James I in which they declared that years earlier the colony had set aside as the "Kings fforest" an 80-square-mile tract of land acquired from the Powhatan Indians. The "Deare and wild Swine" roaming on these acres thus belonged to the Crown, not the Company, but they lacked protection from the "continuall havocke and spoile that is and wilbe made of them and their brood." Martin and the other petitioners humbly requested, without going quite so far as to nominate themselves, that His Majesty appoint some men to enforce the royal prerogative. When Company officials got wind of this scheme, they hastily informed James that the "Kings fforest" was "a name happily knowne to Capt. Martin and his Associates but not to the Company" and the land on which it purportedly sat included Jamestown and several private plantations. The wild swine to be found there were "no other then the breed of such as have bin transported thither by the Companie" and so belonged to it as well.[68]

Formal opposition to Company ownership may have been rare, but less well-organized challenges abounded as individuals simply took whatever wild livestock they wanted. Hungry colonists especially targeted the ubiquitous wild swine. One colonist went so far as to indicate that his fellow settlers regarded wild hogs "as of the Deare in Virginia things belonginge to noe man" and evidently no joint-stock company.[69] Beleaguered officials, struggling to cope with Indian conflicts and colonists' appalling rates of mortality from malaria and other diseases, had little time or energy to contest this redefinition of Company property as common goods. Moreover, by 1624 the Virginia Company had sunk into bankruptcy and a royal commission had begun investigating its dismal affairs. Judging its finances to be beyond repair, the commission recommended that the Company be dissolved and the foundering colony put under royal control.[70]

Thenceforth the Crown assumed ownership of the Company's wild livestock but had just as much trouble compelling colonists to respect its rights. Most infractions involved wild hogs, the easiest animals to pilfer. A 1632 statute prohibited anyone from killing wild swine without the governor's permission unless the animal had wandered onto the hunter's plantation. An additional exception applied to colonists who killed wolves. Any colonist who could prove that he had performed this public service (by bringing in the wolf's head as evidence) was allowed "to kill also one wild hogg and take the same for his owne use." The statute reaffirmed the Crown's privileges, and in the process made wild swine legally off-limits to all but wolf hunters and the governor's cronies. Planters sitting in the assembly had a particular interest in denying servants and slaves access to the creatures. They did not want to make it any easier for workers to come up with an alibi if one of their master's pigs went missing, or make free pork available to hungry runaways. Yet neither the Assembly nor the Crown cared to extend the royal prerogative to include New World animals in a manner similar to the king's claim to deer in royal forests. The burgesses allowed anyone to kill "deare or other wild beasts or fowle in the common woods, forests, or rivers," on the grounds that hunting honed colonists' military skills and kept Indians away from plantations. By making deer and other indigenous fauna freely available to any hunter, the burgesses also avoided the knotty problem of defining the scope of Indians' hunting rights, even as they preserved livestock's special status as chattel.[71]

Yet over the long run the House of Burgesses demonstrated little sustained interest in defending royal rights to wild livestock. A 1643 law stipulated sharply different penalties for killing tame and wild hogs: killing a tame pig brought a charge of felony, but dispatching a wild one merely earned the offender "censure" from the governor and Council. The assembly then ignored the whole issue for the next 62 years, at which point it passed a measure requiring anyone who killed a wild hog simply to report the fact within three months to a justice of the peace.[72]

Technically the Crown's possessions, wild swine for all intents and purposes became another form of game much like deer, raccoons, and foxes. Gentleman hunters vied with poor colonists in stalking the wild gangs roaming the woods.[73] The same fate may eventually have befallen wild cattle and horses. In 1674 a note appeared in the Accomack County records stipulating that hunters needed the governor's permission to pursue wild cattle, but there is no corroborating colony statute. Not long before this, the county court had ordered Thomas Tracker and John Lecatt to pay restitution for a wild steer they had killed on their fenced land but only because the steer's owner was subsequently identified.[74] There is little else to suggest that magistrates cared much about the fate of any kind of wild livestock or felt compelled to defend the royal prerogative in this regard.

Wild livestock's standing as chattel in Virginia ultimately rested on the rather shaky foundation of an unenforced royal claim. The Crown's prerogative meant little in a practical sense. Officials tried to find the owners of unmarked livestock, but did little to defend the king's right to creatures that went unclaimed. No one, either in England or Virginia, advocated using or selling the animals to serve royal interests. Yet the Crown's putative title was no less important for being largely symbolic. Royal rights to feral livestock, however tenuously upheld, preserved the animals' status as property. This ensured that even in their wild state the creatures still served as representatives of English occupation.

The fate of wild livestock provoked a sharper debate in Maryland. Controversies over the animals' status became entangled in the ongoing confrontation between proprietary and settler interests. From the start the proprietor Cecilius Calvert, as second Lord Baltimore, assumed a prerogative right to the animals, which he believed King Charles I had transferred to his family through the colony's charter. The Calverts expected the governors whom they appointed (and who were usually relatives) to regulate access to wild livestock on their behalf. Governors periodically issued proclamations reminding colonists that they needed to secure licenses before they could hunt wild hogs or cattle. Such licenses often stipulated that the hides and tallow of dead animals had to be reserved "for his lordships use," a purely symbolic gesture added to remind colonists to whom they owed fealty.[75]

Maryland's charter also allowed the Calverts to grant manors to prominent individuals who would in turn recruit English tenants to work them. On the few such estates that appeared, the proprietary claim to wild livestock devolved upon the lord of the manor. Thus Thomas Gerard of St. Clement's Manor insisted on his right to wild hogs even if the creatures roamed on land he had leased to others. Luke Gardiner, one of Gerard's tenants, learned the hard way that his landlord was serious about what might have seemed a trivial perquisite. In 1659 Gardiner was hauled before the St. Clement's manorial court and fined 1,000 pounds of tobacco "for catchinge two wilt hoggs & not restoringe the one half" to Gerard, "which hee ought to have done." The judges took offense not only at Gardiner's unsanctioned hunting but also "for his contempt therein."[76]

Selectively granting permission to hunt wild livestock was a matter of patronage. In the highly contentious atmosphere of Maryland politics, the Catholic Calverts deployed every instrument at their command to buttress the position of their coreligionists against a restive Protestant majority. After allowing settlers to retrieve their own cattle from the wild herds, Maryland governors appointed small groups of handpicked favorites to deal with the rest, so long as they saved some of their catch as well as tallow and hides for the Calverts. By the 1680s the Provincial Council, whose members were appointed by the proprietor, periodically issued commissions to rangers to kill or capture "all wild unmarkt Cattle, horses, Mares, Colts, and Swine" and keep or sell them as they pleased. Not surprisingly, several recipients of the council's largess, including George Talbot and Henry Darnall, were Calvert cousins. These men frequently appointed deputies in turn, allocating them a portion of the kill and extending the web of patronage even further.[77]

Not all Marylanders, however, willingly granted the proprietor an exclusive right to wild livestock. More men hunted the animals than sought licenses to do so. Genuine need drove some colonists to risk prosecution to get meat for their families; sheer obstinacy inspired others to take to the woods with their guns. The persistent rivalry between the proprietary party and ordinary settlers also guaranteed that some men regarded poaching as a political statement. It surprised no one when a spate of illegal hunting erupted during the early 1650s while Calvert and his appointees struggled to keep the colony from slipping into Protestant hands. In 1653, an exasperated Governor William Stone denounced the "bould Contemptious unwarrantable" behavior of several men who deprived the proprietor of his rightful property and also demonstrated "Contempt of the Government here Settled under him" with their unlicensed hunting. To the besieged governor, these actions smacked of sedition more than simple theft.[78]

Controversy over the proprietor's right to wild livestock erupted again 40 years later in the midst of an equally momentous political upheaval. The Glorious Revolution in England, which toppled James II from the throne, deprived the Calverts of their principal patron and led to Maryland becoming a royal colony under the new Protestant monarchs, William and Mary. Bereft of political power, the Calverts retained land and economic privileges and, in an effort to lay claim to every perquisite they thought their due, reasserted their right to stray animals. This pronouncement launched a fierce dispute that lasted three years.[79] In May 1692 the Maryland Assembly led the charge on behalf of the colonists, vehemently arguing that the Calverts' claim "can no ways Suit with the Nature and Constitution" of the colony. In Maryland, "the whole Stock of the country run promisc[u]ously one amongst the other . . . Some Mens Stocks wandering Ten or Twenty Miles from their Plantation" as "the Law of Necessity" required. If the proprietary claim were upheld, "his

Lordship would Entitle himself and Engross into his hands the whole Stock of the Province, and destroy every Mans property in the Same." Marked animals, no matter how far they strayed, belonged to their owners. Turning to the status of wild unmarked livestock, the assemblymen made an audacious claim of their own. Up to this point, they asserted, the legislature had freely given the proprietor rights to "unmarked wild Cattle Horses and Hogs" in order "to avoid the Contentions that happened about the Property having no Mark" to identify an owner. What the assembly gave, the assembly could take away. Now that Maryland was a royal colony, the legislature transferred "all the Title his Lordship can pretend to such Unmarked Cattle" to William and Mary.[80]

For months various declarations from both sides slowly made their way through the imperial bureaucracy in London until the debate reached the Lords of Trade and Plantations, the king's advisory body on colonial affairs. In February 1693 the Provincial Council back in Maryland received word of its findings. The proprietor had no legitimate claim, the Council learned, either to marked stray livestock (which remained the property of their owners) or to unmarked wild beasts. Neither did the Assembly have the right to give wild livestock to the proprietor or anyone else. The animals indeed belonged to the Crown, but by virtue of royal prerogative, not the Assembly's gift. Since the Maryland legislature had already accepted the idea of royal ownership, this decision should have aroused little opposition. But the proposed grounds for establishing the royal claim to feral animals sparked an unexpected controversy. London officials had decided that "the Right to them is in the Crowne as being fferae Naturâ," a conclusion that Marylanders simply could not abide.[81]

Creatures that were *ferae naturae* or "wild in nature" by definition belonged to no one, but under certain conditions could be converted into property. If captured and tamed, wild creatures became chattel so long as they bore some physical marker (such as a red collar) denoting their changed status. They might also, by "reason of privilege," be considered the property of the owners of the land where they roamed.[82] The Crown's legal advisers apparently drew upon this last provision in asserting the monarch's right to feral livestock. Since the Crown technically owned all colony land not granted to the proprietor or individual settlers, it could lay claim to the wild livestock living on its domain.[83] But royal attorneys buttressed this justification with an additional feature that became the source of contention. Officials in

England had somehow gotten the idea that feral livestock were "wild by nature, and in being" in Maryland before the original 1632 charter had been granted. This reasoning converted English animals into native creatures, making them part of the American natural world.[84]

In May 1695, the assembly formally objected that the king's solicitor general "was not well informed" if he thought that livestock were New World animals. He obviously did not know "that there were no horses, Beeves or hoggs in this Country" before the colonists arrived. As imported creatures, livestock could not be considered *ferae naturae*. Marylanders could only accept royal ownership of wild livestock on the grounds that the creatures were "in the nature of Waifes and Strayes." In England, waifs (property found without an owner) and strays (animal property that had wandered away from owners who neglected to retrieve them) traditionally belonged to the Crown. Treating feral livestock like strays seemed most consistent with English practice and best preserved the creatures' identity as English animals. Since the Crown had renounced any claim to marked free-range livestock, colonists had no reason to worry that this designation would jeopardize their hold on their animal property.[85]

The colonists' extraordinary sensitivity on this issue was surely heightened by the circumstances surrounding the debate. Marylanders had been forced publicly to acknowledge the unorthodox character of their livestock husbandry and defend it before an audience of England's highest officials. By rejecting *ferae naturae* as the grounds for royal title to feral livestock, colonists denied that the New World had the power to transform English creatures into a new order of beings. The opinion of the Lords of Trade, though limited to the issue of wild livestock's status, raised the unwelcome specter of English people being similarly altered through contact with a new environment. No colonist could admit as much to an English audience, much less to himself. Livestock could no more become *ferae naturae* than colonists could become Indians.[86]

The Marylanders may have won their case. With the establishment of a new royal government after 1691, Maryland's executive defended the Crown's rights to wild livestock by requiring prospective hunters to obtain licenses from him. The wording of one such document hinted at a rhetorical victory for the colonists. In October 1692, when Governor Lionel Copley authorized Edward James to hunt any wild livestock "adjudg[e]d and allowed to be Strays belonging to and the just right of their Majestys," he employed the colonists' preferred terminology. The Assembly accepted the governor's authority to grant such licenses, and further agreed that as the monarch's representative he could distribute captured or killed animals as he saw fit. Copley required rangers to turn two of every three animals over to him, allowing them to keep the remainder for their "Care and pains" in the chase. Colonists may have evaded these licensing restrictions just as frequently as ever, but they did not challenge the royal prerogative in principle. In Maryland as in Virginia, the Crown's claim to wild livestock settled the issue of the animals' status as property and preserved their character as English fauna distinct from the truly wild creatures of the New World.[87]

By defending wild livestock's standing as property and as English, Chesapeake colonists in effect defended themselves. They never expected that it would be so much harder to transfer animal husbandry than actual animals to America. Feral livestock, to an even greater degree than free-ranging creatures, confused familiar categories into which animals were normally placed and thus emphasized the colonists' divergence from English ways. When European observers decried the runty appearance of Chesapeake cattle or relegated wild livestock to the status of native American animals, they either explicitly or implicitly characterized change as degeneration. The colonists' task was to convince their critics, and themselves, that appearances were deceiving.

Colonists insisted that livestock's Englishness was immutable and depended as much on domestication as on biology. Not only were there no "horses, Beeves or hoggs" in the Chesapeake prior to English settlement, there were no domestic animals of any kind. Domestication, however much attenuated, differentiated English animals from native fauna just as civility distinguished English people from Indians. Changes in husbandry practices had indeed produced superficial alterations in livestock and their behavior, but colonists regarded "tameness" in their animals (like civility in themselves) as inherent. People's misdeeds might drive livestock to act against their nature, but for the most part only temporarily. The New World environment alone lacked the power to effect permanent changes in the animals' natural condition as domesticated beasts.

Chesapeake colonists likewise maintained that livestock's status as chattel was unalterable. They simply could not conceive of livestock, even feral livestock, as anything but possessions and if no individual owner could be identified, the Crown offered a reasonable alternative. The colonists' anxiety on this point revealed how much free-range husbandry had magnified the importance of property above other elements linking planters with their animals. Having abandoned the ideals of stewardship that informed English husbandry, colonists relied on legal title to demonstrate a connection that was otherwise hard to prove. Property became the slender thread by which dominion was preserved in an agricultural regime that otherwise appeared to liberate animals from their masters.

Colonists who acknowledged royal rights to wild livestock even as they hunted feral hogs without a license managed to live with the contradiction. Affirming the principle of ownership was far more important than enforcing it. With livestock relegated to a separate category from New World creatures, colonists did not have to worry so much about how their animals actually looked or behaved. Convinced that their beasts could not forfeit their identity as English chattel, colonists could safely regard domestic animals as extensions of themselves. Even the scrawniest cow wandering aimlessly through the woods advanced the cause of civilizing the wilderness.

Chapter Five

A World of Pastures and Pounds

Raising Livestock in Early New England

$\mathcal{T}$homas Danforth's 1663 petition to the Massachusetts General Court aroused the deputies' suspicions almost as soon as they laid eyes on it. The document's obsequious tone failed to disguise its problematic contents. Danforth was well known to the deputies; he not only represented Cambridge in the upper house of the Bay Colony legislature but also served as treasurer of Harvard College and recorder of deeds for Middlesex County. He may have presumed that his civic prominence would lend weight to his request, and he took care to embed it in a context he thought his fellow magistrates would find commendable. In accordance with English imperial goals, Danforth had tried "to further Civility and dilligent labour in the Indians" by helping them to learn how to farm properly. He had "enterteined one of them into a parcell of land, & lent Him out cattle" to improve it. But instead of working hard, the Indian absconded, owing his generous patron more than £7. Other colonists captured and imprisoned the fugitive, but Danforth was loath to incarcerate "so poore a creature" because the man's wife and child would also suffer. Danforth instead made a deal with the Indian: release from prison and cancellation of the debt in return for the sale of a thousand acres "in the Nipnop [Nipmuck] Country" of western Massachusetts. In his petition, Danforth "Humbly" asked the Court to approve the arrangement, promising in advance his "thankfull acknowledgment" of their favor.[1]

The deputies saw through Danforth's scheme, considering it a thinly veiled attempt to circumvent longstanding prohibitions against individual purchases of land from Indians. They determined that it was "not meet to graunt this petition," a decision ratified by Danforth's fellow Assistants in the upper house of the legislature. Much as they objected to his proposed land grab, however, the lawmakers had no quarrel with Danforth's assumption that farming with livestock could promote diligence and civility among the Indians. This was no more than a reiteration of a familiar theme first propounded by John Winthrop decades earlier. By 1663 thousands of colonists had brought "tame Cattle to improve the Land" and implicitly offered themselves as models from whom Indians could learn a great deal. Danforth expressed the right sentiments on this matter, but when the opportunity for illicit gain presented itself he gave in to temptation and put self-interest ahead of the Indian family's self-improvement.[2]

Danforth's gambit, although unsuccessful, revealed that New Englanders, like Chesapeake settlers, accorded livestock an integral role in their colonial enterprise. The assumptions that introduced Danforth's petition echoed the sentiments in Virginia's wolf bounty act. In each case, livestock stood both as symbols of the superior character of English agriculture and as actual instruments of its establishment in the New World. Like the burgesses in Virginia, Danforth presumed that Indians could be induced, whether by the gift of a cow or the loan of land and animals, to improve themselves by emulating colonial farmers. Although Chesapeake planters turned out to be rather poor models in this regard, the same could not be said of New Englanders.

New England farmers more successfully reproduced English methods of husbandry because they settled in towns rather than on isolated plantations. As in England itself, communal regulations augmented individual efforts to supervise livestock, specifying how animals ought to be managed and how recalcitrant farmers would be punished if they did not behave properly. People kept an eye not just on their neighbors, but on their neighbors' cattle, horses, and hogs, in the interest of keeping good order in their communities. Towns allocated scarce resources, from natural meadows for common pasture to precious funds for herders' fees, to promote good husbandry. If control over livestock in the end remained incomplete, it was not for lack of trying on the colonists' part.

New Englanders had no staple crop like tobacco to divert their attention from the care of animals, but even so they too found that a limited supply of labor relative to the amount of land to be developed prevented them from fully reproducing English husbandry practices. And, like Chesapeake farmers, they worried about how the gap between what they practiced and what they preached impinged on their status as civilized people. Ignoring their own deficiencies, Southern colonists explained away changes in the appearance and behavior of their animals as superficial and reversible, incapable of undermining the animals' identity as English creatures and as property. New Englanders, who kept their livestock under tighter rein, had fewer reasons to defend their animals against charges of degeneration. Instead they worried about unwelcome changes in themselves. New England colonists who fretted too much about the fate of their livestock put undue emphasis on the concerns of this world, imperiling their commitment to the Christian principles that governed their relationships with animals and with each other.

🐂   🐂   🐂

Livestock were even more important to New England's survival than they were in the Chesapeake. Indeed, New Englanders came to see domestic animals as the only meaningful form of agricultural capital outside of land itself. By the late eighteenth century, as Samuel Deane explained in *The New England Farmer,* the conflation of cattle and capital was complete. When English farmers used the word "stock," Deane noted, they meant "the quantity of money or wealth a farmer should have, to enable him to hire and cultivate a farm to advantage." But to New Englanders, the word had come to mean "only live stock, or the beasts that are kept upon a farm." In a place where other forms of capital were hard to come by, livestock made all the difference between owning a plot of land and having a working farm.[3]

The centrality of livestock in early New England was more the product of accident than design. Early on, John Smith predicted that fishing would be the region's economic mainstay. Yet valuable as the fisheries turned out to be, they never engaged more than a fraction of the local population. Most New England colonists took up a life of farming. Lacking a staple crop like tobacco to foster commercial agriculture and create a vigorous market for servants, New Englanders resorted to a mixed agrarian regime reminiscent of English wood-pasture farms and relied on their families for labor. But as their efforts to transplant English cereal crops met with disappointment, colonists' dependence on livestock grew.[4]

At first, reports of great success with familiar crops filtered back to England. Francis Higginson happily announced in 1630 that English grains grew "verie well" in Plymouth Colony, an opinion corroborated in 1634 by William Wood. Plymouth colonists had yet to raise beans or wheat in any quantity, Wood admitted, but he was sure that they would "grow as well as any other grain" before long.[5] Such optimism proved unwarranted. Neither the climate nor the soil of coastal New England favored wheat cultivation, and barley and oats fared only slightly better. Wheat flourished mainly in the rich lands of the upper Connecticut Valley, where John Pynchon soon grew enough to ship more than a thousand bushels a year to Boston. But beginning in the 1640s, catastrophes all too reminiscent of biblical plagues struck New England wheat fields. First, armies of caterpillars ate their way through ripening stalks. Then the "blast" withered the leaves of wheat plants before the grain had matured. The cause was black stem rust, a European fungus that grew on barberry bushes colonists brought from England. The upshot was that wheat, the dominant cereal of English agriculture, did not serve New England farmers nearly so well.[6]

Colonists instead depended on corn, learning how to cultivate it from Indians who had done so for centuries. Francis Higginson praised the grain in terms that his fellow colonists could especially appreciate. "Little children here by setting of Corne," he observed, "may earne much more then their own maintenance."[7] Their mothers baked bread from "Injun" and rye, mixing corn with the one imported cereal that took well to New England's soil. Corn even served as currency when an extreme scarcity of specie in the 1630s drove the Massachusetts government to make the grain legal tender for payment of debts and taxes. What it could not do was supply New England with an export crop. It took more than a century for Europeans to consume corn in any quantity, and even then it was scorned as peasant fare. There was little point for New England farmers to grow more than their own families could use.[8]

Thus most colonists aimed to produce enough to meet family needs on farms large enough to sustain their economic independence, preferably into the next generation. Modest as it was, this goal could not have been achieved without the assistance of livestock. In Plymouth Colony, domestic animals comprised between a quarter and a half of the value of a farmer's estate, proportions that likely matched the experience of colonists elsewhere in the region at a time when most land remained undeveloped. Unlike Chesapeake settlers, New Englanders employed livestock in ways that more fully replicated English practice, keeping a variety of domestic animals and putting them to as many uses as possible.[9]

Cattle and hogs predominated in New England as they did in the Chesapeake, reproducing rapidly to help feed an equally prolific settler population. By the 1650s, Edward Johnson could report that meat was "no rare food, beef, pork, and mutton being frequent in many houses" throughout the region.[10] New Englanders also regularly consumed dairy products of their own making. If seventeenth-century milk yields approached those of the late eighteenth century, cows could be counted on to produce a gallon a day— two to four times the output of Chesapeake cows and enough to warrant investment in dairy equipment. In Essex County, Massachusetts in 1670, at least one out of three households contained milk tubs, butter churns, and cheese presses as well as women or girls who knew how to use them. Although few seventeenth-century houses had separate dairies or butteries, many had cellars where dairy products could be chilled but would not freeze in winter. Colonial families consumed these products and traded them with neighbors. Thomas Minor of Stonington, Connecticut, frequently paid off debts in butter, sometimes 60 or 70 pounds of it at a time, and in "good murchatabell [merchantable] Cheese." Rhode Islanders, at least in 1678, could pay their taxes with butter.[11]

Oxen were as important as milk cows to New England family farms. The region's stony soils defied easy cultivation.[12] Colonial farmers relied on oxen's brute strength to clear trees and brush and then to break up the soil. As one observer in neighboring New Netherland explained, "in new lands, full of roots, oxen go forward steadily under the plough," while "horses stand still, or with a start break the harness in pieces." Even oxen's strength was occasionally put to the test. William Wood described areas in Massachusetts where land was "so tough and hard that I have seen ten oxen toiled, their iron chains broken, and their shares and colters much strained." Colonists were eager to switch from using hoes for corn, as the Indians did, to oxen and plows so they could increase yields. Edward Johnson admitted that "it was with sore labour that on[e] man could Plant and tend foure Acres" by hand. Once the number of oxen increased, New Englanders could cross-plow their fields by digging furrows perpendicular to one another and setting seed corn where the rows intersected. With plow and oxen, Johnson reckoned, a farmer could cultivate 30 acres of corn, more than seven times what he could manage without a team.[13]

Farmers who did not own oxen borrowed them or hired a man with a team. Twice in December 1653, Thomas Minor lent his neighbor a pair of oxen to break up soil for the next spring's planting. In Springfield, Massachusetts, John Pynchon routinely leased oxen along with land to his tenants, so the farmers could produce enough of a surplus to pay the rent. A Plymouth Colony statute further testified to the animals' indispensability. Magistrates specifically exempted the "Beast of the Plough or Draught" from seizure in cases of debt, so long as there were other livestock that could be taken. To seize a debtor's ox was to deprive him of the means to make good his obligation.[14]

Crucial to agriculture, oxen proved equally valuable for other productive endeavors. Shipbuilding, which became a leading sector of the New England economy, made extensive demands on the labor of oxen as well as men. Visiting New Hampshire in 1687, the Boston merchant Samuel Sewall marveled at the sight of 36 ox teams—72 beasts in all—hauling one enormous white pine to a sawmill, where it would be trimmed into a ship's mast. Harvesting timber for any number of uses would have been virtually impossible without animal power. Thus when Capt. John Mason set up his sawmill at Piscataqua, he prudently stocked it with more than a hundred oxen.[15]

Because New Englanders did not eat horses or plow with them, the animals were at first less ubiquitous than hogs or cattle. One out of three farmers in parts of Connecticut got along without one, even as late as in the 1680s. Colonists mainly used horses for riding and carting goods, although the proximity of New England towns to each another made the animals less important for transportation than they were on dispersed Chesapeake plantations. New England horses may have been status symbols as much as working animals, owned more often than not by older, more prosperous men. Scarce at first, horses eventually increased enough to cause worries about their proliferation. In Plymouth Colony, according to John Josselyn, horses multiplied "exceedingly" after midcentury. Tiny Rhode Island was all but overrun with them. William Harris went so far as to boast to a London acquaintance in 1675 that Rhode Island contained "so many horses that men know not what to do with them."[16]

New Englanders knew precisely what to do with sheep and wanted as many as possible, more for wool than meat. During the 1640s and 1650s, when civil war and political turmoil in England disrupted overseas trade, colonists became painfully aware of their inability to produce clothing. The Massachusetts General Court spared no effort in portraying the colony's bleak situation. Poor people without woolen garments suffered "much could & hardship, to the impairing of some of their healths, and the hazarding of some of their lives." Their shivering children, clad only in flimsy cotton, clustered around the hearth and were "scorched with fire, yea, divers burnt to death." A home-grown supply of wool was the only remedy, but not easily obtained. Wherever wolves and bears roamed, sheep tended to disappear. The tall grasses of New England's rough meadows also proved less enticing to sheep than to other kinds of livestock. Cattle could fend for themselves because they ate by wrapping their tongues around grass and pulling at it, but sheep would only graze on short grasses. Thus, as Edward Johnson observed, "untill the Land be often fed with other Cattell Sheepe cannot live"; nor could sheep-owners see a good return on their investment.[17]

A sense of urgency drove colonists to confront these environmental challenges. Local and provincial officials joined forces to encourage colonists to destroy wolves by offering bounties of ten shillings, twenty shillings—even as much as five pounds for the "great gray woolfe that hath done so much mischeife" in Warwick, Rhode Island. Bay Colony magistrates urged inhabitants to procure wolfhounds and some towns, such as Newport and Portsmouth in Rhode Island, organized highly successful communal wolf hunts.[18] Colony officials likewise directed townsmen to clear wooded areas where wolves and other "noyesome beasts" skulked and where sheep refused to graze. For a time in Connecticut all males above the age of 14 had to work one day each year cutting bushes and undergrowth near their towns to improve pasturage for sheep, or risk a five-shilling fine for noncompliance. Rough browse that sustained cattle and swine, not to mention deer, had to be eliminated for the sake of more delicate sheep.[19]

Colony governments passed other measures designed to increase sheep populations and the supply of wool. Massachusetts authorities allowed farmers to pasture sheep on any town common, fixed prices to protect owners' investments, and offered cash bounties for the production of woolen cloth. Connecticut magistrates at one point exempted sheep from taxation.[20] The Bay Colony legislature in 1654 prohibited the exportation of ewes or ewe lambs essential for reproduction. Lawmakers also forbade the slaughter of rams or wether sheep (castrated males) less than two years old so that the creatures could be sheared twice before being dispatched. No other domestic animal inspired this kind of protective legislation.[21]

After about 1660 sheep flourished in parts of New England to an extent not seen in the Chesapeake until the eighteenth century. Colonists who had raised sheep in England may have worked hardest to establish the animals on New England farms. Flocks typically remained small, often no more than a dozen creatures. But some men of means, presented with an irresistible opportunity for profit, accumulated substantial flocks. John Pynchon enjoyed unusual success raising sheep in the Connecticut Valley.[22] Prosperity also came to those who commandeered islands as pastures. Once cleared of wolves, islands became sanctuaries where sheep could reproduce with abandon. Sheep eventually abounded on Nantucket, eastern Long Island, and several small islands in Boston Harbor. John Winthrop, Jr., converted Fishers Island off the Connecticut coast into a private reserve for sheep and other livestock. William Coddington had advised Winthrop that sheep on the island would "ordaneriely duble in a yeare, and more for the Lambes have Lambes when they are a yeare ould." Coddington no doubt extrapolated from his experience in Rhode Island, where sheep flourished more spectacularly than anywhere else in New England. This was one colony that never found it necessary to offer incentives to get its inhabitants to invest in sheep.[23]

In sharp contrast to the experience of other livestock, the history of goats in New England was short and not particularly sweet. Colonists deposited them everywhere from Maine and New Hampshire to islands off Connecticut's shore. John Winthrop, Jr., stocked Fishers Island with them, and William Coddington kept goats on his Rhode Island estate. Although they were ideal colonizing animals, able to subsist on the roughest of vegetation, goats quickly wore out their welcome.[24] Regarded with "great esteeme at their first comming," goats were "almost quite banished" by 1650, undone by their voracious appetites. As in the Chesapeake, goats in New England gnawed on precious apple trees, endangering the colonists' source of cider. They also chewed on the hedges that some farmers laboriously planted to bound their fields. Colonists went after goats with a zeal that nearly matched their ferocious campaigns against wolves, even though they were responsible for bringing the animals in the first place. As early as 1639 residents of Cambridge were enjoined to impound all goats found wandering at large.

Three years later Boston's selectmen ordered residents to "remoove all their goates" and "never more to keepe any of them" in town. Warwick, Rhode Island, townsmen went so far as to declare that after 3 June 1650 "it shalbee lawefull for any person or persons to destroy" goats found on the town common. Useful livestock were welcome in New England, but an animal that brought more trouble than it was worth was doomed.[25]

Producers of meat and milk, providers of power and transport, the right mix of livestock gave even the crudest New England farm a shot at viability. Livestock figured prominently among the "moveable" goods that young brides brought to their marriages as necessary complements to the land their husbands' families provided. Several prominent supporters of New England colonization further underscored the value of livestock—and of cattle in particular—by supplying them as a form of poor relief for indigent settlers. Richard Andrews, a London haberdasher, sent 16 heifers to Massachusetts in the 1630s to help "godly poore men whoe have none of theire owne" and who would be willing eventually to return half the animals' increase to their patron. The Londoner also sent steers to be given to struggling ministers. The merchant James Sherley performed a similar service for the poor of Plymouth. One cow would hardly guarantee prosperity, but as a form of property capable of reproducing itself, the creature could make all the difference between eking out a hardscrabble existence and sinking into utter destitution.[26]

Livestock were not only helpmeets on colonial farms but also commodities to buy and sell. Farmers interested in enlarging their herds or diversifying their livestock holdings bargained with neighbors to obtain desired animals. Edward Johnson reported that by the 1640s it had become "the common practice of those that had any store of Cattel, to sell every year a Cow or two, which cloath'd their backs, fil'd their bellies with more varieties then the Country of it self afforded, and put gold and silver in their purses beside." Unlike other commodities, livestock had the distinct advantage of being able to transport themselves to market. Local authorities helped to coordinate sales and exchanges by establishing regular market days and semiannual fairs in larger towns such as Boston, Salem, Watertown, Plymouth, New Haven, and Hartford. On such occasions, the roads linking village to village were clogged with drovers herding hundreds of cattle, horses, and hogs to be sold to butchers and merchants. Towns licensed certain individuals to maintain bridges and ferries to accommodate the traffic, allowing them to charge separate tolls for people and animals.[27]

Boston itself absorbed many animals arriving from the countryside. Because they lived on a small peninsula, at most two miles long and a mile wide, Bostonians almost immediately faced a scarcity of agricultural land. Pasture was in especially short supply; as early as the mid-1630s hay had to be imported by boat to feed the town's animals. "Those that live here upon their cattle," William Wood admitted, "must be constrained to take farms in the country or else they cannot subsist" given the amount of grazing land in town. Within another decade, most of Boston's livestock had been moved to pastures in Muddy River (now Brookline) and Pullen Point across the bay. Merchants and craftsmen increasingly resorted to purchasing meat and dairy products rather than trying to raise their own animals. Farmers in surrounding towns wasted little time in satisfying urban demand. Dedham's butchers, observed Samuel Maverick in 1660, "have Vent enough for their Commodities in Boston," and Ipswich farmers likewise supplied the town "with good Beefe."[28]

The extent of the colonists' trade in meat and livestock gradually spread outward over greater and greater distances. From New England villages the commerce in animals soon encompassed neighboring New Netherland. Dutch farmers never managed to provision their colony adequately, so English colonists obligingly filled their needs. Officials in Holland strenuously objected when they found out that their colonists purchased English livestock while Dutch animals fell "into disrepute." Governor William Kieft tried to "prevent, as much as possible, the sale here of any English cows or goats," but the trade in animals continued. Too many Dutch farmers were convinced that English livestock were hardier, "better suited to this country than those from Holland," requiring "less trouble, expense and attention" than Dutch animals.[29]

Tensions between English and Dutch officials stemming from the livestock trade increased after English settlers began moving to the eastern end of Long Island. By 1649, English towns under nominal Dutch jurisdiction contained an estimated 30,000 cattle and horses. Officials complained that the nearly 5,000 English residents in New Netherland "live only by trade in grain and cattle," selling animals to Manhattan and other Dutch settlements. Repeated efforts to close off that trade, even those initiated when England and Holland were at war with one another, aroused opposition from Dutch colonists anxious about a scarcity of meat.[30] Dutch officials further suspected, with good reason, that some English merchants used the commerce in cattle as a subterfuge for horning in on the fur trade. This was certainly the case when John Pynchon joined William Hawthorne of Salem and several Boston merchants in 1659 to form the Hawthorne Company. Ostensibly founded to provision Dutch traders at Fort Orange, the company also aimed to divert furs into English hands. This enterprise and similar schemes provoked an indignant Governor Peter Stuyvesant to complain that the English "sell their cattle, corn, bacon, meat and other commodities for beavers" to take back to their villages on Long Island and sell to merchants. The trade persisted even after New Netherland became New York in 1664, prompting the English officials then in charge to object to "the *New-England* Mens Trading at *Albany* with Horses & Cattle for Beaver."[31]

By the middle of the seventeenth century, the extent of New England's meat and livestock trade reached even farther. Colonists from Newfoundland to Virginia ate New England-raised beef and pork, as did sailors whose ships took on provisions in Boston, Salem, or Newport. The greatest bonanza by far came after the 1640s with the opening of trade to the West Indies. Caribbean settlers "had rather buy foode at very deare rates than produce it by labour, soe infinite is the profitt of sugar workes," a Barbados planter informed John Winthrop. The Bay Colony governor proceeded to thank the Lord for this unexpected windfall. Vessels laden with barrels of salted pork and beef, as well as with live animals, began making regular runs from New England ports to Barbados, Jamaica, and other island destinations. Merchants scrambled for advantage in this highly lucrative enterprise. In the late 1650s, for instance, John Hull of Boston joined with four Rhode Island entrepreneurs to buy 12 square miles of prime meadow land from the Narragansett Indians in order to raise cattle to sell in the Caribbean. By 1660, according to Samuel Maverick, "many thousand Neate Beasts and Hoggs are yearly killed" for the export market. Live animals, particularly horses, were also in demand for transportation and to work in sugar mills.[32]

When New England farmers assessed their livestock holdings, they thought first and foremost about meeting their families' needs. Aiming for something close to self-sufficiency, they diversified their animal property to an extent not generally seen on seventeenth-century Chesapeake plantations. Because they never could achieve self-sufficiency, farmers sold goods and services to obtain whatever they wanted but could not produce themselves. Livestock figured prominently in these exchanges as a form of property that reliably generated a surplus for owners and for which there was a growing demand. The sale of a calf, a few sheep, or some hogs enabled a farmer to come back from market with a bolt of imported cloth in his cart, some coarse earthenware for the dairy or the kitchen, or a religious pamphlet to guide his meditations and instruct his children. Many small sales such as this, combined with the large-scale enterprises of a Pynchon or Coddington, made New England a significant exporter of animals and meat. By the eighteenth century only fish surpassed livestock in value as an export commodity from the region. What tobacco offered to the Chesapeake and sugar to the West Indies, livestock supplied to New England: a staple to sustain its agricultural economy and enmesh it in an extensive commercial network.[33]

Careful husbandry increased the chances that a family could feed itself and have surplus livestock to exchange. Shrewd management entailed not just deciding which animals to sell and when, but organizing the physical space of farms and the work schedules of farmers to maximize the use and production of domestic creatures. New Englanders who tried to recreate a semblance of England's mixed-farming practices in the New World did not replicate English practices in every detail, but paid considerably more attention to ideals of stewardship than did Chesapeake planters.

Thomas Minor's experience testified to the challenges faced by New England farmers. Minor arrived in Boston in 1630 as a 22-year-old bachelor, and after marrying and living briefly in several towns, ended up in the part of New London that eventually became Stonington, Connecticut. With the help of his wife Grace and their ten children, he toiled for over 40 years to convert a land grant into a working farm. Hardly a day went by when Minor did not wield a hoe, an axe, or a pitchfork as he went about his duties. But unlike most of his neighbors, he also regarded pen and paper as useful tools for a conscientious farmer. Minor began to keep a diary in November of 1653, and for the next 31 years he made a record of his activities and preoccupations as he enacted on a small scale the larger project of English imperial expansion.[34]

Minor's assiduous record keeping testified to his desire to be a good farmer. By taking note of when and where he planted certain crops, how much he harvested, and how many offspring his livestock produced, he tallied his accomplishments and preserved valuable information for planning the work of seasons to come.[35] As he went about his labors, Minor faced conditions that no English farmer of his era encountered. New Englanders typically selected abandoned native village sites for their new towns, attracted by cleared land and proximity to the coastline or rivers. Even so, the woods were never far away, and some colonists ended up on the outskirts of their towns. Such was the fate of Thomas Minor, whose neighbors complained that he lived "so remote that they can have no sosietie" with him "but as an heathen or an Indean." As the populations of New London and nearby Stonington steadily grew, the Minors' isolation diminished, but the effort required to establish a farm in "so remote" a location was daunting.[36]

New Englanders like Thomas Minor, who literally built their farms from the ground up, gradually introduced elements of English plant and animal husbandry to the region. They grew wheat, rye, oats, and peas, albeit with mixed success, along with acres of Indian corn. Orchards produced apples and other fruit from saplings and grafts carefully transported from England. The Minors, along with many colonists, grew flax and hemp, to be processed into homespun linen and rope. To make these gains, they had to adjust to a climate with colder winters and hotter summers than England had. This meant waiting until March or April to plow instead of doing so in February and, depending on where they lived, looking for signs of frost as early as in October. Colonists could nevertheless reassure themselves as the seasons passed that they were making progress in improving the land.[37]

Thomas Minor's style of livestock husbandry, like his choice of crops, revealed English roots and differed from Chesapeake practices. Northern farmers whose livelihood was intimately tied to the successful increase of their animals (especially true of Minor, who raised horses for sale in Rhode Island) could not afford to release their animals into the woods and hope for the best. English husbandry practices, however, had to be modified to accommodate environmental challenges and a persistent shortage of labor, which made it difficult for colonists to adhere to the highest standards of stewardship. For farmers like Minor, success lay in achieving a delicate balance between good intentions and limited means.

The physical layout of New England farms attested to their owners' efforts to protect their investment in domestic animals. Once farmers completed dwellings for themselves, they erected barns and sheds for their livestock. During blizzards and deep freezes, colonists sheltered their most vulnerable livestock in barns, where the creatures stayed warm from the accumulated heat of their huddled bodies. The main function of these structures, however, was to store fodder, which was even more essential than shelter in guaranteeing that livestock would make it through the winter.[38]

The common complaint that Chesapeake planters did not "know what it is to save hay" could not be lodged against New England farmers.[39] Hay became a veritable obsession among them, the prize won by prospective town founders with a keen eye for the lay of the land. The founders of Sudbury shrewdly selected a site with a vast stand of meadow, nearly 3,000 acres in extent, where the grass in some places grew higher than a man's waist. Haverhill's settlers nurtured "an over-weaning desire" for meadow that induced them "to grasp more into their hands" than they could possibly use. Coastal salt marshes, with tall grasses and few trees, attracted special attention as places where farmers could cut hay to bring back to their farms. The availability of salt marsh "did intice" the inhabitants of Hampton as well as founders of other towns to choose a particular destination. Land prices further testified to the priority colonists placed on livestock sustenance. In places like Hingham, Massachusetts, fresh and salt meadow was assessed at twice the value of arable land.[40]

Native grasses were ample in supply but low in nutrients. Salt hay provided 10 to 20 percent less food value than an equivalent amount of English hay, with the result that cattle fed on it grew slowly and produced less milk. One colonist admitted that animals supplied only with native forage grew "lousy" and were "much out of heart and liking."[41] Because increasing the quantity of poor-quality fodder would not make up for its nutritional defects, some colonists introduced English grasses to improve pastures. Livestock at first inadvertently helped this process along. Fed aboard ship on English hay, newly arrived animals deposited grass seeds along with their dung as they wandered through meadows and woods. William Wood noticed that as early as 1634 "in such places where the cattle use to graze, the ground is much improved in the woods, growing more grassy and less weedy." A few years later Edmund Browne reported that "in some places our E[nglish] clover is found" and it "feedeth cattle very well." By 1672, the invasion of English grasses had advanced to the point that John Josselyn recognized 22 European plants growing in Massachusetts and realized that they had "spring up since the English Planted and kept Cattle in New-England." Because these plants had evolved in a world where livestock were commonplace, they flourished better than native grasses ill adapted to constant grazing and trampling.[42]

The improvement of New England meadows was too important to trust to chance. Rhode Islanders, more heavily involved with livestock husbandry than most colonists, led the way in importing clover and other English grasses. Newport's founder, William Coddington, purchased seed for his own meadows and distributed it to neighboring farmers. Following up on a request from John Winthrop, Jr., Roger Williams arranged for his brother to send the Connecticut governor 12 bushels of grass seed to amend the pasturage on Fishers Island. Williams added suggestions on how best to sow the seeds that, at five shillings a bushel, were more than twice as expensive as corn. By the 1650s the Pynchon family, always on the lookout for ways to increase the output of their Connecticut Valley domain, had likewise invested in English grasses.[43]

Such a concerted effort to improve meadows for the benefit of livestock would not take place in the Chesapeake until the middle of the eighteenth century. Long before then even ordinary New England farmers engaged in the practice. By the 1650s, Thomas Minor had fenced in a patch for clover, and sowing hay seed had become a springtime ritual.[44] Colonists also planted other fodder crops. The Minors harvested as much as 460 sheaves of oats a year, mostly to feed horses. They also grew an abundance of turnips—45 bushels in 1657 alone—most of which probably ended up in feeding troughs rather than the stew pot. In addition, farmers saved anything that their animals might eat: straw left over from threshing grains, turnip and parsnip tops, and chopped cornstalks, which they regarded as particularly "good Fodder for Cattle given them for Change sometimes after Hay."[45]

As agricultural experiments go, the colonists' efforts to grow clover and turnips hardly counted as bold innovations when compared to contemporary English projects involving exotic crops like coleseed, saffron, and mulberries.[46] But given the abundance of native hay for their livestock, it is remarkable that farmers with so many other claims on their time and energy bothered to plant English grasses and root crops at all. The labors of men like Thomas Minor indicated their awareness of recent agricultural developments in England and a determination to adopt at least those practices with proven benefits for livestock. Even if these efforts took place on a smaller scale in New England, they had important ramifications for the viability of the region's agricultural economy.[47]

As livestock emerged as the centerpiece of New England's agrarian regime, the animals' survival and proliferation preoccupied colonial farmers.

The region's long, cold winters presented the greatest danger. Had livestock been forced to subsist on what they could find on frozen or snow-covered ground, most would have perished. An early contingent of Connecticut settlers learned this hard lesson when many of their cattle starved during the winter of 1635-36. Exposure to the perils of that same New England winter doomed the stray cow that Chickwallop and his men found. These circumstances explained New Englanders' greedy appropriation of natural meadows and their desire to supplement native hay with cultivated grasses, cornstalks, and root crops. Harvested not for year-round use but as winter fodder, hay and turnips sustained livestock until they could safely be sent to pasture in April or May. Pregnant females fed over the winter also had a better chance of producing healthy progeny in the spring and having enough milk for them. Foddering was indeed a matter "of high consequence" to New England farmers, as one eighteenth-century commentator observed.[48]

Since it was easier to lead animals to fodder than to carry food to them, farmers brought livestock home from distant pastures during the winter. John Winthrop, Jr., noted that colonists often put returning cattle into fenced cornfields after the harvest so they could graze for a few weeks on the stubble. With enough winter fodder, colonists could then pen their animals for the season. Over the years Thomas Minor and his sons constructed a patchwork of pens on his property—one each for goats, sheep, cows, and calves. Even without fences, livestock could be kept nearby with regular feeding. Once animals learned when and where food might appear, they lingered about the farm of their own accord.[49]

So long as livestock remained close by, owners could monitor the animals' welfare to an extent that was impracticable the rest of the year. Thomas Minor discovered that his cow Browne was ill during February of 1657, a month when his dairy cattle were penned in the yard. Losses and gains in herds and flocks were also easier to measure. One April morning in 1659, Minor beheld the gruesome consequences of a wolf's nocturnal attack on his sheep. Similar attacks occurred when animals grazed in distant meadows, but farmers did not discover the results quite so dramatically. At the same time, no Chesapeake planter could note with confidence, as Minor did, the specific days when his cows produced calves and his mares foaled, or precisely calculate that in one month "we had 22 Kids and 9 lambs and 3 Calvs" born. New Englanders made springtime expeditions into their yards, not the woods, to find, mark, and castrate young livestock. The animals had weeks to grow accustomed to contact with people before departing for newly green pastures. By then the process of domestication was well underway, to be reinforced each autumn when the animals returned to the protection of the farmyard and regular contact with their owners.[50]

The advantages of seasonal foddering were not limited to livestock survival and domestication, but also helped to address the problem of soil exhaustion. During the seventeenth century (and much of the eighteenth), New England was tied to a pattern of extensive economic development. When faced with declining soil fertility—a particular problem with cornfields— farmers tended to clear new land rather than improve the quality of existing tracts. Geographic expansion did not dramatically increase crop yields so much as compensate for declining harvests and help farmers keep pace with an extraordinary rate of population growth.[51] Unable to break free from this pattern, New Englanders nevertheless tinkered with it at the margins by taking advantage of a valuable byproduct of penning animals during the winter.

Nearly every November, Thomas Minor and his sons heaped mounds of "muck" into a cart and carried it out to planting fields. Deposited by penned livestock the previous winter, the dung had cured for the better part of a year, which helped to eliminate weeds. The supply was limited to what the animals produced between November and April, but added up to as much as 45 cartloads annually. New Englanders applied manure when and where they could, sometimes supplementing it with ashes or fish. If supplies were particularly low, farmers might painstakingly plant a bit of dung with each grain of corn instead of spreading it over the entire field. Animals allowed to graze on the stubble in cornfields also left fertilizer in their wake. Farmers may not have enriched every field each year, but they did the best they could. Eighteenth-century advocates of agricultural improvement, never sparing in their criticism, disparaged their forebears' methods of applying manure but never chided them for ignoring its virtues altogether.[52]

Dung, observed Samuel Deane in 1790, was "of almost the same importance to the farmer, as stock in trade is to the merchant."[53] Though never bought and sold (so far as we know), it was indeed a form of capital: property capable of producing wealth. For European and colonial farmers alike the application of manure constituted one of a very few known methods to enhance soil fertility and increase agricultural productivity. In seventeenth-century New England, it helped make the difference between a relatively stagnant agrarian economy and one capable of modest growth. Manured fields yielded better harvests of corn and other crops that sustained growing livestock populations over the winter. With more livestock, colonists could clear and fertilize more land to produce more crops. Increased yields of fodder crops in turn made it possible for farmers to raise surplus livestock to sell to merchants. Without winter foddering and the seasonal availability of manure, New England could not so quickly have become a significant exporter of meat and live animals.[54]

New England farmers gradually transformed tangled woods into a more familiar landscape. Performing tasks they thought representative of a superior English agrarian culture, colonists sought not just profit but good order. Farmers such as Thomas Minor implicitly understood what their responsibilities were, but New Englanders knew too much about human weakness to expect all colonists to abide by the standards of good husbandry. The management of domestic animals, like the suppression of sin, was too important to be left to the discretion of hard-pressed farmers. As a result, the community assumed responsibility for keeping order on farms just as it did for encouraging good behavior within farmhouses.

In late October 1648, New Haven selectmen offered John Cooper the job of "general pounder" for the coming year, responsible for inspecting town fences and impounding any wandering cattle he found. Cooper was interested, but if this was to be "his whole imployment" he wanted £30 in salary. His effort to exploit the region's labor scarcity for his own advantage failed when the selectmen made it clear they could not afford his price, and Cooper ended up with a part-time job with less compensation.[55] Had he pressed for a better deal, the selectmen would likely have approached another candidate. They would not, however, have let the job go vacant. Animal control in the Chesapeake (to the extent that it existed at all) may have been a private affair, but New Englanders conceived of it as a communal responsibility undertaken to ensure that the region's livestock remained as thoroughly disciplined as its people.

When it came to managing livestock, good fences indeed made good neighbors. Seventeenth-century farmers usually avoided building stone walls, which took too much time to construct and could not be moved, and instead erected split rail fences to protect crops from animal incursions. As in the Chesapeake, so too in New England: farmers who failed to keep fences in good repair could not sue livestock owners for damage from trespassing animals. In Rhode Island, Portsmouth's selectmen were unusually precise in defining how a good fence ought to look. It should, they insisted, be four and a half feet high with the rails no more than four inches apart. Anyone who cared to go to the trouble of building a stone wall had to make it equally tall.[56]

Beyond the fences that surrounded planting fields, New Englanders' commitment to managing their livestock was visible in other ways. The meetinghouse, used for worship and political gatherings, shared its strategic position near the town center with the town common, a tract of land set aside for livestock. As central to the community's sense of good order as the meetinghouse was to its religious and civic affairs, the common rivaled the building in symbolic weight. Chesapeake livestock grazed well away from colonists' plantations; in New England animals stood near the heart of the town.[57]

At first virtually every proprietor, or original owner of land in a town, could place livestock on the common. Inhabitants with more land or larger herds often had the right to put more beasts there than less affluent residents could, but inequality produced little controversy so long as human and animal populations within town remained low.[58] Livestock also grazed together after the harvest on stubble in the arable fields that lay beyond the common. Farmers possessed pieces of such fields as private property, but since one man's parcel adjoined his neighbor's plot, convenience dictated cooperative management. Men discussed when to plant and harvest, and when livestock could graze at the end of the season. Pooling their labor, inhabitants generally erected one fence around the common and one around each large planting field instead of enclosing individual holdings. In Dorchester, Massachusetts, the number of animals a farmer put on the common determined how much fence he had to build and maintain, at a rate of 20 feet per cow. Ipswich's inhabitants took into account a man's acreage when assigning fencing duties. Common grazing lands gave livestock a special space within towns; common fences kept them in their place.[59]

As herds increased and put pressure on the fixed supply of grass, townsmen eventually began to restrict access to the common. Newcomers could no longer automatically pasture their animals there but had to lease grazing rights from earlier proprietors. Following English practice, colonists in virtually every town sooner or later voted to "stint" the commons, or limit the numbers of animals allowed to graze there. As early as 1646, Bostonians permitted only 70 dairy cattle on the common. New Haven's leaders first urged inhabitants to "seasonally regulate & moderate themselves" but ultimately had to set grazing limits. Several Marblehead men charged with stinting their town commons in 1671 concluded that there was enough pasture for just 50 cattle and assigned a limit to each of 44 families. If someone preferred to place a horse there, that counted for two cows; four goats or sheep counted as one cow. More often than not, farmers used the conveniently located common for dairy cattle and oxen, which they needed almost every day, and looked elsewhere for pastures for other livestock.[60]

Colonists in particular sought places with natural features that would confine animals and offer protection from predators. Islands were perfect for this purpose, peninsulas or "necks" of land a second-best alternative that reduced the amount of fencing to be built. Connecticut's legislature explicitly instructed several men in February 1641 to consider where there would be "le[a]st chardge of fencing" as they surveyed possible sites for common pastures. Whether streams that bounded some prospective commons were sufficient to deter intrepid animals was a matter of speculation. Two Salem men, asked in 1668 if a certain creek would serve, reported seeing several feet of water at high tide and thick mud when the tide was out. Just to be sure, the men "thrust in a rod pole eight or ten feet into the mire" and concluded that it was "a sufficient fence against ordinary cattle" including hogs. Colonists nevertheless grew to appreciate some animals' ingenuity. At one point New Haven inhabitants discovered that "yonge cattle & hoggs" refused to be thwarted by a gate erected across a neck of land and simply swam around it to "doe damadge" on the other side.[61]

The opening of new pastures away from the town center allowed colonists to segregate different species of livestock in separate meadows. The advantages were obvious to anyone who had ever had his horse gored by an ox, or whose cows went hungry because sheep had nibbled the grass right down to the dirt. Crowding several species together hastened overgrazing and provided opportunities for aggressive behavior. When swine ran free in meadows, their rooting transformed smooth ground into an obstacle course of holes and hills that imperiled cattle and horses.[62] Many towns separated animals not only by species but also by function. Often the dry herd (steers and heifers) went to different pastures than dairy cattle. In Cambridge working oxen received their own common. Farmers with large numbers of sheep sequestered them in separate meadows. By 1648 residents of the English village of East Hampton, Long Island, had moved their flocks away from other animals to Montauk Point.[63]

No matter where they grazed, livestock could not be depended on to behave themselves. Because colonists could hardly keep constant watch over animals, they pooled resources to hire town keepers. If Cambridge's 1636 agreement with William Patten was typical, the job of serving as a dry herd keeper was lonely and not particularly lucrative. Patten was to take a hundred cattle across the Charles River and stay with them six days a week for seven months. At the end of his time, Patten received 20 pounds, half paid in money, half in corn. Men hired to herd dairy cattle to the town common at least slept in their own beds at night. Contracts usually specified that every day from May until after harvest these keepers had to be out just after sunrise to gather the town's herd, bringing the cattle back home a half hour before sunset. In Hempstead on Long Island, such work earned keepers 12 to 15 shillings a week, part of it—fittingly—paid in butter, and part either in wampum or grain. Although neither the duties nor the salary rendered the job of cowkeeper particularly attractive, one distinctive feature testified to its indispensability. Livestock herders were about the only New Englanders excused from Sabbath services so that they could go to work.[64]

Herders proved only as reliable as the men, and sometimes boys, hired to do the job. Sheer tedium and unpleasant working conditions often diverted herders' attention from their duties. One hapless livestock keeper in Lynn, Massachusetts, became so deeply immersed in conversation with a neighbor that he failed to notice that the cattle under his charge had strayed into a cornfield. In New Haven, Thomas Osborne came to regret seeking shelter one rainy day instead of getting soaked along with the herd under his care, for he subsequently had to answer in court for losing a cow. Although the judges ultimately decided that the cow's owner had to accept his loss "as an afflicting providence of God," Osborne's predicament revealed the limits of communal livestock control.[65]

Herdsmen were just one line of defense against wayward livestock. Reinforcements came in the form of an array of local officials charged with keeping animals (and their owners) in line. Fenceviewers, sometimes called haywards, routinely examined town fences and either repaired them and charged the person responsible for upkeep or ordered him to do the job himself. Hogreeves went after fractious swine and instructed the animals' owners to pen them. Poundkeepers like New Haven's John Cooper rounded up wandering livestock and confined them, charging owners a fine to get the beasts released. With a handful of men in each town overseeing the community's animals, everyone else could carry on with the other business of farming.[66]

Some animals proved harder to control than others. Swine were perhaps the most recalcitrant beasts. Allowed to run loose around town because they ate refuse tossed into streets and alleys, hogs nevertheless posed risks to the community. In 1658 exasperated selectmen in Boston accused swine of threatening children's lives and causing "elder people . . . greatt hurt" whenever they dared to step outdoors. The selectmen eventually ordered owners to keep their hogs penned, a restriction that officials in Warwick, Rhode Island, also adopted. But hog owners in both towns vehemently complained that they could not afford to feed penned hogs year-round. Officials then insisted that swine could run at large only if yoked and ringed. Placing a ring in each pig's nose prevented it from digging, while fastening a wooden yoke around its neck hindered the animal from crawling under fences. In some places, frequent violations of such ordinances required yet another approach. Inspired perhaps by expedients directed against religious dissenters, several towns resorted to banishment. In 1635 the Massachusetts General Court ruled that swine without a keeper had to stay at least a mile away from any English settlement. Dorchester selectmen increased that to two miles, even for swine with keepers. New Haven's magistrates exiled hogs "8, 10, or 12 mile distanc from the towne" so that there was no chance they could damage property.[67]

Horses could be just as troublesome, but because they were more valuable than hogs and needed for travel, colonists could not easily send them away. New Hampshire owners who could not keep their horses penned had to fetter them, a requirement that colonists elsewhere probably imposed too.[68] Because bulls may have been the most dangerous animals of all, colonists sharply restricted their numbers. Communities typically designated a couple of men to keep "town bulls" that everyone else could use for a fee. Prominent individuals who possessed the means to pen and feed a bull year-round added this responsibility to their other public duties. The practice not only promoted public safety but also permitted modest experiments in selective breeding. Hartford officials, for instance, specifically charged two men to examine several bull calves and choose only those "they shall thinck ffitt" for the job of siring the town's cattle.[69]

Livestock ownership may have been a private affair in early New England, but livestock management definitely was not.[70] Communities decided which animals grazed in which pastures, who built each section of a fence, under what conditions swine could run at large, and how many bulls each town should have. Herders and pounders supervised animals much as constables and tithingmen monitored people. Anyone who flouted communal livestock regulations faced fines and other punishments, just like any malefactor. The only escape from communal oversight was for a farmer to keep his animals confined on his own land and make sure that they stayed there. But few seventeenth-century farmers had sufficient improved land and a reliable enough supply of labor to go it alone. For at least the first generation or two, colonists regarded cooperation as the only practical way to keep order among the domestic animals in their towns.

New Englanders' victory over disorder, however, proved only partial. The commons at the heart of their towns were at best islands of comparative calm within a sea of confusion. The outskirts of communities became refuges for wandering cattle and aggressive swine, whose opportunistic behavior often defeated the colonists' best efforts at maintaining dominion from a distance. Well-supervised town commons represented only one aspect of New England husbandry; free-ranging livestock in surrounding woods and meadows were an equally significant, and far more unsettling, feature that had unintended consequences for the region's development.[71]

Except for the animals grazing on the common, livestock management in early New England was essentially a seasonal affair. Residents could only keep an eye on dry herds, sheep, and sometimes horses, between November and April or May, when the creatures stayed near town for winter foddering. From May until harvest time, colonists had no choice but to move the creatures to distant pastures, hoping that fences, herders, or simply the availability of food in unfenced meadows would encourage livestock to stay put. Pigs, which typically roamed at large all year round, were rarely subject even to modest supervision except when keepers escorted them out of town. Imperfect oversight of livestock inevitably meant that animal trespass cases filled court dockets. Adjudication was the preferred means of resolving disputes, although some colonists were not above taking direct action against offending beasts. Indeed, trespassing swine proved so obnoxious that in 1633 the Massachusetts government permitted colonists to kill errant pigs first and inform the animals' owners later.[72]

On the edges of town conditions differed little from the Chesapeake woods and, not surprisingly, some of the same problems with livestock emerged. The physical appearance of free-ranging New England animals bore witness to their owners' negligence. Sheep forced to graze in rough pastures carried "Lumps of dirt" in their fleeces. They bred at too young an age, producing lambs that were smaller than they ought to have been. Poor nutrition and promiscuous breeding contributed to the "smalness and badness" of horses. The diminished size of cattle in Plymouth likewise testified to lax husbandry.[73]

Free-ranging animals also wandered farther from their homes than they were supposed to. If they happened to cross town boundaries, disputes over damages could set communities as well as individuals against one another. The Bay Colony legislature tried to minimize contention with a 1634 measure stipulating that trespassing swine would be dealt with according to the rules of the town in which the animals had been found, but this did not help aggrieved parties discover where the beasts actually belonged. Thus in 1647 the General Court required owners to paint a symbol with pitch on the flanks of livestock designating the town where they lived. Just as earmarks labeled livestock as private property, these town marks, or in some cases brands, identified them as animal members of a community. Yet town marks also symbolized the attenuated control of each community over its animals' whereabouts.[74]

Such measures could not prevent losses of livestock. Thomas Minor devoted entire days to searching for lost animals, only to come home empty-handed. But no one questioned the necessity of trying to find valuable animal property. In 1646, New Haven officials went so far as to excuse Samuel Marsh for missing two militia training days because he was out "seeking cowes, it being in the spring" when cattle were "lyable to be swampt." To help people find their animals, virtually every town required inhabitants to bring stray livestock to the pound. The constable then gave public notice of the beasts lodged there so owners could retrieve them. This procedure helped colonists find animals that had wandered onto someone else's property, but was of little use in locating missing livestock that ranged well away from town.[75]

At least few New Englanders suspected their neighbors of being livestock rustlers. Supervision of animals, however inefficient, evidently discouraged widespread pilfering. Statutes specifically addressing theft of livestock—even hogstealing—are conspicuously absent from seventeenth-century records. At most, Bay Colony magistrates expressed concern that "the temptation may be too great on some persons in remote Towns and Farms" to keep strays instead of seeking out the animals' owners. Servants occasionally chased after swine with dogs, perhaps as much for amusement as for anything else, but officials saw no cause to single them out as a particularly malicious group. Only in Rhode Island, where communal oversight over neighbors was weakest, did magistrates order anyone who killed swine or goats to show the earmarks to a designated town official to prove ownership of the animals.[76]

Colonists also enjoyed a greater sense of security about animal property because there were few feral livestock in New England to complicate the issue of ownership. This result owed more to climate than to careful husbandry. Left on their own over the winter, grazing animals such as cattle and horses starved before they could produce feral offspring. Only omnivorous and far more prolific swine, able to subsist on almost anything—from nuts to shellfish and even carrion snatched from jaws of wolves—went wild. Settlers noticed them in Massachusetts as early as 1631, but New England's feral swine never came close to rivaling the wild gangs of the Chesapeake woods.[77]

Devoting little energy to debating the fate of New England's wild swine, magistrates simply assumed the creatures were fair game. In 1636, Bay Colony officials decreed that any hogs running loose without some sort of physical restraint "shalbee accounted as wild swine, & it shalbee lawfull for any man to take them, either alive or dead, as he may." All the captor had to do was have two neighbors assess the value of his prize so that a portion of the sum could be paid as a fee to the colony treasurer. Within two months, the General Court suspended the application of this order to tame swine, no doubt because of protests from hog-owning constituents, but colonists remained at liberty to kill wild pigs. A Connecticut law, designed to prevent colonists from hunting tame swine on the "pretence" that they were "Wild Hoggs," similarly implied that feral beasts were free for the taking.[78]

Unlike in the Chesapeake region, no legislature in New England debated whether feral livestock were royal property, and no governor required hunters of wild swine to obtain licenses. No one seemed to worry whether the beasts could be considered *ferae naturae* or if their status as English and as property had been compromised. Too few in number to spark much interest in colonies where royal authority was kept at a distance anyway, the creatures attracted attention only insofar as they caused trouble in towns. Colonists neither doubted that the animals remained English nor disputed magistrates' decision to award them to whoever caught them.

Ironically, anxiety about the potentially degenerative effects of moving to the New World arose when colonists thought about tame livestock, not feral creatures, and the objects of concern were not animals, but people. Even before the flood of migration to the region had ebbed, colonists appeared to be developing an excessive regard for their animal property. Self-interest threatened to overshadow the communal spirit that was supposed to make New England a model Christian commonwealth. Colonists who put the increase of their animals before all else seemed to care little about the integrity of the towns they had themselves founded. Evidence of such an unwelcome shift in attention was not hard to find.

As early as the mid-1630s, inhabitants of such places as Cambridge, Watertown, Dorchester, and Roxbury raised a chorus of complaints that they were running out of room. These towns occupied large tracts of land and each as yet contained perhaps 50 to 100 families. Overcrowding of people was obviously not the problem; rather, a perceived "straitnes of accommodation" for livestock drove farmers to make their protest. Their complaints were by no means frivolous. Even large towns often lacked enough of the right kind of land to sustain free-ranging livestock in spring and summer and to provide hay for winter fodder. Towns could sometimes be cajoled into sharing precious meadows with their neighbors, but this was at best a short-term expedient and could foster contention as easily as cooperation. When farmers in the border town of Hingham grumbled about their "great neede of hay," the Massachusetts General Court aggravated an existing dispute by allowing them to mow land claimed by Plymouth Colony. Competition for meadow and the potential for discord would only increase as herds multiplied.[79]

Farmers could not easily follow the Chesapeake solution and let livestock find their own places to graze. Early New England towns bordered on one another, leaving little pasture land outside of some community's jurisdiction. Furthermore, authorities frowned on colonists using land that had not yet been allocated to any town. Because they wanted territory occupied in an orderly fashion, magistrates prohibited individuals from squatting on land they did not own, trying to buy it from Indians without permission to do so, or arranging questionable deals like Thomas Danforth's bargain with his debtor. At the same time, officials recognized the legitimacy of farmers' concerns, and tried to address them without losing control of the process of settlement.

New England colonization proceeded town by town, rather than farm by farm, to ensure that godly people settled alongside Christian neighbors. Families and individuals had to organize themselves into groups and petition the legislature to start a town. The first town grants provided homes for the constant stream of immigrants from England, but it was not long before established settlers appealed for permission to start new communities in order to have hay for livestock. Magistrates saw little alternative but to heed such petitions, and a procedure designed to regulate human settlement became the preferred means of accommodating domestic animals. The beginnings of Ipswich, Concord, Dedham, and Sudbury in Massachusetts, as well as Duxbury in Plymouth Colony, lay in their founders' quest for hay. These towns bordered on existing villages, but the pattern of contiguous settlement was disrupted when colonists heard about the lush meadows of the Connecticut Valley. Cambridge residents cited a need for pasture to justify their removal to what became Hartford. Rev. Thomas Hooker, who accompanied them, may have had spiritual reasons to distance himself from Massachusetts, but he too deemed it prudent to emphasize the welfare of livestock over other motives. The establishment of Wethersfield and Windsor along the Connecticut River by livestock farmers from Watertown and Dorchester reaffirmed the power of this argument to bring the desired results.[80]

By granting these requests, legislators maintained the illusion of control over the progress of settlement. They guaranteed that people would continue to build towns, not isolated farmsteads, but could not dictate when or where those towns would appear. Some colonists, including several respected leaders, discerned in this swift expansion of settlement a cause for alarm. They could not help but notice that the intense scramble for meadow beginning in the mid-1630s corresponded to a sharp rise in the price of livestock. Thousands of immigrants arriving each year of that decade expected to purchase domestic animals in New England for their farms. High demand for relatively scarce livestock drove prices to exorbitant levels. John Winthrop could hardly conceal his amazement that by 1633 cows sold for £20 apiece—"yea, some at £24, some £26"—while a horse fetched as much as £35. Even a goat cost £4. The same was true in other New England colonies. No wonder farmers who already possessed animals wanted the means to raise more. But where some colonists saw an unexpected bonanza, others detected the insidious influence of Satan.[81]

Rev. Nathaniel Ward, for one, believed that farmers who coveted Connecticut Valley meadows cared little how their towns and churches might suffer from their departure for greener pastures. Determined "to seeke the good of their cattell more then of com[monweal]th," Ward lamented, they had succumbed to the lure of worldliness. William Bradford agreed that the ostensible "benefit" of high prices actually inflicted "hurt" on profit-seeking colonists. The Plymouth governor grieved that "no man now thought he could live except he had cattle and a great deal of ground to keep them, all striving to increase their stocks." Those who abandoned Plymouth to pursue advantage elsewhere rendered their former abode "almost desolate," its people and church divided. Bradford harbored little hope that the pattern of dispersal evident as early as 1632 would be reversed. It would be "the ruin of New England, at least of the churches of God there," he warned, "and will provoke the Lord's displeasure against them."[82]

The Lord's displeasure manifested itself even sooner than Bradford could have guessed and in a form that revealed a divine sense of irony. Profit-seeking colonists had scarcely begun to build their houses and barns in new meadow-rich towns when, in 1640, the livestock market collapsed and a general economic depression ensued. Sustained only by the constant influx of newcomers from England, prices plummeted and the supply of money shrank when the troubles preceding civil war encouraged hopeful Puritans to stay home. By December 1640, John Winthrop reported, a "good cow" brought at most £8; six months later that figure was halved. Thus "God taught us the vanity of all outward things," he added, in case anyone had missed the point. According to Bradford, a few prescient colonists had anticipated a price decline, but had "thought it would be by degrees, and not be from the highest pitch at once to the lowest as it did, which was greatly to the damage of many and the undoing of some." Unable to resist a bit of humor even at the expense of distraught farmers, Rev. Samuel Danforth quipped:

> That since the mighty *Cow* her crown hath lost,
> In every place she's made to rule the roast.[83]

Dwindling fortunes were no laughing matter to colonists who had uprooted themselves to take advantage of an escalating market. Some of them contemplated yet another move to start new towns in more "commodious" places, to check out Long Island, to return to England, even to head for the struggling Puritan colony on Providence Island in the Caribbean. The vast majority remained behind, however, to listen to magistrates and ministers chastise them for losing sight of New England's original purpose by putting greed ahead of God. The economic crisis warned everyone how easy it was to confuse getting by with getting ahead and what the inevitable consequences would be.[84]

If, during the 1630s, livestock enticed restless colonists to value profit more than community, in the following decade the animals represented—at least for a few young men—temptation of another sort altogether. Leaders noted with horror that on top of its other troubles, New England had fallen victim to an outbreak of bestiality. Between 1640 and 1647, eight men were accused of the crime and four were executed—one each in Massachusetts, Plymouth, Connecticut, and New Haven. Although this hardly constituted a crime wave, given that the non-Indian population in 1640 exceeded 13,000, bestiality prosecutions were more common in New England during the seventeenth century than in other English colonies or England itself. Only one case each occurred in early Virginia and Bermuda, and none in Maryland. It seems unlikely that New Englanders were unusually prone to a behavior that occurred in many rural societies with domestic animals. Instead, colonists were especially eager to report what they saw, or thought they saw, and the authorities were quick to prosecute the accused. Two New Haven men (including the unfortunately named Thomas Hogg) landed in court only because observers thought the accused bore an uncanny resemblance to deformed newborn piglets and thus must have sired the animals. Magistrates joined apprehensive colonists in their concern that something had gone terribly wrong in New England.[85]

The timing of the bestiality panic was hardly coincidental. The defendants were usually unmarried young men, who were relatively more numerous in New England in the early 1640s than at any other time in the century. Many young men were what William Bradford called "untoward servants," laborers who had been recruited for their physical strength, not their piety.[86] The 1640s also witnessed economic dislocation and, as England plunged into civil war, religious and political uncertainty. Puritan luminaries and parliamentary leaders focused their attention on matters at home, relegating New England to an uncomfortably marginal position. All of these factors provoked intense reflection in colonists already prone to introspection. They knew corruption and pride could take many forms. That it took shape as bestiality among a people who so recently identified livestock as false temptations in another sense may have come as no surprise.[87]

The bestiality panic soon waned, but anxiety about New England's deviation from the path of righteousness persisted. Worldliness remained a chief concern, and the pursuit of self-interest at the expense of community its principal manifestation. The fall in the price of cattle, as well as the end of the migration from England, slowed the dispersal of settlers during the 1640s, but the recovery of the livestock market with the opening of the West Indies trade in the 1650s revived interest in acquiring more meadow. Plymouth farmers used the threat of departure to coerce the colony government into allocating their town additional pasture. Elsewhere colonists gave in to the "over eager pursuit of the fruits of the earth" and moved on, even though, as Edward Johnson admonished, their quest took them "out so far in this Wilderness" that they were beyond reach of church and congregation. Content "to celebrate their Sabbaths in the chimney-corner, horse, kine, sheep, goats, and swine being their most indeared companions," these restless colonists, like loose threads, seemed capable of unraveling the whole fabric of a godly society.[88]

The likelihood that New Englanders would fail to live up to the founders' standards was virtually guaranteed, given the loftiness of their goal to establish righteous communities in a corrupt world. Yet few people could have expected livestock to play such an important role in leading colonists astray. The dynamic of geographic expansion, which leaders regarded as destabilizing and attributed to selfishness, originated in the colonists' need to accommodate their animals. Until they had time and labor enough to enclose and improve pastures, farmers had little choice but to act as they did. Their accommodations, moreover, brought important benefits to saints and sinners alike. In an economic sense, if perhaps not a spiritual one, the colonists' willingness to move for the sake of their animals was the salvation, not the undoing, of English settlement in New England.

English people who regarded the New World as a land made for livestock never doubted that domestic animals would become their partners in colonization. Colonists expected the creatures to make good use of vast unpopulated meadows, converting grass into meat, milk, labor, and profit.

Improving the land by their very presence, livestock would establish English rights to territory that Indians did not seem to need. In the colonies as in England, husbandmen who understood how animals ought to be raised would construct fences, plant clover, save manure, and exercise dominion over beasts that God had placed on the earth for human use. As these efforts proceeded, cows would become powerful symbols of civility, representing the means by which proper farmers improved themselves and the land at the same time. Colonists took it for granted that Indians would recognize the superiority of an English agrarian regime once they saw how it worked.

But colonists underestimated the difficulty of transplanting English methods of animal husbandry to the New World. The work of enclosing pastures and supervising livestock demanded more effort than hard-pressed settlers could muster so long as they had land to clear, houses to build, crops to plant, and, in the Chesapeake, tobacco to raise. Apologists for English imperialism had reckoned on colonists readily transforming lands that Indians held in common into private property through enclosure and intensive use, but that is not what happened. At least at first, the material improvements signifying English settlement were less extensive than they might have been, visible mainly on small portions of Chesapeake plantations and near the centers of New England towns. Much of the territory claimed by colonists during the seventeenth century remained uncleared and unfenced, the domain of free-ranging animals and not sedentary settlers. Colonists in effect appropriated Indian common lands to serve as their own commons.

Indians would be puzzled by this turn of events, wondering how the colonists' use of the land created rights superior to native claims. The only difference seemed to be that the English had substituted tame animals for wild ones. And even that distinction proved hard to maintain. For the most part, the cattle and hogs roaming through woods and meadows behaved just like deer and other wild beasts, and some livestock actually became wild. Only a small proportion of English creatures appeared to be subject to the colonists' dominion; the remainder did little to advertise the advantages of civility. For native peoples confronted by growing numbers of colonists and livestock, negotiating the differences between what the English said and how they acted emerged as one of the more confusing challenges of the seventeenth century.

Part Three

Contending with Animals

Chapter Six

Forgiving Trespasses

Living with Livestock in Early America

In October 1626, a group of Accomack Indians killed several hogs they found wandering on the Eastern Shore of Chesapeake Bay. The Indians may have hunted the animals for meat or, since it was harvest season, retaliated against the swine for damage they had caused in ripening cornfields. Whatever the reason, the Accomacks surely did not expect their action to arouse such an angry response from English colonists with whom, up to that point, they had maintained friendly relations. A blustering Capt. William Epps confronted them on behalf of the aggrieved hog owners and "demanded satisffaction." The Indians agreed to pay damages in corn, but Epps would not let the matter rest without a stern warning. Should the Accomacks repeat their misdeed, he threatened, "it will be an occasion of the breatch of the peace betweene us." Thus did the Accomacks learn that the English would interpret attacks on their animals as signs of hostility.[1]

Five years later, in June 1631, the Massachusett sachem Chickataubut stood accused of a similar offense, killing one of Sir Richard Saltonstall's pigs. Chickataubut, who had a crippled arm, could not have done the deed himself, but since colonial authorities held sachems responsible for the misconduct of their followers, he had to answer the charges. The hog might once again have provoked the Indians by rooting in a cornfield; if that were true, however, the terms of a Bay Colony law passed just a month earlier required Saltonstall to pay restitution to the Indians. The magistrates ignored this possibility and instead held Chickataubut to account under the terms of his recent agreement to make amends for any wrongs his men perpetrated against the English or their livestock. By fining him one beaver skin, Bay Colony authorities expected the Massachusett leader and his followers to understand that they must refrain from killing the colonists' animals no matter what the provocation.[2]

It comes as no surprise that swine figured prominently in each of these episodes. More prolific and more unruly than other livestock species, hogs seemed to cause trouble wherever they roamed. Less predictable were the responses of the human participants in these small dramas. The potential for further violence, which could easily be directed against people as well as animals, dissipated through exchanges of goods and warnings. The Indians agreed to pay restitution, acknowledging that what they had done was offensive to the English. Richard Saltonstall and Eastern Shore hog owners, who could have sought vengeance on their own, instead allowed the authorities to settle matters on their behalf. In neither instance did minor grievances escalate into uncontrollable hostility, although such an unhappy outcome was certainly conceivable.

The comparatively peaceful resolution of these disputes nevertheless exposed an uneven balance of power. The colonists' response, particularly in Virginia, included threats of harsh retribution should the Indians destroy livestock again. Negotiations took place on English terms to protect English interests, with colonial officials in charge. Indians were familiar with the practice of paying restitution to victims of crime in their own villages, but may not have fully comprehended the nature of their offenses in these cases. If the hogs had caused them injury in the first place, the Indians may have regarded their reactions as swift justice meted out to the real culprits. Encounters with English animals had not yet become commonplace, however, and the novelty of the situation may have encouraged the Accomacks and Chickataubut to accede to English demands in the interest of keeping peace. Whether the Indians derived as much "satisfaction" from the results as the colonists did remains unclear.[3]

The colonists got their way in these disputes, but that did not mean that English authority in New England and around Chesapeake Bay was absolute or that Indian submission was guaranteed. For much of the seventeenth century, relations between Indians and colonists remained fluid as each side gathered information about the other, assessing strengths and testing weaknesses. The outcome of one encounter seldom predicted the nature of the next. Yet during the first century of colonization, one consistent theme did emerge from the welter of Anglo-Indian interactions in the two regions. In terms of the sheer number of incidents involved, nothing brought Indians and colonists into contact more frequently than livestock.

Rare at first, encounters between Indians and English animals became routine as livestock populations boomed. These meetings often generated friction, but also provided Indians and colonists with opportunities for peaceful negotiation. Each group had much to learn about how to live with livestock in the New World. Indians confronted the challenge of incorporating new animals and a new conception of animal property into their ways of thinking. Colonists, compelled to adopt new and less stringent husbandry practices, puzzled over how to prevent livestock from antagonizing Indians whom they hoped to impress with their cultural superiority. Neither group exercised much control over free-ranging livestock, and as a result, both of them contended with similar problems of animal trespass. If Indians, less familiar with domesticated animals, had further to go in embracing livestock as part of their world, there was, at least at first, no reason to think that they and the colonists could not meet on common ground.

By the time these hog-killing incidents occurred, Indians and colonists each had reason to ponder the significance of seemingly random acts performed by members of the other group. In 1626 English and native peoples in Virginia had been feasting, trading, negotiating, and fighting with one another for nearly two decades. The Massachusetts Bay Colony may have been just one year old in 1631 when its leaders called Chickataubut to account, but this was hardly the sachem's first meeting with Englishmen. He had already dealt with Plymouth settlers for at least nine years, and had come away from one encounter with his elbow shattered by a bullet.[4] Disputes over livestock, like exchanges related to other issues, cannot be separated from the main story of colonization. Both Indians and colonists associated livestock with Englishness, leading them to invest quarrels over animals with greater meaning than the actual events might seem to warrant. Participants assessed the significance of such occurrences in light of the general tenor of their relations and reacted accordingly. The Virginians' testy encounter with the

Accomacks and the less aggressive Bay Colony summons to Chickataubut revealed that contrasting patterns of intercultural contact had already emerged in the two colonial regions. Depending on the circumstances, a pig pierced by an arrow could signify enmity, malice, or a mistake.

English settlers on the Eastern Shore had reason to be nervous about the Accomacks' intentions in 1626, for they were among the few local Indians still friendly with the colonists. Geographically isolated from the center of English settlement along the James and York rivers and unaffiliated with the Powhatan chiefdom, the Accomacks played little role in the unfolding drama on the western edge of Chesapeake Bay. For two years following the establishment of Jamestown in April 1607, colonists interacted warily but peacefully with Powhatan and the various groups under his authority. But good relations broke down under pressure from unceasing English demands for corn and the Powhatans' growing dissatisfaction with the colonists' approach to trade. The result was a war that lasted from 1609 to 1614.[5]

With the outbreak of conflict, Indians first began targeting livestock for destruction. One colonist alleged that Powhatan "and his people destroyed our Hogs, (to the number of about six hundred)." That toll was surely exaggerated, reflecting the reporter's fear of starvation as much as his sense of indignation. Yet Powhatan, keenly aware that the colonists had trouble feeding themselves, doubtless intended to aggravate such worries. Upset at having their corn confiscated by the colonists, he and his men deliberately turned against a food source precious to the English. Thus depredations against livestock came to be seen by both sides as acts of war, and their cessation a condition of peace. When colonists formed an alliance with the Chickahominies at the conflict's end, they made the Indians agree "neither to kill nor detaine any of our men, nor cattell, but bring them home."[6]

Military stalemate brought an uneasy peace that lasted eight years. During this period, English settlement expanded rapidly, fueled by constant immigration and the beginnings of tobacco cultivation. Twenty-three plantations lined the James River in 1619; by 1622 the number had doubled. Colonists also spread for the first time to the Eastern Shore. For every acre cleared for corn or tobacco, another five or ten (or more) in the surrounding area became the domain of free-ranging cattle and hogs. Just when the Powhatans found it more difficult than ever to avoid colonists and their animals, their own numbers may have begun to diminish due to the appearance of European diseases against which they had no immunity.[7]

Once again, tensions erupted into violence. Outraged at the colonists' murder of the military and spiritual leader Nemattanew and more generally frustrated by English expansion, the Powhatans launched a preemptive attack on their adversaries. Led by Opechancanough, Powhatan's kinsman and successor as chief, the Indians struck plantations along the James River on the morning of 22 March 1622. Over 300 colonists—perhaps a quarter of the English population—perished. Untold quantities of livestock were also killed in the assault. The Indians "fell uppon the Poultry, Hoggs, Cowes, Goats and Horses whereof they killed great nombers," one witness reported. Even the Chickahominies, erstwhile English allies, slaughtered English animals. When frantic colonists sought refuge within Jamestown's fort, they abandoned many other creatures to their fate, some of which escaped to the woods and went feral.[8]

Ten years of sporadic but brutal fighting ensued. Despite enormous losses, colonial forces rallied to descend on dozens of native villages. Many Virginians believed that "now we have just cause to destroy them by all meanes possible" and acted accordingly. As the second anniversary of the initial attack approached, Virginia legislators coolly ordered inhabitants to prepare to "fall upon their adjoyning salvages as we did last yeare." Though planters scarcely needed encouragement to seek revenge, Governor Francis Wyatt reminded them that the extirpation of the Indians would not only protect colonists but also make Virginia safe for beleaguered livestock. With victory the colonists would "gain the free range of the country for increase of Cattle, swine, etc." Only Capt. John Martin, a noted troublemaker, dared publicly to suggest otherwise. Observing that Indians "have ever kept down the woods and slayne the wolves, beares, and other beasts," he argued that "we shalbe more opressed in short tyme by their absence, then in their liveing by us both for our owne securitie as allso for our Cattle." Martin's comments fell on deaf ears, but if he and Wyatt disagreed about the effects of the Indians' disappearance they began with a similar premise. Both men assumed that the fates of planters and their livestock were closely intertwined.[9]

Because the Accomacks' killing of hogs occurred during this cycle of violence, the colonists must have been relieved to negotiate a peaceful resolution so that fighting did not spread to the Eastern Shore. Elsewhere native raids against the English and their animals continued until 1632, when the two sides agreed to a peace that established English dominance over much of the eastern Tidewater. In 1644, an aging Opechancanough organized one final, desperate assault during which native warriors slew nearly 500 colonists and many livestock, but the English had grown numerous enough by then to absorb this blow without the survival of the colony being seriously endangered. Colonists captured and killed Opechancanough, and in 1646 imposed a peace treaty that effectively crushed the Powhatan chiefdom as a political entity.[10]

From this point on, the Indians of the eastern Chesapeake interacted with colonists from a position of weakness, though hardly one of complete submission. Their relations would involve, as they had from the start, negotiations over the place of English animals in the New World. The colonists' relative strength guaranteed that livestock would proliferate in the region, but could not determine how Indians would respond to the animals' growing presence. Attacks on livestock in wartime indicated that Indians knew how much the colonists relied on their animals but they were not necessarily meant to express native peoples' enmity towards the creatures in their own right. Whether Indians would come to depend on livestock as the English did and in the process—as the burgesses hoped when they drew up the wolf bounty act in 1656—adopt Christianity and other attributes of civility, remained to be seen.

Early relations between Indian and English settlers in New England followed a different, less consistently confrontational path, largely because one important effect of contact with the Old World preceded colonization there. Between 1616 and 1619 an outbreak of smallpox and other European diseases struck native groups living near the coast who had begun trading with French and English visitors. These epidemics exacted an appalling toll: estimated mortality rates ranged from 75 to 90 percent among the Abenakis, Massachusetts, Pawtuckets, and Wampanoags. Reeling from this disaster, survivors not only faced the enormous tasks of physical recovery and village reorganization but also confronted a changed political landscape. No powerful chiefdom on the order of Powhatan's organization existed in New England; instead various peoples maintained allegiance to sachems whose jurisdictions covered fairly limited territories. The outbreak of disease, by striking some villages and not others, magnified political fragmentation and the potential for aggression. Groups unaffected by these early epidemics, including Micmacs, Narragansetts, and Pequots, looked for opportunities to take advantage of their stricken neighbors who, in turn, scrambled for allies to counter such threats.[11]

Into this volatile situation stepped the first English settlers. Pleasantly surprised when a handful of Indian leaders, including Chickataubut and the Wampanoag sachem Massasoit, came forward in apparent friendship, colonists did not appreciate the extent to which these overtures were meant to help offset rivalries with other Indians. Yet relations between Chickataubut and a group of colonists who settled near his village soon went sour when the English began demanding corn from Indians who had little to spare. A violent altercation in 1622 left Chickataubut with an abiding distrust of Plymouth settlers as well as a broken elbow, but the Massachusetts in their weakened condition could not afford to forgo English allies altogether. When the Bay Colony was founded in 1630, Chickataubut approached its leaders to conclude an alliance that he hoped would protect the Massachusetts Indians from the Pilgrims as much as from the Narragansetts.[12]

Under the circumstances, it seems unlikely that the Massachusetts intended the killing of Sir Richard Saltonstall's pig to signify belligerence or that the colonists interpreted it as such. The two groups relied on each other too much for trade, defense, and information in these early years to let grievances rankle to the point of outright hostility. The potential for serious tensions also diminished when it became clear that Bay colonists could provision themselves and would not demand food from the Indians. But the relationship between the two groups was scarcely equal. Chickataubut and many of his people succumbed to smallpox in 1633, foreshadowing the colonists' imminent demographic dominance in the region. Even before the balance of population tipped in their favor, colonists asserted political authority over neighboring Indians, resorting to their own laws when dealing with animal trespasses and other problems. Yet magistrates did not altogether ignore considerations of equity. When it became clear in November 1632 that Sir Richard Saltonstall's cattle had invaded an Indian cornfield, the court ordered the colonial gentleman to render satisfaction in the form of a barrel of corn to Sagamore John, sachem of the Pawtuckets. Likewise in 1634, colony officials responded to a complaint by the sagamore of Agawam by requiring inhabitants of Charlestown to pay restitution for damages caused by their trespassing cattle.[13]

Even so, wherever colonists failed to develop strong diplomatic ties with Indians, they were inclined to act without inquiring into the Indians' side of the story. In 1636, for instance, commissioners in Maine ordered Saco inhabitants to "apprehend, execute or kill any Indian that hath binne known to murder any English, kill ther Cattell or any waie spoyle ther goods or do them violence & will not mack satisfaction." Settlers who felt uneasy about exacting summary justice risked paying fines as punishment for their scrupulousness.[14] Indian tempers could also flare in places where the reach of law and diplomacy stretched thin, and livestock as well as people again suffered as a result. The most notable early example of such a crisis occurred in Connecticut in the mid-1630s when Pequot Indians took aim at English animals as a way of sending an angry message to the colonists.

Once the most powerful native group in eastern Connecticut, the Pequots suffered a series of setbacks beginning in 1633, including a devastating smallpox epidemic and worsening relations with local Dutch traders. They subsequently tried to counter threats from Dutch and native enemies by allowing Bay colonists to come to Connecticut, a strategy they soon had cause to regret. The English, delighted to settle near abundant meadows, arrived in droves but demanded submission as the price of an alliance—too high a price, as far as the Pequots were concerned. Choosing to strike before their adversaries outnumbered them, the Pequots launched an attack on Wethersfield in April 1637 that left nine colonists and 20 cattle dead, the first casualties of a brief but bloody war.[15]

Pequot tactics revealed a keen understanding of colonial dependence on livestock even though English settlement in the region had barely begun. Capt. Lion Gardiner recalled hearing Pequots boast that they had "killed Englishmen, and can kill them as mosquetoes, . . . and we will take away the horses, cows and hogs." Colonists suspected Pequots of trying to lure the Narragansetts into an alliance by promising that they would not have to fight the English in open battle but could simply "fire their houses, kill their cattle, and lie in ambush for them as they went abroad upon their occasions." The alliance never materialized—the Narragansetts ended up siding with the English—but in at least one instance the Pequots indeed waited for a group of colonists to venture out to gather hay and surprised them. Yet they could not hold out for long against a better-armed adversary. In May 1637 the English and their native allies launched an astonishingly brutal assault on a Pequot fort that left hundreds of Indians dead, including many women and children. Shortly thereafter, the conflict ended with the Pequots defeated and Connecticut open for further settlement by colonists and their cattle.[16]

Nearly a generation of relative peace between Indians and colonists in southern New England followed the Pequot War. As various native groups, particularly the Narragansetts and Mohegans, vied with one another to establish a new balance of power in the region, they necessarily incorporated colonists into their political and diplomatic calculations. At the same time, colonists continued to arrive in great numbers; by 1640, over 13,000 had settled in New England. Once the Great Migration ended in 1642, natural increase more than compensated for the lack of new immigrants. By 1650, there were more than 22,000 colonists and in parts of eastern Massachusetts and the Connecticut Valley they outnumbered Indians. Demographic advantage, however, did not translate into outright dominion. These English majorities were highly localized and thus colonists were as eager as Indians to seek protection through alliances.[17]

Both sides reaped other benefits from cooperation. To an extent that had not existed before the Pequot War, and would not outlast the century, Indians and colonists constructed a web of mutually advantageous trade relations. Connecticut Valley Indians acted as key players in New England's fur trade, from which they and colonists such as William and John Pynchon profited. The Narragansetts and Wampanoags enhanced their political positions with economic dominance in the production of wampum, shell beads that colonists briefly used as currency and that Indians exchanged for European goods. Indians earned wages working for English employers, and colonists negotiated with native leaders for purchases of land. Taking advantage of this stable environment, Puritan missionaries began proselytizing among Indians. Even surviving Pequots regained a foothold in Connecticut. From the vantage point of 1640, there seemed little reason to doubt that amicable relations could persist.[18]

This is not to suggest that conflict between Indians and colonists utterly disappeared, even in the short run. During the 1640s, New England colonies worried enough about a rumored alliance between the Narragansetts and Mohawks to form their own defensive league. Hostilities erupting between native groups, most notably the Narragansetts and Mohegans, likewise alarmed English settlers. Following Opechancanough's defeat in 1646, Anglo-Indian relations in the Chesapeake calmed down, although sporadic fighting broke out in Maryland in the 1640s and Virginia in 1656.[19] Even so, Indians and colonists in each region followed somewhat different trajectories to reach a *modus vivendi* that seemed to reduce the chances for large-scale conflict on the order of the early wars. In good part this was due to the fact that native autonomy had diminished and demographic trends favored the colonists. Yet at the same time it appeared that both groups increasingly saw advantages to making accommodations instead of war with each other.

To a considerable extent, those accommodations involved learning to live with livestock as well as with each other. As colonists adapted their husbandry to take advantage of abundant land and compensate for scarce labor, they altered the world in which Indians also lived. The English alone judged the New World as incomplete without livestock in it. To Indians, the environmental integrity of America had never been in doubt and indeed the arrival of livestock disrupted a place that functioned perfectly well without them. Yet native peoples could not avoid these animal intruders simply by staying away from English settlements. Livestock's free-ranging habits inevitably brought them into contact even with distant Indian villages, extending the geographic area affected by colonization well beyond the boundaries of plantations and towns. North and south, colonial husbandry practices forced native peoples to come to terms with animals they did not necessarily welcome. An era of relative calm gave Indians time to consider whether livestock could be made to serve them as well as they did the colonists.

The adaptations that colonists made in adjusting to life in the New World, extensive though they were, paled in comparison with the changes imposed upon Indians. If the arrival of European diseases had the greatest impact on native societies, the introduction of Old World animals proved at least as wide-ranging in its effects. Livestock presented conceptual challenges to Indians who had to incorporate domesticated creatures into a world where virtually all other fauna were wild. The new animals helped to transform the local environment and inspired colonists to make changes on their behalf. Livestock interfered with native subsistence practices in ways that could neither be ignored nor easily remedied and may even have exacerbated the epidemiological crises that periodically afflicted native villages. English animals, along with the people who brought them, reconfigured the Indians' world into a very different place from what it had been before the newcomers arrived.

The Indians' initial impulse to regard English animals as variations of familiar American beasts fell afoul of the colonists' insistence that the two kinds of creatures remain distinct. And because colonists were willing to enforce their views through legal and other means, Indians had little choice but to go along. Native hunters who got in trouble for shooting hogs learned not to think of the creatures as analogous to any American animal, no matter how close the resemblance, or even to use the same word to describe them. Indians soon invented new names for different livestock species, acknowledging the animals' alien character. Narragansetts, who once called pigs *ockqutchaun* (woodchuck), began referring to them as *pígsuck* or *hógsuck*. Cows became *côwsnuck* and goats *gôatesuck*, hybrid names that linked an English root with a Narragansett suffix. "This Termination *suck*, is common in their language," Roger Williams explained, "and therefore they adde it to our *English* Cattell, not else knowing what names to give them." John Eliot's study of the Massachusett language, an eastern Algonquian dialect similar to Narragansett, revealed that the suffix *og* (possibly pronounced *uck* by Narragansetts) formed the plural of nouns representing animate beings. Massachusett speakers who referred to the *oxesog* and *horsesog* on English farms also affirmed the animals' foreign provenance. Yet the Indians' verbal compromise went only so far. Their refusal simply to adopt the colonists' names for livestock implied a deliberate rejection of complete English linguistic supremacy.[20]

Pigs and cows, whatever names they were called, rapidly made themselves at home in the Indians' physical as well as their mental world. Over time, livestock not only infiltrated places where Indians dwelled but also changed them. By grazing selectively on certain plants, domestic animals eventually altered the composition of meadows and forests, compacting the soil in areas where they congregated in significant numbers. Livestock shipped from abroad deposited the seeds of European weeds as well as grasses with their dung. Colonists who cleared woodlands to improve grazing for sheep hastened soil erosion that in turn altered stream patterns through sedimentation. Some indigenous creatures, such as wolves, squirrels, and crows, may have proliferated due to a steady diet of English livestock or grains. Others, including deer, suffered from changes in their habitat and either declined in numbers or moved away, or both.[21]

Many of these environmental transformations, however, lay well in the future. For much of the seventeenth century colonists and their animals occupied fairly limited areas, lessening the overall impact of broad ecological shifts. Whether they moved to New England or the Chesapeake, colonists at first staked out farms where they could catch a whiff of salt in the air, or at least be near rivers that emptied into the Atlantic. Practical reasons—especially, in the Chesapeake, access to waterways useful for transporting tobacco to market—largely dictated these choices, but the distribution of colonial homesteads may also have reflected a nostalgic urge to stay close to the same sea that washed the shores of England. Along seacoasts and riverbanks, existing open spaces and forest clearings immediately attracted the colonists' attention as the best sites for planting fields and the most luxuriant grasslands for livestock. The surrounding woods could be harvested for firewood and building material, and only later would settlers have to embark on large-scale clearing of trees and brush for additional crop land. Like deer and other wildlife, English settlers and their animals thrived in edge habitats where a diversity of resources could be found.[22]

These were also the places Indians chose for their settlements. In New England, the largest native villages appeared in the Connecticut Valley. Smaller communities clustered along the coast, especially near Narragansett and Massachusetts Bays, Cape Cod, and southern Connecticut, and on the largest offshore islands. To the south, Indians concentrated their villages along the network of waterways feeding into Chesapeake Bay. The salt marshes that attracted cattle-owning colonists in both regions sheltered an abundance of plants and animals that sustained Indian populations. Many of the clearings that colonists assumed were natural features perfect for grazing livestock were in fact produced by Indians who burned selected areas to improve the habitat for game. With different ideas of land use in mind, colonists flocked to precisely the same areas preferred by Indians.[23]

Some places once inhabited by Indians lay vacant, their residents lost to disease or displaced by bouts of warfare with colonial forces. Survivors may have been in no hurry to return to scenes of such devastation, yet the establishment of colonial settlements on these sites rendered them permanently off-limits to use by native peoples. As much as contagion and conflict reshaped the human geography of New England and the Chesapeake, however, these factors did not relegate colonists and Indians to living in distinct zones. There emerged instead a mosaic of native and English communities situated along seashores and inland waterways. In many cases, particularly in New England, Indian villages and colonial settlements sat cheek by jowl with one another.[24]

Neither group confined its subsistence activities to the bounds of its actual settlements. Indians, whose more flexible notion of territoriality encompassed use rights to diverse environments, regularly ventured beyond their houses and planting fields into surrounding areas to hunt, fish, and gather wild plants. The colonists spent most of their time on their privately held lands, but sent livestock to forage in many of the same places that Indians used for a variety of purposes. It was in these interstices between their respective settlements where environmental changes caused by colonization were concentrated and where Indian and English settlers really learned what it meant to have each other as neighbors.[25]

These were also the places where indigenous fauna most frequently confronted roaming livestock. The effects of these encounters on deer—an animal that supplied Indians with skins for clothing, bones and antlers for tools, and much of the meat in their diet—are difficult to assess. Until colonists turned to large-scale land clearing and more intensive farming practices, which did not occur until the eighteenth century at the earliest, deer and livestock shared the woods and open spaces at the edges of settlements. Very selective eaters, deer sought out a variety of seasonally available, highly digestible forage. In the spring they grazed on young grass; in summer they consumed other herbaceous ground covers. Their diet in autumn and winter consisted of fruit, nuts, mushrooms, leaves, and twigs. These food sources appealed to livestock too. Cattle and horses grazed in natural meadows and on the undergrowth in the woods. Swine gnawed the roots of plants that produced leaves and bark for deer and, in autumn, joined deer in scouring the forest floor for acorns and other nuts. Even so, during most of the seventeenth century competition from English animals probably had limited impact on deer populations. Free-ranging livestock were not yet numerous enough and for the most part were too widely dispersed to deprive deer of sufficient forage, except perhaps in the immediate vicinity of English settlements. If deer populations declined during this period, severe weather and overhunting, not competition from livestock, were the likeliest causes.[26]

A different threat may have come from diseases that livestock introduced to America, yet once again the extent of the impact is unclear. Although anthrax, tuberculosis, influenza, and various bovine viruses accompanied livestock across the Atlantic and eventually afflicted deer populations, it is difficult to know if any of these maladies plagued New World animals before European contact. At the very least the arrival of livestock intensified the disease environment by providing additional hosts for dangerous germs and new avenues of infectious transmission. American and European animals shared parasites as well. Deer and livestock both grew debilitated from infestations of lungworms, meningeal worms, liver flukes, and other organisms.[27]

New World peoples, not just fauna, may also have fallen victim to livestock-borne diseases. Several of the deadliest afflictions, including smallpox, diphtheria, and measles, required human-to-human contact in order to generate epidemics, but tuberculosis and influenza could be contracted from domestic animals. Some forms of tuberculosis may have existed in the New World prior to European contact, but bovine strains arriving with cattle increased the chance of infection. Swine, the animals most frequently encountered by Indians, carried tuberculosis bacilli as well as flu viruses and the trichina worm. Thus Indians may have been justified in reasoning, as one colonist reported, that meat from livestock was "Unwholsom for their Bodies, filling them with sundry Diseases." Some English settlers also suggested that Indians were unusually susceptible to what they described as colds and "consumption." Those who survived an initial bout of disease often emerged in a weakened state, vulnerable to subsequent ailments that would not necessarily have imperiled a healthy individual.[28]

The germs that wreaked havoc on Indian populations were invisible intruders; their livestock hosts, however, were not only visible but increasingly ubiquitous. Indians did not understand exactly how English animals could be sources of contagion any more than colonists did, but they came to regard the creatures as troublesome for different reasons. Livestock may not initially have competed much with deer and other wildlife, but they posed a direct threat to Indians. From the moment they arrived in the New World, English animals intruded upon nearly every activity that contributed to Indians' subsistence. Shut out of colonial fields by fences and exiled from English communities during the growing season, hungry livestock did not have to travel far to find native lands ripe for the picking.

Indian women, responsible for horticultural production in their villages, learned to despise the roaming livestock that heralded a new English plantation or town in the vicinity. The fields of corn, beans, and squash native women tended as meticulously as gardens could be devastated in a matter of hours. Approaching their fields with hoes in hand, they found cornstalks and other plants stripped bare or trampled to the ground. Uprooted crops and mounds of dirt offered telltale signs that gangs of hogs had come and gone. If the perpetrators remained at the scene of destruction, they were as likely to keep on eating as run away at the approach of indignant farmers. Such nonchalance added insult to injuries that could amount, even by colonists' self-interested reckoning, to as much as 30 bushels of corn at a time. As if spoiling crops in the field were not enough, hogs figured out how to dig their way into the Indians' buried baskets of harvested grains and "rob their garners." Exasperated native women enlisted the help of their menfolk "to roll the bodies of trees" over these storage pits to thwart "those pioneers whose thievery they as much hate as their flesh."[29]

Moving beyond the bounds of their planting fields, Indian women encountered further evidence of the destructive potential of English livestock. When they traveled to the usual places to collect materials for weaving mats and baskets, the women might find bare or trampled spaces instead of thick marsh grasses and reeds. In New England, the scythes of fodder-gathering colonists left even larger swaths of stubble. Sometimes the tender bark of willow and other trees used for basketry showed signs of gnawing by livestock. Groups of Indian women and children making autumn expeditions into the woods to gather nuts and berries occasionally discovered that hogs had gotten there first. In coastal areas, native women hurried to beaches at low tide to dig for clams, trying to beat rooting swine to the shellfish. The omnivorous beasts, reviled by Narragansett women as "filthy cut throats," could in short order make significant inroads on one of the Indians' most important winter food sources.[30]

Indian men had equally compelling reasons to resent the way livestock infiltrated hunting grounds. Accidental shootings were probably more common than suspicious colonists, inclined to accuse Indians of deliberate malice, were willing to admit. When Virginia's House of Burgesses granted the Chickahominies and Pamunkeys "free liberty of hunting in the woods without the English fenced plantations," the legislators neglected to consider the possible consequences for livestock foraging in the same regions. Deer and cattle grazing side by side in tall grass or thick brush presented confusing targets for native bowmen still grappling with the unfamiliar notion that one creature was legitimate game but its companion was not. Large communal hunts, during which as many as two or three hundred native men surrounded herds of deer or drove them towards water, might sweep up hogs or cows at the same time. Cattle and swine, the latter attracted by the acorns often used as bait, also became ensnared in traps meant for wild creatures. In the autumn, New England Indians might set as many as 50 traps within the bounds of just a few miles. Plymouth governor William Bradford, who once ended up hanging in the air by one leg after stepping into one of these "very pretie devise[s]," could testify to the hidden dangers lurking in seemingly innocuous stretches of forest. As if in retaliation, hungry swine that avoided capture might devour the carcasses of ensnared deer before native trappers could retrieve them.[31]

It is hardly surprising that angry Indians often fought back against the creatures that caused so much trouble. Eastern Shore Indians who engaged in a "Continuall Trade of killing of hogs" outside Chesapeake plantations defended themselves against relentless invaders of their villages. The eight native women in southern Connecticut who surrounded and killed one of the colonists' "great fatt swine" around "the tyme of greene eares of corne" probably retaliated for its attack on the fruits of their labor. The women looked on with satisfaction as their male companions dispatched nine more of the despised beasts. New Haven officials, aware of similar episodes, reluctantly acknowledged a direct link between "our trespassinge uppon their corne, & their killing our swinne." So too did Mattagund, a native leader in Maryland, who announced, "Let us have no Quarrels for killing Hogs no more than for the Cows Eating the Indians Corn."[32]

Yet Indians' confidence that killing livestock was a justifiable act of retribution aroused sustained colonial protest. No amount of provocation, in the colonists' view, warranted the deliberate destruction of animal property. As a result, the precarious peace between the two peoples threatened to disintegrate under the pressure of disagreements about how to confront what was rapidly becoming a major problem. The most direct solution of confining livestock in fenced pastures and pens was for the time being beyond the means of colonial farmers. Yet they could hardly expect Indians to tolerate animal trespasses until they could do so. The stakes on each side—the safeguarding of food supplies—were high enough to compel collaboration in managing a crisis that would not go away on its own. The challenge for everyone involved lay in figuring out how to reduce the incidence of animal incursions and to forgive whatever trespasses still occurred.

Nursing separate grievances, Indians and colonists struggled to resolve the seemingly intractable problems that livestock created. Progress depended on each group's willingness to concede the legitimacy of the other's complaints and accept the necessity of compromise. Though dominant in southern New England and the Chesapeake, colonists did not wield sufficient power to impose a solution upon native peoples disinclined to help with enforcement. Indians, in turn, were in no position to make demands that colonists refused to endorse. Proceeding in an unsystematic, ad hoc fashion, the two peoples groped their way toward expedients that helped to reduce friction, if not to eliminate its root cause. In the end, their efforts in this regard partook as much of diplomacy as of law.

Trespass problems mostly affected Indians and colonists who lived near one another, and who interacted not just as neighbors and trading partners but also as allies. Their leaders knew that minor disputes, if left to fester, could weaken mutually beneficial economic and political connections. Thus trespass accusations, which colonists treated among themselves as private legal matters, became public affairs whenever Indians and colonists were involved. Sachems and magistrates intervened as representatives of their respective communities, agreeing on general procedures and determining specific remedies. English authorities typically retained the upper hand, making sure that agreements were written down in their own language and insisting that colonial officials serve as final arbiters. Even so, native leaders recognized opportunities to enhance their own prestige through such negotiations. Every successfully resolved dispute advertised their skill at defending native interests against English encroachments. Chiefs who received corn or goods in recompense for trespass damages could redistribute them as largess to their followers. For leaders who had subordinated themselves to English rule, yet did not regard their condition as subjugation, such public displays offered evidence that native authority had not been totally compromised by the shifting balance of power.[33]

Indians never doubted that their lands deserved protection from English animals but colonists, who often exaggerated the extent of native mobility in order to undermine Indians' territorial claims, needed a bit of coaxing to concede the point. Because land occupied by native peoples lacked the permanent dwellings, fences, and other improvements that the English associated with private property, colonists tended to see it as free for them to appropriate. They proved willing, however, to make an exception for Indian cornfields, which showed enough evidence of the application of labor to make good native claims to ownership. It thus became the colonists' responsibility, as Massachusetts legislators admitted in 1640, to "keepe their cattle from destroying the Indians corne in any ground where they have a right to plant."[34]

When colonists tried to shift the burden to Indians by suggesting that they build fences around their cornfields, native people insisted that they did not know how to do so. Indians in fact knew how to erect defensive palisades around their villages, but apparently did not care to go to so much trouble to protect planting fields. They replied that the only kind of fence they used was made by "tying strings of bark from pole to pole round the field" to frighten birds. Fluttering strips of bark, however, were no deterrent for livestock. Colonists would have to teach Indians how to make animal-proof barriers. A Massachusetts law accordingly obliged teams of colonists to work with Indians "in felling of Trees, ryving & sharpning railes, and holing of posts." When the rails were ready, colonists would "draw the fencing into place for them." Selectmen in Warwick, Rhode Island, appropriately enough taxed cattle to raise money to build fences for the Indians and ordered one member of every English family to help with construction. In Virginia, the governor appointed commissioners to arrange for the Indians' instruction; once they got the hang of it, Indians would be expected to erect their own fences.[35]

Unruly livestock, however, tended to treat fences as a challenge, not a deterrent. When such beasts broke into native fields, Indians had permission to seize and impound them. Native peoples living near Rehoboth in Plymouth Colony, which suffered from a plague of unmanageable livestock, got plenty of experience in chasing after pigs and cows. Colonial officials told them either to drive trespassing animals to Rehoboth's pound and demand satisfaction from the owners or, if a neighboring town's pound was closer, to bring the beasts there. In a telling aside that revealed how far free-range livestock could go, Plymouth magistrates allowed Indians to collect double damages if they had to drive the errant beasts more than eight miles to the nearest pound. There is less evidence of colonial authorities instructing Indians to impound trespassing animals in the Chesapeake, where few English settlements even had such enclosures. Yet in at least one instance,

Maryland's Provincial Court ordered colonists to help Indians near Portobacco build a pound and required one of the Charles County commissioners to make sure native farmers received restitution for trespass damage.[36]

Indians and colonists encountered each other often enough as they went about their daily routines but rarely worked together at common tasks, especially ones that brought Englishmen into native villages for days at a time. As native men labored alongside colonists hewing logs and heaving rails into place, they were doubtless impressed by the inconvenience of such tedious endeavors. Colonists, when the work was finished, may have congratulated themselves on making the Indians' cornfields look a bit more civilized. From their perspective, the new fences served as tokens of the Indians' introduction to English farming practices. Perhaps the next step would be to encourage Indians to get some cows and hogs of their own, which would allow them to abandon their wintertime hunting expeditions. Native men would then be free to work the fields, and native women to retreat to their houses to perform domestic duties. As an inducement to make Indians maintain the fences that had symbolic as well as practical uses, colonial authorities awarded damages for animal trespass only to native plaintiffs who could prove that unruly livestock had broken through intact barriers. It also seemed fair to the English that the same conditions that governed their ability to obtain restitution for animal trespass among themselves be applied to Indians as well.[37]

But fairness, like beauty, lay in the eyes of the beholder. Indians who were being told to adopt English remedies to deal with problems introduced by the colonists in the first place were in a better position to appreciate the irony of the situation. Procedures for awarding compensatory damages revealed other limits to the colonists' impartiality. Colonial magistrates alone judged the validity of native complaints and chose Englishmen to view damaged crops and determine the amount of compensation. Only once, in Plymouth Colony in 1660, were Indians permitted to select the "indifferent man of the English" who would investigate their case. Colonists stipulated the form in which recompense would be paid—usually corn, sometimes wampum, rarely money. No evidence survives of any decision being subject to negotiation. In the Bay Colony, before they could even begin the process of obtaining redress, aggrieved Indians had to identify the specific town where trespassing livestock belonged. No community wanted to pay if its own animals were not at fault, and so it was up to the Indians to look for paint or brand marks on the creatures and learn which mark belonged to which town.[38]

New Englanders may not have made it easy for Indian plaintiffs to obtain restitution, but they were more accommodating than Chesapeake colonists who scarcely bothered to consider native grievances at all.[39] Part of the problem stemmed from the planters' own disorganization when it came to livestock control. Lacking the town-centered institutions that governed such matters in New England, Chesapeake settlers quarreled with one another constantly over animal trespass and theft. This background inevitably hampered Indians in their pursuit of justice. If they went ahead and procured their own compensation in the form of the offending animals, Indians risked summary execution, often without even a warning. The legacy of warfare in early Virginia, which prompted colonists to see livestock-killing as evidence of belligerent intentions, surely encouraged such a violent response. Yet Maryland's comparatively amicable Indian relations proved no better at fostering peaceful negotiation. Dealing with trespass problems through treaties rather than court proceedings, which reinforced the impression that these were diplomatic matters, Chesapeake officials obligated native signers to leave livestock alone. They generally stipulated that Indians who stole or killed livestock were to be turned over to colonial magistrates to be punished like colonists convicted of the same offense. But some treaties, especially if the signatories included native peoples of uncertain loyalties, abandoned the principle of equal treatment. In the1660s Marylanders' suspicions about the Delaware Indians inspired unusually harsh treaty provisions that allowed colonists to shoot any of them caught killing cattle or hogs, as if they were wolves and not humans. No treaty balanced the penalties against Indians with the requirement that colonists compensate them for damage to native cornfields.[40]

These treaties, which ignored the specific circumstances of any dispute, were clumsy instruments for dealing with animal trespass. Having subordinated themselves to English rule, however, Tidewater-area Indians had little room to maneuver for better terms with colonists lacking any inclination to grant them. In the end both sides relied, rather optimistically, on physical separation to reduce the chances of trespass problems. Following the English colonists' victory over the Powhatans in 1646, Virginia's government relocated Indian survivors to lands north of the York River and simultaneously required colonists to remove any livestock located there. In the rare instances when Indians had the power to do so, they made similar demands in an effort to protect their fields from English animals. Machoatick Indians in Virginia's Northumberland county, for example, agreed to let Isaac Allerton occupy some of their land in 1650 only if he kept his cattle and hogs across a river.[41]

All of these measures aimed to make Indian planting grounds off-limits to colonial livestock. Yet even if every cornfield were surrounded by an indestructible fence or located across a wide river, English animals would still have annoyed Indians. Native peoples subsisted not only on the crops they grew, but also on the plants they gathered and the meat they caught in the forest. Livestock were no more welcome there than they were in cornfields. Getting the English to look at the situation from the Indians' point of view, however, was virtually impossible. Colonists who grudgingly acknowledged exclusive native rights to planting fields and were willing to pay restitution for damaged crops simply could not conceive of the woods as the Indians' exclusive domain.

The colonists' position did not reflect a lack of imagination so much as an impulse to think about the New World in light of English experience. The closest analogy to the American woods that colonists could think of were the wooded areas in English villages known as "waste." Custom dictated that such places could be used in common by villagers for such activities as gathering wood, hunting small animals, and fishing, with the understanding that no one squandered the resources to be found there. Having made this connection, no doubt noting that Indians used the woods much as English people exploited waste land, colonists took the next logical step and concluded that the American forest should be available for common use by Indians and colonists alike.[42]

The colonists may have reasoned from ethnocentric principles, but their notion of sharing the woods nevertheless represented a rare moment of serendipity in a relationship more often plagued by misunderstanding and antagonism. Indians, like the English, had a well-established tradition of common use rights to uncultivated territory.[43] If they proved equally willing to share the woods with the colonists, each group in effect extending its customary practices to include the other, the two peoples could avoid destructive competition for land. The only potential complication lay in the colonists' insistence that letting livestock loose to forage constituted an appropriate use of the woods. For a time, however, Indians were willing to entertain the notion that the problems caused by livestock in the forest were not so serious as to preclude coexistence.

In the expectation that their interests could be compatible, colonists and Indians forged agreements to use uncultivated land jointly. As with matters of trade and diplomacy, these arrangements invoked the principle of reciprocity to reinforce existing alliances. Generally good relations between Providence settlers and Pautuxet Indians north of Narragansett Bay provided the context for one joint-use deal between Benedict Arnold and the Pautuxet sachem, Sockananoco, in 1644. The native leader sold a piece of land to Arnold and allowed him to gather wood and graze his cattle on adjacent native territory so long as in return the Englishman fenced Pautuxet cornfields.[44] Tunxis Indians reached a similar understanding with colonists in Connecticut's Farmington Valley in 1650, although native negotiators there operated at a disadvantage. As tributaries of the more powerful Suckiags, they had to abide by land sales made a decade earlier by Sequassen, the Suckiags' chief sachem, which transferred the whole of the Farmington Valley to Hartford settlers. The 1650 treaty required the Tunxis Indians to exchange a tract of cultivated land with the colonists for another piece of ground. In return, the Indians could hunt, fish, and cut wood within the English town of Farmington, so long as it "be not dun to the breach of any orders in the country to hurt cattle." Explicitly identifying the waste as open to all, the document further declared that fishing, hunting, and fowling would be "equally free to English and Indians."[45]

During the middle decades of the seventeenth century, glimpses of Indian hunters or fishermen going about their business in New England towns were commonplace occurrences. This was especially true near Mohegan settlements in Connecticut. The Mohegans, valuable allies of the Connecticut and Massachusetts Bay colonies, had supported the English against the Pequots in 1637 and the Narragansetts in the 1640s. This friendship earned Mohegan men the freedom to hunt and fish almost anywhere on uncultivated land in southeastern Connecticut where herds of English cattle and hogs also foraged. Colonists did ask that the Indians respect Puritan sensibilities and refrain from such activities on the Sabbath.[46]

Joint-use arrangements appeared in the Chesapeake as well, although their terms reflected the region's different pattern of colonization. Because shared woodlands lay at large rather than being assigned to individual towns as in New England, agreements were sometimes vague about the geographic areas involved. One deal negotiated in Virginia in 1652 simply confirmed the Indians' "libertye of all Waste and unfenced Land" for their hunting without specifying precise boundaries. Detailed descriptions may have seemed irrelevant to the colonial legislatures making these arrangements, so long as Indians understood that the colonists' precious tobacco and cornfields were off-limits. Magistrates also made sure that Indians agreed to leave livestock alone in return for the freedom to hunt on the open range.[47]

Chesapeake officials, like New England townsmen, restricted joint-use deals to native groups with whom they maintained good relations. Virginians cooperated with Powhatans and other Tidewater Indians who had submitted to English authority. In Maryland, provisions for sharing uncultivated land appeared in formal articles of peace negotiated with Piscataways, Choptanks, and various Eastern Shore peoples. At times the reciprocal nature of these arrangements was merely implied. One treaty with Eastern Shore Indians in 1659 announced that colonists could graze their cattle on native lands but did not specifically guarantee the Indians' right to hunt in the same places. Another agreement negotiated between Marylanders and 12 native groups in 1666 quite explicitly declared that the Indians' freedom of "hunting Crabbing fishing & fowleing" would be preserved "inviolably" while the colonists' liberty to let their animals loose on the same land was presumed but not written down.[48]

What colonists meant by the inviolability of native hunting rights changed over time. Colonial authorities who offered such broad protection apparently equated hunting with the chase, not with trapping animals. Trapping may have conjured up unsavory images in English minds of poachers furtively setting snares on someone else's property. Although colonists did not directly refer to Indian trappers as poachers, native men who snared deer and other animals for food doubtless suffered from an implicit comparison with England's lower orders.[49] In the end, however, the colonists' move to restrict trapping derived less from its negative image and more from the frequency with which native traps captured livestock, a concern that Indians shared for different reasons.

Because Indian hunters set traps on waste land within New England towns, the problem was most visible there and the consequences measurable to northern farmers who kept better track of their animals. Indians had to pay for livestock hurt or killed in traps even though there was little they could do to prevent such accidents. One Indian who found the remains of a cow in a trap near Barnstable in August 1643 impressed Plymouth magistrates when he "did so ingenuously & playnely confesse the fault, and made dilligent enquiry" to find the cow's owner. However laudable his behavior, the native trapper still owed the owner 50 shillings in damages.[50] More interested in prevention than reparations, New England authorities began to curtail the Indians' freedom to set traps. According to an agreement made with Plymouth officials in 1648, a group of Wampanoags retained "free leave and liberty to hunt" in Barnstable so long as they visited their traps daily and "speedyli" released any ensnared livestock. Elsewhere colonial magistrates prohibited this method of hunting altogether. As early as 1640 Rhode Island authorities refused to allow Narragansetts to place traps on Aquidneck island. Mohegans, despite their alliance with Connecticut settlers, faced the same restrictions. Suspecting that the Indians intentionally set traps where cattle grazed, colonists limited the Mohegans' freedom to hunt within English towns to the use of bows and arrows.[51]

Indians must have puzzled over agreements that simultaneously guaranteed their liberty to hunt and yet placed restrictions on the methods they could use. It only became clear with time that colonists regarded Indians' freedom to hunt and indeed to share the use of waste land at all not as rights but as privileges granted by a sovereign English authority. In Virginia in 1661, for instance, Indians who wished to gather oysters or wild fruit near English plantations had to obtain a licence from county justices before proceeding.[52] Privileges, unlike rights, could be revoked. When sachems made their marks on deeds and treaties specifying joint use of land, they probably assumed that the documents ratified existing native claims, unaware that English signatories regarded those claims as contingent.

This peremptory attitude notwithstanding, the middle decades of the seventeenth century witnessed genuine efforts at cooperation as Indians and colonists dealt with a world that livestock had changed. The fact that each group believed its subsistence was at stake lent urgency to their negotiations. Together they agreed that crop lands deserved protection from trespassing animals and found ways to make that happen. Beyond the bounds of cultivated fields, Indians and colonists defined common ground where they could meet as neighbors, not competitors. Unanticipated (and probably unrecognized) convergences in cultural practices, from a shared understanding of use rights to a belief in the importance of paying restitution for injuries suffered, facilitated collaboration. While colonists did dominate the process of seeking compromise by insisting on using their own legal procedures, defining Indians' rights as revocable privileges, and threatening to enforce native compliance through violence, their actions nevertheless testified to a preference for peaceful solutions over confrontation. For a time, there was hope that the accommodation of one group of people need not require the displacement of the other.

      🐂   🐂   🐂

That mutual hope was founded upon two quite different sets of expectations. Indians tolerated livestock because they saw no alternative, not because they welcomed the changes that the animals introduced to the New World. Every concession Indians made, from building fences to checking for cattle ensnared in their traps, was a defensive measure, with the underlying goal of preserving native sovereignty and culture as completely as possible. Yet colonists anticipated precisely the opposite result from their efforts to accommodate the Indians' interests. They viewed their own concessions as temporary expedients, not evidence of a belief that Indian and English practices were equally deserving of protection. Colonists looked forward to the day, which they hoped was not too far distant, when Indians acknowledged the superiority of English culture and adopted it as their own. Only then would England's imperial vision for the New World be fulfilled.

    Convincing Indians to take up livestock husbandry figured prominently in these plans as a means of inculcating respect for animals as property and promoting steady habits, particularly among Indian men. As these and other outward changes took effect, colonists believed, Indians would become fit disciples of Christianity as they could not be in their original state. Yet despite their eagerness to advance the Indians' cultural and spiritual evolution, English authorities acted with caution when choosing the means by which they promoted native livestock husbandry. Rather than simply giving or selling animals to Indians, colonists preferred to dole them out as rewards for good behavior. They also relied heavily on the power of their own example to inspire change among the Indians. These indirect methods of familiarizing Indians with animal husbandry sometimes conferred substantial benefits on colonial farmers, making such practices even more appealing to those who resorted to them.

    By the middle of the seventeenth century, for instance, magistrates in several colonies undertook to enlist Indian aid in exterminating wolves, a campaign directly related to the expansion of livestock husbandry. Colonists expected to be the main beneficiaries of such an effort, but the elimination of predators also removed an important obstacle to the Indians' eventual acquisition of domestic animals. The timing and terms of hiring arrangements in different places reflected the prevailing level of colonial confidence in native loyalties. English officials were wary of letting armed Indians wander near farms and plantations until they were sure that their bullets or arrows would be aimed only at wolves. Although by 1642 other New England colonies distrusted the Narragansetts, Rhode Island's government still regarded them as allies and sent Roger Williams to solicit their help in destroying wolves on Aquidneck island. Later on Plymouth magistrates felt comfortable offering Wampanoags powder and shot as a reward for each wolf head brought in. More suspicious of local Indians whom they had subdued by force, Chesapeake authorities waited until the 1650s to hire native hunters and, far from providing them with ammunition, prohibited them from using English weapons at all. Virginia's burgesses may have been the only legislators to offer a cow as a wolf bounty, but in so doing they merely made explicit a link between wolf eradication and the Indians' adoption of livestock that colonists elsewhere took for granted.[53]

Colonial farmers soon discovered another way to exploit Indian labor and simultaneously offer native workers training in animal husbandry. They began to employ Indians as livestock keepers. Hiring Indians for this job, especially in New England, released scarce English laborers for other pressing tasks. Thomas Minor frequently engaged Indian workers on his Connecticut farm to care for cattle and otherwise supplement the labor he extracted from his sons. In the Chesapeake, Indian keepers as often as not performed a duty that otherwise went undone. Most native keepers were hired help, not indentured servants or slaves. Colonists preferred Indian youths for the job, in part because they could be assigned other outdoor tasks, but also perhaps to reinforce the notion that livestock husbandry was principally a male responsibility. Indian workers who absorbed this idea while working for colonists would presumably replicate the same division of labor once they returned to their villages and acquired their own animals. In this way, lessons in livestock husbandry furthered the Indians' general education in civility. On occasion they produced striking results. In May 1665 residents of the Plymouth Colony town of Rehoboth were so impressed with the transformation wrought in "Sam, the Indian that keeps the cows" that they voted to admit him as an inhabitant of their community. Tending cattle had helped to transform Sam into someone whom townspeople were willing to accept as a neighbor.[54]

Hiring native workers to keep cows sent a message that these particular animals ought to be the focus of the Indians' transition to livestock husbandry. Comparatively docile and quite versatile in their uses, cattle ideally instilled habits of industry and stewardship in their owners. One way for colonists to channel Indian preferences in the right direction was to supply cattle to chiefs, which marked the beasts as prestigious and hence desirable property. Giles Brent of Virginia may have had this result (and not just the chance to make a good bargain) in mind in August 1658 when he offered the Potomacs' chief a cow and a calf in return for clear title to land that Brent had already patented and apparently paid for. The chief might also have regarded this as a shrewd investment, since he obtained property that could reproduce itself.[55]

Colonial authorities were more reluctant—and Indian leaders more eager—to see native villages supplied with horses. English settlers used the animals for military purposes, and did not want to see Indians doing the same. In 1656 Massachusetts quite explicitly encouraged New England colonies to enact a comprehensive ban against selling horses to Indians in the interest of mutual defense. At various points, Plymouth officials either prohibited such sales altogether or banned only the sale of mares, to prevent Indian purchasers from acquiring breeding stock. The wholesale prohibition was in effect when the Wampanoag chief Metacom, known to the English as King Philip, made an "earnest request" to buy a horse in 1665. Unwilling to offend an influential native leader by denying his wish and yet averse to making an exception to the law, the Plymouth government decided to give him one rather than permit a purchase. The designated gift horse, formerly ridden by the trumpeter in the Governor's troop, may not have been the best the colony had to offer, but Metacom could still interpret the magistrates' gesture as a bow to his chiefly status. For their part officials gambled that, by substituting a diplomatic gift for a purchase, they forestalled the prospect of Metacom asking for another exemption. The level of calculation in their response only became evident when, that same day, Plymouth magistrates voted to allow an ordinary Indian named Keencomsett to buy a horse. Whereas the sachem's possible motives for desiring a mount invited misgivings, Keencomsett was a safer bet: he lived in Barnstable, wanted the horse "for his use in husbandry," and would remain under English supervision.[56]

Keencomsett, who had taken up English-style farming, offered a better model of the kinds of behavior the colonists hoped to instill than did Metacom. The Wampanoag sachem continued to live like an Indian and gave no indication that ownership of a horse might trigger any sort of cultural transformation in him or his followers. He could perhaps be trusted with a trumpeter's nag, but colonial officials had no interest in encouraging further acquisitions unless Metacom changed his ways. The last thing that colonists wanted to see was livestock roaming around Indian villages whose inhabitants lived much as they always had. The creatures were supposed to act as a catalyst for change, not a supplement to hunting and gathering. Thus English authorities tried to regulate the circumstances under which Indians acquired domestic animals to ensure that they helped to promote a new way of life.

By far the most vigorous demonstration of this policy occurred in New England, where a handful of ministers and laymen established 14 "praying towns" for Indians interested in Christian proselytization and training in civility. Between 1651 and 1674, over 2,000 Indians moved to praying towns in Massachusetts Bay and Plymouth, and on the offshore islands of Nantucket and Martha's Vineyard. Comprising perhaps a tenth of the native population of southern New England, these recruits included a number of survivors disoriented by devastating epidemics in their former homes. Rev. John Eliot, the foremost proponent of praying towns, took advantage of their misery by hinting that conversion to Christianity and civility might offer Indians protection from future onslaughts of disease. The possibility of maintaining good health, however, was but one of several advantages that Eliot and other colonial leaders dangled before prospective converts.[57]

Eliot had not at first anticipated that special communities would be needed; he hoped that Indians interested in hearing the Word of God could simply be induced to settle near the English. When it became clear that potential converts worried about their cornfields being overrun by livestock, Eliot concluded that a place "some what remote from the English" had to be found. Natick, situated on the western border of the Bay Colony town of Dedham, became the first of several such "remote" villages and the focus of Eliot's proselytizing energies. Hoping mainly to inspire Indian conversions, Eliot also intended to see that native residents were instructed "in Letters, Trades, and Labours" sufficient to bring them up to English standards.[58] Those labors included livestock husbandry, which the minister represented as a blessing as well as a duty. If the Indians worked just as hard as the English did, Eliot advised, they "should

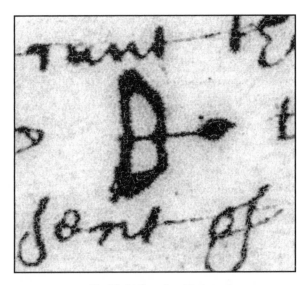

Natick Indians' cattle brand.
Courtesy of Massachusetts Archives

have cloths, houses, cattle, riches as [the English] have, God would give you them."[59]

Financial supporters of the praying towns accordingly provided livestock, plows, ox bells, and other equipment to launch native residents on a new way of life. The inhabitants learned to plow, cut hay, erect fences, and build barns, as well as to construct sturdier housing, wear English clothing, and worship in meetinghouses.[60] Their towns included plenty of meadow for livestock and visitors commented on native farmers' successful transition to animal husbandry. John Josselyn reported that the hogs raised and sold by Christian Indians "are counted the best in *New-England.*" Cattle and swine flourished in every praying town, despite one observer's assessment of native owners as "very far short of the English both in diligence and providence." Natick's herds had grown sufficiently numerous by 1670 that its inhabitants petitioned the Massachusetts General Court to assign them a town brand to distinguish their animals from those belonging to neighboring settlements. Although some form of the initial letter of a town's name customarily served as a brand mark for English communities, magistrates designated a bow and arrow for Natick—an ambiguous symbol at best, suggesting that no amount of acculturation would fully erase from English minds the sense that Indians remained fundamentally different from colonists.[61]

Because livestock husbandry introduced native practitioners to a hierarchical set of relations between people and animals, it intersected with
missionaries' religious as well as secular goals. Exemplifying a divinely
ordained human dominion over other creatures, it challenged Indian beliefs
in animals' spiritual equivalence and power. Members of Eliot's audience
may have been loath to alter their understanding of the natural world in such
a significant way. One of them confronted the minister directly on this issue,
asking "Why have not beasts a soul as man hath, seeing they have love, anger,
&c. as man hath?" In his published account of this exchange, Eliot did not
record his response, doubtless assuming his English readers had little need
of an explanation.[62]

Indians who accepted Christianity must in some measure have come to
terms with this new way of thinking about animals and may have helped to
spread the word to skeptical compatriots. In his *Indian Dialogues,* Eliot
depicted a Massachusett spokesman, Waban, expounding at length to his
fellow Indians about Creation and the way that God had given man "dominion
over all his works in this world." Although it presented imaginary dialogues
between Christians and unbelievers rather than actual debates, this work
reflected Eliot's deep familiarity with the kinds of questions posed by Indian
audiences. And it was no accident that the minister featured Waban so
prominently in this particular exchange. Eliot's first convert and one of the first
native preachers, Waban had embraced Christian teaching and could safely
be assigned the task of bringing his fellow Indians to a similar understanding.[63]

Whether Christianity fully superseded native religious beliefs, even for
Waban, remains an open question. Indian converts who succeeded in convincing Puritan ministers of their spiritual transformation described their progress
(through interpreters) in ways that resembled but did not replicate the
narratives of English believers. Focusing less on abstract theological concepts
and more heavily on their relationships with God and fellow Indians, converts'
testimony revealed an adherence to principles of moral reciprocity that were
as central to native religious culture as they were to Christianity. Such
convergences in belief smoothed Indians' path toward conversion yet also
provided room for familiar ideas to persist under the guise of change.[64] To what
extent their acknowledgment of animals' spiritual power, often expressed in
terms of reciprocity, survived the transition to a new faith is unclear. While
one prospective convert decried his former worship of "the Sun, Heavens,
Beasts, Trees, and everything in the world," and Natick residents were less

inclined than other New England Indians to use animal imagery in decorating baskets, pipes, and other material objects, deeply embedded ideas about animals may have endured. Yet even Natick Indians who wholeheartedly accepted Christian teachings about animals' place in the world would have puzzled over one element of Eliot's instruction—his stern admonition against the sin of bestiality. The minister's pronouncement revealed far more about the English and their livestock than he may have intended. For native peoples possessing limited experience with domesticated animals, the very idea of bestiality was at least bewildering and almost certainly abhorrent.[65]

No counterpart to the praying town appeared in the seventeenth-century Chesapeake. Indian children on occasion went to live in planters' households but were more likely to be exploited as laborers than educated as Christians. Some of these native youths would have been exposed to the planters' minimalist style of animal husbandry, but not as part of a concerted effort to encourage their acculturation. Chesapeake settlers were as fully committed as New Englanders to the notion that Indians ought to become civilized and that cattle could help make them Christians; they simply preferred to let matters take their own course rather than invest time and money in an enterprise that might not bring much in the way of quick returns.[66]

Colonists did not necessarily expect that it would be easy to convince Indians to alter their beliefs and behavior in response to English example and preaching. Yet of all the changes they hoped to effect, encouraging Indians to keep livestock probably seemed one of the easier projects. Indians who might have trouble understanding the finer points of Christian doctrine, or balk at seeing men instead of women hoeing cornfields, would surely recognize the advantages of animal husbandry once they learned how it worked. Colonial officials appeared to worry more that Indians would readily adopt this one English practice and ignore the rest of the civilizing agenda. It was thus important for Indians to acquire livestock under close supervision to ensure that their progress toward civility and Christianity continued. Colonists could not imagine that, in the long run, peaceful relations between the two peoples could endure unless Indians reshaped their lives and ceased being Indians.

The colonists' vision of the future was hardly one that Indians shared. Native peoples adapted to the English presence, but never with the intent of abandoning their own culture outright. Even Christian Indians, the most acculturated group of all, clung to native practices in spite of colonists' disapproval.[67] As it became clear that colonists intended for Indian livestock-keeping to spawn a host of other changes, the animals provoked even more native resentment than what was already generated by the creatures' prodigious ability to make nuisances of themselves. Symbols of civility to the English, livestock threatened to become symbols of cultural annihilation to Indians. For a time, Indians and colonists approached the problems posed by livestock as localized disputes best addressed in piecemeal fashion, allowing tensions to dissipate through negotiation and compromise. As years passed and those problems not only persisted but spread to new regions and affected new Indian groups, lasting solutions became harder to reach.

In 1641, one unusually prescient Narragansett sachem took stock of the changes that had occurred in southern New England in less than a lifetime and predicted disaster for his people. Miantonomi had supported the English four years earlier in the Pequot War, only to be horrified by the colonists' ruthless slaughter of Pequot women and children during that conflict. Relations between the English and the Narragansetts worsened after the war as colonial leaders, especially in Massachusetts and Connecticut, sought to dominate their erstwhile native allies. Fed up with this treatment, in the summer of 1641 Miantonomi visited the Montauks on the eastern tip of Long Island—where colonists and their animals had recently settled—to urge them to join in an attack against the English. In so doing, Miantonomi made one of the first known pleas for pan-Indian unity. He argued that Narragansetts and Montauks ought to put aside their differences and regard themselves as "all Indians as the English are, and say brother to one another; so must we be one as they are, otherwise we shall be all gone shortly."[68]

Miantonomi could have recited any number of examples of English perfidy—the murder of Pequot women and children, the refusal to give Pequot survivors and use of Pequot land to the Narragansetts as promised, holding Narragansetts responsible for misdeeds perpetrated by other Indians—to gain Montauk support. But these were grievances specific to the Narragansetts; to make his case he had to convince the Montauks that they too faced imminent danger. Miantonomi wisely chose the one issue sure to strike a nerve among the Montauks: the destruction that followed in the wake of the English and their livestock as surely as night followed day.

> [You] know our fathers had plenty of deer and skins, our plains were full of deer, as also our woods, and of turkies, and our coves full of fish and fowl. But these English having gotten our land, they with scythes cut down the grass, and with axes fell the trees; their cows and horses eat the grass, and their hogs spoil our clam banks, and we shall all be starved; therefore it is best for you to do as we.

He suggested a plan of attack, which included giving the English a taste of their own medicine by killing their women and children along with their soldiers. But the victims of Indian wrath would, for the time being, include "no cows, for they will serve to eat till our deer be increased again."[69]

Lt. Lion Gardiner, a veteran of the Pequot War, heard about Miantonomi's appeal from the Montauks who, instead of heeding the Narragansetts' call to arms, reported it to colonial authorities. Gardiner duly recorded the speech, but even in his recounting it bears eloquent witness to Indian, not English, fears. By 1641 livestock had ranged in Narragansett country for only half a dozen years and in neighboring Plymouth for less than two decades. Colonists regarded the animals' steady proliferation and the environmental alterations settlers made on the creatures' behalf as sources of pride, not concern. They scarcely noticed the disappearance of wildlife, which at any rate was nowhere near as far advanced as it would eventually be. If Gardiner had intended to invent, rather than record, an inflammatory speech, he would surely have emphasized Miantonomi's innate depravity or lust for power, themes that spoke more directly to English prejudices than a sachem's anxiety about cows replacing deer in the forest.

Miantonomi was a prophet, and like so many prophets found that he was without honor in his own country. The Montauks cast their lot with the colonists, hoping to advance their own interests through cooperation rather than conflict. So too did the Mohegans, the Wampanoags, and other Indians throughout southern New England who believed that artful negotiation and forms of resistance more subtle than warfare could avert the calamity that Miantonomi foretold. Indian peoples throughout the eastern Chesapeake whose world was also being transformed by English settlers and their animals likewise hoped that accommodation would prove a successful strategy for survival. The Narragansett sachem had no such illusions. But like many prophets, he did not live long enough to see his prediction come to pass. In the summer of 1643 he was captured by Uncas for plotting the

Mohegan chief's death and turned over to colonial officials for punishment. The English wished to protect their Mohegan allies but had no desire to execute Miantonomi themselves. So they returned him to Uncas with instructions to take the Narragansett leader back to Mohegan territory and put him to death there. A blow from a Mohegan club crushed Miantonomi's skull and silenced his voice. Yet his prophecy about the fate of Indian country would return like a ghost to haunt his enemies and friends alike.[70]

Chapter Seven

A Prophecy Fulfilled

*From Cooperation
to the Displacement of Indians*

*L*ess than 50 years after Miantonomi's death, Assateague Indians living hundreds of miles to the south of Narragansett country on Maryland's Eastern Shore witnessed the fulfillment of the northern sachem's ominous prediction. English settlers encroached on their lands from every direction except the east, where the ocean offered no avenue of escape. The comfortable subsistence Indian ancestors had enjoyed in a region with abundant resources gave way to fears of starvation. Slowly but inexorably, colonists appropriated native hunting territory, stripping away trees and undergrowth to make tobacco plantations. Livestock foraged as freely through Assateague cornfields as they did through the woods. No longer just passive companions of colonial farmers, as they had been in Miantonomi's day, by the 1680s the creatures functioned as highly effective instruments of English dominion.

During that decade Edward Hammond, a prominent Maryland planter, repeatedly directed his livestock toward an Assateague town as if they were artillery, intending to inflict widespread devastation. Choatam, the Assateagues' leader, reported that the trouble began with Hammond's complaint that Indian dogs had killed his swine. Slaying ten of those dogs and threatening to burn down the Indians' "Court house" did not suffice as revenge. Hammond and an accomplice then "drove their Cattle in our Town against our wills," Choatam claimed, and when the Indians erected barriers to stop them, the two Englishmen "broke them downe three severall times." Still enraged, Hammond prepared to deploy his heaviest weaponry. He announced his intention to "drive horses in our Towne in summer," Choatam declared, so that "we shall make noe corne." Such relentless aggression betrayed Hammond's real motives. Avenging dead hogs served as the flimsiest of pretexts for such belligerence. Hammond drew upon his animal arsenal in order to drive the Assateagues from their land.[1]

These assaults distressed the Assateagues mightily, for they had labored to maintain good relations with Maryland. The very fact that they refrained from answering Hammond's provocation with violence of their own and instead trusted the Provincial Council to see "that we may have Justice" testified to their forbearance. They had made every possible accommodation to the colonists' presence, submitting to the Proprietor's authority, settling permanently in towns with "Court houses," fencing their fields, and even acquiring their own pigs and horses. The English had responded with formal recognition of native title to the lands within those towns, but moved slowly in defending Indian rights against the likes of Edward Hammond and other recalcitrant planters. Joining with Pocomokes, Monoakins, and other belea-guered Eastern Shore peoples, the Assateagues protested in May 1686 that they were "daily and continually molested, troubled and perplexed with injurious breakeing in upon them of greate numbers of Cattle, horses and hoggs to the destruction of their Corne Fields." This recitation of current woes served equally well as a forecast of future troubles.[2]

Edward Hammond was unusually forthright in expressing his hostility toward Indians, but he was not alone in using livestock to displace them. Colonists elsewhere in the Chesapeake and in southern New England favored the same tactic, particularly wherever they enjoyed a substantial population advantage over local Indians. After 1660 it became clear that the mechanisms of negotiation and accommodation that had prevailed for decades rested upon an exceedingly fragile foundation. As calculations of self-interest were revised and good will evaporated, cooperation gave way to competition and, eventually, peace gave way to war.

Livestock were unwitting participants in this unfolding drama, as they had been since the beginnings of English colonization. Much of the impetus for English expansion derived from the colonists' concern for their animals' sustenance, a fact that Indians grasped only too clearly. That numerous Indian communities acquired their own livestock, turning the colonists' rationale against them in a futile attempt to preserve native control over land, bespeaks both the irony and the tragedy of the story. An adaptation that colonists had encouraged, and ought thus to have applauded, instead produced friction when it became obvious that Indians intended to pick and choose among the items on the English agenda for native cultural transformation. Owning cows did not make them Christians, much less apprentice Englishmen.

Seeing their plans go awry and feeling the pressure to sustain their own growing populations, colonists moved toward a new understanding of their imperial enterprise and the role of livestock in it. Less important as tools for introducing Indians to a civilized way of life, domestic animals assumed far greater significance as the means by which colonists established exclusive control over more and more territory. As agents of empire, livestock occupied land in advance of English settlers, forcing native peoples who stood in their way either to fend the animals off as best they could or else to move on. Before long a new generation of Indians glimpsed the same dismal future that Miantonomi had predicted decades earlier. Taking up arms to defend themselves against a rising tide of colonists and livestock, Indians discovered that it was too late for it to be turned.

Almost from the moment they arrived in the New World, English settlers urged Indians to acquire livestock, believing, like Roger Williams, that this would help native peoples to progress "from Barbarisme to Civilitie."[3] Convinced that such a project could only produce positive results, colonists gave little thought to possible adverse consequences. They merely wanted to supervise native peoples' transition to livestock ownership so as to ensure that other desirable cultural changes would accompany it. As events turned out, however, the colonists' wishes were only partially fulfilled. Indians indeed obtained livestock, but not in a manner that accorded with English plans.

Driven by colonial interference with their hunting and environmental alterations that may have reduced populations of indigenous fauna, Indians turned to livestock as an alternative source of meat. They not only hunted

English animals—much to the settlers' displeasure—but also assembled herds of their own. Native peoples living close to English settlements were the first to do so; as colonial settlements spread so too did the incidence of Indian livestock ownership. The Patuxents in Maryland may have obtained stocks of hogs as early as the 1640s. Other Chesapeake-area Indians, including Chopticos, Assateagues, Powhatans, and Weanocks, acquired them in the 1650s and 1660s. In southern New England, Shawomets, Wampanoags, Mohegans, and Montauks acquired swine at about the same time. Metacom, the Wampanoag sachem to whom Plymouth authorities reluctantly gave a horse, already owned pigs in the 1660s, as did Awashunkes, the "squaw sachem" of Saconet. Indians in Oyster Bay on Long Island circumvented colonial restrictions to obtain horses. Virtually every one of these native groups found ways to procure livestock without resorting to English intermediaries.[4]

Colonists had not anticipated that Indians would be so resourceful. But free-range husbandry, even in its seasonal New England version, frustrated attempts to dole out livestock to Indians in carefully controlled settings where Englishmen could impress native recipients with other attractions of civilized life. The animals were ubiquitous, for the most part untended, and their status as someone else's property appeared more hypothetical than real. Colonists typically assumed that Indians who possessed livestock were thieves, a questionable assumption given the frequency with which English settlers gave up on trying to recover animals lost to woods and swamps. It is just as likely that Indians assembled their herds from wandering livestock abandoned by colonial owners. Moreover, particularly in the Chesapeake, there was a plentiful supply of feral livestock available for Indians to tap. That was precisely what one Choptico chief did in the spring of 1660. Encountering a wild sow that had recently farrowed, the Indian killed the fierce adult and took the piglets to raise for his own stock.[5]

From the colonists' perspective, this was a frustrating evasion of English plans, but it might have been overlooked had livestock ownership spurred Indians toward civility. Instead of complying with English expectations for cultural change, however, Indians found ways to incorporate livestock into their lives with minimal disruption. Nothing revealed their conservative strategy more clearly than their distinct preference for hogs over other livestock species.[6] Though Indians prized horses, the animals' dietary requirements and general boisterousness, along with their relative scarcity

in certain colonies, discouraged significant native investment in the creatures. Cattle—the animals identified by colonists as the likeliest to foster
civility—were also deemed more trouble than they were worth, particularly
in New England where they could not survive without winter fodder and
shelter. Indians saw no reason to replace skilled women farmers with oxen
and plows, and a tendency toward lactose intolerance eliminated any interest
in raising cows for their milk.[7] A supply of meat was what Indians wanted,
ideally obtained with no greater effort than hunting normally required. Hogs
fit the bill better than any other kind of livestock.

The Choptico chief who brought the wild piglets back to his village had
learned enough about domestication to make an important distinction
between English animals and American fauna: he probably never raised
fawns or bear cubs for food. But he and other Indians who acquired livestock
had observed colonists long enough to see that swine could be used in this
way. What made hogs particularly appealing was their ability to fit niches
occupied by animals already familiar to Indians. Pigs, like dogs, could
scavenge in native villages. Indians who threw food scraps to swine, like
colonists who lured livestock back to their farms with corn, kept the beasts
in a semidomesticated state. The fences that Indians built around their
cornfields at the colonists' behest deterred native-owned hogs as readily as
English ones. If any of their own hogs broke through a fence they could be
dispatched without fear of penalty. Native hunters tracked down swine that
took to the woods in the same way that they pursued deer or other prey,
which is how colonists often retrieved their hogs. At least where swine were
involved, Indians not only adopted a colonial creature but also the colonists'
highly attenuated form of animal husbandry.

Once they had been slaughtered, pigs could be put to many of the same
uses as American prey animals, and not just as meat. Colonial observers
watched Indian women in southern Connecticut treat hog carcasses like bear
flesh, boiling them to render the fat and make "pummy." The solidified fat
could be eaten on its own or mixed into stews of meat and vegetables. In this
case, however, the enterprising Indian women filled bottles with the pummy
and sold it to Mohegans.[8] Daniel Gookin, reporting on changing Indian
practices in 1674, mentioned another way that pigs substituted for bears.
Indians "used to oil their skins and hair with bear's grease heretofore," he
noted, "but now with swine's fat." Hogs, like deer, supplied raw material for
leather. Several New Englanders noticed Indians wearing moccasins fash-

ioned from "green [i.e., untreated] hogs skinns."[9] From the Indians' point of view, swine were by far the most versatile of English livestock.

They were also by far the most prolific. Cows and mares would generally not begin to reproduce until they were three years old, and then almost always bore just one offspring at a time. Pigs bore litters of three to seven young as early as their second year. Thus even if the Choptico chief brought home only three or four feral piglets in the spring of 1660, within a couple of years they could easily have produced a herd of several dozen animals. Indians intent on acquiring livestock to augment diminished meat supplies from indigenous animals could not have chosen a better creature for such a purpose than the hog.[10]

Colonists were by no means impressed with this display of Indian adaptability. Pigs were the least prestigious of livestock species, reviled by English farmers for their filthy habits and nasty dispositions.[11] The Indians' preference for such a creature over cattle did not speak well for their capacity to make good choices. Colonists furthermore knew that swine would do little to induce native owners to embrace an English way of life. Hog-keeping would not encourage Indian men to take their wives' places in tilling cornfields, as the adoption of oxen and plows would do. Because swine required little care or supervision, they failed to instill in their owners a strong sense of stewardship. About the only advantage to be gained from native hog-keeping was that Indians became accustomed to the notion that living animals could be considered property. Colonists had from the start reasoned that ownership of animals and other property would discourage Indians from contemplating aggression against the English. According to this logic, even lowly pigs could promote the cause of peace.[12]

Once again Indian ingenuity confounded colonial expectations. Indians viewed their new possessions not only as food but also as trade goods. From Massachusetts to Virginia, they began selling meat to colonial consumers, directly competing with English farmers. Outraged colonists denounced their rivals for stealing the creatures whose flesh they sold, which sometimes no doubt was true. But since native entrepreneurs frequently appeared in places where Indians were known to have their own animals, larceny need not always have been involved. In 1651 English farmers from Hempstead on Long Island accused Indians of selling meat from stolen livestock to Dutch consumers on Manhattan, horning in on a market the English preferred to keep to themselves. Marylanders similarly charged Indians during the 1660s with taking colonists' animals and selling the meat. Maryland officials actually subverted the civilizing agenda by insisting that Indians stick to hunting wild animals; they could supply colonists with "venison or wild fowle" but not beef or pork. In 1669 Plymouth settlers, vexed to find themselves outmatched by sharp Indian traders, took perhaps the most drastic step of all. To discourage Indians from carrying pork to Boston and selling it there "att an under rate" (that is, at a lower price than Plymouth merchants charged), magistrates proposed renewing the suspended trade in arms. Indians apparently used the proceeds of their pork sales in Boston to buy guns from licensed Bay Colony merchants. If they could acquire weapons locally, Plymouth officials surmised, Indians would cede the intercolonial pork trade to Plymouth producers. Providing Bostonians with cheap meat, however, was not part of the deal. The aim of Plymouth's policy was to ensure that the pork trade "may fall into the hands of some of our people, and soe the prise may be kept up."[13]

Embedded in these unintentional testimonials to Indian entrepreneurialism were hints of other strategic adaptations. Native traders doubtless drove their animals to market, but since colonists complained about sales of meat, not live creatures, Indians must have butchered the beasts once they arrived and in a manner that purchasers found acceptable. Colonists never mentioned if all of the meat was sold fresh; if Indians ever salted it to appeal to colonial tastes, they would have mastered a food preservation technique unknown to native peoples before colonization. Indian traders had certainly divined the most efficient ways to attract buyers. If the timing of colonial complaints—mid- to late spring—reflected the dates when Indians showed up with their animals in tow, native sellers knew when colonists' supplies of salted meat had run low and thus when their appetites for fresh beef and pork were keenest. Moreover, Indians correctly identified Boston and Manhattan as particularly lucrative markets. Where grazing limitations and other constraints discouraged town residents from raising their own livestock, opportunities for meat merchants were greatest.[14]

Native ownership of livestock stimulated competition for land as well as trade. Colonial authorities who were willing to share waste land with Indian hunters balked at sharing it with Indian hog owners. The most glaring example of this double standard applied to the aptly named Hog Island off the coast of Portsmouth, Rhode Island. In June 1669 Portsmouth's selectmen were dismayed to learn that Metacom, the Wampanoags' leader, had ferried some of his swine to the place where colonists let their own animals graze. Instead of encouraging him further to emulate English ways, they accused Metacom of "intrudeinge on the Rights of this Towne" and ordered him to remove his hogs to avoid prosecution. The sachem evidently did so, since there is no record of further complaint, but in the process grasped an important lesson about English duplicity. The same point was brought home to Indians on Nantucket who faced stiff colonial resistance to sharing grazing rights to the island's limited supply of pasture.[15]

Although Indians may have preferred to continue sharing waste land, the colonists' growing insistence on exclusive control inspired native peoples to follow suit. Indians in Plymouth Colony who exchanged land among themselves occasionally drew up English-style deeds specifying that the right to graze "any kind of cattle" belonged solely to the purchaser. Such provisos may indicate increasing friction among Indians over access to pasture, a problem that more typically generated disputes between Indians and colonists.[16] In less formal ways, and in defense of collective rather than individual property rights, native peoples may have cited their possession of livestock among other reasons to counter English expansion. Eastern Shore Indians who negotiated with Maryland authorities in the 1670s for official recognition of native land rights could certainly have pressed such a case. And even if they refrained from doing so explicitly, Indians who placed livestock on their lands offered an implicit challenge to any colonial justification for seizing the same territory. Colonists who argued that "to clear, plant, and tend an Acre of Ground with Corn, or to build an House, and keep a stock of Cattle, for one whole year together" sufficed to confirm a landowner's rights could hardly deny that livestock-owning Indians had fulfilled every condition. Or they could only deny it by turning a blind eye to the inconvenient evidence that lay before them.[17]

Once native peoples obtained livestock, it was no longer possible for anyone automatically to assume that all domestic creatures wandering through the woods had to be colonists' property. How to distinguish between Indian and English livestock eventually became a matter of debate in colonial legislatures. Indians knew that colonists identified their animals by earmarks; whether native owners would be allowed to do the same remained an open question for several decades. A story that probably originated in Virginia and later circulated in England suggested that by the 1650s earmarks had at least become a topic of conversation between Indians and colonists. Informed by

irate Englishmen that his followers had been stealing hogs, a sachem reportedly countered that colonists had been just as busy killing the Indians' deer.
The English reminded him that earmarks identified the hogs as private
property but deer displayed no comparable sign of ownership. "Tis true indeed,
none of my deer are marked," the Indian coolly replied, "and by that [you] may
know them to be mine: and when you meet with any that are marked, you may
do with them what you please; for they are none of mine."[18] Possibly
apocryphal, the anecdote nevertheless fairly represented Indian wit and
addressed a topic of current interest to both parties.

Once Chesapeake-area Indians owned swine, the virtues of marking them
became self-evident. Unmarked hogs offered tempting targets for colonial
thieves, who needed only to clip the ears of such creatures to claim them as
their own. Given the propensity of colonists to steal livestock from one another,
this was no idle threat. Earmarks also distinguished Indian hogs from feral
swine. Native owners could have marked their beasts at any time, but these
marks would not provide genuine protection until colonial authorities recognized them as legitimate symbols of private property. Virginia's legislature did
not make such a concession until 1674 when, in a measure aimed at curbing
Indian theft of English animals, it ordered county courts to designate "a
perticuler marke" for inhabitants of each native town to use on their swine.
Assigning a mark to towns instead of individuals may have indicated that
Indians regarded swine as common property, or simply that the burgesses
failed to make distinctions among native owners. Whether earmarks actually
enabled Indians to defend their animal property is unclear.[19]

Oddly enough, when faced with the same circumstances, New England
magistrates adopted precisely the opposite tactic. Although there is evidence
to suggest that some Indians in Rhode Island took the initiative to begin
marking their swine, one by one New England legislatures moved to prohibit
the practice. Between 1666 and 1672, Rhode Island, Plymouth, and Massachusetts all ordered that "noe Indian shall give any eare marke to his swine
upon the penalty of the forfeiture of such swine." Indian hogs brought to
market had to have uncut ears; native sellers of pork likewise had to produce
intact ears to prove ownership. The ostensible reason for this policy was to
prevent Indians from profiting from stolen English swine, but its more
obvious effects were to complicate Indians' market activity and to render
Indian animals vulnerable to unscrupulous colonists who merely had to mark
the creatures' uncut ears and claim possession. There was also no way for

Indians to distinguish their swine from feral beasts that, if less numerous in New England than in the Chesapeake, still roamed the woods and were regarded by colonists as fair game. If Christian Indians in Natick, allowed to have a town brand for their animals, were exempted from the earmark prohibition in recognition of their efforts at acculturation, they would have been the exception that proved the rule. New England magistrates otherwise denied Indians use of the acknowledged symbol of legitimate ownership, as if it ought to signify their progress toward civility rather than their hogs' status as private property.[20]

Yet Indians who adopted livestock clearly intended to do so on their own terms and not those dictated by colonists. Frustrated by the Indians' refusal to make all the changes necessary to move away from "Barbarisme" and surprised by the unforeseen problems that emerged, English settlers judged native hog-keeping a failed experiment. Instead of bringing the two peoples closer, it brought into sharp focus their disparate goals: the Indians' effort to preserve their culture versus the colonists' desire to replace it. These goals had also informed strategies for cooperation but in a much less visible way. That native traders often beat the colonists at their own game only made matters worse. By the 1660s some disillusioned colonists went so far as to declare that "Indians ought not to keepe hoggs" at all because of the unexpected complications.[21] With the maturing of a new generation of colonists and Indians, the struggle for dominion intensified in a land that no longer seemed to have enough room for both of them.

By the third quarter of the seventeenth century, only the most optimistic colonists still believed that the English could live side by side with native peoples. The colonial population had burgeoned by 1670 to more than 50,000 in New England and over 40,000 in the Chesapeake, and the numbers of their livestock vastly exceeded those figures.[22] Demographic growth, though perhaps most significant, was not the only factor eroding confidence in the possibility of coexistence. The colonists' response to the scarcity and expense of labor, especially their adoption of long-fallow farming and free-range animal husbandry, increased their demand for land far beyond what anyone reasoning from English experience could have imagined. Together these developments generated a powerful dynamic for geographical expansion against which Indians scrambled to mount a defense. Disquieting enough on its own, English settlers' land hunger intensified just at the time when fragile mechanisms that had once encouraged cooperation with Indians began to break down.

The expansion of English settlement appeared all but unstoppable. By the 1670s, a steady stream of immigrant servants allowed planters to extend tobacco cultivation around the entire Chesapeake coast and up to a hundred miles inland along major rivers. Population growth was so rapid that the legislatures of Maryland and Virginia had to create seven new counties in the decade after 1654 to accommodate frontier settlements. New England's expansion was just as dramatic. In Massachusetts and Plymouth, new towns appeared at a rate of one a year between 1650 and 1675. Some were carved out of existing communities, but others signaled the colonists' advance into new areas. Four more towns sprouted up in the Connecticut Valley to join Springfield, and half a dozen others extended the line of more-or-less contiguous English settlement 40 miles west of Boston. Scarcely any land in Plymouth Colony remained unclaimed by colonists.[23]

English expansion necessarily occurred at the expense of Indian territorial holdings. Colonists coveted not just lands around Indian settlements, but within native villages. Visiting a Nottoway town in 1650, Edward Bland described the area as "a rich levell, well timbered, watered, and very convenient for Hogs and Cattle"—a virtual real estate advertisement aimed at his fellow Virginians. Even lands set aside specifically for the Indians attracted the notice of colonists facing the consequences of long fallow agriculture and proliferating livestock herds. In 1648, a group of Virginians cited "the mean produce of their labours upon barren and over-wrought grounds and the apparent decay of their cattle and hoggs for want of sufficient range" to justify their petition to the House of Burgesses for permission to move onto what had been an Indian preserve north of the Rappahannock River. Although the burgesses later recognized that Indians could be forced "into such narrow Streights, and places That they Cannott Subsist" to such a point that "they may bee Justlye Driven to dispaire," their solution was to require colonists who hungered after Indian land to obtain "full Leave" from the governor and Council before making their move. They furthermore offered to help displaced Indians settle elsewhere, ignoring the likelihood that this might locate refugees on lands claimed by other native groups. Subsequent legislative efforts to confirm existing Indian landholdings and prohibit further sales to colonists resembled holding actions rather than permanent solutions.[24]

The situation in Maryland was no better. In 1663, the "Queene" or female chief of Portoback informed colonial authorities that her people had "not only left their Towne standing by the water, but have removed themselves farther of[f] even to their utmost bownds of their land" so the English could settle in the deserted village. The colonists remained unsatisfied, she reported, and "Doe still take up land and Seate themselves very nigh unto the said Indians." Making matters worse, livestock wandered away from these new plantations and into native cornfields. The magistrates' decree that English settlers stay at least three miles away from native villages may have offered the Indians some brief respite, but in the long run could not halt the onslaught of colonists.[25]

In New England, the acquisitive impulse took hold with particular urgency in Plymouth and Rhode Island, two colonies confined to narrow borders by more powerful English neighbors in Connecticut and Massachusetts. Plymouth authorities negotiated some sort of land deal with local Indians nearly every year during the two decades after 1655, often mentioning the colonists' dearth of pasture as their reason for doing so. In June 1655, for instance, the town of Plymouth bought Indian land "to winter cattle upon"; seven years later, the legislature authorized Thomas Willett to arrange for the purchase of Saconet Neck, the kind of peninsula where colonists typically placed their livestock to minimize fence construction. Rhode Island's requirement that purchasers of Indian land first obtain the government's permission helped to regularize such transactions, not to discourage them. In 1659, the assembly rather bluntly granted the town of Providence "liberty to buy out and cleare off Indians" within its bounds. During the same session, legislators also authorized a committee to buy a town-sized tract from the Narragansetts. Employing a tactic that other Rhode Islanders no doubt found useful, Samuel Wildbore at one point staked a preemptive claim to native lands "by building and bringing cattell" under the assumption that his actions would receive retroactive approval from the authorities. Even the inhabitants of praying towns in the Bay Colony, who might have expected protection from aggressive neighbors, suffered from unwanted intrusions. Visiting Okommakamesit, situated next to Marlborough, Daniel Gookin found that its native residents "do not much rejoice under the English men's shadow; who do so overtop them in their number of people, stocks of cattle, &c. that the Indians do not greatly flourish, or delight in their station at present."[26]

Every new Chesapeake plantation or New England town brought colonists into closer proximity to Indian villages and hunting grounds. As English and native settlements increasingly abutted one another, pressure grew to survey their respective boundaries to clarify what belonged to whom. The House of Burgesses in effect created Powhatan reservations in 1658 by setting aside tracts of land, allocated at 50 acres per native bowman, for Indian towns. The burgesses called for surveys of Accomack and Chickahominy territory as well in the early 1660s. Plymouth authorities responded to similar pressures at about the same time. In 1662, surveyors marked the boundary between Barnstable and Sandwich, "to end any difference that is betwixt them and the Indians about any graunt of lands." The following year, another team set out to mark the line between Taunton and Seekonk, again "to prevent damage that might arise to the Indians by the neglect thereof."[27]

Lines on a map were easily enough ignored by land-hungry Englishmen; they meant nothing at all to foraging livestock. Unless insurmountable barriers blocked their path, colonists' animals did not respect boundaries. Beyond the official borders of nearly every New England town or Chesapeake plantation lay a penumbra of land, often several miles wide, that livestock effectively claimed as their own. Their ranging magnified the impact of expanding colonial settlements ever further, introducing trespass problems to new areas. Plymouth authorities reluctantly acknowledged that, as time went on, Indians "liveing in remote places from any townshipes have received great damage by the horses and hoggs of the English," the kinds of livestock receiving the least supervision from New England farmers. Afflicted by similar woes, Maryland Indians turned to the colony's legislature for redress. Mattagund, representing the Patuxents and other local groups, made an eloquent plea in the spring of 1666 that summed up the Indians' predicament. "Your hogs & Cattle injure Us," he declared, "You come too near Us to live & drive Us from place to place. We can fly no farther[,] let us know where to live & how to be secured for the future from the Hogs & Cattle."[28]

Though hardly deaf to such complaints, colonial authorities felt little compulsion to make amends. Their willingness to cooperate with Indians had always reflected careful considerations of self-interest; they knew that it did not pay to alienate military allies or trading partners. But as time went on, the colonists judged local Indians less useful for the services they could render. Until about 1660 in New England, trade in furs and wampum enmeshed Indians and colonists in a web of mutually beneficial exchange strong enough to withstand periodic tension over issues of land and diplomacy. The virtual extinction of fur-bearing animals in southern New England due to overhunting, however, dissolved one important strand in that economic relationship. Another gave way with the decline in the colonists' demand for wampum. An increase in overseas commerce (generated in part by the growing livestock trade with the West Indies) brought more hard currency to New England, allowing colonists to cease accepting wampum as legal tender. These economic shifts had diplomatic repercussions that further weakened the bargaining position of southern New England Indians. The Narragansetts and their native allies had for decades wielded influence as intermediaries between the English and the Mohawks, the easternmost members of the powerful Iroquois confederation. New England Indians exchanged wampum with the Mohawks for furs to supplement the diminishing local supply sold to the colonists. With the English conquest of New Netherland in 1664, colonial merchants and officials pursued direct connections with the Mohawks, undermining the diplomatic leverage of the Narragansetts and other southern New England native peoples.[29]

A strikingly similar set of developments occurred in the Tidewater Chesapeake region at about the same time. Already weakened by earlier clashes with colonists and relegation to tributary status, many eastern Chesapeake peoples saw their remaining ties with the English unravel after 1660. As the local beaver trade diminished from overhunting, colonial merchants with an eye on the main chance pursued contacts with Indians living further to the west with deerskins to exchange. Wampum, never as important to Anglo-Indian relations in the Chesapeake as it was in New England, became even less significant as it declined in value relative to English currency. The most serious blow to the Tidewater Indians' position, however, occurred in the realm of diplomacy. English officials responded to growing rivalries with the Dutch (before 1664) and the French by negotiating alliances with more powerful native groups like the Iroquois and the Susquehannocks. Such maneuvers pushed the Algonquian-speaking peoples of the Tidewater to the margins, leaving them isolated and frustrated.[30]

Shifting their diplomatic attention to a different and larger stage, colonial authorities in the Chesapeake and New England no longer devoted much effort to resolving such mundane problems as Indian complaints about animal trespass. They instead ordered local officials to handle what were now considered matters of law enforcement rather than diplomacy. In

Virginia and Maryland the task devolved to county commissioners.[31] New England legislatures assumed that townsmen were best able to judge the validity of Indian grievances in their communities and left it up to them to keep the peace. Trespass complaints involving Indians happened so frequently in Plymouth, however, that in 1671 the colony government appointed standing committees in each town to deal with them.[32]

Leaving the resolution of such disputes up to local residents had the unhappy effect of entrusting men who may have owned the offending livestock with the responsibility for making impartial judgments. Legislatures had few sanctions to impose if townsmen reached biased conclusions, or if they failed to answer Indians' complaints altogether. A protracted exchange between the Wampanoags and the town of Rehoboth fully exposed the shortcomings of local self-policing. The Indians went all the way to Plymouth to lodge complaints about trespassing Rehoboth livestock at least five times between March 1653 and June 1660, to little avail. Each time the legislature referred the matter back to Rehoboth. Townsmen confronted with the problem at first claimed to "know nothing of yt," then insisted that they had built sufficient fences (ignoring the fact that horses and cattle could swim around one part of the barrier). Colony officials instructed the Indians in 1656 to impound the errant beasts, only to discover the following year that Rehoboth had no pound. Wamsutta, who preceded Metacom as the Wampanoags' sachem, and later Metacom led regular delegations to Plymouth to plead for redress that they never managed to obtain.[33]

Rehoboth lay 35 miles west of the colonial government in Plymouth, and this distance surely encouraged townsmen in their stubborn refusal to address Indian grievances. But timing was also a factor. By the 1660s, colonists were generally less interested in conciliating their Indian neighbors, seeing little point in strengthening relations with peoples whom they regarded as essentially useless for trade and insignificant as allies. Moreover, these same Indians had not only offended colonists by resisting prescribed cultural transformations but, with their procurement of swine, also emerged as unwelcome competitors in the marketplace. The townspeople of Rehoboth, along with the inhabitants of many colonial villages and plantations, had evidently decided that they had little to lose by ignoring Indian complaints and perhaps even something to gain.

A combination of factors encouraged colonists to imagine a world where Indians who refused to become civilized would be displaced, not placated. The English realized that land constituted the Indians' single remaining asset, and land—without Indians on it—was what they wanted. They also knew that as other economic opportunities diminished, Indians needed the revenue that land sales could supply. Colonists made deals with an array of sachems and individual Indians whose authority to dispose of collectively owned lands was suspect. Merchants seized native lands in payment for debts, and magistrates did the same to punish Indians convicted of crimes.[34] The easiest and cheapest method of all, however, was for colonists to let livestock do the job for them. Experience suggested that Indians thoroughly frustrated by persistent trespass problems might simply move away. Thus colonists' willful disregard for Indian complaints may be seen less as evidence of negligence than as a deliberate strategy for land acquisition. Whether Indians, confined to shrinking amounts of territory barely able to support them, would make a graceful exit became less clear as time went on.

Like wounds left to fester, disputes about livestock plagued Indians and colonists alike. No remedy seemed capable of alleviating one group's distress without worsening the condition of the other. The English feared that their growing populations would overwhelm available resources unless they continually spread out with their animals into new communities. Relentless English expansion, in turn, threatened Indians with nothing less than extinction. Anxiety bred indifference to each other's plight, reducing the incentive to seek common ground. With leaders either unable or unwilling to take charge, individual colonists and Indians took matters into their own hands, engaging in defiant acts of sabotage that only made the situation more intolerable for everyone.

The potential for violence that lay at the heart of nearly every livestock dispute was realized with alarming frequency as the seventeenth century wore on. Emboldened by demographic preponderance and confidence in their superior claim to the land, some English settlers tried to antagonize Indians to the point where they would abandon their territory in order to find peace and quiet. Samuel Wildbore, for instance, thought nothing of shooting at Narragansett Indians who opposed his settlement and placement of livestock on their lands. Wildbore must have known that the Narragansetts would report his actions to Rhode Island authorities, as they did in September 1662, but the slim possibility of punishment scarcely deterred him. The following year, equally obstreperous Connecticut farmers harassed Indians near Niantic by burning the fences around their cornfields. Once the rails had been reduced to ashes, livestock could continue the assault by invading unprotected grounds.[35]

Colonists in the Chesapeake occasionally delivered the same contemptuous message to neighboring Indians. In 1666, a delegation of native leaders complained to the Maryland Assembly of losing an entire crop of corn to marauding livestock after colonists destroyed the surrounding fences. Although the magistrates agreed that any colonist who committed such an act ought to pay damages, it was unclear how guilty parties would be identified and brought to justice. At the same time, beleaguered Indians would not have missed the ironic symbolism of this new form of harassment. Native peoples had learned to build fences in response to pressure from colonists. When belligerent colonists targeted fences for destruction, they struck out at the whole notion of harmonious coexistence. In addition, by enlisting livestock in their campaign of abuse, colonists guaranteed that Indians would blame English animals along with English people when they saw their efforts at accommodation lying in ruins.[36]

Taking aim at another token of the Indians' selective acculturation, malicious Plymouth colonists began to kill Indian hogs. Accused of snatching one near Mattapoisett in 1668, Francis Wast claimed that the pig had earmarks contrary to the law, and thus the animal was forfeit anyway. Colony authorities, responding to a petition for justice from Metacom himself, ignored Wast's spurious excuse and referred the case to Taunton's selectmen for resolution, adding that if the case "bee not by them ended" it ought to be referred back to Plymouth. This was hardly a vote of confidence in the efficacy of local adjudication and, sure enough, the case reappeared on the colony court's agenda seven months later. Plymouth judges ordered the offending colonists in this and similar cases to pay damages, but frequent repetitions of the original complaints revealed that matters often remained unsettled.[37]

Indians thus learned that colonial courts, which regularly punished them when they owed debts to English creditors or broke English laws, failed to provide the same swift justice when native plaintiffs accused colonists of misdeeds. The Indians' willingness to resort to legal action—an effort that at least left a paper trail marking a worsening situation—diminished accordingly. Colonists, however, did not hesitate to report hostile acts directed against them by Indians. The preponderance of evidence therefore suggests that colonists were the chief victims of aggression, but it represents just one side of a vigorous and increasingly angry debate conducted in deeds as well as words. Only rarely would colonists concede, as Virginia's burgesses did in 1662, that "the mutuall discontents, complaints, jealousies and ffeares of English and Indians proceed chiefly from the violent intrusions of diverse English" onto Indian lands.[38] Indians who answered violence with more violence were under no illusion that they could drive the colonists back to England. They instead acted in self-defense, raising the costs to colonists of ignoring native grievances in the hope of restoring balance to their relations.

Indians principally directed their vengeance against colonial property, not persons. And no form of property offered a more tempting or appropriate target than livestock. After decades of contact, Indians knew how much colonists relied on their domestic animals, and thus what a blow they could deliver by stealing or destroying the creatures. Moreover, livestock had amply earned the Indians' enmity in their own right. Indians trusted that colonists would comprehend the clear symbolic intent of their actions. By choosing these emblems of English civility as their target, Indians signaled their defiant rejection of the civilizing agenda that called for their wholesale transformation into docile cattle-raising farmers.

Native attacks against livestock were nothing new, having formed part of the Indians' offensive strategy since the first conflicts with colonists. Indians knew that even the threat of such violence sent chills up colonists' spines. The Narragansetts had deftly wielded this rhetorical weapon in 1645 when their conflict with the Mohegans seemed likely to engulf the Mohegans' English allies. According to Plymouth's governor William Bradford, Narragansett leaders promised to "lay the English cattle on heaps as high as their houses, and that no Englishman should stir out of his door to piss, but he should be killed." In offering this bold challenge, the Narragansetts exploited their leverage over colonists who needed their help with trade and Indian diplomacy. War with the English was indeed averted, but the Narragansetts' inflammatory speech burned in colonists' memories for decades thereafter. Once the balance of population and power shifted in the colonists' favor, such threats no longer produced the same effect. Indians frustrated by colonial indifference to their complaints saw no alternative but to take direct action.[39]

The Narragansetts, keenly aware that their power to influence English policy was on the wane, began to supplement threatening speeches with physical intimidation. According to the testimony of Thomas Minor and other

Englishmen, the catalogue of Narragansett offenses during one altercation in 1662 included harassing colonists at work, throwing stones at them, and seizing cattle and horses to hold for ransom. Minor was especially incensed that Indians had caught his horses and threatened to take his life. When a similar incident occurred six years later, Narragansetts added burning hay and beating horses "with Clubs and staves" to their list of "insolencies." Fueling the Narragansetts' wrath was intense anxiety over having been forced to mortgage land to colonial speculators in order to pay off a fine. That the colonists' horses came in for particular abuse, however, suggests an additional grievance. After England's government levied a tax on horse exports beginning in 1654, New Englanders—including Thomas Minor and the truculent Samuel Wildbore—rushed to produce a homegrown supply to sell in the West Indies. By the 1660s, much to the Narragansetts' dismay, their territory was fast becoming both a giant pasture and a thoroughfare for horses driven to the bay for shipment overseas.[40]

More often than not, colonists characterized these and other assaults against livestock as evidence of Indian "insolency" or arrogance. Attributing them to native depravity doubtless reinforced colonists' sense of their own moral superiority.[41] Yet the impulse to place blame wholly on the Indians blinded English settlers to the episodes' full significance. Colonists interpreted these attacks as crimes against their property, not rejections of their overweening power. They responded with judicial procedures and admonitory legislation, not diplomatic discussions. The symbolic message that Indians were trying to send was lost in the colonists' translation of their campaign of resistance into random acts of malicious mischief.

The lax supervision of colonial livestock guaranteed that animals might disappear for any number of reasons, but colonists on the whole preferred to accuse Indians of stealing them. Edmund Scarborough insisted in 1663 that Indians living south of the James River pilfered his and fellow Virginians' hogs on a daily basis. Marylanders were convinced that, "under pretence of killing wild Hoggs," local Indians habitually made off with tame creatures. In Massachusetts, colonists felt equally certain that they had "just reason to suspect the Indians to have stolne" their animal property even though "it be very difficult to proove such thefts." Plymouth's inhabitants joined in the chorus of complaint.[42]

As if filching animals were not provocation enough, colonists accused Indians of trafficking in stolen goods. They were convinced that unwary consumers who bought pork or beef from native traders probably purchased flesh from their own animals or those of their neighbors. Marylanders also fretted that "forreigners and strangers" offered particularly easy marks for this illicit commerce. Legislation requiring Indian sellers to produce earmark evidence—or, in the case of Plymouth, "good Testimonies" from Englishmen—proving that they owned the creatures for sale appeared in due course in nearly every colony.[43]

English suspicions about Indian theft and commerce in stolen meat may often have been justified even if they could not be substantiated. Robbing colonists of their troublesome creatures doubtless struck many Indians as an unusually appropriate way of making their displeasure known, particularly if the animals in question had invaded native lands. Tricking settlers into buying meat from their own animals may likewise have proven irresistible. In effect exactions of retributive justice, these expedients fit with concepts of fairness common to native cultures, which focused on restitution for the aggrieved party. Since the colonists and their courts so rarely satisfied native victims of livestock incursions, they may simply have decided to collect their own damages. The frequency and ubiquity of colonists' accusations of theft, appearing everywhere from Massachusetts to Virginia, reinforces the impression that Indians indeed committed such attacks with some regularity. If so, however, they undertook these actions not as opportunistic adventures but as reasoned responses to a shared predicament.[44]

Native peoples signaled their exasperation with the state of affairs most vigorously when they killed livestock outright. Colonists treated some incidents as relatively minor infractions, such as when two Indian boys in Maryland tried to run away after dispatching a hog and taking its flesh, or when a pair of Indians near Boston confessed to having killed a cow for "want of provisions." Offenders in such cases received fines and corporal punishment.[45] When significant numbers of animals were involved, however, and particularly when Indians left behind the unbutchered carcasses of the beasts, colonists understood that more than petty thievery was involved. English settlers on the eastern end of Long Island, for instance, could hardly misinterpret the aggressive intent of a group of "ensolent" Indians who in 1651 drove cattle into the ocean "and soe drowned them to the great damage of the owners." A few years later, Indians near New Haven chose swine as well as cows for destruction. During the 1660s, Marylanders protested that Indians set their dogs on colonists' hogs and sometimes swooped down on remote plantations to attack women and children along with any livestock found on the premises. The Maryland episodes were deemed serious enough to elicit calls for military campaigns, not judicial action.[46]

The Marylanders' response indicated that colonists were fully capable of interpreting unusually violent depredations against livestock, not to mention the murder of English settlers, as belligerent acts. Characterizing these incidents as unprovoked assaults, however, they failed to look for connections between the Indians' behavior and their own conduct. Lack of knowledge about what was going on in other colonies further hampered their ability to appreciate the scope of the problems they faced. The New England colonies, which had formed a defensive confederation as early as 1643, did share information about Indian affairs, but attacks on livestock rarely attracted the organization's attention. Moreover, the decision to exclude Rhode Island because of its inhabitants' unorthodox religious views limited the confederation's knowledge of Indian affairs in a particularly crucial locale.[47] And there were no regular lines of communication at all between the New England and Chesapeake colonies to alert English settlers in the two regions to their common plight.

The tendency to regard attacks on livestock as isolated local problems prevented colonists from appreciating the extent to which the Indians' conduct amounted to a guerrilla campaign of opposition to English expansion. Native peoples may not have coordinated their attacks against offending English people and animals, but the effect might not have been much different had they done so. Two features of the Indians' response in particular linked separate episodes into a common pattern of resistance. First, Indians increasingly concentrated their attacks on newly colonized areas. In New England these sites included the Connecticut Valley in western Massachusetts, "inland plantations" begun in the 1650s and 1660s, and villages located near the disputed border between Connecticut and Rhode Island.[48] Chesapeake colonists venturing into the upper part of Northampton county on the Eastern Shore, the south side of the James River, the head of Chesapeake Bay itself, and the "frontier" of Baltimore county likewise felt the sting of Indian raids.[49] The recent movement of English settlers into all of these places introduced new groups of Indians to troublesome livestock, sparking similar acts of retaliation. In some cases, native refugees from areas colonized earlier found to their dismay that the plague of cattle and swine had caught up with them, provoking them to strike out in anger and frustration at the detested beasts.

Second, judging from colonists' complaints, Indians most frequently singled out hogs for destruction. Colonists accused Indians of stealing them, shooting them, or leaving wounded and dead pigs lying around to be found by their owners. In Charles County, Maryland, Robert Troop observed an Indian dog gnawing away on a neighbor's sow, an attack that may not have been an accident since Indians were often charged with goading their dogs to attack livestock. In this case, the dog had "eat of[f] her hed from her bodie," leaving little for Troop to salvage.[50] Colonists probably exaggerated the total number of these incidents because they generally suspected that all Indian-owned hogs or stray pigs had been stolen. In a rare about-face, a group of Marylanders who in 1674 had accused Indians of destroying livestock were forced to retract their charge when several of the creatures in question wandered home.[51] But there is little reason to doubt that hogs were indeed special targets of Indian attacks. By far the most numerous of livestock species and the least easily controlled, swine inflicted the greatest amount of damage on Indian villages. Retaliatory attacks on individual pigs caught rooting in cornfields might be dismissed as isolated incidents, but larger scale assaults against an entire community's swine constituted a proxy war in which the real enemies included the animals' English owners.

By the 1670s, tensions that had simmered for years approached the boiling point. The Indians' campaign against livestock had produced no major victories, and scarcely any minor ones. Colonists showed little inclination to control their animals, let alone to slow their inexorable advance onto native territory. If the past offered any indication of what lay ahead, Indians faced a dismal future of repeated displacement. No matter where they sought refuge, livestock would eventually appear, giving advance warning of an occupying army of colonists soon to follow. Cooperation, negotiation, even acts of violence failed to halt the juggernaut of English people and animals. Scorned by Indians from the start as advertisements of English cultural superiority, livestock were now hated more than ever for being agents of English imperial dominion.

Despite the increase in tensions, no one could have predicted that in 1675 cataclysmic conflict between Indians and colonists would simultaneously erupt in two separate locations. Nearly everyone was taken by surprise when a disaster on the scale of King Philip's War broke out in New England that June and when a seemingly minor altercation between Doeg Indians and Virginia colonists in July set off a chain of events leading to the Susquehannock War and Bacon's Rebellion. By the time hostilities diminished in August 1676 in New England and October of the same year in Virginia, thousands of Indians and colonists lay dead. Whole towns and plantations had been reduced to rubble and ashes, and untold numbers of Indian villages lay in ruins. Countless livestock carcasses littered the woods and fields.

The incidents that sparked these two catastrophes gave little indication of the horrors to come, for they resembled previous encounters that had been settled short of war. In Plymouth, a calamitous train of events was set in motion when a colonial jury sentenced three Wampanoag men to death for murdering John Sassamon, a native interpreter who had reported rumors of Wampanoag plans to attack the English. This was hardly the first time that Indians chafed at the workings of colonial justice or that colonists heard warnings about imminent Indian aggression. And while the sachem Metacom expressed intense frustration with this latest manifestation of English dominance, he had always before submitted to colonial assertions of authority.[52] Likewise on the border between Virginia and Maryland, the Doeg Indians were unlikely protagonists in the opening scene of a brutal confrontation between English and native peoples. Signatories of a peace treaty with Maryland in 1666, the Doegs had maintained relatively amicable relations with colonists for almost a decade.[53] Their eagerness to trade with English settlers, in fact, led to their undoing. When Thomas Mathew, a Virginia planter, failed to pay Doeg traders for goods he had purchased from them, they seized a few of his hogs to settle the debt. Mathew and several colonists pursued the Indians, killing some of them, and recovered the swine. The Doegs responded with a raid of their own, which led to the slaying of Mathew's herdsman. The militia's decision to avenge the Englishman's death turned a dispute over pigs first into an Indian war and then a revolt of colonists against their government.[54]

Like all human conflicts, King Philip's War (as it was known to colonists) and Bacon's Rebellion each originated in a tangled weave of human decisions and actions. Although neither confrontation was inevitable, each reflected a general trend on the part of Indians and colonists toward intransigence instead of cooperation. Intent on transforming local Indians into subject peoples, colonists ignored their grievances and insisted that political submission, a willingness to part with land, and religious conversion (especially in New England), were prerequisites for native influence in a colonial world. Most Indians opposed surrendering their autonomy in so abject a fashion and defied English attempts at subordination. By the time war broke out, relations among the various peoples living in New England and the Chesapeake were sufficiently complicated that antagonists could not easily be divided into English and Indian camps. Internal divisions pitted Christian Indians against unconverted native peoples and set moderate colonists against firebrands intent on eliminating Indian adversaries once and for all.[55]

From the moment they arrived in the New World, livestock repeatedly intruded upon the affairs of Indians and colonists, and matters were no different during the crises of 1675-76. Livestock acted in several ways as necessary, if not wholly sufficient, causes for these tragic confrontations. The free-ranging animals' subsistence requirements overshadowed every other factor driving the colonists' insatiable quest for land, which emerged as a key source of discord. Shrinking territorial holdings, compounded by damage from trespassing livestock on what remained of native lands, eroded the material foundations of Indian independence as never before. The increasingly acrimonious character of livestock disputes, which set Indians and colonists at odds more often than any other single issue, created an atmosphere of mistrust and anxiety. Unresolved grievances pertaining to animal trespass, destroyed fences, and related problems gave Indians little cause to expect fair treatment from the English. Acts of sabotage perpetrated by both sides had already cast a pall of violence over the countryside years before the outbreak of war in New England and Virginia.

That animals could help to incite a war between human combatants was eminently clear to New Englanders by the early 1670s. Angry Massachusetts colonists in a newly settled part of Dedham nearly attacked Wampanoag Indians in the spring of 1671 over a trespass dispute. English families had recently driven the Wampanoags from the area, and displaced Indians apparently took their revenge on roaming livestock. Urging forbearance from the Dedham settlers, the Bay Colony's Indian superintendent, Daniel Gookin, pleaded that it was not worth *"fighting with Indians about horses and hogs, as matters too low to shed blood."* If the colonists would keep their animals on their own land, Gookin advised, similar losses could be avoided and peace preserved.[56]

Metacom managed to calm his followers as well, but he could add the Dedham episode to a lengthening list of bitter encounters with the English. From the moment he became sachem in 1662, Metacom had done his best to safeguard his people's autonomy even as he witnessed the Wampanoags' influence with their Plymouth allies and other colonists steadily diminish. Despite his efforts, new English towns established in Plymouth, Rhode Island, and Massachusetts hedged ancestral Wampanoag lands in on all sides and rendered his people unusually vulnerable to encroachments by colonists and livestock. Metacom was no stranger to livestock ownership, having acquired pigs of his own, but this earned him no credit with colonial authorities. Because he failed to adopt other attributes of civility, especially Christianity, colonists viewed his incomplete acculturation more as a challenge to their dominance than a reasoned preference for selective accommodation. Plymouth magistrates were convinced that Metacom harbored hostile intentions, and summoned him three times between 1667 and 1671 to answer charges of plotting insurrection. At the third meeting, on 29 September 1671, he reaffirmed his submission to English authority. But, given his experience with English unresponsiveness in dealing with livestock disputes and other problems, he must have gritted his teeth as he promised to refer future complaints arising between Wampanoags and colonists to Plymouth's governor for resolution.[57]

Following the execution of John Sassamon's alleged murderers in June 1675, rumors of war again swept through the countryside. In an eleventh-hour attempt to avert hostilities, John Easton, Rhode Island's deputy governor, arranged a meeting with Metacom. Asserting that his people "had dun no rong" but that "the English ronged them," the Wampanoag leader supplied a litany of grievances that recalled past quarrels and stressed intractable problems involving sovereignty, land, and animals. He accused colonists of plying Indians with alcohol to cheat them out of land. When the Indians later protested that they had not intended to sell so much territory, colonists insisted that written deeds were more accurate than native memories. If one sachem refused to sell property, the English would "make a nother king that wold give or seell them there land." Incessant quarrels over animal trespass provided an equally powerful justification for war. Because "the English Catell and horses still incresed" and roamed at large, when Indians "removed 30 mill [miles] from wher English had anithing to do, they Could not kepe ther coren from being spoyled." Easton, Metacom assumed, was fully aware that the

Wampanoags could no longer put so much distance between themselves and English neighbors. With rising indignation, the sachem fumed that his people expected that "when the English boft [bought] land of them that thay wold have kept ther Catell upone ther owne land."[58]

Easton's peace mission failed, and war commenced with a Wampanoag raid on Swansea. The town was an obvious target, and not just because it bordered Metacom's home base on Mount Hope peninsula in Rhode Island. Swansea had split off in 1668 from Rehoboth, a village notorious among Wampanoags for its trespassing cattle. Metacom had sold land he owned there in 1669 and again in 1671, with the proceeds of the second transaction most likely helping to pay a fine levied as punishment for his rumored conspiracy against the English. The attack in June 1675, which began with Indians "plundering and destroying cattle," may not actually have been intended as a declaration of war so much as another act of sabotage similar to those that had plagued the countryside in recent years. Even contemporaries suspected that Metacom had not ordered it, but that some of his followers had taken matters into their own hands. The colonists' decision to flee to garrisons for safety and request military support, however, helped to transform a plundering raid into the opening act of an astonishingly bloody war.[59]

Within months, the Narragansetts joined in the fighting against the colonists, entering the kind of pan-Indian alliance that their former sachem, Miantonomi, had once advocated.[60] But instead of sparing livestock until deer populations rebounded, as Miantonomi had suggested, this new generation of Indians made English animals special targets of their wrath. During a raid near Brookfield, native warriors "made great spoyle of the cattel belonging to the inhabitants." They "drove away many cattell & h[or]ses" from Rehoboth, "killd neer an hundred cattell" at Providence, and took away "at the least a thousand horses & it is like two thousan Cattell And many Sheep" from Narragansett country.[61] Despite their best efforts, English forces failed to prevent Metacom's escape from Mount Hope in late July and only managed to capture "six, eight, or ten young Pigs" from the sachem's herds.[62]

Indians took a much larger toll on English animals. By November 1675, Connecticut magistrates worried so much about livestock losses that they advised inhabitants to "kill and salt up what of their cattell were fitt to kill" lest Indians take them first.[63] It also became clear that colonists who tried to keep their animals safe exposed themselves to peril. Early in the war, Indians assaulted five Rhode Islanders rounding up their cattle on Pocasset Neck. Colonists fled with their animals to garrison houses with palisaded yards only to discover that fodder supplies often dwindled before danger disappeared. Metacom and his men, quite familiar with livestock appetites and the seasonal rhythms of the colonists' animal husbandry, knew they only had to wait. In March 1676 near Groton, Indians "laid an Ambush for two Carts, which went from the Garison to fetch in some Hay." Two Concord men on a similar errand were caught in an attack that left one of them dead. The growth of new spring pastures brought no relief. When Hatfield residents let livestock out to graze in May 1676, 70 cattle and horses fell victim to Indians who had anticipated the move.[64]

English families were not the only ones to watch their animal property disappear. Christian Indians, whose possession of cattle testified to their cultural transformation as much as their Puritan faith and woolen garments did, suffered devastating losses at the hands both of warring Indians and angry colonists who questioned the converts' allegiance to the English cause. Informing colonial authorities that his family and congregation had been driven to desperation, Joseph Tuckapawillin, Hassanamesit's Indian minister, described how "the English have taken away some of my estate, my corn, cattle, my plough, cart, chain, and other goods," and "enemy Indians have also taken a part of what I had." Protective measures, however, likewise forced Christian Indians into poverty. An August 1675 order confining them to their homes prevented them from hunting, harvesting, or caring for livestock. Two months later, Massachusetts's decision to intern Natick Indians in squalid conditions on Deer Island in Boston Harbor only made a bad situation worse.[65]

Those who raided Christian Indians' livestock attacked symbols as well as living beasts. To native combatants who rejected the colonists' call for cultural transformation, the animals signified the converts' contemptible eagerness to mimic the despised English in hopes of gaining influence with them. Colonists, driven by fear and prejudice to suspect all Christian Indians of treachery, now regarded livestock as misplaced emblems of civility that did not belong with savage owners. The symbolic connection between livestock and Englishness only intensified as warfare tore New England apart. A surprising testimonial to its power to reassure colonists whose world had turned upside down appeared in Mary Rowlandson's account of her three-month-long captivity with enemy Indians in 1676. Enduring a forced march through the northern Massachusetts woods in late winter, she recalled, "I saw a place where *English* cattle had been: that was comfort to me." Only in a profoundly disordered world would a glimpse of trampled earth or perhaps just heaps of manure provide such solace to a woman who until then had taken cattle for granted all of her life.[66]

The creatures that reminded Rowlandson of her English identity aroused intense hatred in many Indians because of that very association. Native combatants accompanied physical attacks with verbal taunts impugning English claims that possession of animal property helped to assure cultural dominance. When a party of Narragansetts seized Joshua Tift and took him captive in Rhode Island, they slaughtered five of his cattle "before his face" and then mocked the terrified colonist by asking, "[W]hat will Cattell now doe you good?" The same insulting message was delivered in a hastily scrawled note stuck in the cleft of a bridge post outside of Medfield just after a devastating raid in February 1676. The crumpled note announced,

> Know by this paper, that the Indians that thou hast provoked to wrath and anger, will war this twenty one years if you will; there are many Indians yet, we come three hundred at this time. You must consider the Indians lost nothing but their life; you must lose your fair houses and cattle.

This defiant challenge to love of property may have disconcerted unusually perceptive colonists with its echo of scriptural warnings about the dangers of covetousness.[67]

When Indians mutilated livestock rather than killing the animals directly, they terrorized colonists at the same time that they deprived them of valuable property. One observer reported that "what cattle they took they seldom killed outright: or if they did, would eat but little of the flesh, but rather cut their bellies, and letting them go several days, trailing their guts after them, putting out their eyes, or cutting off one leg." Increase Mather related an incident when Indians near Chelmsford "took a Cow, knocked off one of her horns, cut out her tongue, and so left the poor creature in great misery." They also put a horse and ox in a "hovil" that they then set ablaze. Convinced that such displays were intended "only to shew how they are delighted in exercising cruelty," colonists misunderstood the episodes' full significance. The choice of cattle and to a lesser extent horses—not the pigs that Indians may have hated but often owned—for mutilation took aim at the most "English" of livestock species. By inflicting tortures similar to those used on human victims, Indians identified the animals as enemies in their own right whose destructive behavior and contribution to English expansion had earned them such treatment.[68]

As the war dragged on, making it virtually impossible to plant crops or to hunt, Indians relied more and more on captured livestock for food. Benjamin Church and a company of English soldiers, happening upon an Indian encampment near an orchard, found the apples gone and puddles of blood on the ground left from "the flesh of swine, which they had killed that day." Church later heard that Indians were raiding colonial farms specifically to "kill cattle and horses for provisions." Alerted in one instance by the sound of Indians shooting at livestock, colonial troops found a camp with "some of the English Beef boiling in their Kettles." These native raids could make significant inroads on the colonists' own food supply. On a retaliatory plundering expedition that occurred toward the end of the war, English soldiers seized "about a thousand Weight of dried Beef, with other Things" from Indian adversaries.[69]

Livestock raids, however, could not sustain the Indians all the way to victory. Shortages of food and weapons, outbreaks of disease, and attacks by Mohawk enemies during the winter of 1675-76 sapped the strength of Metacom's forces. The following August, English soldiers with native allies overwhelmed the straggling band of Indian fighters who had returned to Mount Hope. Metacom's death at the hands of a Christian Indian effectively ended a war that may have cost up to 3,000 English and 7,000 Indian lives. Damage to property was also extensive, including as many as 1,200 houses destroyed and "8000 head of cattle, great and small, killed" by Indians whose own losses were immeasurable.[70]

When conflict erupted in Virginia within weeks of the outbreak of King Philip's War, some people feared that a universal Indian uprising was in progress. The escalation of hostilities in the Chesapeake, however, owed more to Virginians' aggression than Indian actions. Militia units followed up on the earlier skirmish with the Doeg Indians by indiscriminately attacking Susquehannocks and then slaughtering several of their leaders during a fake peace parley. Before long, a vicious cycle of warfare tore through the countryside as Susquehannocks sought revenge on frontier plantations and colonial volunteers led by the recently arrived Nathaniel Bacon attacked any and all Indians they could find.[71]

Bacon drew his followers from the ranks of Virginia's young, propertyless men who coveted Indian lands and despised their own leaders, whom they regarded as a self-aggrandizing elite intent on denying the multitude any chance for economic independence. Prominent among their complaints against the government were high taxes levied to help build defensive forts along the frontier. Upset at seeing a line drawn between English and Indian territory in this way, discontented young men wanted instead to be given a free hand in exterminating Indians and appropriating their lands. Bacon championed their cause, less out of sympathy for their plight than to redress personal grievances against Governor William Berkeley. Under their intemperate leader's guidance, armed colonists descended not only on Susquehannocks but also on subject Indian peoples like the Pamunkeys and Occaneechees whose lands lay conveniently near existing plantations. When Berkeley declared Bacon and his followers to be rebels, the Indian war was absorbed into an internecine conflict of even larger proportions. As confusing as it was violent, the rebellion disintegrated quickly after Bacon died of dysentery in October 1676.[72]

Disentangling the Indian war from the rebellion itself remained difficult even after a measure of calm returned to Virginia. Unlike New Englanders, who rushed into print with numerous self-justifying histories of King Philip's War, Virginians preferred to forget the recent past rather than analyze it.[73] The Indians' side of the story is even more elusive, especially since no leader comparable to Metacom emerged to explain longstanding grievances against the colonists. Yet in its basic outlines, the story was familiar enough, and at least where fighting between colonists and Indians was concerned, it bore a striking resemblance to New England's experience. Once again, a burgeoning English population coveted Indian land, in this case to make room for tobacco as well as free-range livestock. Economic distress, including bad harvests and low tobacco prices, heightened the colonists' anxiety about their futures at an inopportune moment. On exposed frontier plantations, where sporadic Indian attacks on people and animals most often occurred, English settlers complained about lack of adequate protection. Other colonists, particularly those who wanted to move to the same areas, took up the cause without acknowledging any connection between native depredations and English entry onto their lands.[74]

No Indian leader in Virginia announced, as Metacom did in New England, that trespassing livestock contributed to the outbreak of hostilities. It was Bacon who implied that recurrent Indian depredations against livestock and other property justified *English* aggression. For years, Bacon charged,

Indians had acted as "Robbers and Theeves and Invaders" of colonial estates, a blanket accusation that included what had in fact been retaliatory acts of sabotage for damages suffered.[75] Those attacks only intensified after the war began, signaling the Indians' identification of livestock as enemies as deserving of destruction as their owners. At first wary Susquehannocks traveled in small parties and killed only "a very few Cattle and Swine" in outlying plantations. When the opportunity presented itself, they seized troopers' horses for food. Soon, however, native raids increased in severity. By August 1675, Doegs and Susquehannocks reportedly ambushed frontier farmers at will and "distroyed severall stocks of cattle in the said upper parts of Stafford County," terrifying inhabitants with surprise assaults. As English attacks spread to the Pamunkeys and other former Indian allies, they too responded with plundering raids on colonists' livestock and other property.[76]

When the chaos of war and rebellion finally subsided, weary colonists counted the "great Destruction of the Stocks" among their many losses. Rappahannock county residents reported that their region lay "a bleeding," with murdered planters and ravaged estates testifying to the Indians' savagery. As late as 1680, magistrates attributed a shortage of provisions in large part to the Indians' wartime destruction of cattle. Even as they complained of Indian depredations, magistrates allowed colonists to keep any goods—doubtless including hogs as well as other property—plundered from the Indians as legitimate spoils of war.[77]

Assigning blame for both of these catastrophes consumed colonists' energies even as they tried to put their lives back together. On the very day that Metacom died, William Harris of Rhode Island complained in a letter to England that some people accused colonists of bringing the disaster on themselves, oppressing Indians by "defrauding them of theyr land" and "trespasing in theyr corne by theyr cattell." Only self-interested scoundrels intent on flattering Indians to induce them to sell land or engage in trade, Harris sneered, would make such a preposterous charge when the Indians were clearly the aggressors. Edward Randolph, sent from England to investigate New England affairs, heard the same rumors but he believed the fault lay with colonists who willingly sold arms to Indians. Whenever the issue of animal trespass came up, New Englanders denied its importance. Defending Plymouth's behavior to the King himself, Nathaniel Morton insisted that "When an English plantation was near a body of Indians the English frequently fenced their fields for them that the cattle might not damnify them, and on complaint of trespass English justice was speedily granted." Morton's selective memory might have been improved by a careful reading of Plymouth's own records. In the end, New Englanders preferred to explain the war as a divine chastisement inflicted on them for their impiety. The colonists decided that their many sins included everything from failing to keep the Sabbath to cursing to wearing unseemly apparel, but had nothing to do with their trespassing livestock or their treatment of Indians.[78]

In Virginia, Governor Berkeley and those who had remained loyal to him were too busy wreaking vengeance on the rebels, 23 of whom were hanged, to delve into the causes of the Indian war. Yet Frances Moryson, one of the royal commissioners charged with investigating the rebellion, had little doubt that the fault lay with colonists who could not curb their lust for Indian land. The treaty that reestablished peace between Virginians and the Pamunkeys, Nottoways, and other subject Indians admitted as much. Article 4 claimed that the "Violent Intrusions of divers *English*" onto native lands had forced Indians "by way of Revenge, to kill the Cattel and Hogs of the *English*," helping to spark "the late unhappy Rebellion." The treaty stipulated that from then on, no English plantation ought to be established within three miles of an Indian village. Neither the admission of guilt nor the proposed solution was new. The treaty language repeated almost verbatim the preamble of a 1662 statute that had similarly discouraged colonists from settling in close proximity to Indians. If the statute had not resolved the problem, why should a treaty be any more effective?[79]

In the wake of these conflicts, everything seemed different, but nothing had changed. Physical damage everywhere attested to the ravages of war, and colonists and Indians alike sustained emotional wounds that never fully healed. Yet the juggernaut of colonial expansion only paused as the victorious English assessed the devastation. Within two decades, New Englanders had resettled destroyed frontier towns and begun occupying new lands. By the end of the century Virginians too claimed new territory for their plantations.[80] But the time that helped the colonists to recover brought no such solace to the Indians of southern New England or the Chesapeake. Suffering from severe population losses and lacking any hope for political influence in the postwar world, Indian survivors ended up in isolated enclaves dangerously vulnerable to English encroachment.[81]

That encroachment again began with invasions of livestock. To Choatam, the Assateague leader who protested when Edward Hammond drove cattle through his village, and to countless other Indians living wherever the English reigned supreme, the specter of past disputes disturbed the present and haunted the future. Even Uncas, the New Englanders' staunch Mohegan ally, could not convince colonists to keep their animals off his lands. After 1675 English livestock were as relentless in their destruction, and colonists as nonchalant in their response, as ever.[82]

The postwar world thus witnessed a resumption of earlier antagonisms and sabotage campaigns. Colonists killed Indian dogs, demolished Indian fences, stole Indian swine, and let their livestock run amok in Indian fields. They goaded Indians with taunts as well as physical aggression. Piscataways in Maryland heartily objected to being blamed for the disappearance of English hogs and then "called Rogues & doggs" to boot. In New England, colonists who had no qualms about enslaving defeated Indians after King Philip's War did not hesitate to circumscribe native behavior in other ways. They prohibited Indians from hunting or fishing in English towns and, after 1679, Indian hunters in Massachusetts could no longer set fires in the woods to clear out underbrush lest they inadvertently set colonists' haystacks ablaze. North and south, victory emboldened colonists to domineer over subject Indians as never before.[83]

Indians retaliated as vigorously as they dared, although now in rearguard actions against an onslaught they knew they could not stop. They mutilated and killed offending livestock, sometimes leaving carcasses as a cautionary message to the beasts' owners. Marylanders complained that Indians never passed by an English settlement "but the inhabitants receive some Signall dammage in their Stocks more then Usuall." In a parody of earmarking, Nanticoke Indians chopped off the ears and tails of trespassing colonial hogs. Such actions prompted Maryland officials to include prohibitions against hurting livestock in virtually every treaty with Indians. Northern colonies did not escape similar attacks. Shinnecock Indians on Long Island killed colonists' horses and buried them, though not so well that the owners could not find them. Outside of Dedham, Massachusetts, Indians repeatedly preyed on trespassing animals. Despite their weakened position, Indians adopted such actions to express their frustration and indignation.[84]

The expansion of English settlement introduced new groups of Indians to the perils of living near livestock and perpetuated the cycle of violence against animals. Colonial authorities in New England and the Chesapeake both accused the Iroquois of violating a newly forged alliance by attacking English cattle and swine, sometimes killing them "afore the faces of the Owners of them." Marylanders charged Delawares and "Northern" (probably Seneca) Indians with perpetrating similar atrocities. There seemed to be no end in sight to the violence. Wherever colonists went with their free-ranging animals, they used the creatures to occupy land and Indians defended themselves by every means possible.[85]

In less than a century a world of possibility had become a world of discord. The sense of wonder that infused early encounters among Indians, colonists, and animals gave way to disillusionment, opportunism, and antagonism. Cooperation diminished as competition—for land, dominance, or justice—intensified. Although livestock could hardly be blamed for every-thing that happened in early America, they certainly helped to shape the course of events. As indispensable to colonial survival as they were inimical to Indian sovereignty, livestock enabled the English to extend their dominion over the New World with remarkable speed and thoroughness. Few colonists would have credited their animals with such a momentous role, but Miantonomi had seen it coming. Long before the bloody conflicts that ended the century had come to pass, he warned his fellow Indians of what effects the colonists' fateful partnership with their animals might produce. For Metacom's generation, and those to follow, Miantonomi's grim prophecy became bitter reality.

Epilogue

Full Circle

*T*he dawn of the eighteenth century brought little change to the lopsided relationship between colonists and Indians in New England and the Chesapeake. Year by year, gradually expanding English settlements threatened to engulf remaining Indian outposts. In only a few instances did Indians, principally in New England, manage to use livestock husbandry as a strategy to protect their territorial claims. Ironically, their success depended on maintaining corporate control of land and animals, in defiance of English exhortations to switch to individual holdings.[1] Such exceptions notwithstanding, the triumphant occupation of the land by colonists and their livestock steadily progressed as the century wore on.

As always, roaming livestock acted as the advance guard of English settlement. The colonists' relaxed mode of husbandry endured so long as labor remained scarce and "empty" land seemed plentiful. New England farmers clung to seasonal free-range husbandry well into the eighteenth century and beyond, much to the despair of a handful of local agricultural improvers. Jared Eliot, who wrote a series of essays on this subject in the 1750s and 1760s, criticized New Englanders for such an extravagant use of land. Farmers in England, he noted, used less than an acre of enclosed pasture for each cow, yet colonists persisted in allocating five or six acres of open range for every animal. Echoing complaints lodged by European visitors more than a century earlier, Samuel Deane observed that New Englanders let their cattle wander so far from home that "the owner entirely loses them; or else spends as much time as they are worth in seeking after them." Competition for poor forage encouraged hungry animals "to leap over fences, or break through them" in search of better grass. Another critic was even more blunt, calling New England husbandmen "the most negligent ignorant set of men in the world." Not until the nineteenth century would a changing labor market and technological improvements permit a more intensive style of husbandry—far too late to ease the plight of New England's Indians.[2]

Free-range husbandry disappeared sooner in the Tidewater Chesapeake, although not until the middle of the eighteenth century. A shift in the labor supply from English indentured servants to African slaves, which accelerated after 1700, and an improving international market for grain worked together to produce the change. Responding to the new commercial opportunities, farmers with large estates and numerous slaves began converting tobacco lands into fields of wheat and corn. Because these crops (unlike tobacco) required plowing, planters invested in greater numbers of draft animals, which they kept in enclosures and fed on grain harvested by slaves. The manure that accumulated in animal pens was applied to grain fields, further increasing yields to be sold and used as fodder. At least on large plantations, the lax practices that had disturbed so many seventeenth-century commentators were on the wane.[3]

Yet the gradual transformation of husbandry regimes in the longest-settled colonial regions did not bring this historical chapter to a close. In subsequent years, the setting changed but the plot remained the same. Colonists moving to frontier areas experienced the identical combination of scarce labor and abundant land that had earlier produced free-range husbandry and accordingly adopted the same expedient as their forebears. New Englanders venturing north into New Hampshire and Maine drove livestock ahead to occupy choice tracts before their owners arrived. Even as Tidewater planters in the Chesapeake abandoned free-range husbandry, migrants to western Virginia and North Carolina set their animals loose. In an ironic twist, wealthy planters such as William Byrd II scorned these frontier settlers as "Indolent Wretches" for the same "ill Management" of livestock that had characterized Byrd's father's generation.[4] As happened before, so too once again Indians bore the brunt of the troubles instigated by free-ranging animals.

The story did not end at the eastern seaboard or with the transition from British colonies to American nation. Free-range husbandry moved westward with American settlers across the Appalachians into the Midwest and beyond. Wherever labor was harder to find than land, animals occupied territory on their own account and their owners dealt with the consequences much as the first English colonists had. After 1776, livestock helped a new national empire to spread across the continent, much as they had enabled England to establish a foothold on the Atlantic coast nearly two centuries earlier.[5]

For Indians too, history repeated itself. And that repetition manifested itself not just in the sudden appearance of strange, voracious animals on native lands but in the earnest entreaties of Americans urging Indians to leave old ways behind and become keepers of livestock. No less a figure than Thomas Jefferson expounded upon the utility of animal husbandry as a mechanism for civilizing Indians. Indeed, he regarded raising cattle as the essential first step in any such plan, for it helped Indians to "acquire a knowledge of the value of property." Although Jefferson spoke in the language of the Enlightenment, his words echoed the sentiments of the seventeenth-century Virginia burgesses who were convinced that cows would turn Indians into Christians.[6]

These were words, and promises, that Indians had heard before. And the outcome was likewise familiar. Many Indians did turn to livestock husbandry to compensate for the environmental and other changes induced by American settlement, but like earlier generations they did so in their own ways, rejecting the entire civilizing agenda that aimed to erase native culture. This partial accommodation served them no better than it did Metacom or other Indians of an earlier era. Even the Cherokees, whose engagement with animal husbandry and many other elements of American culture exceeded that of nearly any other Indian group, suffered the loss of their land and forced displacement. No wonder that expressions of Indian resistance, in the nineteenth century as before, took the form of attacks on livestock as hated symbols of American encroachment. With such experiences, the narrative of the intertwined histories of Indians, colonists, and animals comes full circle.[7]

At various times, Indians and Euro-Americans shared a genuine interest in cooperation when it came to dealing with livestock, but in nearly every instance that desire fell victim to two irrepressible forces. Indians who learned to live with livestock did so because they wished to remain Indians, a preference that English colonists and their American descendants could neither understand nor abide. Yet for colonists and their successors, even limited efforts to reach accommodation with Indians evaporated when the consequences of their husbandry methods became clear. It was their own insatiable drive for land, fueled by demographic growth and the steady increase in their herds, that overwhelmed the possibility for harmonious coexistence. Therein lies the tragedy of this story. Indians found room in their world for livestock, but the colonists and their descendants could find no room in theirs for Indians.

Notes

Works frequently cited have been identified
by the following abbreviations:

AHR	*American Historical Review*
Ct. Recs.	J. Hammond Trumbull, ed. *The Public Records of the Colony of Connecticut,* 15 vols. Hartford, 1850–90.
JAH	*Journal of American History*
Mass. Bay Recs.	Nathaniel B. Shurtleff, ed. *Records of the Governor and Company of the Massachusetts Bay in New England.* 5 vols. Boston, 1853–54.
Md. Arch.	William Hand Browne, ed. *Archives of Maryland.* 72 vols. Baltimore, 1883–1972.
MHS *Colls.*	Massachusetts Historical Society, *Collections.*
NEQ	*New England Quarterly*
New Haven Recs.	Charles J. Hoadly, ed. *Records of the Colony and Plantation of New Haven, From 1638 to 1649.* 2 vols. Hartford, 1857–58.
Plym. Col. Recs.	Nathaniel B. Shurtleff and David Pulsifer, eds. *Records of the Colony of New Plymouth in New England.* 12 vols. Boston, 1855–61.
R.I. Recs.	John Russell Bartlett, ed. *Records of the Colony of Rhode Island and Providence Plantations in New England.* 10 vols. Providence, 1856–65.
Va. Statutes	William Waller Hening, ed. *The Statutes at Large; Being a Collection of All the Laws of Virginia, . . .* 13 vols. Richmond, 1819–23.
VMHB	*Virginia Magazine of History and Biography*
WMQ	*William and Mary Quarterly*

Limited alterations have been made in quotations from seventeenth-century sources to correspond with modern usage. Such changes included substituting "i" for "j," "v" for "u," and "th" for "y" and expanding abbreviations. Otherwise, spelling and punctuation have been reproduced from the original texts.

PROLOGUE: SEEING BANQUO'S GHOST

1. Duxbury became a separate town in 1637. For its origins, see William Bradford, *Of Plymouth Plantation, 1620–1647,* ed. Samuel Eliot Morison (New York, 1952), 253.
2. Neal Salisbury, *Manitou and Providence: Indians, Europeans, and the Making of New England, 1500–1643* (New York, 1982),110–52.
3. Alfred W. Crosby, Jr., *The Columbian Exchange: Biological and Cultural Consequences of 1492* (Westport, 1972) and *Ecological Imperialism: The Biological Expansion of Europe, 900–1900* (New York, 1986). Other key works focusing on English colonization include William Cronon, *Changes in the Land: Indians, Colonists, and the Ecology of New England* (New York, 1983); Carolyn Merchant, *Ecological Revolutions: Nature, Gender, and Science in New England* (Chapel Hill, 1989); Timothy Silver, *A New Face on the Countryside: Indians, Colonists, and Slaves in South Atlantic Forests, 1500–1800* (New York, 1990). For a more expansive examination of the topic by a nonhistorian, see Jared Diamond, *Guns, Germs, and Steel: The Fates of Human Societies* (New York, 1997).
4. Daniel Richter's masterful synthesis, *Facing East From Indian Country: A Native History of Early America* (Cambridge, Mass., 2001), provides an excellent overview of the scholarship that has informed the present study.
5. For a general discussion of the cultural implications of agriculture, see Frieda Knobloch, *The Culture of Wilderness: Agriculture as Colonization in the American West* (Chapel Hill, 1996).
6. Richard White, *The Middle Ground: Indians, Empires, and Republics in the Great Lakes Region, 1650–1815* (New York,

CHAPTER ONE: CHICKWALLOP AND THE STRANGE BEAST

1. Letter from John Pynchon to John Winthrop, Jr., dated 5 March 1668/69 in Carl Bridenbaugh, ed., *The Pynchon Papers,* 2 vols. (Boston, 1982–85), 1:79–80. I thank Kevin Sweeney for this reference.
2. Suggestive evidence about the origins of this charge appears in a subsequent letter from Pynchon to Winthrop; see Bridenbaugh, ed., *Pynchon Papers,* 1: 83. For information on Jeremy Adams, see Robert Charles Anderson, ed., *The Great Migration Begins: Immigrants to New England 1620–1633,* 3 vols. (Boston, 1995), 1:6–11. For the often tense relations between Indians and colonists in the Connecticut Valley, see Peter A. Thomas, *In the Maelstrom of Change: The Indian Trade and Cultural Process in the Middle Connecticut River Valley, 1635–1665* (New York, 1990), 144–55.
3. Yasuhide Kawashima, *Puritan Justice and the Indian: White Man's Law in Massachusetts, 1630–1763* (Middletown, 1986), 130–33; James P. Ronda, "Red and White at the Bench: Indians and the Law in Plymouth Colony, 1620–1691," *Essex Institute Historical Collections,* 110 (1974): 200–15.

4. Bridenbaugh, ed., *Pynchon Papers,* 1:79, 80. The elder John Winthrop men-
    tioned heavy winter snowfalls in 1635 and 1636 in his journal; see Richard S.
    Dunn, James Savage, and Laetitia Yeandle, eds., *The Journal of John Winthrop
    1630–1649* (Cambridge, Mass., 1996), 137–38, 141, 161.

5. See Mary Midgley, *Beast and Man: The Roots of Human Nature,* 2nd ed. (London
    and New York, 1995).

6. William Strachey, *The Historie of Travell Into Virginia Britania* (1612), ed. Louis
    B. Wright and Virginia Freund, The Hakluyt Society, 2nd ser., no. 103 (London,
    1953): 193; Roger Williams, *A Key into the Language of America* (1643), ed.
    John J. Teunissen and Evelyn J. Hinz (Detroit, 1973), 173; John Eliot, *The Indian
    Grammar Begun* . . . (Cambridge, Mass., 1666), 9. On the difficulty in recovering
    Indian ideas about the natural world, see Richard White, "Indian Peoples and
    the Natural World: Asking the Right Questions," in Donald L. Fixico, ed.,
    Rethinking American History (Albuquerque, 1997), 87–100; I thank Jim Drake
    for this reference. A general treatment of colonial responses to native languages
    may be found in Edward G. Gray, *New World Babel: Languages & Nations in
    Early America* (Princeton, 1999).

7. Strachey, *Historie,* 55; Glenn W. LaFantasie, ed., *The Correspondence of Roger
    Williams,* 2 vols. (Hanover and London, 1988), 1:146.

8. Thomas Hariot, *A Briefe and True Report* (1588) in David Beers Quinn, ed., *The
    Roanoke Voyages, 1584–1590,* The Hakluyt Society, 2nd ser., no. 104 (London,
    1955), 373; Edward Winslow, *Good Newes from New England,* . . . (1624) in
    Alexander Young, ed., *Chronicles of the Pilgrim Fathers of the Colony of Ply-
    mouth, from 1602 to 1625* (Boston, 1841), 356; William S. Simmons, *Spirit of the
    New England Tribes: Indian History and Folklore, 1620–1984* (Hanover, 1986),
    38–41, 172–234. Kiehtan was also known as Cautantowwit or Kautántouwit.

9. Strachey, *Historie,* 102; Helen C. Rountree, *The Powhatan Indians of Virginia:
    Their Traditional Culture* (Norman, Okla., and London, 1989), 131; Paul J.
    Lindholdt, ed., *John Josselyn, Colonial Traveler: A Critical Edition of Two
    Voyages to New England* (Hanover, 1988), 97; Edward Johnson, *Johnson's
    Wonder-Working Providence 1628–1651* (1654), ed. J. Franklin Jameson (New
    York, 1910), 263.

10. Henry Whitfield, *Strength Out of Weaknesse; or a Glorious Manifestation of the
    Further Progresse of the Gospel among the Indians in New England* (1652), in
    MHS *Colls.,* 3rd ser. (1834) 4:187; see also Simmons, *Spirit of the New England
    Tribes,* 91.

11. On this point, see James Axtell, *The Invasion Within: The Contest of Cultures
    in Colonial North America* (New York, 1985), 16; Colin G. Calloway, *New Worlds
    for All: Indians, Europeans, and the Remaking of Early America* (Baltimore,
    1997), 72–73; Clara Sue Kidwell, "Science and Ethnoscience: Native American
    World Views as a Factor in the Development of Native Technologies," in Kendall
    E. Bailes, ed., *Environmental History: Critical Issues in Comparative Perspec-
    tive* (Lanham, 1985), 277–87.

12. Kathleen J. Bragdon, *Native People of Southern New England, 1500–1650* (Norman, Okla., 1996), 188–90; William S. Simmons, "Cultural Bias in the New England Puritans' Perception of Indians," *WMQ*, 3rd ser., 38 (1981): 56–72; Karen Ordahl Kupperman, *Indians & English: Facing Off in Early America* (Ithaca, 2000), ch. 4.

13. Williams, *Key*, 191. For discussions of the concept of *manitou*, see Constance A. Crosby, "From Myth to History, or Why King Philip's Ghost Walks Abroad," in Mark P. Leone and Parker B. Potter, eds., *The Recovery of Meaning: Historical Archaeology in the Eastern United States* (Washington, D.C., 1988), 183–209; Bragdon, *Native People*, 184–90.

14. Williams, *Key*, 173, 174, 225; Bragdon, *Native People*, 145.

15. On meat in the Indian diet, see M. K. Bennett, "The Food Economy of the New England Indians, 1605–75," *Journal of Political Economy*, 63 (1955): 387–88; John R. Swanton, *The Indians of the Southeastern United States* (Washington, D.C., and London, 1946; reprinted 1979), 295. Perhaps the best known historical study of Indian perceptions of the spiritual power of animals is Calvin Martin, *Keepers of the Game: Indian-Animal Relationships and the Fur Trade* (Berkeley, 1978). Martin's thesis about the effects of European contact and the fur trade on the Indian-animal relationship has sparked considerable criticism, but his description of precontact relations remains useful. For Martin's critics, see Shepard Krech III, ed., *Indians, Animals, and the Fur Trade: A Critique of Keepers of the Game* (Athens, Ga., 1981). There are numerous examples of Indian conceptions of animals' spiritual power in Bruce G. Trigger, ed., *Northeast*, vol. 15 of *Handbook of North American Indians*, ed. William Sturtevant (Washington, D.C., 1978), 84, 139, 192, 319.

16. Bragdon, *Native People*, 97–98; Williams, *Key*, 182, 210–14.

17. Bragdon, *Native People*, 187–88.

18. Lindholdt, ed., *John Josselyn*, 20–21; Bragdon, *Native People*, 187–88.

19. A 1533 Parliamentary statute required English villagers to keep nets to catch crows; see Keith Thomas, *Man and the Natural World: A History of the Modern Sensibility* (New York, 1983), 274. For the Narragansetts, see Williams, *Key*, 163–64; for White's painting, see Paul Hulton, *America 1585: The Complete Drawings of John White* (Chapel Hill, 1984), plate 36, p. 66.

20. See Karen Ordahl Kupperman, *Settling with The Indians: The Meeting of English and Indian Cultures in America, 1580–1640* (Totowa, N.J., 1980), ch. 2; and her "Presentment of Civility: English Reading of American Self-Presentation in the Early Years of Colonization," *WMQ*, 3rd ser., 54 (1997): 193–228; Bernard Sheehan, *Savagism and Civility: Indians and Englishmen in Colonial Virginia* (New York, 1980), 48–51; Joyce E. Chaplin, *Subject Matter: Technology, the Body, and Science on the Anglo-American Frontier, 1500–1676* (Cambridge, Mass., 2001), 138–39.

21. Philip L. Barbour, ed., *The Complete Works of Captain John Smith (1580–1631)*, 3 vols. (Chapel Hill, 1986), 1:149, see also 160–61; William Wood, *New En-*

gland's Prospect (1634), ed. Alden T. Vaughan (Amherst, 1977), 84. For similar descriptions, see James Rosier, *A True Relation . . .* (1605) in David B. Quinn and Alison M. Quinn, eds., *The English New England Voyages 1602–1608,* The Hakluyt Society, 2nd ser., no. 161 (London, 1983): 268–69; Williams, *Key,* 185–87.

22. Wood, *New England's Prospect,* 85; "Observations by Master George Percy, 1607," in Lyon G. Tyler, ed., *Narratives of Early Virginia 1606–1625* (New York, 1907), 19; Barbour, ed., *Works of John Smith,* 1:161.

23. *The Discoveries of John Lederer . . .* (1672), in Clarence Walworth Alvord and Lee Bidgood, eds., *The First Explorations of the Trans-Allegheny Region by the Virginians 1650–1674* (Cleveland, 1912), 143, 154.

24. Julian Franklyn and John Tanner, *An Encyclopaedic Dictionary of Heraldry* (Oxford, 1970), 207; Stephen Friar, ed., *A Dictionary of Heraldry* (New York, 1987), 218, 312.

25. For the absence of totemism among most southern New England Algonquians, see Bragdon, *Native People,* 185–86.

26. Barbour, ed., *Works of John Smith,* 1:170; Strachey, *Historie,* 74; Wood, *New England's Prospect,* 85.

27. Williams, *Key,* 127; Patricia E. Rubertone, *Grave Undertakings: An Archaeology of Roger Williams and the Narragansett Indians* (Washington, D.C., 2001), 150–51, 156; Charles C. Willoughby, *Antiquities of the New England Indians* (Cambridge, Mass., 1935), 106–10, 164, 166, 169–70; Bragdon, *Native People,* 118–19, 187.

28. L. Daniel Mouer, "Chesapeake Creoles: The Creation of Folk Culture in Colonial Virginia," in Theodore R. Reinhart and Dennis J. Pogue, eds., *The Archaeology of 17th-Century Virginia,* Special Publication No. 30 of the Archeological Society of Virginia (Richmond, 1993), 129–35; Rountree, *Powhatan Indians,* 134; Barbour, ed., *Works of John Smith,* 1:173–74. For Powhatan's mantle, see Gregory A. Waselkov, "Indian Maps of the Colonial Southeast," in Peter H. Wood, Gregory A. Waselkov, and M. Thomas Hatley, eds., *Powhatan's Mantle: Indians in the Colonial Southeast* (Lincoln, 1989), 306–8.

29. Robert Beverley, *The History and Present State of Virginia,* ed. Louis B. Wright (Chapel Hill, 1947; reprinted Charlottesville, 1968), 190.

30. Barbour, ed., *Works of John Smith,* 1:164; Wood, *New England's Prospect,* 105. On the spiritual implications of hunting, see Bragdon, *Native People,* 133–34. For the significance of archery in early English colonization, see Chaplin, *Subject Matter,* ch. 3.

31. Barbour, ed., *Works of John Smith,* 1:164; Strachey, *Historie,* 113; Regina Flannery, *An Analysis of Coastal Algonquian Culture* (Washington, D.C., 1939), 135; Frank G. Speck, "Chapters on the Ethnology of the Powhatan Tribes of Virginia," *Indian Notes and Monographs,* vol. 1, no. 5 (1928): 347; Rountree, *Powhatan Indians,* 85. Speck's evidence for the Pamunkey feast derived from

early twentieth-century observations, but may well reflect a much older tradition.

32. Barbour, ed., *Works of John Smith*, 1:164, 263; Williams, *Key*, 224. For general accounts of Indian hunting, see Bragdon, *Native People*, 117–18; William Cronon, *Changes in the Land: Indians, Colonists, and the Ecology of New England* (New York, 1983), 38, 46–48, 50, 63–65, 107, 163; Neal Salisbury, *Manitou and Providence: Indians, Europeans, and the Making of New England, 1500–1643* (New York, 1982), 32, 34, 39; Rountree, *Powhatan Indians*, 38–42, 44, 57, 79, 87, 88.

33. Wood, *New England's Prospect*, 105.

34. Barbour, ed., *Works of John Smith*, 1:164; see also Williams, *Key*, 224.

35. Barbour, ed., *Works of John Smith*, 1:171.

36. Salisbury, *Manitou and Providence*, 35; Colin G. Calloway, *The Western Abenakis of Vermont, 1600–1800: War, Migration, and the Survival of an Indian People* (Norman, Okla., 1990), 49–50; Rountree, *Powhatan Indians*, 136.

37. Barbour, ed., *Works of John Smith*, 1:165.

38. "A Letter from Mr. John Clayton, Rector of Crofton at Wakefield in Yorkshire, to the Royal Society, May 12, 1688," in Peter Force, ed., *Tracts and Other Papers, Relating Principally to the Origin, Settlement, and Progress of the Colonies in North America, From the Discovery of the Country to the Year 1776*, 4 vols. (Washington, D.C., 1836–44; reprinted, Gloucester, 1963), 3:§12, 35.

39. The description of the moose hunt in this and succeeding paragraphs is based on Josselyn's account in Lindholdt, ed., *John Josselyn*, 98–99.

40. John Josselyn, *New-Englands Rarities Discovered: In Birds, Beasts, Fishes, Serpents, and Plants of that Country* (London, 1672), 20; Adrian Tanner, *Bringing Home Animals: Religious Ideology and Mode of Production of the Mistassini Cree Hunters* (New York, 1979), 155–56; Robert A. Brightman, *Grateful Prey: Rock Cree Human-Animal Relationships* (Berkeley, 1993), 110–13, 117, 120, 123; for the Crees' gendered division of labor in butchering game, see 123–32.

41. Adriaen Van der Donck, *A Description of the New Netherlands*, ed. Thomas F. O'Donnell (Syracuse, 1968), 120; John Lawson, *A New Voyage to Carolina*, ed. Hugh Talmage Lefler (Chapel Hill, 1967), 58. Modern Crees hang animal bones in trees, or boil or burn them, to keep them from dogs and show respect to the animal's soul; see Brightman, *Grateful Prey*, 118–19, 132–33.

42. Letter from Peter Wynne to Sir John Egerton (1608) in Philip Barbour, ed., *The Jamestown Voyages Under the First Charter 1606–1609*, 2 vols., The Hakluyt Society, 2nd ser., no. 136 (Cambridge, Eng., 1969): 246; Strachey, *Historie*, 79–80.

43. Lindholdt, ed., *John Josselyn*, 91; Daniel Gookin, *Historical Collections of the Indians in New England* (1674) (Boston, 1792; facsimile reprint New York, 1972), 5; William Hubbard, *A General History of New England, From the*

Discovery to MDCLXXX (New York, 1972; reprinted from MHS *Colls.*, ser. 2, vols. 5–6), 25; Beverley, *History and Present State of Virginia*, 17.

44. Jared Diamond, *Guns, Germs, and Steel: The Fates of Human Societies* (New York, 1997), 142, 167, 213; Alfred W. Crosby, Jr., *The Columbian Exchange: Biological and Cultural Consequences of 1492* (Westport, 1972), 74–75; Frederick E. Zeuner, *A History of Domesticated Animals* (London, 1963), 436–39; Marion Schwartz, *A History of Dogs in the Early Americas* (New Haven, 1997).

45. Diamond, *Guns, Germs, and Steel*, 46–47, 170–73; Shepard Krech III, *The Ecological Indian: Myth and History* (New York, 1999), ch. 1; Zeuner, *History of Domesticated Animals*, 37; Juliet Clutton-Brock, *Domesticated Animals from Early Times* (London and Austin, 1981), 15–16, 130–34, 172–74.

46. Clutton-Brock, *Domesticated Animals*, 19–20; Zeuner, *History of Domesticated Animals*, 23–35, 55–63; Diamond, *Guns, Germs, and Steel*, 167.

47. On the availability of protein from wild food sources and the low population densities among eastern Indians, see Cronon, *Changes in the Land*, 39–41, 45–48; Timothy Silver, *A New Face on the Countryside: Indians, Colonists, and Slaves in South Atlantic Forests, 1500–1800* (New York, 1990), 35–37, 39. For the timing of plant domestication among Algonquians, see Bragdon, *Native People*, 77–79; Stephen R. Potter, *Commoners, Tribute, and Chiefs: The Development of Algonquian Culture in the Potomac Valley* (Charlottesville, 1993), 101.

48. For the Narragansetts' use of hawks, see Williams, *Key*, 166. Dogs were the first creatures to be domesticated by humans, an innovation that appeared independently about 12,000 years ago in southwest Asia, China, and North America. See Diamond, *Guns, Germs, and Steel*, 167.

49. Barbour, ed., *Jamestown Voyages*, Hakluyt Society, 2nd ser., no. 136: 246; Lindholdt, ed., *John Josselyn*, 91; Barbour, ed., *Works of John Smith*, 1:155; Lawson, *New Voyage to Carolina*, 44; Josselyn, *New-Englands Rarities*, 15.

50. Helmut Hemmer, *Domestication: The Decline of Environmental Appreciation* (New York, 1990), 38–44; Zeuner, *History of Domesticated Animals*, 102–5; Clutton-Brock, *Domesticated Animals from Early Times*, 39–40; Schwartz, *History of Dogs*, 15–18.

51. Thomas, *Man and the Natural World*, 101–8.

52. Zeuner, *History of Domesticated Animals*, 63; Clutton-Brock, *Domesticated Animals from Early Times*, 39.

53. Schwartz, *History of Dogs*, 31–39, 46–55, 92; Trigger, ed., *Northeast*, 382, 686, see also 734–35, 764; Barbour, ed., *Jamestown Voyages*, Hakluyt Society, 2nd ser., no. 136: 246. Dogs are absent from the list of southeastern Indian foods, see Swanton, *Indians of the Southeastern United States*, 295; for the possibility that eastern Algonquians ate them in famines, see Flannery, *Analysis of Coastal Algonquian Culture*, 32–33, 178.

54. Juliet Clutton-Brock, "Dog," in Ian L. Mason, ed., *Evolution of Domesticated Animals* (London and New York, 1984), 204–5; Zeuner, *History of Domesticated*

Animals, 39–42, 83–85; Swanton, *Indians of the Southeastern United States,* 345; Lawson, *New Voyage to Carolina*, 44. The animal ecologist I. Lehr Brisbin, who has studied what he believes are descendants of early Indian dogs, has identified a "pariah niche" occupied by semiwild dogs that subsist largely from scavenging near human settlements. This may apply to the situation of seventeenth-century Algonquian dogs; see Scott Weidensaul, "Tracking America's First Dog," *Smithsonian,* 29 (March, 1999): 46.

55. William Bradford, *Of Plymouth Plantation 1620–1647,* ed. Samuel Eliot Morison (New York, 1952), 64; John Mason, "A Brief History of the Pequot War," in Charles Orr, ed., *History of the Pequot War: The Contemporary Accounts of Mason, Underhill, Vincent, and Gardener* (Cleveland, 1897), 27.

56. Howard M. Chapin, *Dogs in Early New England* (Providence, 1920), 5. Indian signature marks were usually bows and arrows or hatchets; for an example of a dog, see *R.I. Recs.,* 1:136.

57. Bragdon, *Native Peoples,* 34; Paul A. Robinson, Marc A. Kelley, and Patricia E. Rubertone, "Preliminary Biocultural Interpretations from a Seventeenth-Century Narragansett Indian Cemetery in Rhode Island," in William W. Fitzhugh, ed., *Cultures in Contact: The European Impact on Native Cultural Institutions in Eastern North America, A.D. 1000–1800* (Washington, D.C., 1985), 123.

58. David J. Silverman, "'We chuse to be bounded': Native American Animal Husbandry in Colonial New England," *WMQ,* 3rd ser., 60 (2003): 517–19. On the basis of Silverman's article and comments from Daniel Richter, I have modified my argument about the incompatibility of domestication with native culture presented in "King Philip's Herds: Indians, Colonists, and the Problem of Livestock in Early New England," *WMQ,* 3rd ser., 51 (1994): 606–7.

59. Christopher L. Miller and George R. Hamell, "A New Perspective on Indian-White Contact: Cultural Symbols and Colonial Trade," *JAH,* 73 (1986–87): 311–28; James H. Merrell, "'The Customes of Our Countrey': Indians and Colonists in Early America," in Bernard Bailyn and Philip D. Morgan, eds., *Strangers Within the Realm: Cultural Margins of the First British Empire* (Chapel Hill, 1991), 131–33; James H. Merrell, *The Indians' New World: Catawbas and Their Neighbors from European Contact through the Era of Removal* (New York, 1989), 32–34.

60. Williams, *Key,* 103, 158, 176, 240.

61. Rubertone, *Grave Undertakings,* 191–97; William A. Turnbaugh, "The Material Culture of RI-1000: A Mid-17th-Century Narragansett Indian Burial Site in North Kingstown, Rhode Island," (Kingston, R.I., 1984), typescript at Tozzer Library, Peabody Museum, Harvard University; Bragdon, *Native People,* 232–33; Elise M. Brenner, "Sociopolitical Implications of Mortuary Ritual Remains in 17th-Century Native Southern New England," in Leone and Potter, eds., *Recovery of Meaning,* 147–81.

62. Edward Winslow, *Good Newes from New England: or a true Relation of things very remarkable at the Plantation of Plimoth in New-England* (1624), in

Alexander Young, ed., *Chronicles of the Pilgrim Fathers of the Colony of Plymouth, from 1602 to 1625* (Boston, 1841), 359; Whitfield, *Strength Out of Weaknesse,* 187; Crosby, "From Myth to History," 183–209.

63. Cronon, *Changes in the Land,* 130.

64. James Lockhart, *The Nahuas After the Conquest: A Social and Cultural History of the Indians of Central Mexico, Sixteenth Through Eighteenth Centuries* (Stanford, 1992), 279–80; Inga Clendinnen, *Ambivalent Conquests: Maya and Spaniard in Yucatan, 1517–1570* (New York, 1987), 137; Strachey, *Historie,* 179; Williams, *Key,* 173–74. Williams also noted that Narragansetts used the term *netasûog* for their own tame birds as well as colonists' cattle, but he then recorded the analogy between hogs and woodchucks. James Trumbull translated *ockqutchuan* as woodchuck; see his *Natick Dictionary,* Bureau of American Ethnology, Smithsonian Institution, Bulletin 25 (Washington, D.C., 1903): 277. Great Plains Indians encountering Spanish cattle in the sixteenth century initially considered them "spotted buffalo"; see John C. Ewers, "Spanish Cattle in Plains Indian Art," *Great Plains Journal,* 16 (1976): 67. Cherokee Indians likened hogs to opossums; see Tom Hatley, *The Dividing Paths: Cherokees and South Carolinians through the Era of Revolution* (New York, 1993), 162. In the nineteenth century, Ojibwa Indians called cattle *pijiki,* or buffalo; see Rebecca Kugel, "Of Missionaries and Their Cattle: Ojibwa Perceptions of a Missionary as Evil Shaman," *Ethnohistory* 41 (1994): 228.

65. Silverman, "'We chuse to be bounded,'" 518.

66. Barbour, ed., *Works of John Smith,* 3:318.

67. Dunn, et al., eds., *Journal of John Winthrop,* 406. For another discussion of Indians imputing spiritual power to European livestock, see Kugel, "Of Missionaries and Their Cattle," 227–44.

68. "The Journeys of Needham and Arthur" [1674], in Alvord and Bidgood, eds., *First Explorations of the Trans-Allegheny Region,* 212–13. John Lawson similarly described Waxhaw Indians feeding a horse with corn "till he is as fat as a Hog"; see Lawson, *New Voyage to Carolina,* 44.

69. Charles Hudson, *Knights of Spain, Warriors of the Sun: Hernando de Soto and the South's Ancient Chiefdoms* (Athens, Ga., 1997), 72–78; Ian K. Steele, *Warpaths: Invasions of North America* (New York, 1994), 14, 31–32. For Carolina Indian leaders' enthusiasm for horses, see Lawson, *New Voyage to Carolina,* 44.

70. Bragdon, *Native People,* 220; Rountree, *Powhatan Indians,* 108–9.

CHAPTER TWO: THE DEER WITH THE RED COLLAR

1. George Francis Dow, ed., *Records and Files of the Quarterly Courts of Essex County, Massachusetts,* 9 vols. (Salem, 1911–75), 8:299–300; Michael Dalton, *The Countrey Justice . . . ,* enlarged edition (London, 1666), 306.

2.　There was no restriction on hunting wild deer in Massachusetts until 1694; see William Cronon, *Changes in the Land: Indians, Colonists, and the Ecology of New England* (New York, 1983), 101.

3.　The charges against Webster were eventually dismissed for unspecified reasons; see Dow, ed., *Essex Quarterly Court Recs.*, 8:299.

4.　For a discussion of this theme as it relates to the nineteenth-century American West, see Richard White, "Animals and Enterprise," in Clyde A. Milner II, Carol A. O'Connor, Martha Sandweiss, eds., *The Oxford History of the American West* (New York and Oxford, 1994), 237–73. I owe this reference to Jon Coleman.

5.　H. Kirke Swann, *A Dictionary of English and Folk-Names of British Birds* (London, 1913), 232; Keith Thomas, *Man and the Natural World: A History of the Modern Sensibility* (New York, 1983), 76–77.

6.　Swann, *Dictionary of English and Folk-Names of British Birds*, 20, 55, 127, 187, 201, 232; for other examples of birds thought to predict rain, see pp. 42, 62, 135, 152, 158, 226. In some of these cases, Swann notes classical or early British sources for these beliefs. See also Stephen Wilson, *The Magical Universe: Everyday Ritual and Magic in Pre-Modern Europe* (Hambledon and London, 2000), 52.

7.　Swann, *Dictionary of English and Folk-Names of British Birds*, 189, 191, 217.

8.　Thomas, *Man and the Natural World*, 75–76; John Worlidge, *Systema Agriculturae; The Mystery of Husbandry Discovered*, 4th ed. (London, 1687), 302–3. On the persistence of weather lore, see also E. Estyn Evans, "The Cultural Geographer and Folklife Research," in Richard M. Dorson, ed., *Folklore and Folklife: An Introduction* (Chicago and London, 1972), 528.

9.　Swann, *Dictionary of English and Folk-Names of British Birds*, 13, 42, 67, 151, 198, 201, 231; Thomas, *Man and the Natural World*, 76–77; Worlidge, *Systema Agriculturae*, 303; Wilson, *Magical Universe*, 383–84, 386, 416–17.

10.　Swann, *Dictionary of English and Folk-Names of British Birds*, 13, 127, 151, 189, 196, 199, 209, 233, 251; Worlidge, *Systema Agriculturae*, 303; Wilson, *Magical Universe*, 289, 384–85.

11.　On the difficulty of assessing the significance of folklore, see D. R. Woolf, "The 'Common Voice': History, Folklore and Oral Tradition in Early Modern England," *Past & Present*, 120 (1988): 26–52; James Obelkevich, "Proverbs and Social History," in Peter Burke and Roy Porter, eds., *The Social History of Language* (Cambridge, Eng., 1987), 45–55.

12.　Thomas, *Man and the Natural World*, 76–77; Worlidge, *Systema Agriculturae*, 289–308; Obelkevich, "Proverbs and Social History," 55–57; Woolf, "The 'Common Voice'," 26–38; on the interconnections between oral and print culture in early modern England, see Barry Reay, *Popular Cultures in England 1550–1750* (London and New York, 1998), ch. 2.

13.　For a summary of recent research on literacy rates in early modern England, see Reay, *Popular Cultures in England*, 39–47.

14. B. A. Botkin, ed., *A Treasury of New England Folklore,* rev. ed. (New York, 1965), 346, 348; Bartlett Jere Whiting, *Early American Proverbs and Proverbial Phrases* (Cambridge, Mass., and London, 1977), 143, 214. Because the skin temperature of hogs follows the temperature of their surroundings, in cooler weather or with increased air circulation they are prone to evaporative heat loss; their sensitivity to wind may thus have given rise to the impression that they could "see" the wind; see L. E. Mount, "Adaptation of Swine," in E. S. E. Hafez, ed., *Adaptation of Domestic Animals* (Philadelphia, 1968), 277, 281–86. For Sewall's notations about swallows, see M. Halsey Thomas, ed., *The Diary of Samuel Sewall 1674–1729,* 2 vols. (New York, 1973), 1:408, 429, 501, 522, 544, 564, 594; 2: 658, 685, 710, 791, 815, 893, 921, 946, 1014, 1046; in many parts of England, April 15 was celebrated as "Swallow Day"; see Swann, *Dictionary of English and Folk-Names of British Birds,* 231. The incident with Charles Chauncy is described in David D. Hall, *Worlds of Wonder, Days of Judgment: Popular Religious Belief in Early New England* (New York, 1989), 83. On the transmission to the colonies of English popular religion (although not animal lore specifically), see Hall, *Worlds of Wonder;* Jon Butler, *Awash in a Sea of Faith: Christianizing the American People* (Cambridge. Mass., and London, 1990), especially chs. 1 and 3. Little has been written about the topic in the Chesapeake region, but see James Horn, *Adapting to a New World: English Society in the Seventeenth-Century Chesapeake* (Chapel Hill, 1994), ch. 9.

15. Thomas, *Man and the Natural World,* 71–78. For a discussion of medieval Europeans' fascination with portents, see Norman R. Smith, "Portent Lore and Medieval Popular Culture," *Journal of Popular Culture,* 14 (1980): 47–59.

16. Swann, *Dictionary of English and Folk-Names of British Birds,* 151, 188–89, 262; Elizabeth Atwood Lawrence, *Hunting the Wren: Transformation of Bird to Symbol* (Knoxville, 1997); Keith Thomas, *Religion and the Decline of Magic* (London, 1971); Reay, *Popular Cultures in England,* 86–90.

17. Swann, *Dictionary of English and Folk-Names of British Birds,* 198–99.

18. The story of the Narragansetts and crows, described in chapter 1, appears in Roger Williams, *A Key into the Language of America,* ed. John J. Teunissen and Evelyn J. Hinz (Detroit, 1973), 164.

19. James Sharpe, *Instruments of Darkness: Witchcraft in England 1550–1750* (London, 1996), 71–74, 137, 283; Robin Briggs, *Witches & Neighbors: The Social and Cultural Context of European Witchcraft* (Harmondsworth, 1996), 29–30, 53, 235; Reay, *Popular Cultures in England,* 101, 124–25; Thomas, *Religion and the Decline of Magic,* 530–31, 592; Malcolm Gaskill, "Witchcraft in early modern Kent: Stereotypes and the Background to Accusations," in Jonathan Barry, Marianne Hester, and Gareth Roberts, eds., *Witchcraft in Early Modern Europe: Studies in Culture and Belief* (Cambridge, Eng., 1996), 265–66. James Sharpe has argued that animal familiars were a distinctive "staple of English witch beliefs"; see his essay, "The Devil in East Anglia: The Matthew

Hopkins Trials reconsidered," in Barry, Hester, and Roberts, eds., *Witchcraft in Early Modern Europe,* 248.

20. Sharpe, *Instruments of Darkness,* 74; Hall, *Worlds of Wonder,* 74; George Lyman Kittredge, *Witchcraft in Old and New England* (New York, 1929; reprinted 1972), 175.

21. John Putnam Demos, *Entertaining Satan: Witchcraft and the Culture of Early New England* (New York, 1982), 167, 173–74.

22. Mather quoted in Kittredge, *Witchcraft in Old and New England,* 178; Demos, *Entertaining Satan,* 45, 140–41, 185; Carol F. Karlsen, *The Devil in the Shape of a Woman: Witchcraft in Colonial New England* (New York, 1987), 8, 11; Dorcas Good quoted in Chadwick Hansen, *Witchcraft at Salem* (New York, 1969), 58, see also 63–64. Witchcraft accusations occurred far less frequently in the seventeenth-century Chesapeake, and often arose from defamation suits; see Horn, *Adapting to a New World,* 411–16.

23. John Smith, *A Map of Virginia* [1612] in Philip L. Barbour, ed., *The Complete Works of Captain John Smith (1580–1631),* 3 vols. (Chapel Hill and London, 1986), 1:169; Edward Winslow, *Good Newes from New England: or a true Relation of things very remarkable at the Plantation of Plimoth in New-England* [1624], in Alexander Young, ed., *Chronicles of the Pilgrim Fathers of the Colony of Plymouth, from 1602 to 1625* (Boston, 1841), 356–57; William Wood, *New England's Prospect,* ed. Alden T. Vaughan (Amherst, 1977), 100–101; Charles Francis Adams, Jr., ed., *New English Canaan of Thomas Morton,* Publications of the Prince Society, XIV (Boston, 1883; reprint, 1967): 150. For English views of Indian religion as witchcraft, see James Axtell, *The Invasion Within: The Contest of Cultures in Colonial North America* (New York and Oxford, 1985), 228–29; William S. Simmons, "Cultural Bias in the New England Puritans' Perception of Indians," *WMQ,* 3rd ser., 38 (1981): 56–72. Witchcraft provided one context, but hardly the only one, within which colonists analyzed Indian religion; for an account of some of the less censorious approaches that sought parallels between Christianity and native spirituality, see Karen Ordahl Kupperman, *Indians & English: Facing Off in Early America* (Ithaca and London, 2000), ch. 4.

24. The most thorough treatment of this subject remains Thomas, *Religion and the Decline of Magic,* although more recent scholarship has suggested that Protestantism's success in England was as much due to the incorporation of certain popular beliefs as their elimination. See the concise overview of the historiography of this topic in Alexandra Walsham, *Providence in Early Modern England* (Oxford, 1999), 3–6.

25. Although the word had roots in Middle English, it gained currency in its modern sense beginning in the 1530s; *Oxford English Dictionary,* s. v. "superstition."

26. Genesis 1:26, 2:7. On the belief in human uniqueness, see Thomas, *Man and the Natural World,* 30–36; quotation from 33.

27. Genesis 1:28, 9:2.

28. Thomas, *Man and the Natural World,* 17–25, 30–31; Joyce E. Salisbury, *The Beast Within: Animals in the Middle Ages* (New York and London, 1994), 4–7.

29. Thomas, *Man and the Natural World,* 32–33; Erica Fudge, *Perceiving Animals: Humans and Beasts in Early Modern English Culture* (London, 2000), 9–10, 34–35, 45–54; Mary Midgley, *Beast and Man: The Roots of Human Nature* (London, 1979), 209–17.

30. Arthur O. Lovejoy, *The Great Chain of Being* (Cambridge, Mass., 1936); Thomas, *Man and the Natural World,* 60–61; Salisbury, *The Beast Within,* 114–17; T. H. White, ed., *The Bestiary: A Book of Beasts* (New York, 1954).

31. Thomas, *Man and the Natural World,* 124–25; these ambiguities are the principal subject of Fudge, *Perceiving Animals.*

32. Walsham, *Providence in Early Modern England,* esp. ch. 4; quotation about Prynne on p. 180. See also Thomas, *Religion and the Decline of Magic,* 90–132. On the general theme of the persistence of "magical" beliefs during and after the Reformation, see Robert W. Scribner, "The Reformation, Popular Magic, and the 'Disenchantment of the World,'" *Journal of Interdisciplinary History,* 23 (1993): 475–94; Ronald Hutton, "The English Reformation and the Evidence of Folklore, *Past and Present,* 148 (1995): 89–116.

33. "Journal of Richard Mather," Dorchester Antiquarian and Historical Society, *Collections,* no. 3 (Boston, 1850), 16; Richard S. Dunn, James Savage, and Laetitia Yeandle, eds., *The Journal of John Winthrop 1630–1649* (Cambridge, Mass., and London, 1996), 32; Virginia DeJohn Anderson, *New England's Generation: The Great Migration and the Formation of Society and Culture in the Seventeenth Century* (New York, 1991), 70–88; Richard S. Dunn, "John Winthrop Writes His Journal," *WMQ,* 3rd ser., 41 (1984): 185–212.

34. Dunn et al., eds., *Journal of John Winthrop,* 715.

35. Nathaniel Morton, *New-Englands Memoriall . . .* (Cambridge, Mass., 1669; facsimile edition, Boston, 1903), 90–91; John Dane, "John Dane's Narrative, 1682," *New England Historical and Genealogical Register,* 8 (1854): 155; *The Diaries of John Hull, Mint-master and Treasurer of the Colony of Massachusetts Bay,* reprinted in *Transactions and Collections of the American Antiquarian Society,* 3 (1857): 210, 228. Michael Winship explores the distinction between elite and popular views of providentialism in "Encountering Providence in the Seventeenth Century: The Experiences of a Yeoman and a Minister," *Essex Institute Historical Collections,* 126 (1990): 27–36.

36. Barbour, ed., *Works of John Smith,* 2:366–68.

37. Kathleen J. Bragdon, *Native People of Southern New England, 1500–1650* (Norman and London, 1996), 62–63, 102–4; M. K. Bennett, "The Food Economy of the New England Indians, 1605–75," *Journal of Political Economy,* 63 (1955): 369–97, especially 392; John R. Swanton, *The Indians of the Southeastern United States* (Washington, D.C., 1946), 265–310, especially 295.

38. Thomas, *Man and the Natural World*, 26; Joan Thirsk, ed., *The Agrarian History of England and Wales*, vol. 4, *1500–1640* (Cambridge, Eng., 1967), 451–52.

39. Roger B. Manning, *Hunters and Poachers: A Cultural and Social History of Unlawful Hunting in England 1485–1640* (Oxford, 1993), 10–11; Swanton, *Indians of the Southeastern United States*, 295; Bennett, "Food Economy of the New England Indians," 387; Williams, *Key*, 224.

40. For Indian hunting, see ch. 1 above. For English hunting, see Thomas, *Man and the Natural World*, 29, 71–72, 145–46; Manning, *Hunters and Poachers*, ch. 1, 36–41.

41. Thomas, *Man and the Natural World*, 21–22; quotation from 22.

42. Thomas, *Man and the Natural World*, 41, 145–47, 153. For Narragansett hunting of wolves that raided deer traps, see Williams, *Key*, 225.

43. Manning, *Hunters and Poachers*, 24–27, 40; Thomas, *Man and the Natural World*, 29; Matt Cartmill, *A View to a Death in the Morning: Hunting and Nature Through History* (Cambridge, Mass., 1993), 61–67.

44. Manning, *Hunters and Poachers*, 26, 28–33, 40. See also the lengthy list of people employed in the upkeep of Windsor Forest, a royal hunting ground, in E. P. Thompson, *Whigs and Hunters: The Origin of the Black Act* (New York, 1975), 35.

45. Manning, *Hunters and Poachers*, 5–22; quotation from James I cited on p. 65.

46. Manning, *Hunters and Poachers*, 58–63; P. B. Munsche, *Gentlemen and Poachers: The English Game Laws 1671–1831* (Cambridge, Eng., 1981), 3–5, 9–14; Patricia Seed, *American Pentimento: The Invention of Indians and the Pursuit of Riches* (Minneapolis, 2001), 47–50.

47. For Indian hunting practices, see Cronon, *Changes in the Land*, 63–65.

48. Manning, *Hunters and Poachers*, 26, 58–59, 84–100; Munsche, *Gentlemen and Poachers*, 5; Thomas, *Man and the Natural World*, 164–65; J. A. Sharpe, *Crime in Early Modern England 1550–1750*, 2nd ed. (London and New York, 1999), 180–81.

49. Gervase Markham, *Country Contentments: Or, The Husbandmans Recreations*, 7th ed. (London, 1654), 26; Manning, *Hunters and Poachers*, 15, 25–26, 35–56, 196–231; Munsche, *Gentlemen and Poachers*, ch. 3; Sharpe, *Crime in Early Modern England*, 179–88; Thompson, *Whigs and Hunters*, 58–59.

50. Thomas, *Man and the Natural World*, 160–64; Allyn B. Forbes et al., eds., *Winthrop Papers, 1498–1654*, 6 vols. (Boston, 1929–1992), 2:165; Manning, *Hunters and Poachers*, 16. See also Cartmill, *View to a Death in the Morning*, ch. 5.

51. "Observations by Master George Percy, 1607," in Lyon Gardiner Tyler, ed., *Narratives of Early Virginia 1606–1625* (New York, 1907), 18; John Smith, *A Map of Virginia* [1612], in Barbour, ed., *Works of John Smith*, 1:164; Rev. Francis Higginson, *New-Englands Plantation with The Sea Journal and Other Writings* (Salem, 1908), 106; Levett quoted in Cronon, *Changes in the Land*, 52;

see also "Bradford's and Winslow's Journal," in Alexander Young, ed., *Chronicles of the Pilgrim Fathers of the Colony of Plymouth, from 1602 to 1625* (Boston, 1841), 363; and Wood, *New England's Prospect*, 112–15. For English impressions of the gendered division of labor in Indian societies, see Kupperman, *Indians & English*, 148–49; Kathleen M. Brown, *Good Wives, Nasty Wenches & Anxious Patriarchs: Gender, Race, and Power in Colonial Virginia* (Chapel Hill and London, 1996), 57–59; Seed, *American Pentimento*, 54–55. Edmund Morgan suggests that Indian men, like the English, conceived of hunting as sport, but offers little substantiation for this claim; see *American Slavery, American Freedom: The Ordeal of Colonial Virginia* (New York, 1975), 51–52.

52. Smith, *Map of Virginia*, in Barbour, ed., *Works of John Smith*, 1:155–56; Smith, *New England's Trials* [1620] in ibid., 1:395; Higginson, *New-Englands Plantation*, n.p.; Morton, *New English Canaan*, 222; "George Percy's *Discourse*," in Philip L. Barbour, ed., *The Jamestown Voyages Under the First Charter 1606–1609*, vol. 1, The Hakluyt Society, 2nd ser., no. 136 (Cambridge, Eng., 1969): 133; see also Francis Magnel's Relation, ibid., 153; Paul J. Lindholdt, ed., *John Josselyn, Colonial Traveler: A Critical Edition of Two Voyages to New-England* (Hanover and London, 1988), 71; Wood, *New England's Prospect*, 53. For general comments on New World abundance, see Cronon, *Changes in the Land*, 22–25; Timothy Silver, *A New Face on the Countryside: Indians, Colonists, and Slaves in South Atlantic Forests, 1500–1800* (New York, 1990), 30–31; Judith Adkins, "Bodies and Boundaries: Animals in the Early American Experience" (Ph.D. diss., Yale University, 1998), 56–60.

53. John Josselyn, *New-Englands Rarities Discovered: In Birds, Beasts, Fishes, Serpents, and Plants of that Country* (London, 1672), 12–13; Wood, *New England's Prospect*, 51; Morton, *New English Canaan*, 214. On the introduction of European rats to America, see Alfred W. Crosby, Jr., *The Columbian Exchange: Biological and Cultural Consequences of 1492* (Westport, 1972), 97.

54. Josselyn, *New-Englands Rarities*, 8, 11, 21, 22; Wood, *New England's Prospect*, 43–52; Lindholdt, ed., *John Josselyn*, 63; Morton, *New English Canaan*, 189–90, 194–95, 200–3, 207–8; Thomas Hariot, *A Briefe and True Report of the New Found Land of Virginia . . .* [1588], in David Beers Quinn, ed., *The Roanoke Voyages 1584–1590*, vol. 1, The Hakluyt Society, 2nd ser., no. 104 (London, 1955): 355; Smith, *Map of Virginia*, in Barbour, ed., *Works of John Smith*, 1:154–55. On the tendency of English colonists, in the seventeenth century and later, to draw parallels between familiar creatures and those they found in other lands, see Thomas R. Dunlap, *Nature and the English Diaspora: Environment and History in the United States, Canada, Australia, and New Zealand* (Cambridge, Eng., and New York, 1999), 23–27.

55. Wood, *New England's Prospect*, 44–45, 50; Morton, *New English Canaan*, 198–99; Smith, *Map of Virginia*, in Barbour, ed., *Works of John Smith*, 1:155. For the various symbolic constructions associated with opossums, see Susan Scott

Parrish, "The Female Opossum and the Nature of the New World," *WMQ,* 54 (1997): 475–514. See also Adkins, "Bodies and Boundaries," 71–85.

56.   Lindholdt, ed., *John Josselyn,* 67, 73; Wood, *New England's Prospect,* 46.

57.   This summary is based on the lists of animals included in the following sources: Hariot, *A Briefe and True Report,* 355–62; Smith, *Map of Virginia,* in Barbour, ed., *Works of John Smith,* 1:154–56; Higginson, *New-Englands Plantation;* Morton, *New English Canaan,* 189–215; Lindholdt, ed., *John Josselyn,* 59–88; Josselyn, *New-Englands Rarities,* 7–40; Wood, *New England's Prospect,* 41–57. For a discussion of contemporary classification schemes, see Thomas, *Man and the Natural World,* 51–58.

58.   Wood, *New England's Prospect,* 48; Higginson, *New-Englands Plantation.*

59.   Hariot, *Briefe and True Report,* 355–62; Higginson, *New-Englands Plantation;* Lindholdt, ed., *John Josselyn,* 59, 61, 62, 63, 65, 67, 70 ("birds for the dish"), 71–73, 76–80; Josselyn, *New-Englands Rarities,* 8–9, 12, 13 (bear), 16 (ounce, or wildcat), 17, 19 (moose), 20, 23–32; Morton, *New-English Canaan,* 190–95, 200–3, 205, 206 (ounce), 207, 210–11; Wood, *New England's Prospect,* 41, 43–45, 47 (otter), 50, 51 (cormorant), 52–53, 55–57.

60.   Henry M. Miller, "An Archaeological Perspective on the Evolution of Diet in the Colonial Chesapeake, 1620–1745," in Lois Green Carr, Philip D. Morgan, and Jean B. Russo, eds., *Colonial Chesapeake Society* (Chapel Hill and London, 1988), 182–87.

61.   Wood, *New England's Prospect,* 47, 54; Morton, *New English Canaan,* 189; Lindholdt, ed., *John Josselyn,* 59, 60, 61, 69, 83; Josselyn, *New-Englands Rarities,* 9, 10, 25, 33, 34, 35, 37.

62.   Lindholdt, ed., *John Josselyn,* xv, 61, 61 n.108, 64, 69, 77, 82. On the doctrine of signatures and the use of animal-based remedies in England, see Thomas, *Man and the Natural World,* 84; Roy Porter and Dorothy Porter, *In Sickness and In Health: The British Experience 1650–1850* (London, 1988), 266–67; Andrew Wear, *Knowledge and Practice in English Medicine, 1550–1680* (Cambridge, Eng., 2000), 78, 84, 92, 98, 100; Doreen Evenden Nagy, *Popular Medicine in Seventeenth-Century England* (Bowling Green, 1988), 48.

63.   Josselyn, *New-Englands Rarities,* 11, 12, 14, 16, 17, 36, 38, 39; Lindholdt, ed., *John Josselyn,* 61, 65, 82.

64.   Lindholdt, ed., *John Josselyn,* 66, 78–79; Josselyn, *New-Englands Rarities,* 35; and for English examples of similar remedies, see Wilson, *Magical Universe,* 280, 286, 319, 350, 357–59, 419. For a general discussion of common maladies in early modern England, see Wear, *Knowledge and Practice in English Medicine,* ch. 3.

65.   Francis Higginson, *New-Englands Plantation,* n.p.; Lindholdt, ed., *John Josselyn,* 86–88; Wood, *New England's Prospect,* 45.

66.   John Smith, *A Description of New England,* . . . [1616], in Barbour, ed., *Works of John Smith,* 1:330; Barbour, ed., *Jamestown Voyages,* 1:101; for similar

comments, see Wood, *New England's Prospect,* 53; Josselyn, *New-Englands Rarities,* 32.

67. Hariot, *Briefe and True Report,* 330; Morton, *New English Canaan,* 202, 205–7; see also Wood, *New England's Prospect,* 47; Lindholdt, ed., *John Josselyn,* 62, 66–67; Smith, *Description of New England,* in Barbour, ed., *Works of John Smith,* 1:336; Barbour, ed., *Jamestown Voyages,* 1:102.

68. Wood, *New England's Prospect,* 51–52. On the colonists' tendency to view the New World in terms of its "merchantable" commodities, see Silver, *New Face on the Countryside,* 68–69; Cronon, *Changes in the Land,* 20–25.

69. Gary L. Francione, *Animals, Property, and the Law* (Philadelphia, 1995), 41; Munsche, *Gentlemen and Poachers,* 10–11; Manning, *Hunters and Poachers,* 58.

70. Dalton, *The Countrey Justice,* 306–7; Francione, *Animals, Property, and the Law,* 40–42; John Locke, *The Second Treatise of Government* [1690], ed. Thomas P. Peardon, (New York, 1952), 18–19, 23 (quotation).

71. For the difference between taming and domestication, see Frederick E. Zeuner, *A History of Domesticated Animals* (London, 1963), 52–59.

72. Josselyn, *New-Englands Rarities,* 9.

73. Lindholdt, ed., *John Josselyn,* 66; Robert Beverley, *The History and Present State of Virginia,* ed. Louis B. Wright (Chapel Hill, 1947; reprinted Charlottesville, 1968), 282; Wood, *New England's Prospect,* 43; on domesticating moose, see also Morton, *New English Canaan,* 200.

74. G. A. Feldhamer and J. A. Chapman, "Other furbearers," in Ian L. Mason, ed., *Evolution of domesticated animals* (London, 1984), 294–95; H. F. Peters, "American bison, and bison-cattle hybrids," and T. J. Fletcher, "Other deer," in ibid., 46–47, 144; Zeuner, *History of Domesticated Animals,* 425–29; Juliet Clutton-Brock, *Domesticated Animals from Early Times* (Austin, 1981), 180–82; Helmut Hemmer, *Domestication: The Decline of Environmental Appreciation* (New York, 1990), 165–66.

CHAPTER THREE: THE COMPANY OF CATTLE

1. "Observations by Master George Percy, 1607," in Lyon Gardiner Tyler, ed., *Narratives of Early Virginia, 1606–1625* (New York, 1907), 3, 18. On the colonists' fascination with gold, see John Smith, *The Proceedings of the English Colonie in Virginia . . .* [1606–1612], in Philip L. Barbour, ed., *The Complete Works of Captain John Smith (1580–1631),* 3 vols. (Chapel Hill, 1986), 1:218.

2. The earls of Northumberland owned vast estates all over England, as well as several great houses in Yorkshire and elsewhere. Northumberland farmers specialized in raising cattle and sheep on open pastures, working in the sort of landscape that Percy clearly imagined for Virginia. See Joan Thirsk, ed., *The Agrarian History of England and Wales,* gen. ed. H. P. R. Finberg, vol. 4, *1500–1640* (Cambridge, Eng., 1967), 4, 36, 283. The tendency of European colonists

and their American descendants to envision the land in terms of their own experiences and economic goals persisted; see, for instance, Elliott West, *The Contested Plains: Indians, Goldseekers, and the Rush to Colorado* (Lawrence, 1998).

3. Philip L. Barbour, ed., *The Jamestown Voyages Under the First Charter 1606–1609,* 2 vols., Hakluyt Society, 2nd ser. I, no. 136 (Cambridge, Eng., 1969): 161; William Bradford, *Of Plymouth Plantation 1620–1647,* ed. Samuel Eliot Morison (New York, 1952), 143; Rev. Francis Higginson, *New-Englands Plantation with The Sea Journal and Other Writings* (Salem, 1908), n. p.; William Wood, *New England's Prospect,* ed. Alden T. Vaughan (Amherst, 1977), 34; see also John Pory's letter to Sir Francis Wyatt in Sydney V. James, Jr., *Three Visitors to Early Plymouth: Letters About the Pilgrim Settlement in New England During its First Seven Years* (Plymouth, 1963), 16; Allyn B. Forbes et al., eds., *Winthrop Papers, 1498–1654,* 6 vols. (Boston, 1929–92), 4:492.

4. Anthony Pagden, *Lords of All the World: Ideologies of Empire in Spain, Britain and France c. 1500–c. 1800* (New Haven and London, 1995), 63–73.

5. Anthony Pagden, "The Struggle for Legitimacy and the Image of Empire in the Atlantic to c. 1700," in Nicholas Canny, ed., *The Origins of Empire,* vol. 1 of *The Oxford History of the British Empire,* ed. Wm. Roger Louis (Oxford and New York, 1998), 34–54; Patricia Seed, *Ceremonies of Possession in Europe's Conquest of the New World 1492–1640* (New York, 1995), 34–35.

6. William Strachey, *The Historie of Travell into Virginia Britania,* ed. Louis B. Wright and Virginia Freund, The Hakluyt Society, 2nd ser., no. 103 (London, 1953): 25; Bradford, *Of Plymouth Plantation,* 25; Robert Cushman, "Reasons and Considerations Touching the Lawfulness of Removing Out of England Into the Parts of America," in Alexander Young, *Chronicles of the Pilgrim Fathers of the Colony of Plymouth, From 1602 to 1625,* (Boston, 1841), 243; Higginson, *New-Englands Plantation,* n. p.; Wood, *New England's Prospect,* 34; see also Forbes et al., eds., *Winthrop Papers,* 2:115.

7. Neal Salisbury discusses the epidemic–almost certainly a European disease–in *Manitou and Providence: Indians, Europeans, and the Making of New England, 1500–1643* (New York, 1982), 102–5. Contemporary accounts include John White, *The Planters Plea* (London, 1630), reprinted in Peter Force, ed., *Tracts and Other Papers, Relating Principally to the Origin, Settlement, and Progress of the Colonies in North America, From the Discovery of the Country to the Year 1776,* 4 vols. (Washington, D.C., 1836–1844; reprinted, Gloucester, 1963), 3: §3, 14; Edward Johnson, *Wonder-Working Providence of Sions Savior in New England 1628–1651,* ed. J. Franklin Jameson (New York, 1910), 41.

8. John Smith, *A Map of Virginia* [1612], in Barbour, ed., *Works of John Smith,* 1:144, 146–48, 157–58, 160. Historians estimate the native population of eastern Virginia at the start of the seventeenth century at 13,000 to 14,000; see Helen C. Rountree, *The Powhatan Indians of Virginia: Their Traditional Culture* (Norman, Okla., and London, 1989), 15.

9. Robert Johnson, *Nova Britannia: Offering Most Excellent Fruites by Planting in Virginia* [1609] in Force, ed., *Tracts,* 1:§6, 11; Bradford, *Of Plymouth Plantation,* 25; Cushman, "Reasons and Considerations," 243; quotation from Robert Gray in Bernard W. Sheehan, *Savagism and Civility: Indians and Englishmen in Colonial Virginia* (New York, 1980), 68.

10. Pagden, *Lords of All the World,* 76–78; John Locke, *The Second Treatise of Government,* ed. Thomas P. Peardon (New York, 1952), 29; John Winthrop, "Reasons to be Considered, and Objections with Answers," in Forbes et al., eds., *Winthrop Papers,* 2:140–41. On the relationship between England's colonial activities and Locke's ideas about property, see Barbara Arneil, "The Wild Indian's Venison: Locke's Theory of Property and English Colonialism in America," *Political Studies* 44 (1996): 60–74.

11. Johnson, *Nova Britannia,* in Force, ed., *Tracts,* 1:§6, 7; Bradford, *Of Plymouth Plantation,* 25. See also Roy Harvey Pearce, *The Savages of America: A Study of the Indian and the Idea of Civilization* (Baltimore, 1953), ch. 1.

12. Winthrop, "Reasons," in Forbes et al., eds., *Winthrop Papers,* 2:141; Strachey, *Historie,* 25–26.

13. Higginson, *New-Englands Plantation,* n.p.; Winthrop, "Reasons," in Forbes, et al., eds., *Winthrop Papers,* 2:141; Johnson, *Nova Britannia,* in Force, ed., *Tracts,*1:§6, 14. See also William Cronon, *Changes in the Land: Indians, Colonists, and the Ecology of New England* (New York, 1983), 56–57.

14. Wood, *New England's Prospect,* 112–16, quotation on p. 113. For similar comments, see Roger Williams, *A Key into the Language of America,* ed. John J. Teunissen and Evelyn J. Hinz (Detroit, 1973), 122, 128, 207; Smith, *Map of Virginia,* in Barbour, ed., *Works of John Smith,* 1:162. Indian women farmers are described in R. Douglas Hurt, *Indian Agriculture in America: Prehistory to the Present* (Lawrence, Kans., 1987), 29, 31, 40. See also Karen Ordahl Kupperman, *Indians & English: Facing Off in Early America* (Ithaca and London, 2000), 148–52.

15. Strachey, *Historie,* 26; White, *Planters Plea,* in Force, ed., *Tracts,* 2:§3, 15.

16. White, *Planters Plea,* in Force, ed., *Tracts,* 2:§3, 15; Seed, *Ceremonies of Possession,* ch. 1.

17. Letters from Ralph Lane and Sir Richard Grenville in David Beers Quinn, ed., *The Roanoke Voyages, 1584–1590,* The Hakluyt Society, 2nd ser., no. 104 (London, 1955): 208, 219; Pory's letter in Tyler, ed., *Narratives of Early Virginia,* 283; Higginson, *New-Englands Plantation,* n. p. For a similar comment from Virginia's Gov. Francis Wyatt, see Susan Myra Kingsbury, ed., *The Records of the Virginia Company of London,* 4 vols. (Washington, D.C., 1906–35), 4:283.

18. Winthrop, "Reasons," in Forbes et al., eds., *Winthrop Papers,* 2:140–41.

19. William P. Cumming, *The Southeast in Early Maps,* 3rd ed., revised and enlarged by Louis De Vorsey, Jr., (Chapel Hill and London, 1998), plates 20, 25, 29; Wilma George, *Animals and Maps* (Berkeley, 1969), 94–100; Peter Benes,

New England Prospect (Boston, 1981), 5–6. An earlier version of the Smith map, published in 1627 before the Winthrop migration brought hundreds of emigrants and domestic animals to Massachusetts, has the imaginary towns, but not the cattle.

20. Keith Thomas, *Man and the Natural World* (New York, 1983), 26; Robert Trow-Smith, *A History of British Livestock Husbandry to 1700* (London, 1957), 233; D. V. Glass, "Gregory King and the Population of England and Wales at the End of the Seventeenth Century," in D. V. Glass and D. E. C. Eversley, *Population in History: Essays in Historical Demography* (London, 1965), 174; G. E. Fussell, *The English Dairy Farmer 1500–1900* (London, 1966), 1–10; Alan Everitt, "Farm Labourers," in Thirsk, ed., *Agrarian History of England and Wales,* 4:412–25. On the difficulties of assessing livestock productivity in this period, see Mark Overton and Bruce M. S. Campbell, "Productivity Change in European Agricultural Development," in Bruce M. S. Campbell and Mark Overton, eds., *Land, Labour and Livestock: Historical Studies in European Agricultural Productivity* (Manchester and New York, 1991), 11–12.

21. John Stow, *A Survey of London, Reprinted from the Text of 1603,* ed. Charles Lethbridge Kingsford, 2 vols. (Oxford, 1908), 1:83, 126, 184; Pauline Frost, "Yeomen and Metalsmiths: Livestock in the Dual Economy in South Staffordshire 1560–1720," *Agricultural History Review,* 29 (1981): 29–41; A. L. Beier, "The social problems of an Elizabethan country town: Warwick, 1580–90," in Peter Clark, ed., *Country Towns in Pre-industrial England* (New York, 1981), 52; Adrienne Rosen, "Winchester in Transition, 1580–1700," in ibid., 147; Michael Reed, "Economic Structure and Change in Seventeenth-Century Ipswich," in ibid., 92, 129; Peter Clark and Paul Slack, *English Towns in Transition 1500–1700* (Oxford, 1976), 18, 27, 49; Rev. William Hudson and John Cottingham Tingey, eds., *The Records of the City of Norwich,* 2 vols. (Norwich and London, 1906–10), 2:205–7.

22. Trow-Smith, *History of British Livestock Husbandry,* chs. 1–2; Julian Wiseman, *A History of the British Pig* (London, 1986), 2–5. On the origins of livestock husbandry in general, see the essays by Brian Hesse, Gil Stein, and Peter Bogucki in Pam Crabtree, Douglas Campana, and Kathleen Ryan, eds., *Early Animal Domestication and Its Cultural Context* (Philadelphia, 1989).

23. The best-known study of highly local agrarian variations is Margaret Spufford, *Contrasting Communities: English Villagers in the Sixteenth and Seventeenth Centuries* (Cambridge, Eng., 1974). For England's agricultural regions, see Joan Thirsk, "The Farming Regions of England," in Thirsk, ed., *Agrarian History,* 4:111–12; see also Mark Overton, *Agricultural Revolution in England: The Transformation of the Agrarian Economy 1500–1850* (Cambridge, Eng., 1996), 47–53; M. L. Zell, "A Wood-Pasture Agrarian Régime: The Kentish Weald in the Sixteenth Century," *Southern History,* 7 (1985): 69–93; J. A. Yelling, *Common Field and Enclosure in England 1450–1850* (London and Hamden, 1977), 26–29, 176–77 quotation about Norfolk is from W. Marshall's *The Rural Economy*

of Norfolk (1787), cited on p. 125. For the wood-pasture origins of colonists, see Virginia DeJohn Anderson, *New England's Generation: The Great Migration and the Formation of Society and Culture in the Seventeenth Century* (New York, 1991), 30–31; David Grayson Allen, *In English Ways: The Movement of Societies and the Transferal of English Local Law and Custom to Massachusetts Bay in the Seventeenth Century* (Chapel Hill, 1981), 87–89, 91, 99, 122; Frank Thistlethwaite, *Dorset Pilgrims: The Story of West Country Pilgrims Who Went to New England in the 17th Century* (London, 1989), 56; Anthony Salerno, "Social Background of Seventeenth-Century Emigration," *Journal of British Studies,* 19 (1979): 41; James Horn, *Adapting to a New World: English Society in the Seventeenth-Century Chesapeake* (Chapel Hill, 1994), 93–97, 106, 113.

24. Gervase Markham, *Markham's Farewel to Husbandry: Or, the Enriching of All Sorts of Barren and Sterile Grounds in our Nation . . . ,* 10th ed. (London, 1676), 115–16.

25. W. S. Holdsworth, *A History of English Law,* 16 vols. (London, 1903–66), 3:378–79. For pig husbandry, see Thirsk, ed., *Agrarian History,* 4:70, 171–72, 193, 416, 616; Trow-Smith, *History of British Livestock Husbandry,* 250–51; Leonard Mascal, *The Government of Cattell, Divided into Three Books, . . .* (London, 1653), 255–72, on 255 ("troublesome to rule"), 272 (cutting sinews); Markham, *Cheape and Good Husbandry,* 99–102, 105–7.

26. Yelling, *Common Field and Enclosure,* 176.

27. Joan Thirsk, "Farming Techniques," in Thirsk, ed., *Agrarian History,* 4:180; Trow-Smith, *History of British Livestock Husbandry,* 255–58. The classic account of this development was articulated by Eric Kerridge, who asserted that a host of agricultural improvements once thought to date from the eighteenth and nineteenth centuries had first appeared 300 years earlier; see his *The Agricultural Revolution* (London, 1967). The book sparked considerable criticism, much of which has addressed not so much the appearance of improvements in the sixteenth and seventeenth centuries as the extent of their practice and the speed of diffusion around the country. For examples of critiques of Kerridge, see Overton, *Agricultural Revolution in England;* Joan Thirsk, *Agricultural Regions and Agrarian History in England, 1500–1750* (Basingstoke and London, 1987), especially ch. 5.

28. Mascal, *Government of Cattell,* 61, 272; see also Thirsk, ed., *Agrarian History,* 4:47, 170–71, 193, 624.

29. Thirsk, ed., *Agrarian History,* 4:205, 654; Thomas Tusser, *Five Hundred Points of Good Husbandry* (London, 1663), 100, see also 47, 49, 68, 87; Markham, *Markham's Farewel to Husbandry,* 122–23; John Worlidge, *Systema Agriculturae; The Mystery of Husbandry Discovered,* 4th ed. (London, 1687), ch. 5. Seventeenth-century farmers also knew about improving soil fertility by rotating crops and letting fields lie fallow; they had also begun experimenting with growing legumes and other crops that improved the nitrogen content of the soil.

See Robert S. Shiel, "Improving soil productivity in the Pre-fertiliser Era," in Campbell and Overton, eds., *Land, labour and livestock,* 51–77.

30. Nicholas Russell, *Like Engend'ring Like: Heredity and Animal Breeding in Early Modern England* (Cambridge, Eng., 1986); Trow-Smith, *History of British Livestock Husbandry,* 176–77, 186, 187, 235–36; Mascal, *Government of Cattell,* 52, 63, 166–68; see also Markham, *Cheape and Good Husbandry,* 71.

31. Juliet Clutton-Brock, *Domesticated Animals From Early Times* (Austin, 1981), 25; Katherine Albro Houpt, *Domestic Animal Behavior for Veterinarians and Animal Scientists,* 3rd ed. (Ames, 1998), 36–43; Mascal, *Government of Cattell,* 52, 64, 255–56, 260–61; see also Tusser, *Five Hundred Points,* 64; Markham, *Cheape and Good Husbandry,* 36; Worlidge, *Systema Agriculturae,* 265–66, 280, 282.

32. Tusser, *Five Hundred Points,* 63, 64; Markham, *Cheape and Good Husbandry,* 33, 71, 101; Markham, *Markham's Farewel to Husbandry,* 121, 123; Mascal, *Government of Cattell,* 52, 67–68, 100, 204, 246, 256; Worlidge, *Systema Agriculturae,* 265–66; Benjamin L. Hart, *The Behavior of Domestic Animals* (New York, 1985), 96–97.

33. Markham, *Cheape and Good Husbandry,* 101; Mascal, *Government of Cattell,* 67–68. See also Tusser, *Five Hundred Points,* 64.

34. Mascal, *Government of Cattell,* 52–53.

35. Markham, *Markham's Farewel to Husbandry,* 112.

36. Ann Kussmaul, *Servants in Husbandry in Early Modern England* (Cambridge, Eng., 1981); Mascal, *Government of Cattell,* 55.

37. This comment by Edmund Spenser was intended to highlight the deficiencies of the Irish; quoted in Wesley N. Laing, "Cattle in Seventeenth-Century Virginia," *VMHB,* 67 (1959): 144.

38. Thirsk, ed., *Agrarian History,* 4:47, 53, 58, 62, 185,193, 616, 749; Francis W. Steer, *Farm and Cottage Inventories of Mid-Essex 1635–1749* (Colchester, Eng., 1950), 54–58; Thomas, *Man and the Natural World,* 95; Kussmaul, *Servants in Husbandry,* 41.

39. Mascal, *Government of Cattell,* 2–5; see also Tusser, *Five Hundred Points,* 63.

40. Thomas, *Man and the Natural World,* 57, 64, 69, 93–98, 113–14; Harriet Ritvo, *The Animal Estate: The English and Other Creatures in the Victorian Age* (Cambridge, Mass., 1987), 18–21; Accomack County Records, Virginia State Library, microfilm reel 4 (1682–97), fol. 181, reel 2, fol. 34; *Md.Arch.* 41:136; George Francis Dow, ed., *Records and Files of the Quarterly Courts of Essex County, Massachusetts,* 9 vols. (Salem, 1911–75), 2:357; 3:427–28; see also 3:361 and Sidney H. Miner and George D. Stanton, Jr., eds., *The Diary of Thomas Minor, Stonington, Connecticut, 1653 to 1684* (New London, 1899), 7.

41. Mascal, *Government of Cattell,* 5–6, 8–49, 58 (quotation), 66–67, 75–90, 106–11, 169–90, 213–29, 232–44, 248–51, 261–69, 273–76, 279–82; Markham, *Cheape and Good Husbandry,* 48–69, 73–84, 88–95, 102–5; Tusser, *Five*

Hundred Points, 42, 62; Worlidge, *Systema Agriculturae,* 223–26; Trow-Smith, *History of British Livestock Husbandry,* 240–41, 248–50, 252.

42. Thomas, *Man and the Natural World,* 96–114; Dow, ed., *Records of the Quarterly Courts of Essex County,* 2:350; Miner and Stanton, eds., *Diary of Thomas Minor,* 22–23.

43. Thomas, *Man and the Natural World,* 109–10, 143–91; Ritvo, *Animal Estate,* ch. 3; William H. Whitmore, ed., *The Colonial Laws of Massachusetts. Reprinted from the Edition of 1672, with the Supplements through 1686* (Boston, 1890), 39; this law first appeared in 1641. Edgar J. McManus's survey of court cases in seventeenth-century New England shows no prosecutions for cruelty to animals; see *Law and Liberty in Early New England: Criminal Justice and Due Process 1620–1692* (Amherst, 1993), Appendix C, 200–10.

44. Mascal, *Government of Cattell,* 209.

45. Thomas, *Man and the Natural World,* 154–57; Calvin quotation on 154.

46. Mascal, *Government of Cattell,* 184; Robin Briggs, *Witches & Neighbors: The Social and Cultural Context of European Witchcraft* (New York, 1996), 85–90, 271; Jim Sharpe, "The Devil in East Anglia: the Matthew Hopkins Trials Reconsidered," in Jonathan Barry, Marianne Hester, and Gareth Roberts, eds., *Witchcraft in Early Modern Europe: Studies in Culture and Belief* (Cambridge, Eng., 1996), 242; Keith Thomas, *Religion and the Decline of Magic* (London, 1971), 541, 620–21, 632–33, 642, 663, 665–66; George Lyman Kittredge, *Witchcraft in Old and New England* (Cambridge, Mass., 1929; reprint New York, 1972), 163–67; David D. Hall, *Worlds of Wonder, Days of Judgment: Popular Religious Belief in Early New England* (New York, 1989), 84–85; John Demos, *Entertaining Satan: Witchcraft and the Culture of Early New England* (New York, 1982), 57–94, 140–41, 145–46, 171–72; Jon Butler, *Awash in a Sea of Faith: Christianizing the American People* (Cambridge, Mass., and London, 1990), 69–70; Richard Godbeer, *The Devil's Dominion: Magic and Religion in Early New England* (New York, 1992), 43, 79, 165–66, 169; Horn, *Adapting to a New World,* 414–16; Paul Boyer and Stephen Nissenbaum, *Salem Possessed: The Social Origins of Witchcraft* (Cambridge, Mass., 1974), 190–209; Carol F. Karlsen, *The Devil in the Shape of a Woman: Witchcraft in Colonial New England* (New York 1987), 6–7, 69–70.

47. Thomas, *Man and the Natural World,* 97–98; City of Boston, *Second Report of the Record Commissioners of the City of Boston* [Boston Town Records] (Boston, 1877), 3; City of Boston, *Fourth Report of the Record Commissioners of the City of Boston* [Dorchester Town Records], 2nd ed. (Boston, 1883), 20, 48, 139; *Mass. Bay Recs.,* 1:215; 2:190; William H. Whitmore, ed., *The Colonial Laws of Massachusetts, Reprinted from the Edition of 1660, with the Supplements to 1672, Containing Also the Body of Liberties of 1641* (Boston, 1889), 130–132; *Md. Arch.* 13:549–50; Benjamin Hicks, ed., *Records of the Towns of North and South Hempstead, Long Island, N.Y.,* 8 vols. (Jamaica, N. Y., 1896–1904), 1:124, 133–34.

48. Thomas, *Man and the Natural World*, 97–98; W. P. Upham, ed., "Town Records of Salem, 1634–1659," *Essex Institute Historical Collections*, 2nd ser., 1 (1868): 41, 130; Howard M. Chapin, *Dogs in Early New England* (Providence, 1920), 6–7; City of Boston, *A Seventh Report of the Record Commissioners of the City of Boston, Containing the Boston Records from 1660 to 1701* (Boston, 1881), 212; *Mass. Bay Recs.*, 2:252.

49. Thomas, *Man and the Natural World*, 97; Esther Cohen, "Law, Folklore and Animal Lore," *Past & Present*, 110 (1986): 6–37; J. J. Finkelstein, "The Ox That Gored," *Transactions of the American Philosophical Society*, 71 (1981): 5–89.

50. Mascal, *Government of Cattell*, 4.

51. Thomas, *Man and the Natural World*, 97–98, 125–28; Cohen, "Law, Folklore and Animal Lore," 21–24.

52. *Mass. Bay Recs.*, 2:252; Hicks, ed., *Recs. of Hempstead*, 1:133–34.

53. Thomas, *Man and the Natural World*, 39, 97–98, 119, 134–35; Erica Fudge, *Perceiving Animals: Humans and Beasts in Early Modern English Culture* (London and New York, 2000), 68, 136–37; John M. Murrin, "'Things Fearful to Name': Bestiality in Colonial America," *Explorations in Early American Culture*, a special supplement to *Pennsylvania History*, 65 (1998): 8–43.

54. Alfred W. Crosby, Jr., *The Columbian Exchange: Biological and Cultural Consequences of 1492* (Westport, 1972), 75–96; Karl W. Butzer, "Cattle and Sheep from Old to New Spain: Historical Antecedents," *Annals of the Association of American Geographers*, 78 (1988): 29–56; Anthony Pagden, ed., *Hernán Cortés: Letters from Mexico* (New Haven and London, 1986), 103, 296, 335; Charles Hudson, *Knights of Spain, Warriors of the Sun: Hernando de Soto and the South's Ancient Chiefdoms* (Athens and London, 1997), 55.

55. Crosby, *Columbian Exchange*, 79, 89–90; David B. Quinn, *North America from Earliest Discovery to First Settlements: The Norse Voyages to 1612* (New York, 1977), 472; H. P. Biggar, ed., *The Works of Samuel de Champlain*, 6 vols. (Toronto, 1922), 1:235.

56. Alfred W. Crosby, *Ecological Imperialism: The Biological Expansion of Europe, 900–1900* (New York, 1986), 175; Biggar, ed., *Works of Champlain*, 2:55, 344; 5:112.

57. Nicolaes Van Wassenaer, *Historisch Verhael*, in J. Franklin Jameson, ed., *Narratives of New Netherland 1609–1664* (New York, 1909), 79, 81–84.

58. David Beers Quinn, ed., *The Roanoke Voyages 1584–1590*, 2 vols., The Hakluyt Society, 2nd ser., nos. 104, 105 (London, 1955), 1:162–63, 176, 187, 219 ; 2:521.

59. Quinn, ed., *North America from Earliest Discovery*, 426. One exception may have been the short-lived outpost at Sagadahoc on the Kennebec River in Maine. See David B. Quinn and Alison M. Quinn, eds., *The English New England Voyages 1602–1608*, The Hakluyt Society, 2nd ser., no. 161 (London, 1983): chs. 7–8; Alfred A. Cave, "Why Was the Sagadahoc Colony Abandoned? An Evaluation of the Evidence," *NEQ*, 68 (1995): 625–40.

60. Smith, *Proceedings of the English Colonie in Virginia,* in Barbour, ed., *Works of John Smith,* 1:273; "The Relation of the Lord De-la-ware, 1611," in Tyler, ed., *Narratives of Early Virginia,* 213; Kingsbury, ed., *Virginia Co. Recs.* 1:257, 269, 392, 420, 423, 618, 625–26.

61. Factionalism within the Plymouth Company may also have hindered its effectiveness in supplying the colony. Altham's letter is in James, ed., *Three Visitors to Early Plymouth,* 24; Bradford, *Of Plymouth Plantation,* 130–31, 141, 174 n. 7; George D. Langdon, Jr., *Pilgrim Colony: A History of New Plymouth 1620–1691* (New Haven, 1966), 9–10, 17–19, 27–29, 35–36.

62. When company officials specified the ratio of animals to "men," it is unclear if they only meant adult males. Many emigrant men headed households, and transporting 20 or so cows for every 75 to 100 households would have left many families without animals. See *Mass. Bay Recs.,* 1:36; Forbes et al., eds., *Winthrop Papers,* 2:225; Richard Dunn et al., eds., *The Journal of John Winthrop 1630–1649* (Cambridge, Mass., and London, 1996), 40–41, 53, 54, 69, 70, 89, 91, 92, 96–97, 100–1, 118, 119, 121, 129, 135, 147, 157, 182, 187, 207.

63. Everett Emerson, ed., *Letters from New England: The Massachusetts Bay Colony, 1629–1638* (Amherst, 1976), 26; Forbes, et al., eds., *Winthrop Papers,* 2:213; inventory of Benjamin Cooper's estate, probate docket no. 4, Suffolk County Registry of Probate, Boston, Mass.; Johnson, *Wonder-Working Providence,* 54.

64. Anderson, *New England's Generation,* 70–88.

65. Emerson, ed., *Letters from New England,* 73; Dunn et al., eds., *Journal of John Winthrop,* 40–41, 70, 91; for other references to animal mortality at sea, see 69, 96–97, 121, 182; and Alison Games, *Migration and the Origins of the English Atlantic World* (Cambridge, Mass., and London, 1999), 66–67.

66. Melvin H. Jackson, "Ships and the Sea: Voyaging to the Chesapeake," in David B. Quinn, ed., *Early Maryland in a Wider World* (Detroit, 1982), 33–57; Dunn et al., eds., *Journal of John Winthrop,* 12, 207; Emerson, ed., *Letters from New England,* 26, 73, 187. On the Irish cattle trade, see Donald Woodward, "The Anglo-Irish Livestock Trade of the Seventeenth Century," *Irish Historical Studies,* 18 (1973): 489–523.

67. Karen Ordahl Kupperman, "The Puzzle of the American Climate in the Early Colonial Period," *AHR,* 87 (1982): 1262–89; Karen Ordahl Kupperman, "Climate and Mastery of the Wilderness in Seventeenth-Century New England," in David D. Hall and David Grayson Allen, eds., *Seventeenth-Century New England* (Boston, 1984), 3–37.

68. Kupperman, "Puzzle of the American Climate," 1264–65; Barbour, ed., *Works of John Smith,* 1:143, 245; Dunn et al., eds., *Journal of John Winthrop,* 43–44, 132; for other references to cold winters see 45, 84, 87, 105, 109.

69. Dunn et al., eds., *Journal of John Winthrop,* 42, 174; James Phinney Baxter, ed., *Documentary History of the State of Maine,* vol. 3, The Trelawny Papers (Portland, Me., 1884), 57, 308–9; Horn, *Adapting to a New World,* 281. On

livestock's ability to tolerate low temperatures, see E. S. E. Hafez, ed., *Adaptation of Domestic Animals* (Philadelphia, 1968), 107, 117, 183, 187, 242, 289; L. E. Mount, *The Climatic Physiology of the Pig* (Baltimore, 1968), 120–21, 123.

70. David W. Stahle et al., "The Lost Colony and Jamestown Droughts," *Science,* 280 (1998): 564–67; Hafez, ed., *Adaptation of Domestic Animals,* 175–76; Karen Ordahl Kupperman, "Apathy and Death in Early Jamestown," *JAH,* 66 (1979): 24–40, especially 35; Carville V. Earle, "Environment, Disease, and Mortality in Early Virginia," in Thad W. Tate and David L. Ammerman, eds., *The Chesapeake in the Seventeenth Century: Essays on Anglo-American Society & Politics* (Chapel Hill, 1979), 96–125.

71. Hafez, ed., *Adaptation of Domestic Animals,* 251–53. Parasites remained a major problem for livestock in the American South into the twentieth century; see Frederick F. Siegel, *The Roots of Southern Distinctiveness: Tobacco and Society in Danville, Virginia, 1780–1865* (Chapel Hill, 1987), 71.

72. Frederick Zeuner, *A History of Domesticated Animals* (London, 1963), 82; Baxter, ed., *Doc. History of the State of Maine,* 3, Trelawny Papers, 141, see also 118, 122, 156, 166, 169, 200, 216, 219, 281; Dunn et al., eds., *Journal of John Winthrop,* 57, see also 39, 40, 101; Wood, *New England's Prospect,* 45; Forbes et al., eds., *Winthrop Papers,* 3:184, 185; Cronon, *Changes in the Land,* 132.

73. For wolf bounties in the Chesapeake, see *Va. Statutes,* 1:199, 395, 456; 2:87; Warren M. Billings, ed., "Some Acts Not in Hening's *Statutes*: The Acts of Assembly, April 1652, November 1652, and July 1653," *VMHB,* 83 (1975): 68, 69; *Md. Arch.,* 1:362–63. For examples of New England bounties, see Henry M. Burt, *The First Century of the History of Springfield,* 2 vols. (Springfield, 1898–99), 1:189; Howard M. Chapin, ed., *The Early Records of the Town of Warwick* (Providence, 1926), 111; *Mass. Bay Recs.,* 1:81, 156, 304; 2:84–85, 103, 252; 3:17, 134, 319; 4, pt. 2, 2, 42; 5:453; John D. Cushing, ed., *Acts and Laws of New Hampshire 1680–1726* (Wilmington, 1978), 219. On the possible expansion of the wolf population following the introduction of livestock, see Timothy Silver, "A Useful Arcadia: European Colonists as Biotic Factors in Chesapeake Forests," in Philip D. Curtin, Grace S. Brush, and George W. Fisher, eds., *Discovering the Chesapeake: The History of an Ecosystem* (Baltimore and London, 2001), 160–61. Roger Williams described two hogs driving a wolf away from its prey in Williams, *Key,* 226.

74. Barbour, ed., *Works of John Smith,* 1:275; *For The Colony in Virginea Britannia. Lavves Diuine, Morall and Martiall, &c.* (1612) in Force, ed., *Tracts,* 3:§2, 15. On the wretched condition of the colonists, see Edmund S. Morgan, *American Slavery, American Freedom: The Ordeal of Colonial Virginia* (New York, 1975), ch. 4, especially 72–73; and Karen O. Kupperman, "Apathy and Death in Early Jamestown," *JAH* 66 (1979): 24–40.

75. Barbour, ed., *Works of John Smith,* 1:263; Ralph Hamor, *A True Discourse of the Present State of Virginia* [1615] (Richmond, 1957), 23; Morgan, *American*

Slavery, 139; Lois Green Carr, Russell R. Menard, Lorena S. Walsh, *Robert Cole's World: Agriculture & Society in Early Maryland* (Chapel Hill, 1991), 47–48, 223, 228, 233, 237.

76. Kingsbury, ed., *Virginia Co. Recs.,* 3: 171–72; Martha W. McCartney, "An Early Virginia Census Reprised," *Quarterly Bulletin of the Archaeological Society of Virginia,* 54 (1999): 179, 181; Edward Waterhouse, "A Declaration of the State of the Colony . . . ," in Kingsbury, ed., *Virginia Co. Recs.* 3:545. Edmund Morgan estimated that Virginia's English population in 1625 stood at about 1,300; see *American Slavery,* 404. Disputes over the number of imported cattle emerged in 1623 as company officials tried to assess the damage to Virginia's herds after the Powhatan attack of 1622; see Kingsbury, ed., *Virginia Co. Recs.,* 4:137–38.

77. Kingsbury, ed., *Virginia Co. Recs.,* 3:612; 4:228–29, 235, 476. The animal muster of 1624/25 is reprinted in Annie Lash Jester and Martha Woodroof Hiden, eds., *Adventurers of Purse and Person: Virginia, 1607–1625,* 2nd ed. (Richmond, 1964), 5–69. This count doubtless omitted animals that had escaped into the woods for good.

78. *Va. Statutes,* 1:153; "A Perfect Description of Virginia . . ." [London, 1649], in Force, ed., *Tracts,* 2:§8, 3, 12; Lewis Cecil Gray, *History of Agriculture in the Southern United States To 1860,* 2 vols. (Washington, D.C., 1932), 1:28–29, 35; Morgan, *American Slavery,* 139–40. For an overview of population growth in the Chesapeake, see Horn, *Adapting to a New World,* 136–39.

79. Wood, *New England's Prospect,* 69; see also 58–62; Percy Wells Bidwell and John I. Falconer, *History of Agriculture in the Northern United States 1620–1860* (Washington, D.C., 1925; reprinted New York, 1941), 27; Forbes et al., eds., *Winthrop Papers,* 3:166; Langdon, *Pilgrim Colony,* 36–37.

80. Howard S. Russell, *A Long, Deep Furrow: Three Centuries of Farming in New England* (Hanover, N.H., 1976), 60; Johnson, *Wonder-Working Providence,* 68–69, 69–70, 72, 74, 99, 110, 189, 197, 211; Carl Bridenbaugh, *Fat Mutton and Liberty of Conscience: Society in Rhode Island, 1636–1690* (Providence, 1974), 42–43; Bidwell and Falconer, *Hist. of Agriculture,* 26; Paul J. Lindholdt, ed., *John Josselyn, Colonial Traveler: A Critical Edition of Two Voyages to New-England* (Hanover, N.H., 1988), 138–39. Daniel Vickers calculated that, in the 1680s, there were between 2 and 2.5 cows per taxable male in three Essex County villages; see *Farmers & Fishermen: Two Centuries of Work in Essex County, Massachusetts, 1630–1850* (Chapel Hill, 1994), 213. Jackson Turner Main's figures for early Connecticut are somewhat higher, with a median of six cattle per household as enumerated in inventories; actual livestock holdings varied by the age and wealth of the decedent; see *Society and Economy in Colonial Connecticut* (Princeton, 1985), 203, 212–13, 215, 218, 222–23.

81. E. B. O'Callaghan, ed., *Documents Relative to the Colonial History of the State of New York, . . . ,* 15 vols. (Albany, 1853–87), 1:419; 2:433; J. Franklin Jameson, ed., *Narratives of New Netherland 1609–1664* (New York, 1909), 423; Russell, *Long, Deep Furrow,* 54, 59–60, 62–63, 113; Bidwell and Falconer, *Hist. of*

Agriculture, 42–44; Darrett B. Rutman, "Governor Winthrop's Garden Crop: The Significance of Agriculture in the Early Commerce of Massachusetts Bay," *WMQ,* 3rd ser., 20 (1963): 396–415.

82. This pattern persisted everywhere Europeans colonized new lands; see Crosby, *Ecological Imperialism,* ch. 8.

CHAPTER FOUR: THE WILD GANGS OF THE CHESAPEAKE

1. *Va. Statutes,* 1:393–96; quotation on 395.

2. On the English colonists' association of civilization with Christianity, see James Axtell, *The Invasion Within: The Contest of Cultures in Colonial North America* (New York, 1985), ch. 7; Bernard W. Sheehan, *Savagism and Civility: Indians and Englishmen in Colonial Virginia* (New York, 1980), 124–26.

3. *Va. Statutes,* 1:393–94. On the nature of leadership among Virginia's Indians, see Helen C. Rountree, *The Powhatan Indians of Virginia: Their Traditional Culture* (Norman, Okla., 1989), 146–49.

4. For descriptions of the material circumstances of life in the early Chesapeake colonies, see Lois Green Carr, Russell R. Menard, Lorena S. Walsh, *Robert Cole's World: Agriculture & Society in Early Maryland* (Chapel Hill, 1991), 36–37, 91, 94, 102–6, 115; James Horn, *Adapting to a New World: English Society in the Seventeenth-Century Chesapeake* (Chapel Hill, 1994), 293–330; Gloria L. Main, *Tobacco Colony: Life in Early Maryland, 1650–1720* (Princeton, 1982), 140–239.

5. For English farm buildings, see Joan Thirsk, ed., *The Agrarian History of England and Wales,* IV, *1500–1640* (Cambridge, Eng., 1967), 744; G. E. Fussell, *The English Dairy Farmer 1500–1900* (London, 1966), ch. 3. Chesapeake farm buildings and fences are discussed in Carr et al., *Robert Cole's World,* 36, 62–63, 66–68.

6. Main, *Tobacco Colony;* Horn, *Adapting to a New World,* 328–33; Carr et al., *Robert Cole's World,* 90–94, 98–114; Edmund Morgan, *American Slavery, American Freedom: The Ordeal of Colonial Virginia* (New York, 1975), 108–13, 141–42. Sandys's remark is in Susan M. Kingsbury, ed., *The Records of the Virginia Company of London,* 4 vols. (Washington, D.C., 1906–35), 3:489.

7. George Alsop, *A Character of the Province of Maryland* (1666), in Clayton Colman Hall, ed., *Narratives of Early Maryland, 1633–1684* (New York, 1910), 347; Robert Beverley, *The History and Present State of Virginia,* ed. Louis B. Wright (Charlottesville, 1968; orig. pub. 1947), 317 (quotation); "A Letter from Mr. John Clayton . . . to the Royal Society, May 12, 1688," in Peter Force, ed., *Tracts and Other Papers, Relating Principally to the Origin, Settlement, and Progress of the Colonies in North America, From the Discovery of the Country to the Year 1776,* 4 vols. (Washington, D.C., 1836–44; reprint, Gloucester, Mass., 1963), 3:§12, 35. See also John Hammond, *Leah and Rachel, or, The Two Fruitfull Sisters Virginia and Mary-Land* (1656) in Hall, ed., *Narratives of Early*

Maryland, 291; Thomas Glover, *An Account of Virginia . . .* , reprinted from *Philosophical Transactions of the Royal Society*, June 20, 1676 (Oxford, 1904), 19; Carr et al., *Robert Cole's World*, 51; Main, *Tobacco Colony*, 62, 72; Lewis Cecil Gray, *History of Agriculture in the Southern United States to 1860*, 2 vols. (Washington, D.C., 1932), 1:207–8; Philip Alexander Bruce, *Economic History of Virginia in the Seventeenth Century . . .* , 2 vols. (New York, 1895), 1:298–99, 376–77; David O. Percy, *Of Fast Horses, Black Cattle, Woods Hogs, and Rat-Tailed Sheep: Animal Husbandry Along the Colonial Potomac*, National Colonial Farm Research Report No. 4 (Accokeek, Md., 1979), 53–63.

8. Gray, *History of Agriculture in the Southern U.S.*, 1:19–20, 28–30; Carr et al., *Robert Cole's World*, 35–36; Main, *Tobacco Colony*, 197–98.

9. Martha W. McCartney, "An Early Virginia Census Reprised," *Quarterly Bulletin of the Archaeological Society of Virginia*, 54 (1999): 181; Ralph Hamor, *A True Discourse of the Present State of Virginia* (1615) (Richmond, 1957), 23; Bruce, *Economic History of Virginia*, 1:200, 223–24; Main, *Tobacco Colony*, 76, 200; Carr et al., *Robert Cole's World*, 35; Gray, *History of Agriculture in the Southern U. S.*, 1:194–95; [Durand of Dauphiné], *A Frenchman in Virginia: Being the Memoirs of a Huguenot Refugee in 1681* (Richmond, 1923), 108. For the English population of Virginia in 1650, see John J. McCusker and Russell R. Menard, *The Economy of British America, 1607–1789* (Chapel Hill, 1985), 136.

10. Main, *Tobacco Colony*, 45, 67, 200 n. 110; Bruce, *Economic History of Virginia*, 1:298, 374, 375; Percy, *Of Fast Horses*, 5–6; Carr et al., *Robert Cole's World*, 137; Gray, *History of Agriculture in the Southern U. S.*, 1:38, 202; "A Perfect Description of Virginia . . ." (London, 1649) in Force, ed., *Tracts*, 2:§8, 3; Kevin P. Kelly, "'In Dispers'd Country Plantations': Settlement Patterns in Seventeenth-Century Surry County, Virginia," in Thad W. Tate and David L. Ammerman, eds., *The Chesapeake in the Seventeenth Century: Essays on Anglo-American Society* (Chapel Hill, 1979), 183–205; [Durand of Dauphiné], *Frenchman in Virginia*, 23; *Va. Statutes*, 2:267, 271.

11. Horn, *Adapting to a New World*, 36–38; Thomas Tusser, *Five Hundred Points of Good Husbandry* (London, 1663), 81; Julia Cherry Spruill, *Women's Life and Work in the Southern Colonies* (New York, 1998; orig. pub. 1938), 3–19; Calvert Papers, *Maryland Historical Society Fund-Publications*, 3 vols. (Baltimore, 1889–99), I (no. 28), 196.

12. Percy, *Of Fast Horses*, 22, 30–33; Main, *Tobacco Colony*, 200; Carr et al., *Robert Cole's World*, 38, 69, 72, 73–74, 95–96; Frederick F. Siegel, *The Roots of Southern Distinctiveness: Tobacco and Society in Danville, Virginia, 1780–1865* (Chapel Hill, 1987), 71; Joanne Bowen, "A Comparative Analysis of the New England and Chesapeake Herding Systems," in Paul A. Shackel and Barbara J. Little, eds., *Historical Archaeology of the Chesapeake* (Washington, D.C., 1994), 161; John Worlidge, *Systema Agriculturae: The Mystery of Husbandry Discovered*, 4th ed. (London, 1687), 172; Wesley N. Laing, "Cattle in

Seventeenth-Century Virginia," *VMHB*, 67 (1959): 154–55; "Letter from Mr. John Clayton," 25; [Durand of Dauphiné], *Frenchman in Virginia*, 116–17; Calvert Papers, *Md. Hist. Soc. Fund-Publications*, I, no. 28, 263 (quotation).

13.   Keith Thomas, *Man and the Natural World: A History of the Modern Sensibility* (New York, 1983), 26; Horn, *Adapting to a New World*, 259.

14.   Henry M. Miller, "An Archaeological Perspective on the Evolution of Diet in the Colonial Chesapeake, 1620–1745," in Lois Green Carr, Philip D. Morgan, and Jean B. Russo, eds., *Colonial Chesapeake Society* (Chapel Hill, 1988), 176–99; [Durand of Dauphiné], *Frenchman in Virginia*, 117–18; Hammond, *Leah and Rachel*, 292; Carr et al., *Robert Cole's World*, 97, 217–18; Main, *Tobacco Colony*, 201–2, 204; Karen Kupperman, "Apathy and Death in Early Jamestown," *JAH*, 66 (1979): 32–33.

15.   Kingsbury, ed., *Va. Co. Recs.*, 3:18, 221; see also Laing, "Cattle in Seventeenth-Century Virginia," 160; Morgan, *American Slavery*, 137; Carr et al., *Robert Cole's World*, 46.

16.   Beverley, *History of Virginia*, 37; Bruce, *Economic History of Virginia*, 1:209–10, 300, 312; Morgan, *American Slavery*, 136–37; Kingsbury, ed., *Va. Co. Recs.*, 3:473; Philip L. Barbour, ed., *The Complete Works of Captain John Smith (1580–1631)*, 3 vols. (Chapel Hill, 1986), 2:242; Hamor, *True Discourse*, 30–31; Lorena S. Walsh, Ann Smart Martin, and Joanne Bowen, "Provisioning Early American Towns; The Chesapeake: A Multidisciplinary Study," Final Performance Report, NEH Grant RO–22643–93 (1997), 32. For the use of islands, see "Letter of Governor Leonard Calvert to Lord Baltimore, 1638," in Hall, ed., *Narratives of Early Maryland*, 154; *A True Declaration of the Estate of the Colonie in Virginia . . .* (London, 1610) in Force, ed., *Tracts*, 3:§1; Barbour, ed., *Works of John Smith*, 1:254; Calvert Papers, *Md. Hist. Soc. Fund-Publications*, I, no. 28, 208.

17.   Calvert Papers, *Md. Hist. Soc. Fund-Publications*, I, no. 28, 196; *Va. Statutes*, 1:228; *Md. Arch.*, 17:422–23; see also Bruce, *Economic History of Virginia*, 1:315; Walsh, et al., "Provisioning Early American Towns," 30. For court cases involving errant swine, see Accomack County Records, Virginia State Library, microfilm, reel 4, fol. 226; *Md. Arch.*, 4:412–13.

18.   "Letter from Mr. John Clayton," 26; Edmund Berkeley and Dorothy S. Berkeley, eds., "Another 'Account of Virginia' by the Reverend John Clayton," *VMHB*, 76 (1968): 419; [Durand of Dauphiné], *Frenchman in Virginia*, 116–17; Morgan, *American Slavery*, 137.

19.   James Blakely and David H. Bade, *The Science of Animal Husbandry*, 4th ed. (Reston, Va., 1985), 106, 125, 394, 586, 587; Katherine A. Houpt, *Domestic Animal Behavior for Veterinarians and Animal Scientists*, 3rd ed. (Ames, Iowa, 1998), 100, 289–90, 319; Siegel, *Roots of Southern Distinctiveness*, 70–71; Lois Green Carr and Russell R. Menard, "Land, Labor, and Economies of Scale in Early Maryland: Some Limits to Growth in the Chesapeake System of Husband-

ry," *Journal of Economic History* 49 (1989): 409, 413; Main, *Tobacco Colony,* 63–64.

20. *Va. Statutes,* 1:244–45, 332; 2:96–97, 100–1; Billings, "Some Acts Not in Hening's *Statutes,*" 58; *Md. Arch.,* 1:96, 344, 413–14; 2:350, 398–99; 13:472–73, 487; 22:477–78. For a description and illustrations of Virginia fences, see Berkeley and Berkeley, eds., "Another 'Account of Virginia,'" 426. For a comparison with English trespass laws, see William Holdsworth, *A History of English Law,* 5th ed., 16 vols. (London, 1942), 3:378–79; Peter Karsten, "Cows in the Corn, Pigs in the Garden, and 'the Problem of Social Costs': 'High' and 'Low' Legal Cultures of the British Diaspora Lands in the 17th, 18th, and 19th Centuries," *Law and Society Review* 32 (1998): 66–67; Bruce, *Economic History of Virginia,* 1:313–15.

21. Alsop, *Character of the Province of Maryland,* 348; Henry Hartwell, James Blair, and Edward Chilton, *The Present State of Virginia, and the College* (1727), ed. Hunter Dickinson Farish (Williamsburg, 1940), 9; Glover, *Account of Virginia,* 13; [Durand of Dauphiné], *Frenchman in Virginia,* 109; Hugh Jones, *The Present State of Virginia . . .,* (1724), ed. Richard L. Morton (Chapel Hill, 1956), 77; Carr and Menard, "Land, Labor, and Economies of Scale in Early Maryland," 407–18; Morgan, *American Slavery,* 141; Carr et al., *Robert Cole's World,* 52; Carville V. Earle, *The Evolution of a Tidewater Settlement System: All Hallow's Parish, Maryland, 1650–1783* (Chicago, 1975), 24–30; Bruce, *Economic History of Virginia,* 1:322; Gray, *History of Agriculture in the Southern U. S.,* 1:198; Main, *Tobacco Colony,* 41–42; Richard L. Bushman, "Opening the American Countryside," in James A. Henretta, Michael Kammen, and Stanley N. Katz, eds., *The Transformation of Early American History: Society, Authority, and Ideology* (New York, 1991), 242–43. Quotations from Glover, *Account of Virginia,* 12–13; "Letter from Mr. John Clayton," 20–21.

22. Hartwell et al., *Present State of Virginia,* 8.

23. Sam B. Hilliard, *Hog Meat and Hoecake: Food Supply in the Old South, 1840–1860* (Carbondale, 1972), 136; Timothy Silver, "A Useful Arcadia: European Colonists as Biotic Factors in Chesapeake Forests," in Philip D. Curtin, Grace S. Brush, George W. Fisher, eds., *Discovering the Chesapeake: The History of an Ecosystem* (Baltimore, 2001), 155; Main, *Tobacco Colony,* 62.

24. "Letter from Mr. John Clayton," 21; [Durand of Dauphiné], *Frenchman in Virginia,* 59; Darrett B. Rutman and Anita H. Rutman, *A Place in Time: Middlesex County, Virginia, 1650–1750* (New York, 1984), 153.

25. Calvert Papers, *Md. Hist. Soc. Fund-Publications,* I, no. 28, 238–39.

26. Silver, "Useful Arcadia," 155, 161. For a discussion of livestock density and ecological change in Mexico, see Andrew Sluyter, "From Archive to Map to Pastoral Landscape: A Spatial Perspective on the Livestock Ecology of Sixteenth-Century New Spain," *Environmental History,* 3 (1997): 508–28. I thank Julia Hobson for this reference.

27. Kelly, "'In dispers'd Country Plantations,'" 183–205; Horn, *Adapting to a New World,* 162–63; Earle, *Evolution of a Tidewater Settlement System,* 138–40; Main, *Tobacco Colony,* 44–45; Rutman and Rutman, *Place in Time,* 209–11.

28. For Chesapeake women's performance of agricultural tasks, see Kathleen M. Brown, *Good Wives, Nasty Wenches & Anxious Patriarchs: Gender, Race, and Power in Colonial Virginia* (Chapel Hill, 1996), 85–88.

29. [Whitaker], *Good Newes from Virginia . . .* (London, 1613; facsimile, New York, n.d.), 41; "The Relation of the Lord De-la-ware, 1611," in Lyon Gardiner Tyler, ed., *Narratives of Early Virginia, 1606–1625* (New York, 1907), 213; "Letter from Mr. John Clayton," 26; [Durand of Dauphiné], *Frenchman in Virginia,* 54, 59, 60, 115–17; Beverley, *History of Virginia,* 291, 318.

30. "Letter from Mr. John Clayton," 25–26. On English farmers' use of sainfoin, see Eric Kerridge, *The Agricultural Revolution* (New York, 1967), 278–80.

31. Glover, *Account of Virginia,* 19; [Durand of Dauphiné], *Frenchman in Virginia,* 54, 116–17.

32. [Durand of Dauphiné], *Frenchman in Virginia,* 113, 116; Beverley, *History of Virginia,* 318; "Letter from Mr. John Clayton," 25; Gray, *History of Agriculture in the Southern U. S.,* 1:200–201.

33. Edward Waterhouse, "A Declaration of the State of the Colony . . . ," in Kingsbury, ed., *Va. Co. Recs.,* 3:545; see also the letter from John Pory in ibid., 3:221.

34. Glover, *Account of Virginia,* 19; Beverley, *History of Virginia,* 291; *Md. Arch.,* 38:11.

35. For estimates of Chesapeake animals' weights, see Main, *Tobacco Colony,* 65; Carr et al., *Robert Cole's World,* 335–36. In 1692, the Maryland Assembly ordered the gelding of horses under 14 hands high, leaving only larger animals to breed in an effort to improve the quality of stock; see *Md. Arch.,* 13:549–50. English comparisons are difficult to find, although evidence suggests that by the late seventeenth century English animals were certainly larger, with 200-pound hogs and 1,000-pound oxen not uncommon. Improved management techniques and specialized breeding in the eighteenth century led to further increases in size and weight. See Mark Overton, *Agricultural Revolution in England: The Transformation of the Agrarian Economy 1500–1850* (Cambridge, 1996), 80; Joan Thirsk, ed., *The Agrarian History of England and Wales, 1640–1750,* V, Pt. 2 (Cambridge, Eng., 1985), 10–11.

36. Ronald R. Keiper, *The Assateague Ponies* (Centreville, Md., 1985), 15–16. Modern free-range cattle also tend to be small; see H. Epstein and I. L. Mason, "Cattle," in Ian L. Mason, ed., *Evolution of Domesticated Animals* (London, 1984), 25; Walsh et al., "Provisioning Early American Towns," 39–40.

37. On the concern about the potential effects of the American environment on English people, see Joyce E. Chaplin, *Subject Matter: Technology, the Body, and Science on the Anglo-American Frontier, 1500–1676* (Cambridge, Mass., 2001), 130–56.

38. *Md. Arch.*, 4:170; 54:396; Susie M. Ames, ed., *County Court Records of Acco-mack-Northampton, Virginia 1632–1640* (Washington, D.C., 1954), 30; Jones, *Present State of Virginia,* 84.

39. H. R. McIlwaine, ed., *Minutes of the Council and General Court of Colonial Virginia,* 2nd ed. (Richmond, 1979), 129; Accomack County Recs., reel 2, fol. 34 (mare), fol. 142 (Edwards's cattle); "Letter from Mr. John Clayton," 20, 25–26 (quotation). Other examples of lost animals in the Accomack records can be found on reel 2, fols. 95, 96, 123, 135–36, 149, 151, 152, 172, 182. See also Glover, *Account of Virginia,*18–19; Earle, *Evolution of a Tidewater Settlement System,* 120.

40. *Md. Arch.,* 4:168; Carr et al., *Robert Cole's World,* 177, 187; Beverley, *History of Virginia,* 318.

41. McCartney, "Early Virginia Census Reprised," 178; *Md. Arch.,* 1:486 (example of use of term "wild gangs"). Only in northernmost England and in Wales could wild cattle or horses be found in the seventeenth-century British Isles; see Thirsk, ed., *Agrarian History of England and Wales,* 4:19, 138, 160, 187.

42. Alfred W. Crosby, *Ecological Imperialism: The Biological Expansion of Europe, 900–1900* (New York, 1986), 174–87; H. Epstein and I. L. Mason, "Cattle," in Mason, ed., *Evolution of Domesticated Animals,* 7, 25; Epstein and M. Bichard, "Pig," in ibid., 146; Tom McKnight, *Feral Livestock in Anglo-America,* University of California Publications in Geography, vol. 16 (Berkeley, 1964), 41; John J. Mayer and I. Lehr Brisbin, Jr., *Wild Pigs of the United States: Their History, Morphology, and Current Status* (Athens, Ga., 1991), 124, 127, 134, 139, 147; H. B. Graves, "Behavior and Ecology of Wild and Feral Swine (Sus Scrofa)," *Journal of Animal Science,* 58 (1984): 484; Keiper, *Assateague Ponies,* 16, 58–59.

43. "Letter from Mr. John Clayton," 35; Beverley, *History of Virginia,* 153–54, 312.

44. Houpt, *Domestic Animal Behavior,* 38, 46–47, 55–56, 173; McKnight, *Feral Livestock in Anglo-America,* 19, 28, 31, 41, 43; Keiper, *Assateague Ponies,* 39; Mayer and Brisbin, *Wild Pigs,* 8–9; G. W. Arnold and M. L. Dudzinski, *Ethology of Free-Ranging Domestic Animals* (New York, 1978), 125; Hilliard, *Hog Meat and Hoecake,* 95; Graves, "Behavior and Ecology of Wild and Feral Swine," 483–90. Quotations from *Md. Arch.,* 10:48; 38:11–12.

45. E. B. O'Callaghan, ed., *Documents Relative to the Colonial History of the State of New-York . . . ,* 15 vols. (Albany, 1853–87), 2:54.

46. [Durand of Dauphiné], *Frenchman in Virginia,* 114.

47. Kingsbury, ed., *Va. Co. Recs.,* 4:283–84. It is unclear whether anyone ever was executed for theft of animals.

48. Hammond, *Leah and Rachel,* 295; *Va. Statutes,* 1:350. See also Virginia DeJohn Anderson, "Animals into the Wilderness: The Development of Livestock Husbandry in the Seventeenth-Century Chesapeake," *WMQ,* 3rd ser., 59 (2002): 396.

49. *Md. Arch.*, 41:161; 53:234–37; 54:42–43, 384. For similar cases, see 10:233–34; 53:206, 237–39, 544–48; 54:369–70; Accomack County Records, reel 4, fols. 130–31, 137, 158, 223–28. See also Raphael Semmes, *Crime and Punishment in Early Maryland* (Baltimore, 1938), ch. 3; and Horn, *Adapting to a New World,* 352, 360–61.

50. Accomack County Records, reel 4, fols. 226, 232–33.

51. *Md. Arch.*, 1:253; 17:135–36; 38:77–78; *Va. Statutes*, 1:465–66. On livestock theft, see also Gray, *History of Agriculture in the Southern U. S.,* 1:143–45; and Bruce, *Economic History of Virginia,* 1:371–72, 379.

52. Kingsbury, ed., *Va. Co. Recs.,* 3:120; *Va. Statutes*, 1:145–46; Morgan, *American Slavery,* 122; *Md. Arch.*, 2:346–47; 5:568–69; 8:36–37; 15:155–56; Semmes, *Crime and Punishment in Early Maryland,* 76.

53. *Va. Statutes,* 1:420–21; Billings, ed., "Some Acts Not in Hening's *Statutes,*" 67–68. On English practice, see Charles M. Andrews, *The Colonial Period of American History,* 4 vols. (New Haven, 1936), 2:208.

54. *Md. Arch.*, 54:42–43.

55. Warren Billings, ed., *The Old Dominion in the Seventeenth Century: A Documentary History of Virginia, 1606–1689* (Chapel Hill, 1975), 90; Barton H. Wise, ed., "Northampton County Records in the 17th Century," *VMHB,* 4 (1897): 406; Gray, *History of Agriculture in the Southern U. S.,*1:144–45; Carr et al., *Robert Cole's World,* 176–77. Horses may also have been branded; especially sensitive to handling around the head and ears, they were not good candidates for earmarks.

56. For earmarking, see *Md. Arch.,*1:295; Wise, ed., "Northampton Co. Recs.," 404; Gray, *History of Agriculture in the Southern U. S.,* 1:144–45; Laing, "Cattle in Seventeenth-Century Virginia," 159–60. Examples of earmarks can be found in the Accomack County Records, reel 2, fols. 267–70; Susie M. Ames, ed., *County Court Records of Accomack-Northampton, Virginia, 1640–1645* (Charlottesville, 1973), 30; Carr et al., *Robert Cole's World,* 176–77. For the Gerard-Evans dispute, see *Md. Arch.*, 41:159–60.

57. *Md. Arch.*, 4:207; 22:554–55; 41:20–21, 523; 54:42–43; *Va. Statutes,*1:244.

58. For the extent of free-ranging livestock's wandering, see Arnold and Dudzinski, *Ethology of Free-Ranging Domestic Animals,* 39–43, 84; E. S. E. Hafez, ed., *The Behaviour of Domestic Animals* (Baltimore, 1962), 372; Houpt, *Domestic Animal Behavior,* 56; Caroline Grigson, "Porridge and Pannage: Pig Husbandry in Neolithic England," in Martin Bell and Susan Limbrey, eds., *Archaeological Aspects of Woodland Ecology,* British Archaeological Reports International Series 146 (Oxford, 1982): 299; *Md. Arch.,*13:313. On the social behavior of domesticable animals, see Frederick Zeuner, *A History of Domesticated Animals* (London, 1963), 37; Juliet Clutton-Brock, *Domesticated Animals from Early Times* (London and Austin, 1981), 15–16.

59. Beverley, *History of Virginia,* 318; *Md. Arch.*, 10:236; 2:277–79; see also 53:545.

60. Clutton-Brock, *Domesticated Animals,* 15; Hafez, ed., *Behaviour of Domestic Animals,* 16–17, 112; Houpt, *Domestic Animal Behavior,* 242, 248; Grigson, "Porridge and Pannage," 303; Graves, "Behavior and Ecology of Wild and Feral Swine," 483.

61. Carr et al., *Robert Cole's World,* 218; Main, *Tobacco Colony,* 63, n. 9.

62. On using food to control animals' movement, see Sytze Bottema, "Some Observations on Modern Domestication Processes," in Juliet Clutton-Brock, ed., *The Walking Larder: Patterns of Domestication, Pastoralism, and Predation* (London, 1989), 44; Grigson, "Porridge and Pannage," 302–3. There is no evidence that colonists used salt for this purpose. See also Bartlett Burleigh James and J. Franklin Jameson, eds., *Journal of Jasper Danckaerts, 1679–1680* (New York, 1913), 134; "Letter from Mr. John Clayton," 26; Hilliard, *Hog Meat and Hoecake,* 99. On penning livestock, see Bruce, *Economic History of Virginia,* 1:379; *Md. Arch.,* 4:412–13, 54:396. On penning farrowing swine as a method of domestication, see Grigson, "Porridge and Pannage," 305.

63. *Md. Arch.,* 10:48–49.

64. For brief descriptions of the turmoil in Maryland, see Carr, et al., *Robert Cole's World,* 11–12; Andrews, *Colonial Period of American History,* 2:308–14.

65. *Md. Arch.,* 10:49.

66. Accomack County Recs., reel 2, fol. 141. Italics added.

67. Ibid.

68. Kingsbury, ed., *Va. Co. Recs.,* 1:502; 2:40–42. For Martin, see scattered references in Andrews, *Colonial Period of American History,* esp. 1:130, 166–67, 177, 186, 190, 195. For a similar debate about wild livestock in colonial Latin America, see Silvio R. Duncan Baretta and John Markoff, "Civilization and Barbarism: Cattle Frontiers in Latin America," *Comparative Studies in Society and History,* 20 (1978): 606.

69. Kingsbury, ed., *Va. Co. Recs.* 3:589; 4:138.

70. Morgan, *American Slavery,* 101–2.

71. *Va. Statutes,* 1:199. On royal hunting rights in England, see E. P. Thompson, *Whigs and Hunters: The Origin of the Black Act* (New York, 1975), 29–31.

72. *Va. Statutes,* 1:244, 3:279.

73. Robert Beverley noted that hunting game and wild hogs yielded "Pleasure, as well as Profit to the Sports-man"; see *History of Virginia,* 153.

74. Accomack County Recs., reel 2, fols. 159, 204. On the hunting of wild horses, see Beverley, *History of Virginia,* 312.

75. *Md. Arch.,* 4:142–43; 10:232; 41:441; 57:115.

76. Andrews, *Colonial Period of American History,* 2:294–97; Carr, et al., *Robert Cole's World,* 5–9; *Md. Arch.,* 41:188–89; 49:575, 586–87; 53:628. Gardiner's fine was subsequently reduced to 200 pounds of tobacco.

77. *Md. Arch.,* 1:418–19; 17:233, 241–42. On the familial connections of Darnall and Talbot, see Newton D. Mereness, *Maryland as a Proprietary Province* (New York, 1901), 34, 61.

78. *Md. Arch.,* 3:295. On the various political struggles between proprietor and colonists in Maryland, see Susan Rosenfeld Falb, *Advice and Ascent: The Development of the Maryland Assembly 1635–1689* (New York, 1986); and Carr et al., *Robert Cole's World,* 19–20.

79. For the Glorious Revolution in Maryland, see Lois Green Carr and David William Jordan, *Maryland's Revolution of Government 1689–1692* (Ithaca, 1974).

80. *Md. Arch.,* 8:313.

81. *Md. Arch.,* 20:26.

82. Michael Dalton, *The Countrey Justice . . . ,* enlarged edition (London, 1666), 306–7; Erica Fudge, *Perceiving Animals: Humans and Beasts in Early Modern English Culture* (London, 2000), 125–27.

83. It is unclear why the Calverts did not enjoy a similar right so long as they owned ungranted land in their colony. This may have been due to the fact that the Crown never explicitly granted such a right in the original Maryland charter; see *Md. Arch.,* 20:26. Also, as in the case of Virginia, no mention is made of Crown ownership of deer or other indigenous animals.

84. *Md. Arch.,* 19:184.

85. *Md. Arch.,* 19:184, and for a similar discussion in early Georgia, see Mart A. Stewart, "'Whether Wast, Deodand, or Stray': Cattle, Culture, and the Environment in Early Georgia," *Agricultural History,* 65 (1991): 1–28.

86. Comparatively few English colonists ended up living with the Indians, with the important exception of colonists captured in wartime. See James Axtell, "The White Indians of Colonial America," *WMQ,* 3rd ser., 32 (1975): 55–88. On English concerns about the transformative power of the American environment, see Chaplin, *Subject Matter,* ch. 4.

87. *Md. Arch.,* 8:392–93, 13:549–50, 20:294.

CHAPTER FIVE: A WORLD OF PASTURES AND POUNDS

1. Mass. Archives, vol. 30, fol. 119; the petition is not dated, but from its placement in the archives it appears to be from 1662 or 1663. For biographical information on Danforth, see *The Dictionary of American Biography on CD-ROM* (New York, 1997), originally published in 1930. A map of the Nipmuck country can be found in Robert S. Grumet, *Historic Contact: Indian People and Colonists in Today's Northeastern United States in the Sixteenth Through Eighteenth Centuries* (Norman, Okla., 1995), 102.

2. Mass. Arch., vol. 30, fol. 119; *Mass. Bay Recs.,* 1:112; John Winthrop, "Reasons to be Considered, and Objections with Answers," in Allyn B. Forbes et al., eds., *Winthrop Papers, 1498–1654,* 6 vols. (Boston, 1929–92), 2:140–41.

3. Samuel Deane, *The New-England Farmer; or, Georgical Dictionary . . .* (Worcester, 1790), 266–67. On the shortage of capital in the early New England agrarian

economy, see Daniel Vickers, *Farmers & Fishermen: Two Centuries of Work in Essex County, Massachusetts, 1630–1830* (Chapel Hill, 1994), 43–47.

4. Philip L. Barbour, ed., *The Complete Works of Captain John Smith (1580–1631),* 3 vols. (Chapel Hill, 1986), 1:330–31; John J. McCusker and Russell R. Menard, *The Economy of British America 1607–1789* (Chapel Hill, 1985), 99–101; Vickers, *Farmers & Fishermen,* 41–77, 85–100, 145–53.

5. Francis Higginson, *New-Englands Plantation with The Sea Journal and Other Writings* [1630] (Salem, 1908), n.p.; William Wood, *New England's Prospect,* ed. Alden T. Vaughan (Amherst, 1977), 36; see also the letter from William Hammond to Sir Simonds D'Ewes in Everett Emerson, ed., *Letters from New England: The Massachusetts Bay Colony, 1629–1638* (Amherst, 1976), 112.

6. Howard S. Russell, *A Long, Deep Furrow: Three Centuries of Farming in New England* (Hanover, 1976), 40–42; Percy Wells Bidwell and John I. Falconer, *History of Agriculture in the Northern United States 1620–1860* (Washington, D.C., 1925; reprinted New York, 1941), 12–13; Darrett B. Rutman, *Husbandmen of Plymouth: Farms and Villages in the Old Colony, 1620–1692* (Boston, 1967), 46; Stephen Innes, *Labor in a New Land: Economy and Society in Seventeenth-Century Springfield* (Princeton, 1983), 33; William Cronon, *Changes in the Land: Indians, Colonists, and the Ecology of New England* (New York, 1983), 154–55.

7. Archaeologists now believe that maize agriculture came relatively late to New England, probably between AD 1000 and 1300; see Kathleen J. Bragdon, *Native People of Southern New England, 1500–1650* (Norman, Okla., 1996), 81–86; Higginson, *New-Englands Plantation,* n. p.

8. Fernand Braudel, *Capitalism and Material Life 1400–1800* (English edition, London, 1973), 113–14; Russell, *Long, Deep Furrow,* 43–44; Bidwell and Falconer, *History of Agriculture,* 9–12, 14; Robert R. Walcott, "Husbandry in Colonial New England," *NEQ,* 9 (1936): 230; *Mass. Bay Recs.,* 1:92, 140, 180, 191, 192.

9. Vickers, *Farmers & Fishermen,* 14–23; Rutman, *Husbandmen of Plymouth,* 46–47.

10. J. Franklin Jameson, ed., *Johnson's Wonder-Working Providence 1628–1651* (New York, 1910), 210; see also letter of John Winthrop, Jr., in MHS *Colls.,* 5th ser., 8 (1882): 65; Bidwell and Falconer, *History of Agriculture,* 26–27; Sarah F. McMahon, "A Comfortable Subsistence: The Changing Composition of Diet in Rural New England, 1620–1840," *WMQ,* 3rd ser., 42 (1985): 34–36, 55; Carl Bridenbaugh, *Fat Mutton and Liberty of Conscience: Society in Rhode Island, 1636–1690* (Providence, 1974), 46–47; Joanne Bowen, "A Comparative Analysis of the New England and Chesapeake Herding Systems" in Paul A. Shackel and Barbara J. Little, eds., *Historical Archaeology of the Chesapeake* (Washington, D.C., 1994), 156–60.

11. Samuel Deane described cheesemaking in *New-England Farmer,* 48–49, and mentioned an expected milk yield of a gallon a day per cow, 63. For dairying

and equipment, see Russell, *Long, Deep Furrow,* 83; Laurel Thatcher Ulrich, *Good Wives: Image and Reality in the Lives of Women in Northern New England 1650–1750* (New York, 1982), ch. 1; David Grayson Allen, *In English Ways: The Movement of Societies and the Transferal of English Local Law and Custom to Massachusetts Bay in the Seventeenth Century* (Chapel Hill, 1981), 59–60, 102. On the sex ratio in early New England, see Virginia DeJohn Anderson, *New England's Generation: The Great Migration and the Formation of Society and Culture in the Seventeenth Century* (New York, 1991): 20–21, 223. Abbott Lowell Cummings describes early cellars in *The Framed Houses of Massachusetts Bay, 1625–1725* (Cambridge, Mass., 1979), 29–30. For Thomas Minor, see *The Diary of Thomas Minor, Stonington, Connecticut, 1653 to 1684,* prepared by Sidney H. Miner and George D. Stanton, Jr. (New London, 1899), 19, 24, 25, 54–55, 58–59, 84, 112, 123, 131, 141. For Rhode Island dairying and taxes, see Bridenbaugh, *Fat Mutton,* 45–46.

12. Gloria L. Main, *Peoples of a Spacious Land: Families and Cultures in Colonial New England* (Cambridge, Mass., 2001), 2–3.

13. E. B. O'Callaghan et al. eds., *Documents Relative to the Colonial History of the State of New* York; . . . , 15 vols. (Albany, 1853–87): 1:368; Wood, *New England's Prospect,* 36; Jameson, ed., *Johnson's Wonder-Working Providence,* 85, 154; Fulmer Mood, "John Winthrop, Jr., on Indian Corn," *NEQ,* 10 (1937): 127–28.

14. Vickers, *Farmers & Fishermen,* 69, 213; Jackson Turner Main, *Society and Economy in Colonial Connecticut* (Princeton, 1985), 77; Miner and Stanton, eds., *Diary of Thomas Minor,* 6, see also 34; Innes, *Labor in a New Land,* 52; John D. Cushing, ed., *The Laws of the Pilgrims: A Facsimile Edition of The Book of the General Laws of the Inhabitants of the Jurisdiction of New-Plimoth, 1672 & 1685* (Wilmington, 1977), 14.

15. M. Halsey Thomas, ed., *The Diary of Samuel Sewall 1674–1729,* 2 vols. (New York, 1973), 1:149; Jeremy Belknap, *The History of New Hampshire,* 2 vols. (orig. publ. 1784–91; reprinted Dover, 1831), 1:22.

16. Rutman, *Husbandmen of Plymouth,* 48; Main, *Society and Economy in Colonial Ct.,* 77–78; Russell, *Long, Deep Furrow,* 62; Bidwell and Falconer, *History of Agriculture,* 30; Vickers, *Farmers & Fishermen,* 69; Walcott, "Husbandry in Colonial New England," 243–44; *Mass. Bay Recs.,* 2:190; *Ct. Recs.,* 2:27–28; Cushing, ed., *Laws of the Pilgrims,* 47; Paul J. Lindholdt, ed., *John Josselyn, Colonial Traveler: A Critical Edition of Two Voyages to New-England* (Hanover, 1988), 132; Bridenbaugh, *Fat Mutton,* 57, 59 (William Harris quotation).

17. *Mass. Bay Recs.,* 2:105; Cronon, *Changes in the Land,* 129; Katherine A. Houpt, *Domestic Animal Behavior for Veterinarians and Animal Scientists,* 3rd ed. (Ames, 1998), 321, 327; Jameson, ed., *Johnson's Wonder-Working Providence,* 115.

18. *Mass. Bay Recs.,* 1:81, 156, 304; 2:84–85; 103, 252; 3:17, 134, 319; 4:153; 5:453; William H. Whitmore, ed., *The Colonial Laws of Massachusetts; Reprinted from the Edition of 1660, with the Supplements to 1672, Containing Also,*

The Body of Liberties of 1641 (Boston, 1889), 202, 228; Henry M. Burt, *The First Century of the History of Springfield,* 2 vols. (Springfield, 1898–99), 1:189; John D. Cushing, ed., *Acts and Laws of New Hampshire 1680–1726* (Wilmington, 1978), 219; Howard M. Chapin, ed., *The Early Records of the Town of Warwick* (Providence, 1926), 111; Cronon, *Changes in the Land,* 132–34; Bridenbaugh, *Fat Mutton,* 16–17.

19. "Essay on the Ordering of Towns," in Forbes et al., eds., *Winthrop Papers,* 3:184–85; *Mass. Bay Recs.,* 3:397; *Ct. Recs.,* 2:139.

20. Walcott, "Husbandry in Colonial New England," 246–47; *Mass. Bay Recs.,* 1:303; 2:251–52; *Ct. Recs.,* 2:34.

21. *Mass. Bay Recs.,*3:355–56; Susan M. Ouellette, "Divine Providence and Collective Endeavor: Sheep Production in Early Massachusetts," *NEQ,* 69 (1996): 355–80. Thanks to Tom Field for explaining the prohibition against slaughtering rams and wethers under the age of two.

22. Russell, *Long, Deep Furrow,* 34, 95, 99, 154; Ouellette, "Divine Providence," 355–80; Vickers, *Farmers & Fishermen,* 69; Bidwell and Falconer, *History of Agriculture,* 28; Jameson, ed., *Johnson's Wonder-Working Providence,* 211; Allen, *In English Ways,* 27, 58–60, 100–1; Rutman, *Husbandmen of Plymouth,* 25, 48; Innes, *Labor in a New Land,* 37.

23. Russell, *Long, Deep Furrow,* 155–56; Main, *Society and Economy in Colonial Ct.,* 78; Edward Byers, *The Nation of Nantucket: Society and Politics in an Early American Commercial Center 1660–1820* (Boston, 1987), 42–43; Rev. William Hubbard, *A General History of New England, From the Discovery to MDCLXXX* (New York, 1972; reprinted from MHS, *Colls.,* 2nd ser., vols. 5, 6 [Boston, 1815]), 672; Samuel Maverick, *A Briefe Discription of New England and the Severall Townes Therein Together with the Present Government Thereof* [1660] (Boston, 1885), 22, 25; Forbes et al., eds., *Winthrop Papers,* 5:150; Bridenbaugh, *Fat Mutton,* 17, 50–55.

24. Bidwell and Falconer, *History of Agriculture,* 18, 32; Russell, *Long, Deep Furrow,* 15–16, 20, 31, 32, 33–34; Walcott, "Husbandry in Colonial New England," 247–48; James Phinney Baxter, ed., *Documentary History of the State of Maine,* vol. 3, The Trelawny Papers (Portland, 1884), 45–46, 48, 57–58, 109, 224, 243, 309, 310; Jeremy Belknap, *The History of New Hampshire,* 2 vols. (orig. publ. 1784–91; reprint Dover, 1831), 1:424, 430; Bridenbaugh, *Fat Mutton,* 19, 41; Richard S. Dunn, *Puritans and Yankees: The Winthrop Dynasty of New England 1630–1717* (Princeton, 1962; reprint New York, 1971), 75.

25. Jameson, ed., *Johnson's Wonder-Working Providence,* 73; Lucius R. Paige, *History of Cambridge, Massachusetts,* 2 vols. (Boston, 1877), 1:41; City of Boston, *Second Report of the Record Commissioners of the City of Boston* [Boston Town Records 1634-1660] (Boston, 1877), 68; Chapin, *Early Records of Warwick,* 52-53.

26. Richard S. Dunn, James Savage, Laetitia Yeandle, eds., *The Journal of John Winthrop 1630–1649* (Cambridge, Mass., 1996), 121, 402; Forbes et al., eds., *Winthrop Papers*, 4:129; "Governor Bradford's Letter Book," MHS *Colls.*, 1st ser., 3 (1794): 35; *Plym. Col. Recs.*, 12:32–33.

27. Jameson, ed., *Johnson's Wonder-Working Providence*, 209; *Plym. Col. Recs.*, 11:32; Whitmore, ed., *Colonial Laws of Massachusetts*, 150; *Ct. Recs.*, 1:91; *New Haven Recs.*, 1:130; William B. Weeden, *Economic and Social History of New England 1620–1789*, 2 vols. (Providence, 1890; reprinted Williamstown, 1978), 1:110–11, 205–6.

28. Karen J. Friedmann, "Victualling Colonial Boston," *Agricultural History*, 47 (1973): 189–205; Darrett B. Rutman, *Winthrop's Boston: A Portrait of a Puritan Town, 1630–1649* (Chapel Hill, 1965), 32–36, 204–7; Bidwell and Falconer, *History of Agriculture*, 46; Russell, *Long, Deep Furrow*, 61–62; Wood, *New England's Prospect*, 59; Jameson, ed., *Johnson's Wonder-Working Providence*, 96; Maverick, *Briefe Discription*, 15.

29. O'Callaghan et al., eds., *Documents Relative to the Colonial History of New York*, 1:203, 277; J. Franklin Jameson, ed., *Narratives of New Netherland 1609–1664* (New York, 1909), 296; see also Adriaen Van der Donck, *A Description of the New Netherlands* [1655], ed. Thomas F. O'Donnell (Syracuse, 1968), 41.

30. O'Callaghan et al., eds., *Documents Relative to the Colonial History of New York*, 1:288, 419; 2:433; 14:216; Jameson, ed., *Narratives of New Netherland*, 423.

31. Innes, *Labor in a New Land*, 31–32; O'Callaghan et al., eds., *Documents Relative to the Colonial History of New York*, 14: 469, 13 (Old Series): 458.

32. Letter from John Winthrop, Jr. [1660] in MHS *Colls.*, 5th ser., 8 (1882): 65; Forbes et al., eds., *Winthrop Papers*, 5:172; Dunn et al., eds., *Journal of John Winthrop*, 692–93; Nathaniel Bouton, ed., *Documents and Records Relating to the Province of New-Hampshire, From the Earliest Period of Its Settlement, 1623–1686* (Concord, 1867), 1:263; Russell, *Long, Deep Furrow*, 54, 59–60, 62–63, 113; Bidwell and Falconer, *History of Agriculture*, 42–44; Darrett B. Rutman, "Governor Winthrop's Garden Crop: The Significance of Agriculture in the Early Commerce of Massachusetts Bay," *WMQ*, 3rd ser., 20 (1963): 396–415; Daniel A. Romani, Jr., "The Pettaquamscut Purchase of 1657/58 and the Establishment of a Commercial Livestock Industry in Rhode Island," in Peter Benes, ed., *New England's Creatures: 1400–1900, 1993 Annual Proceedings of the Dublin Seminar for New England Folklife* (Boston, 1995), 45–60; Innes, *Labor in a New Land*, 33; Maverick, *Briefe Discription*, 26; Bridenbaugh, *Fat Mutton*, 58, 66, 120, 122–24.

33. Carole Shammas, "How Self-Sufficient Was Early America?" *Journal of Interdisciplinary History*, 13 (1982): 247–72. On the sorts of material goods that might be found in New Englanders' homes, see Gloria L. Main, "The Standard of Living in Southern New England, 1640–1773," *WMQ*, 3rd ser., 45 (1988): 124–34. Comparative values for New England exports in the eighteenth century can be found in McCusker and Menard, *Economy of British America*, 108.

34. For a brief sketch of Minor's life, see Robert Charles Anderson, *The Great Migration Begins: Immigrants to New England 1620–1633*, 3 vols. (Boston, 1995), 2:1262–67. See also Miner and Stanton, eds., *Diary of Thomas Minor*. This is the only substantial extant diary of a seventeenth-century New England farmer.

35. One of Minor's sons also kept a diary; see Frank Denison Miner and Hannah Miner, eds., *The Diary of Manasseh Minor, Stonington, Conn. 1696–1720* (n. p., 1915).

36. Main, *Peoples of a Spacious Land*, 40; Joseph S. Wood, "Village and Community in Early Colonial New England," *Journal of Historical Geography*, 8 (1982): 333–46; Anthony N. B. Garvan, *Architecture and Town Planning in Colonial Connecticut* (New Haven, 1951), 62; Forbes et al., eds., *Winthrop Papers*, 6:242.

37. Miner and Stanton, eds., *Diary of Thomas Minor*, passim; Karen Ordahl Kupperman, "Climate and Mastery of the Wilderness in Seventeenth-Century New England," in David D. Hall and David Grayson Allen, eds., *Seventeenth-Century New England* (Boston, 1984), 3–37.

38. Russell, *Long, Deep Furrow*, 88–89; Rutman, *Husbandmen of Plymouth*, 17, 33; Miner and Stanton, eds., *Diary of Thomas Minor*, 18.

39. [Durand of Dauphiné], *A Frenchman in Virginia: Being the Memoirs of a Huguenot Refugee in 1686* (privately printed, 1923), 115.

40. Sumner Chilton Powell, *Puritan Village: The Formation of a New England Town* (Middletown, 1963), 78; Jameson, ed., *Johnson's Wonder-Working Providence*, 188, 234–35; Henry Follansbee Long, "The Salt Marshes of the Massachusetts Coast," *Historical Collections of the Essex Institute*, 47 (1911): 1–19; Allen, *In English Ways*, 59.

41. Long, "Salt Marshes of the Massachusetts Coast," 8; Bridenbaugh, *Fat Mutton*, 31; Rutman, *Husbandmen of Plymouth*, 59; Emerson, ed., *Letters from New England*, 214.

42. Wood, *New England's Prospect*, 34; Letter from Edmund Browne in Emerson, ed., *Letters from New England*, 227; John Josselyn, *New-Englands Rarities Discovered* . . . (London, 1672), 85–86; see also letter from Isaack de Rasieres in Sydney V. James, Jr., ed., *Three Visitors to Early Plymouth* (Plymouth, 1963), 67; Cronon, *Changes in the Land*, 142.

43. Forbes et al., eds., *Winthrop Papers*, 5:148–49, 165–66, 168; Bridenbaugh, *Fat Mutton*, 31–33; Daniel A. Romani, Jr., "'Our *English Clover-grass* sowen thrives very well': The Importation of English Grasses and Forages into Seventeenth-Century New England," in Peter Benes, ed., *Plants and People: 1995 Annual Proceedings of the Dublin Seminar for New England Folklife* (Boston, 1996), 25–37; Innes, *Labor in a New Land*, 8–9; Rutman, *Husbandmen of Plymouth*, 59.

44. For Chesapeake practices, see Lewis Cecil Gray, *History of Agriculture in the Southern United States To 1860*, 2 vols. (Washington, D.C., 1932), 1:177–78; Miner and Stanton, eds., *Diary of Thomas Minor*, 6, 29, and passim.

45. Miner and Stanton, eds., *Diary of Thomas Minor,* 26, 64, and passim; Bidwell and Falconer, *History of Agriculture,* 14, 16; Russell, *Long, Deep Furrow,* 89; Mood, "John Winthrop, Jr., on Indian Corn," 129.

46. Joan Thirsk, "Patterns of Agriculture in Seventeenth-Century England," in Hall and Allen, eds., *Seventeenth-Century New England,* 39–54.

47. On English agricultural developments in this period, see Mark Overton, *Agricultural Revolution in England: The Transformation of the Agrarian Economy 1500–1850* (Cambridge, Eng., 1996).

48. E. S. E. Hafez, ed., *The Behaviour of Domestic Animals* (Baltimore, 1962), 87–88; Dunn et al., eds., *Journal of John Winthrop,* 174; Deane, *New-England Farmer,* 100, 101.

49. Mood, "John Winthrop, Jr., on Indian Corn," 129; Miner and Stanton, eds., *Diary of Thomas Minor,* 21, 32, 36, 53; Vickers, *Farmers & Fishermen,* 50–51.

50. Miner and Stanton, eds., *Diary of Thomas Minor,* 7, 12, 22, 23, 27–28, 32, and passim.

51. Daniel Vickers, "The Northern Colonies: Economy and Society, 1600–1775," in Stanley L. Engerman and Robert E. Gallman, eds., *The Cambridge Economic History of the United States,* 3 vols. (New York, 1996), 1:226–27; Richard L. Bushman, "Opening the American Countryside," in James A. Henretta, Michael Kammen, and Stanley N. Katz, eds., *The Transformation of Early American History: Society, Authority, and Ideology* (New York, 1991), 239–56; Cronon, *Changes in the Land,* 152–53.

52. Miner and Stanton, eds., *Diary of Thomas Minor,* 37, 42, 81, 87, 93, 99, 106, 120, 138, 140; John Worlidge, *Systema Agriculturae; The Mystery of Husbandry Discovered,* 4th ed. (London, 1687), 69–70; Rutman, *Husbandmen of Plymouth,* 40; Russell, *Long, Deep Furrow,* 43; Mood, "John Winthrop, Jr., on Indian Corn," 128; Emerson, ed., *Letters from New England,* 227; Deane, *New-England Farmer,* 79–80. Cronon argues that New England farmers could not use manure because they did not house their livestock, but frequent mentions of manuring and the practice of winter foddering suggest otherwise; *Changes in the Land,* 151.

53. Deane, *New-England Farmer,* 76.

54. Donald Woodward, "'An essay on manures': Changing attitudes to fertilization in England, 1500–1800," in John Chartres and David Hey, eds., *English rural society, 1500–1800: Essays in honour of Joan Thirsk* (Cambridge, Eng., 1990), 251–78; Overton, *Agricultural Revolution in England,* 16. The free-range husbandry of the Chesapeake postponed a similar development in livestock production and use until the eighteenth century; see Lois Green Carr and Russell R. Menard, "Land, Labor, and Economies of Scale in Early Maryland: Some Limits to Growth in the Chesapeake System of Husbandry," *Journal of Economic History,* 49 (1989): 407–18.

55. *New Haven Recs.,* 1:406–7.

56. Russell, *Long, Deep Furrow,* 37; Cronon, *Changes in the Land,* 119–20; David Thomas Konig, *Law and Society in Puritan Massachusetts: Essex County, 1629–1692* (Chapel Hill, 1979), 118–19; *Mass. Bay Recs.,* 2:14–15; Clarence S. Brigham, ed., *The Early Records of the Town of Portsmouth* (Providence, 1901), 160–61; Whitmore, ed., *Colonial Laws of Massachusetts,* 131.

57. See, for instance, the map of Sudbury in Powell, *Puritan Village,* 77, 106–7.

58. Rutman, *Husbandmen of Plymouth,* 17; Russell, *Long, Deep Furrow,* 73; Burt, *History of Springfield,* 1:158; City of Boston, *Fourth Report of the Record Commissioners of the City of Boston* [Dorchester Town Records], 2nd ed. (Boston, 1883), 37–38.

59. Russell, *Long, Deep Furrow,* 73; Bidwell and Falconer, *History of Agriculture,* 21–23; City of Boston, *Fourth Report of Record Commissioners,* 1–2; George Francis Dow, ed., *Records and Files of the Quarterly Courts of Essex County, Massachusetts,* 9 vols. (Salem, 1911–75), 4:227.

60. Rutman, *Husbandmen of Plymouth,* 17; Bidwell and Falconer, *History of Agriculture,* 21; City of Boston, *Second Report of Record Commissioners,* 88–89; *New Haven Recs.,* 1:157, 186, 209; Dow, ed., *Essex Court Recs.,* 5:279–80. For other examples of stinting, see City of Boston, *Fourth Report of Record Commissioners,* 295, 300; J. Wickham Case, ed., *Southold Town Records,* 2 vols. (New York, 1882–84), 1:326–27, 329, 331–32; Benjamin Hicks, ed., *Records of the Towns of North and South Hempstead, Long Island, N.Y.,* 8 vols. (Jamaica, N.Y., 1896–1904), 1:28–29. On the general trend toward restricting rights to the initial group of town proprietors, see John Frederick Martin, *Profits in the Wilderness: Entrepreneurship and the Founding of New England Towns in the Seventeenth Century* (Chapel Hill, 1991), ch. 6.

61. Bidwell and Falconer, *History of Agriculture,* 22; Herbert B. Adams, "Salem Meadows, Woodland, and Town Neck, *Essex Institute Historical Collections,* 20 (1883), 59–61; *Ct. Recs.,* 1:60, 436–37; Dow, ed., *Essex Court Recs.,* 4:69; *New Haven Recs.,* 1:312.

62. Dorchester officials complained in 1642 that, when cattle were all pastured together, milk cows were injured by steers and oxen; see City of Boston, *Fourth Report of Record Commissioners,* 47; Leonard Mascal, *The Government of Cattell, Divided into Three Books . . .* (London, 1653), 69–70, 270.

63. Rutman, *Husbandmen of Plymouth,* 18–19; Bidwell and Falconer, *History of Agriculture,* 21–22; City of Boston, *Second Report of Record Commissioners,* 88; *New Haven Recs.,* 1:197; Paige, *History of Cambridge,* 1:13; Bridenbaugh, *Fat Mutton,* 49, 53.

64. Russell, *Long, Deep Furrow,* 74; Bidwell and Falconer, *History of Agriculture,* 22; Paige, *History of Cambridge,* 1:38–39; Hicks, ed., *Records of Hempstead,* 1:40–42, see also 1:22–24. For other examples of livestock keepers' agreements, see Chapin, ed., *Early Records of Warwick,* 42–43; City of Boston, *Fourth Report of Record Commissioners,* 11, 61–62, 74–75; W. P. Upham, ed., "Town Records

of Salem 1634–1659," *Essex Institute Historical Collections,* 2nd ser., vol. 1, pt. 1 (1868): 41–42, 66, 99, 100, 101, 182–83, 197–98, 206–7.

65. Dunn et al., eds., *Journal of John Winthrop,* 267; *New Haven Recs.,* 1:308–9. Herders were hired to supervise as many as a hundred head of cattle; see Hicks, ed., *Recs. of Hempstead,* 1:18–19, 21–22, 62–64; Upham, ed., "Town Records of Salem," 182–83.

66. John Fairfield Sly, *Town Government in Massachusetts (1630–1930)* (Cambridge, Mass., 1930), 40–42.

67. City of Boston, *Second Report of Record Commissioners,* 145, 147, 151–52; Chapin, ed., *Early Records of Warwick,* 97, 101–2; City of Boston, *Fourth Report of Record Commissioners,* 37–38, 299–300; *Mass. Bay Recs.,* 1:157; *New Haven Recs.,* 1:407. For other orders about restraint of swine, see *Plym. Col. Recs.,* 1:38–39; *Ct. Recs.,* 1:131, 214, 557–58; Case, ed., *Southold Town Records,* 1:328–29, 330; Burt, *History of Springfield,* 1:188–89, 191–92; 2:61; Upham, ed., "Town Records of Salem," 130, 238–39; Paige, *History of Cambridge,* 1:41; Horatio Rogers, George Moulton Carpenter, and Edward Field, eds., *The Early Records of the Town of Providence,* 21 vols. (Providence, 1892–1915), 17:9.

68. John D. Cushing, ed., *Acts and Laws of New Hampshire 1680–1726* (Wilmington, 1978), 215.

69. City of Boston, *Fourth Report of Record Commissioners,* 10; *New Haven Recs.,* 1:428; City of Boston, *Second Report of Record Commissioners,* 130; Hicks, ed., *Records of Hempstead,* 140; Hartford officials' comment quoted in Bidwell and Falconer, *History of Agriculture,* 23–24.

70. The one exception to private ownership occurred in Plymouth. Until 1627, colony livestock was communal property. See Rutman, *Husbandmen of Plymouth,* 6.

71. In making a distinction between livestock management at the centers and on the peripheries of towns, I modify my argument in "King Philip's Herds: Indians, Colonists, and the Problem of Livestock in Early New England," *WMQ,* 3rd ser., 51 (1994): 601–24.

72. For examples of trespass cases, see *New Haven Recs.,* 1:293–94; Dow, ed., *Essex Court Recs.,* 1:14, 16, 333–34, 415–16; *Ct. Recs.,* 1:51, 2:309; "Records of the Particular Court of Connecticut 1639–1663," *Collections of the Connecticut Historical Society,* 22 (1928): 3, 7, 8, 80, 83, 86, 89, 114, 185, 208. Colonists' formal and informal methods of dealing with trespassing animals are addressed in Peter Karsten, "Cows in the Corn, Pigs in the Garden, and 'the Problem of Social Costs': 'High' and 'Low' Legal Cultures of the British Diaspora Lands in the 17th, 18th, and 19th Centuries," *Law & Society Review,* 32 (1998): 66–68, 74–75. The Massachusetts statute of 1633 appears in *Mass. Bay Recs.,* 1:106.

73. Whitmore, ed., *Colonial Laws of Massachusetts,* 191, 243; Cushing, ed., *Laws of the Pilgrims,* 46; Lindholdt, ed., *John Josselyn, Colonial Traveler,* 132; Deane, *New-England Farmer,* 42, 99, 134, 156; Jared Eliot, *Essays Upon Field Hus-*

bandry in New England and Other Papers 1748–1762, ed. Harry J. Carman and Rexford G. Tugwell (New York, 1934), 19, 27.

74.   *Mass. Bay Recs.,* 1:119; 2:190, 225. Connecticut also required town marks. Thomas Minor, in fact, once served as Stonington's "brander of horses"; see Miner and Stanton, eds., *Diary of Thomas Minor,* 207.

75.   Miner and Stanton, eds., *Diary of Thomas Minor,* 6, 8, 10, 25, 26, 28, 40, 41, 49, 59, 90, 125; *New Haven Recs.,* 1:270. For examples of colonial ordinances about impoundment of strays, see Cushing, ed., *Laws of the Pilgrims,* 46; *Ct. Recs.,* 1:556–57; *Mass. Bay Recs.,* 4, pt. 2:319–20; *R.I. Recs,* 1:68.

76.   Whitmore, ed., *Colonial Laws of Massachusetts,* 237; Dow, ed., *Essex Court Recs.,* 4:15, 194n; *R.I. Recs.,* 1:117, 151. Theft cases in general (not just those involving livestock) rarely comprised more than 10 to 15 percent of court actions; see Edgar J. McManus, *Law and Liberty in Early New England: Criminal Justice and Due Process 1620–1692* (Amherst, 1993), 201–10.

77.   In winter, the caloric needs of livestock dramatically increased, at a time when species dependent on grazing found the least to eat. See Hafez, ed., *Behaviour of Domestic Animals,* 87–88. Roger Williams described hogs feasting on shellfish and chasing a wolf away from a deer carcass; see his *A Key into the Language of America,* ed. John J. Teunissen and Evelyn J. Hinz (Detroit, 1973), 182, 226. For the earliest mention of wild swine in Massachusetts, see *Mass. Bay Recs.,* 1:87.

78.   In May 1631, Massachusetts prohibited anyone from killing wild swine "without a generall agreement att some Court," but this may have been an effort to protect the fledgling colony's food supply. There is no evidence that this restriction persisted for long. See *Mass. Bay Recs.,* 1:87, 181–82, 187; *Ct. Recs.,* 2:51.

79.   *Mass. Bay Recs.,* 1:122, 129, 210, 257; Dunn et al., eds., *Journal of John Winthrop,* 146–47; Frank Thistlethwaite, *Dorset Pilgrims: The Story of West Country Pilgrims Who Went to New England in the 17th Century* (London, 1989), 96–97.

80.   For the town-based land distribution system, see Anderson, *New England's Generation,* 90–100. For the maintenance of cattle as a motive for creation of new towns, see Powell, *Puritan Village,* 76; Dunn et al., eds., *Journal of John Winthrop,* 115, 126–27, 146–47; William Bradford, *Of Plymouth Plantation, 1620–1647,* ed. Samuel Eliot Morison (New York, 1952), 253.

81.   Dunn et al., eds., *Journal of John Winthrop,* 102, 200; Bradford, *Of Plymouth Plantation,* 301; Main, *Society and Economy in Colonial Ct.,* 62; Glenn W. LaFantasie, ed., *The Correspondence of Roger Williams,* 2 vols. (Hanover and London, 1988), 1:123. On magistrates' efforts to enact price controls, see Innes, *Creating the Commonwealth,* 102, 178–82.

82.   Forbes et al., eds., *Winthrop Papers,* 3:217; Bradford, *Of Plymouth Plantation,* 253–54.

83.   Dunn et al., eds., *Journal of John Winthrop,* 328, 339, 342, 353; Bradford, *Of Plymouth Plantation,* 310; Morison included the Danforth rhyme in note 7. See

also Marion H. Gottfried, "The First Depression in Massachusetts," *NEQ,* 9 (1936): 655–78.

84. Bradford, *Of Plymouth Plantation,* 314–15, 333–34; Dunn et al., eds., *Journal of John Winthrop,* 414; Karen Ordahl Kupperman, *Providence Island 1630–1641: The Other Puritan Colony* (New York, 1993), 320–25.

85. John M. Murrin, "'Things Fearful to Name': Bestiality in Early America," *Pennsylvania History,* special supplement to vol. 65 (1998), 8–43; Robert F. Oaks, "'Things Fearful to Name': Sodomy and Buggery in Seventeenth-Century New England," *Journal of Social History* 12 (1978): 268–81; Keith Thomas, *Man and the Natural World: A History of the Modern Sensibility* (New York, 1983), 119. For New England's estimated population in 1640, see McCusker and Menard, *Economy of British America,* 103.

86. Murrin, "'Things Fearful to Name,'" 23; Bradford, *Of Plymouth Plantation,* 321.

87. Richard Godbeer, *Sexual Revolution in Early America* (Baltimore, 2002), 64–67; John Canup, *Out of the Wilderness: The Emergence of an American Identity in Colonial New England* (Middletown, 1990), 33–48.

88. *Plym. Col. Recs.,* 2:170; Jameson, ed., *Johnson's Wonder-Working Providence,* 253.

CHAPTER SIX: FORGIVING TRESPASSES

1. H. R. McIlwaine, ed., *Minutes of the Council and General Court of Colonial Virginia,* 2nd ed. (Richmond, 1979), 116; Helen C. Rountree and Thomas E. Davidson, *Eastern Shore Indians of Virginia and Maryland* (Charlottesville and London, 1997), 51–52.

2. *Mass. Bay Recs.,* 1:86, 87, 88; Neal Salisbury, *Manitou and Providence: Indians, Europeans, and the Making of New England, 1500–1643* (New York, 1982), 187.

3. On notions of justice in native culture, see Daniel K. Richter, *Facing East from Indian Country: A Native History of Early America* (Cambridge, Mass., 2001), 64.

4. Salisbury, *Manitou and Providence,* 130.

5. Rountree and Davidson, *Eastern Shore Indians,* 50–52; Christian F. Feest, "Nanticoke and Neighboring Tribes," in *Handbook of North American Indians,* ed. William C. Sturtevant, vol. 15: *Northeast,* ed. Bruce G. Trigger (Washington, D.C., 1978), 240–43; Martin H. Quitt, "Trade and Acculturation at Jamestown, 1607–1609: The Limits of Understanding," *WMQ,* 3rd ser., 52 (1995): 227–58; Helen C. Rountree, *Pocahontas's People: The Powhatan Indians of Virginia Through Four Centuries* (Norman, Okla., and London, 1990), 29–55; J. Frederick Fausz, "An 'Abundance of Blood Shed on Both Sides': England's First Indian War, 1609–1614," *VMHB,* 98 (1990): 3–55.

6. *A True Declaration of the Estate of the Colonie in Virginia . . .* [1610] in Peter Force, ed., *Tracts and Other Papers, Relating Principally to the Origin, Settle-*

ment, and Progress of the Colonies in North America, From the Discovery of the Country to the Year 1776, 4 vols. (Washington, D.C., 1844; reprint, Gloucester, 1963), 3:§1, p. 17; John Smith, *The Generall Historie of Virginia, the Somer Iles, and New England . . .* [1624], in Philip L. Barbour, ed., *The Complete Works of Captain John Smith (1580–1631),* 3 vols. (Chapel Hill, 1986), 2:246.

7. Fausz, "An 'Abundance of Blood Shed on Both Sides,'" 50–51; Edmund Morgan, *American Slavery, American Freedom: The Ordeal of Colonial Virginia* (New York, 1975): 90; E. Randolph Turner, "Socio-Political Organization within the Powhatan Chiefdom and the Effects of European Contact, A.D. 1607–1646," in William W. Fitzhugh, ed., *Cultures in Contact: The European Impact on Native Cultural Institutions in Eastern North America, A.D. 1000–1800* (Washington, D.C., and London, 1985), 212.

8. J. Frederick Fausz, "George Thorpe, Nemattanew, and the Powhatan Uprising of 1622," *Virginia Cavalcade,* 28 (1979): 111–17; Rountree, *Pocahontas's People,* 71–74; Susan Myra Kingsbury, ed., *The Records of the Virginia Company of London,* 4 vols. (Washington, D.C., 1906–35), 2:375 (quotation); 3:612; 4:118, 138.

9. For quotations, see Smith, *Generall Historie,* in Barbour, ed., *Works of John Smith,* 2:298; *Va. Statutes,* 1:128; Wyatt quoted in Richter, *Facing East,* 75; Kingsbury, ed., *Va. Co. Recs.,* 3:706. For a discussion of the 1622–32 conflict, see Rountree, *Pocahontas's People,* 75–81.

10. H. R. McIlwaine, ed., *Minutes of the Council and General Court of Colonial Virginia,* 2nd ed. (Richmond, 1979), 190; *A Perfect Description of Virginia . . .* [1649], in Force, ed., *Tracts,* 2:§8, p. 11; Neal Salisbury, "Native People and European Settlers in Eastern North America, 1600–1783," in Bruce G. Trigger and Wilcomb E. Washburn, eds., *The Cambridge History of the Native Peoples of the Americas,* vol. 1, *North America,* (New York, 1996), pt. 1: 414–15.

11. Russell Thornton, *American Indian Holocaust and Survival: A Population History Since 1492* (Norman, Okla., 1987), 70–71; Salisbury, "Native People and European Settlers," 402–3; Richter, *Facing East,* 60–61; Kathleen J. Bragdon, *Native People of Southern New England, 1500–1650* (Norman, Okla., 1996), 140–51.

12. Salisbury, *Manitou and Providence,* 120–33. Until 1623, Chickataubut went by the name of Obtakiest.

13. Richard S. Dunn, James Savage, and Laetitia Yeandle, eds., *The Journal of John Winthrop 1630–1649* (Cambridge, Mass., 1996), 101; *Mass. Bay Recs.,* 1:102, 121, 133; Bert Salwen, "Indians of Southern New England and Long Island: Early Period," in Trigger, ed., *Handbook of North American Indians,* 15: 170–71; Salisbury, *Manitou and Providence,* 183–86.

14. Charles Thornton Libby et al., eds., *Province and Court Records of Maine,* 5 vols. (Portland, 1928–1960), 1:3–4.

15. The most comprehensive recent account of this conflict is Alfred A. Cave, *The Pequot War* (Amherst, 1996).

16. "Leift Lion Gardener his relation of the Pequot Warres," in Charles Orr, ed., *History of the Pequot War* (Cleveland, 1897), 128–29, 132 (quotation); William Bradford, *Of Plymouth Plantation 1620–1647,* ed. Samuel Eliot Morison (New York, 1952), 294; see also John Mason, *A Brief History of the Pequot War,* and John Underhill, "News from America," in Orr, ed., *History of the Pequot War,* 6, 66. For an account of the Mystic fort fight, see Cave, *Pequot War,* 148–51.

17. For population figures, see John J. McCusker and Russell R. Menard, *The Economy of British America 1607–1789* (Chapel Hill, 1985), 103; Bragdon, *Native People,* 28.

18. Neal Salisbury, "Indians and Colonists in Southern New England after the Pequot War: An Uneasy Balance," and Jack Campisi, "The Emergence of the Mashantucket Pequot Tribe, 1637–1975," in Laurence M. Hauptman and James D. Wherry, eds., *The Pequots in Southern New England: The Fall and Rise of an American Indian Nation* (Norman, Okla., 1990), 81–95, 117–140; Alden T. Vaughan, *New England Frontier: Puritans and Indians 1620–1675,* revised ed. (New York, 1979), chs. 7–10.

19. For a useful chronology of Anglo-Indian conflicts during the seventeenth century, see S. G. Drake, *The Old Indian Chronicle; . . .* (Boston, 1836), 147–73.

20. Roger Williams, *A Key into the Language of America* (1643), ed. John J. Teunissen and Evelyn J. Hinz (Detroit, 1973), 173–74; John Eliot, *The Indian Grammar Begun . . .* (Cambridge, Mass., 1666), 9; Ives Goddard, "Eastern Algonquian Languages," in Trigger, ed., *Handbook of North American Indians,* 15: 72. For the simultaneous development of pidgin English in New England, see Ives Goddard, "Some Early Examples of American Indian Pidgin English from New England," *International Journal of American Linguistics* 43 (1977): 37–41.

21. William Cronon, *Changes in the Land: Indians, Colonists, and the Ecology of New England* (New York, 1983), 101, 142–48; Timothy Silver, *A New Face on the Countryside: Indians, Colonists, and Slaves in South Atlantic Forests, 1500– 1800* (New York, 1990), 177–80.

22. Kevin P. Kelly, "'In Dispers'd Country Plantations': Settlement Patterns in Seventeenth-Century Surry County, Virginia," in Thad W. Tate and David L. Ammerman, eds., *The Chesapeake in the Seventeenth Century: Essays on Anglo-American Society & Politics* (Chapel Hill, 1979), 183–205; Carville V. Earle, *The Evolution of a Tidewater Settlement System: All Hallow's Parish, Maryland, 1650–1783* (Chicago, 1975), 19–24, 59–61; Lorena S. Walsh, "Land Use, Settlement Patterns, and the Impact of European Agriculture, 1620–1820," in Philip D. Curtin, Grace S. Brush, and George W. Fisher, eds., *Discovering the Chesapeake: The History of an Ecosystem* (Baltimore, 2001), 220–24; Gloria L. Main, *Peoples of a Spacious Land: Families and Cultures in Colonial New England* (Cambridge, Mass., 2001), 40–42; Cronon, *Changes in the Land,* 51.

23. Bragdon, *Native People,* 55–79; Peter A. Thomas, "Contrastive Subsistence Strategies and Land Use as Factors for Understanding Indian-White Relations

in New England," *Ethnohistory,* 23 (1976): 1–18; Henry M. Miller, "Living Along the 'Great Shellfish Bay': The Relationship between Prehistoric Peoples and the Chesapeake," in Curtin et al., eds., *Discovering the Chesapeake,* 117–24; Frederic W. Gleach, *Powhatan's World and Colonial Virginia: A Conflict of Cultures* (Lincoln, 1997), 23, 171; Wayne E. Clark and Helen C. Rountree, "The Powhatans and the Maryland Mainland," in Helen C. Rountree, ed., *Powhatan Foreign Relations 1500–1722* (Charlottesville, 1993), 115; Cronon, *Changes in the Land,* 51; Silver, *New Face on the Countryside,* 59–64.

24. For maps showing settlement patterns, see Clark and Rountree, "Powhatans and the Maryland Mainland," 115; Robert S. Grumet, *Historic Contact: Indian People and Colonists in Today's Northeastern United States in the Sixteenth Through Eighteenth Centuries* (Norman, Okla., 1995), 98–99, 102, 107–8, 112–13, 119–21, 131–33, 141–42, 155–56.

25. For Indian ideas about territoriality, see Cronon, *Changes in the Land,* 62–65; see also Thomas, "Contrastive Subsistence Strategies," 5.

26. Lowell K. Halls, ed., *White-tailed Deer: Ecology and Management* (Harrisburg, 1984), 70–71, 112, 188, 313–14, 374–75; Ilo Hiller, *The White-tailed Deer* (College Station, 1996), 18–19, 21; Silver, *New Face on the Countryside,* 179; Cronon, *Changes in the Land,* 101. Although the earliest prohibitions against deer hunting appeared in the seventeenth century, it is difficult to link them to declining deer populations caused by competition from livestock. Rhode Island officials, who banned deer hunting for two months in 1646, worried that deer carcasses attracted wolves; Virginia's first such measure, in 1699, specified overhunting of pregnant does as the cause. See *R.I. Recs.,* 1:84; *Va. Statutes,* 3:180. I thank Roy Roath of Colorado State University for help with this paragraph.

27. Halls, ed., *White-tailed Deer,* 176–81; Rory Putman, *The Natural History of Deer* (Ithaca, 1988), 126–28.

28. Susan E. Aiello, ed., *The Merck Veterinary Manual,* 8th ed. (Whitehouse Station, N.J., 1998), 490–92, 1106, 1263; Alfred W. Crosby, Jr., *The Columbian Exchange: Biological and Cultural Consequences of 1492* (Westport, 1972), 35–58; William H. McNeill, *Plagues and Peoples* (New York, 1976), ch. 5; Jared Diamond, *Guns, Germs, and Steel: The Fates of Human Societies* (New York, 1997), 206–7; William Hubbard, *The History of the Indian Wars in New England, from the First Settlement to the Termination of the War with King Philip, in 1677,* ed. Samuel G. Drake (Roxbury, 1865; reprinted New York, 1969), 215; Sherburne F. Cook, "The Significance of Disease in the Extinction of the New England Indians," *Human Biology,* 45 (1973): 485–508; Guy A. Settipane, ed., *Columbus and the New World: Medical Implications* (Providence, 1995), 1, 20, 26; Robert R. Gradie, "New England Indians and Colonizing Pigs," in William Cowan, ed., *Papers of the Fifteenth Algonquian Conference* (Ottawa, 1984), 159–62; Daniel Gookin, *Historical Collections of the Indians in New England* (1674; reprinted New York, 1972), 33. Skeletal remains excavated in native cemeteries offer evidence of a greater incidence of tuberculosis among

Indians in the postcontact period; see Marc A. Kelley, Paul S. Sledzik, and Sean P. Murphy, "Health, Demographics, and Physical Constitution in Seventeenth-Century Rhode Island Indians," *Man in the Northeast,* 34 (1987): 1–25, especially 16–17. Little comparable information survives for the Chesapeake region, in part because burial practices often included burning; see, for instance, Robert L. Stephenson and Alice L. L. Ferguson, *The Accokeek Creek Site: A Middle Atlantic Seaboard Culture Sequence* (Ann Arbor, 1963) and the essays by Hodges, and Turner and Opperman, in Theodore R. Reinhart and Dennis J. Pogue, eds., *The Archaeology of 17th-Century Virginia* (Richmond, 1993).

29. William Wood, *New England's Prospect,* ed. Alden T. Vaughan (Amherst, 1977), 113 (quotation). Indian complaints about trespassing livestock abound in colonial records. For examples, see *Md. Arch.,* 2:196–97; 3:489; 49:139; *Va. Statutes,* 2:13–14, 138–39; *New Haven Recs.,* 2:104–7; *Plym. Col. Recs.,* 3:21, 106, 119–20, 132, 167, 192; 4:68; *Mass. Bay Recs.,* 1:121, 133; *Ct. Recs.,* 2:165; Allyn Forbes et al., eds., *Winthrop Papers,* 6 vols. (Boston, 1929–92), 5:246–47; 6:34.

30. On native women's nonhorticultural economic roles, see Wood, *New England's Prospect,* 112–14; Cronon, *Changes in the Land,* 45–46; Thomas, "Contrastive Subsistence Strategies," 10–11, 14; Helen C. Rountree, *The Powhatan Indians of Virginia: Their Traditional Culture* (Norman, Okla., 1989), 44–48, 60–61. For the materials used in native weaving, see Charles C. Willoughby, *Antiquities of the New England Indians, With Notes on the Ancient Cultures of the Adjacent Territory* (Cambridge, Mass., 1935), 244–58; Laurel Thatcher Ulrich, *The Age of Homespun: Objects and Stories in the Creation of an American Myth* (New York, 2001), 47–48, 73; Edward Byers, *The Nation of Nantucket: Society and Politics in an Early American Commercial Center 1660–1820* (Boston, 1987), 59. On shellfish, see Williams, *Key,* 182 (quotation); Bragdon, *Native People,* 62–63, 110–11.

31. *Va. Statutes,* 1:468; *Plym. Col. Recs.,* 2:60; 4:57, 82–83; *New Haven Recs.,* 1:150; John Noble, ed., *Records of the Court of Assistants of the Colony of the Massachusetts Bay 1630–1692,* 3 vols. (Boston, 1901–28), 1:52; Williams, *Key,* 224, 226; Henry Martyn Dexter, ed., *Mourt's Relation or Journal of the Plantation at Plymouth* (Boston, 1865), 24–25. On Indian hunting techniques, see also Rountree, *Powhatan Indians of Virginia,* 39–41; Bragdon, *Native People,* 117–18. On deer's tendency to ignore grazing cattle, see Halls, ed., *White-tailed Deer,* 165.

32. *Md. Arch.,* 2:15 (quotation), 3:279; Rountree and Davidson, *Eastern Shore Indians,* 63–64; Forbes et al., eds., *Winthrop Papers,* 6:34; *New Haven Recs.,* 1:208. For other examples of Indian attacks on troublesome livestock, see *Md. Arch.,* 1:136; 3:95–96; *Plym. Col. Recs.,* 9:111; E. B. O'Callaghan, ed., *Documents Relative to the Colonial History of the State of New-York,* 15 vols. (Albany, 1853–87), 1:150–51.

33. On the chiefs' role in redistributing goods, see Richter, *Facing East,* 52. By the 1640s, Indians who had subordinated themselves to English rule included

Massachusetts, Mohegans, Wampanoags, and Quinnipiacs in New England, and Powhatans, Patuxents, Nanticokes, Piscataways, and Accomacks in the Chesapeake. See Salisbury, *Manitou and Providence*, 184, 225–26; Feest, "Nanticoke and Neighboring Tribes," 243; Rountree, *Pocahontas's People*, 87; James H. Merrell, "Cultural Continuity Among the Piscataway Indians of Colonial Maryland," *WMQ*, 3rd ser. 36 (1979): 548–70.

34. *Mass. Bay Recs.*, 1:293; see also 3:281–82.

35. Joseph Ewan and Nesta Ewan, eds., *John Banister and His Natural History of Virginia 1678–1692* (Urbana, 1970), 382 (quotation); William H. Whitmore, ed., *The Colonial Laws of Massachusetts; Reprinted from the Edition of 1660, with the Supplements to 1672, Containing Also, the Body of Liberties of 1641* (Boston, 1889), 162 (quotation); Howard M. Chapin, ed., *The Early Records of the Town of Warwick* (Providence, 1926), 80, 89, 94–95, 167; *Va. Statutes*, 2:139–40; see also *Mass. Bay Recs.*, 1:99; *Plym. Col. Recs.*, 11:137–38, 143, 219; *Md. Arch.*, 1:431; *Ct. Recs.*, 2:174; Yasuhide Kawashima, *Puritan Justice and the Indian: White Man's Law in Massachusetts, 1630–1763* (Middletown, 1986), 62–65.

36. *Plym. Col. Recs.*, 3:106, 192; 11:123; *Md. Arch.*, 49:139; see also *Ct. Recs.*, 3:42–43; James P. Ronda, "Red and White at the Bench: Indians and the Law in Plymouth Colony, 1620–1691," *Essex Institute Historical Collections*, 110 (1974): 208–9.

37. *Va. Statutes*, 2:139–40; Whitmore, ed., *Colonial Laws of Massachusetts*, 162.

38. For the awarding of restitution to Indians, see *Mass. Bay Recs.*, 1:121, 133; 2:293–94; Leonard Bliss, Jr., *The History of Rehoboth, Bristol County, Massachusetts . . .* (Boston, 1836), 44; Joseph H. Smith, ed., *Colonial Justice in Western Massachusetts (1639–1702); The Pynchon Court Record* (Cambridge, Mass., 1961), 243; *Plym.Col. Recs.*, 3:132, 192 (quotation), 5:47; Chapin, ed., *Early Recs. of Warwick*, 89; *Ct. Recs.*, 3:42–43; *New Haven Recs.*, 2:106–7; "Records of the Particular Court of Connecticut 1639–1663," in Connecticut Historical Society, *Collections*, 22 (1928): 129, 171, 208.

39. For a couple of rare exceptions, see *Md. Arch.*, 3:363; 49:139.

40. Susan Rosenfeld Falb, *Advice and Ascent: The Development of the Maryland Assembly 1635–1689* (New York, 1986), 332–33; Rountree, *Pocahontas's People*, 94; J. Frederick Fausz, "Merging and Emerging Worlds: Anglo-Indian Interest Groups and the Development of the Seventeenth-Century Chesapeake," in Lois Green Carr, Philip D. Morgan, and Jean B. Russo, eds., *Colonial Chesapeake Society* (Chapel Hill, 1988), 47–91; *Md. Arch.*, 3:431–33, 486, 549–50; 5:30; 15:170.

41. *Va. Statutes*, 1:323–25; "Isaac Allerton and the Indians," *William and Mary College Quarterly*, 8 (1899): 24. On the overall policy of separation, see Martha W. McCartney, "Seventeenth-Century Apartheid: The Suppression and Containment of Indians in Tidewater Virginia," *Journal of Middle Atlantic Archaeology*, 1 (1985): 51–80.

42. Peter Karsten, *Between Law and Custom: "High" and "Low" Legal Cultures in the Lands of the British Diaspora—The United States, Canada, Australia, and New Zealand, 1600–1900* (New York, 2002), 125–28; E. P. Thompson, *Customs in Common: Studies in Traditional Popular Culture* (New York, 1993), 128–29.

43. Cronon, *Changes in the Land,* 62–67.

44. Horatio Rogers, George Moulton Carpenter, and Edward Field, eds., *The Early Records of the Town of Providence,* 21 vols. (Providence, 1892–1915), 160–62. The Pautuxets were probably tributaries of Rhode Island's more powerful native allies, the Narragansetts; Grumet, *Historic Contact,* 129–30. For a similar land-sharing arrangement, see Chapin, ed., *Early Recs. of Warwick,* 23–24.

45. Kenneth L. Feder, "'The Avaricious Humour of Designing Englishmen': The Ethnohistory of Land Transactions in the Farmington Valley," *Bulletin of the Archaeological Society of Connecticut,* no. 45 (1982): 29–40, quotations on p. 36; see also Victor Hugo Paltsits, ed., *Minutes of the Executive Council of the Province of New York,* 2 vols. (Albany, 1910), 1:450–51. On the Indians' active role in the negotiation of such agreements, see Peter S. Leavenworth, "'The Best Title That Indians Can Claime': Native Agency and Consent in the Transferal of Penacook-Pawtucket Land in the Seventeenth Century," *NEQ* 72 (1999): 275–300.

46. *Ct. Recs.,* 1:186; on the Mohegans, see Grumet, *Historic Contact,* 143, 146–47; Michael Leroy Oberg, *Uncas: First of the Mohegans* (Ithaca, 2003). Connecticut settlers tolerated Narragansett hunters near their plantations in the late 1640s; see Forbes et al., eds., *Winthrop Papers,* 5:255.

47. Warren M. Billings, ed., "Some Acts Not in Hening's *Statutes:* The Acts of Assembly, April 1652, November 1652, and July 1653," *VMHB,* 83 (1975): 68, 72–73; "Underwood Family of Virginia," *VMHB,* 38 (1930): 391–92.

48. *Md. Arch.,* 2:25–27; 3:362–64.

49. Roger B. Manning, *Hunters and Poachers: A Cultural and Social History of Unlawful Hunting in England 1485–1640* (Oxford, 1993), 25. The negative image of trapping did not apply to Indians when fur-bearing animals were involved.

50. *Plym. Col. Recs.,* 2:60; see also 4:57, 82–83; *Mass. Bay Recs.,* 1:143; *Ct. Recs.,* 1:19.

51. *Plym. Col. Recs.,* 2:130–31; Howard M. Chapin, *Documentary History of Rhode Island,* 2 vols. (Providence, 1916–19), 2:101–2; *Ct. Recs.,* 1:186; *New Haven Recs.,* 1:150; see also Bliss, *History of Rehoboth,* 49.

52. *Va. Statutes,* 2:140. For documents that made explicit use of the language of privilege, see *Md. Arch.,* 2:15, 25. The term "liberty" carried the same conno-tation.

53. *R. I. Recs.,* 1:124–25; *Va. Statutes,* 1:395, 457; *Md. Arch.,*1:362–63; *Plym. Col. Recs.,* 4:6; see also *Mass. Bay Recs.,* 3:134; Massachusetts Archives, 1:18.

54. Forbes et al., *Winthrop Papers,* 5:280; *Plym. Col. Recs.,* 10:436; *New Haven Recs.,* 2:67; *Md. Arch.,* 3:281; Sidney H. Miner and George D. Stanton, Jr., *The Diary of Thomas Minor, Stonington, Connecticut, 1653 to 1684* (New London, 1899), 51; Bliss, *History of Rehoboth,* 60. Information on the use of

Indian labor in the seventeenth century is limited, but see Yasuhide Kawashima, "Indian Servitude in the Northeast," and Peter H. Wood, "Indian Servitude in the Southeast," in *Handbook of North American Indians,* ed. William C. Sturtevant, vol. 4: *History of Indian-White Relations*, ed. Wilcomb E. Washburn (Washington, D.C., 1988), 404–6, 407–9; Lawrence W. Towner, "'A Fondness for Freedom': Servant Protest in Puritan Society," *WMQ,* 3rd ser., 19 (1962): 201–19.

55. "Col. Gerard Fowke and the Indians," *William and Mary College Quarterly,* 8 (1899): 23–24. A cow and calf were worth about 400 to 700 pounds of tobacco, depending on their condition; see Morgan, *American Slavery, American Freedom,* 140, n. 28. Note, too, that sachems were the intended recipients of cows given as wolf bounties in Virginia.

56. Williams, *Key,* 149; *Mass. Bay Recs.,* 3:398; *Plym. Col. Recs.,* 4:93. For similar concerns about Indians with horses, see John Cox, Jr., ed., *Oyster Bay Town Records,* 6 vols. (New York, 1916–31), 1:659.

57. Key works on praying towns include Richter, *Facing East,* 95–96, 126–29; James Axtell, *The Invasion Within: The Contest of Cultures in Colonial North America* (New York, 1985), 139–66; Michael Leroy Oberg, *Dominion & Civility: English Imperialism & Native America, 1585–1685* (Ithaca, 1999), 124–27; Jean M. O'Brien, *Dispossession by Degrees: Indian Land and Identity in Natick, Massachusetts, 1650–1790* (New York, 1997); Vaughan, *New England Frontier,* 260–308; Richard W. Cogley, *John Eliot's Mission to the Indians Before King Philip's War* (Cambridge, Mass., 1999); Neal Salisbury, "Red Puritans: The 'Praying Indians' of Massachusetts Bay and John Eliot," *WMQ,* 3rd ser., 31 (1974): 27–54; Harold W. Van Lonkhuyzen, "A Reappraisal of the Praying Indians: Acculturation, Conversion, and Identity at Natick, Massachusetts, 1646–1730," *NEQ* 63 (1990): 396–428; James P. Ronda, "Generations of Faith: The Christian Indians of Martha's Vineyard," *WMQ,* 3rd ser. 38 (1981): 369–94.

58. Edward Winslow, "The Glorious Progress of the Gospel, Amongst the Indians in New England," (1649), in MHS *Colls.,* 3rd ser., 4 (1834): 81. A map of seventeenth-century praying towns appears in O'Brien, *Dispossession by Degrees,* 29.

59. Thomas Shepard, "The Clear Sun-shine of the Gospel Breaking Forth upon the Indians in New-England," (1648), in MHS *Colls.,* 3rd ser. 4 (1834): 58.

60. *Plym. Col. Recs.,* 10:167; William Kellaway, *The New England Company 1649–1776: Missionary Society to the American Indians* (New York, 1961), 69; O'Brien, *Dispossession by Degrees,* 45, 52; Van Lonkhuyzen, "Reappraisal of the Praying Indians," 406–7; Cogley, *John Eliot's Mission,* 106–7. Christian Indians on Martha's Vineyard, far outnumbering English colonists there, were under much less pressure to adopt colonial practices, including livestock husbandry, during the seventeenth century; see David J. Silverman, "Conditions for Coexistence, Climates for Collapse: The Challenges of Indian Life on Martha's Vineyard, 1524–1871" (Ph.D. diss., Princeton University, 2000), 138–39.

61. Gookin, *Historical Collections*, 44, 45 (quotation), 49; Paul J. Lindholdt, ed., *John Josselyn, Colonial Traveler: A Critical Edition of Two Voyages to New-England* (Hanover, 1988), 105; *Mass. Bay Recs.*, 2:225 (brand marks for English towns); 4, pt. 2:459 (Natick's brand).

62. Winslow, *Glorious Progress of the Gospel*, 91.

63. Henry W. Bowden and James P. Ronda, eds., *John Eliot's Indian Dialogues: A Study in Cultural Interaction* (Westport, 1980), 97. On Waban's career, see Cogley, *John Eliot's Mission*, 61, 73; O'Brien, *Dispossession by Degrees*, 49, 52–55, 57–58; Van Lonkhuyzen, "Reappraisal of the Praying Indians," 399–402.

64. Richter, *Facing East*, 110–29; O'Brien, *Dispossession by Degrees*, 51–60; Ronda, "Generations of Faith"; Charles L. Cohen, "Conversion Among Puritans and Amerindians: A Theological and Cultural Perspective," in Francis J. Bremer, ed., *Puritanism: Transatlantic Perspectives on a Seventeenth-Century Anglo-American Faith* (Boston, 1993), 233–56.

65. Quotation is from [John Eliot], *A Further Account of the Progress of the Gospel Amongst the Indians in New England* (London, 1660), cited in Cohen, "Conversion Among Puritans and Amerindians," 250; Van Lonkhuyzen, "Reappraisal of the Praying Indians," 412; Shepard, "Clear Sun-shine," 40.

66. W. Stitt Robinson, Jr., "Indian Education and Missions in Colonial Virginia," *Journal of Southern History* 18 (1952): 152–68.

67. O'Brien, *Dispossession by Degrees*, 44–51; James P. Ronda, "'We Are Well As We Are': An Indian Critique of Seventeenth-Century Christian Missions," *WMQ*, 3rd ser., 34 (1977): 66–82.

68. "Leift Lion Gardener His Relation," in Orr, ed., *History of the Pequot War*, 142; see also Paul A. Robinson, "Lost Opportunities: Miantonomi and the English in Seventeenth-Century Narragansett Country," in Robert S. Grumet, ed., *Northeastern Indian Lives 1632–1816* (Amherst, 1996), 13–28.

69. "Leift Lion Gardener His Relation," in Orr, ed., *History of the Pequot Warr*, 142–43; for Montauk problems with colonial livestock, see John A. Strong, "The Imposition of Colonial Jurisdiction over the Montauk Indians of Long Island," *Ethnohistory* 41 (1994): 567–68; and in New Netherland and Long Island more generally, see James Homer Williams, "Great Doggs and Mischievous Cattle: Domesticated Animals and Indian-European Relations in New Netherland and New York," *New York History* 76 (1995), 245–64.

70. For an account of Miantonomi's death, see Oberg, *Uncas*, 103–7.

CHAPTER SEVEN: A PROPHECY FULFILLED

1. *Md. Arch.*, 17: 348–49.

2. Hammond further infuriated the Assateagues by robbing their sachems' graves. For this grievance and other troubles, see *Md. Arch.*, 5:482–84 (quotation 482), 517–19. For an overview of relations between Marylanders and Eastern Shore

Indians, see Helen C. Rountree and Thomas E. Davidson, *Eastern Shore Indians of Virginia and Maryland* (Charlottesville, 1997), 96–97, 106–8, 114, 120–21, 137; the authors suggest that the planter may have been Edmund, not Edward, Hammond; see 293, n. 92.

3. Glenn W. LaFantasie, ed., *The Correspondence of Roger Williams,* 2 vols. (Hanover and London, 1988), 2:413.

4. For evidence of Indian livestock ownership, see *Md. Arch.,*4:409, 53:630; *Va. Statutes,* 2:316–17; Lewis R. Binford, "An Ethnohistory of the Nottoway, Meherrin and Weanock Indians of Southeastern Virginia," *Ethnohistory* 14 (1967): 163; Massachusetts Archives, 30:18; Howard M. Chapin, ed., *The Early Records of the Town of Warwick* (Providence, R. I., 1926), 102, 171; *Plym. Col. Recs.,* 4:66, 92–93; 5:6, 22, 85; *R.I. Recs.,* 2:172–73; E. B. O'Callaghan, ed., *Documents Relative to the Colonial History of the State of New-York . . .,* 15 vols. (Albany, 1853–1887), 3:169–70; Clarence S. Brigham, ed., *The Early Records of the Town of Portsmouth* (Providence, 1901), 149–50; John Cox, Jr., ed., *Oyster Bay Town Records,* 6 vols. (New York, 1916–1931), 1:659; Jasper Danckaerts, "Journal of a Voyage to New York in 1679–80," *Memoirs of the Long Island Historical Society,* 1 (1867): 126; Robert S. Grumet, *Historic Contact: Indian People and Colonists in Today's Northeastern United States in the Sixteenth Through Eighteenth Centuries* (Norman, Okla., 1995), 150; Joseph H. Waters, "Animal Remains From Some New England Woodland Sites," *Bulletin of the Archaeological Society of Connecticut,* 33 (1965): 7–8. In 1672, Awashunkes was ordered to pay back a debt with pork; see Jeremy Dupertuis Bangs, *Indian Deeds: Land Transactions in Plymouth Colony, 1620–1691* (Boston, 2002), 434.

5. *Md. Arch.,* 53:630.

6. Virtually every reference cited in note 4 above specifies swine as the Indians' animal property.

7. On Indians' lactose intolerance, see Alfred W. Crosby, *Ecological Imperialism: The Biological Expansion of Europe, 900–1900* (New York, 1986), 27.

8. Allyn B. Forbes et al., eds., *Winthrop Papers, 1498–1654,* 6 vols. (Boston, 1929–1992), 6:34; Howard S. Russell, *Indian New England Before the Mayflower* (Hanover, 1980), 91; John R. Swanton, *The Indians of the Southeastern United States* (Washington, D.C., 1946), 370–72. Chesapeake-area Indians also rendered deer suet in this way; see Helen C. Rountree, *The Powhatan Indians of Virginia: Their Traditional Culture* (Norman, Okla., and London, 1989), 57.

9. Daniel Gookin, "Historical Collections of the Indians in New England" (1674), MHS *Colls.,* 1st ser., 1 (1792): 153; *Mass. Bay Recs.,* 4, pt. 2:360. The incidents in which Indians used hogs to make pummy and moccasins involved stolen livestock, but native-owned swine were doubtless used in similar ways.

10. Calculating reproductive rates for seventeenth-century livestock involves a great deal of guesswork, but for the most careful investigation of the topic, see Lois Green Carr, Russell R. Menard, Lorena S. Walsh, *Robert Cole's World: Agricul-*

ture & Society in Early Maryland (Chapel Hill, 1991), 219, 228, 237. For reproductive rates of present-day feral swine, see H. B. Graves, "Behavior and Ecology of Wild and Feral Swine (Sus Scrofa)," *Journal of Animal Science* 58 (1984): 484.

11.   Keith Thomas, *Man and the Natural World: A History of the Modern Sensibility* (New York, 1983), 57, 64, 69.

12.   This was the explicit rationale for the Virginians' wolf bounty act of 1656 bestowing cows on compliant sachems; see *Va. Statutes*, 1:393–96.

13.   O'Callaghan, ed., *N.Y. Col. Docs.*, 2:157; *Md. Arch.*, 1:450; 2:130; *Plym. Col. Recs.*, 5:11–12; 9:281; *Mass. Bay Recs.*, vol. 4, pt. 2: 512–13. For the arms trade in colonial New England, see Patrick M. Malone, *The Skulking Way of War: Technology and Tactics Among the New England Indians* (Lanham, Md., 1991), 47–51.

14.   For Indians' unfamiliarity with salting meat, see Russell, *Indian New England*, 90–91; Rountree, *Powhatan Indians of Virginia*, 52. For seasonality of meat consumption in colonial diets, see Sarah F. McMahon, "A Comfortable Subsistence: The Changing Composition of Diet in Rural New England, 1620–1840," *WMQ*, 3rd ser., 42 (1985): 36; Henry M. Miller, "An Archaeological Perspective on the Evolution of Diet in the Colonial Chesapeake, 1620–1745," in Lois Green Carr, Philip D. Morgan, and Jean B. Russo, eds., *Colonial Chesapeake Society* (Chapel Hill, 1988), 184–85. On the domestic market for meat in Boston, see Karen J. Friedmann, "Victualling Colonial Boston," *Agricultural History* 47 (1973): 189–205.

15.   Brigham, ed., *Early Recs. of Portsmouth*, 149–50; Edward Byers, *The Nation of Nantucket: Society and Politics in an Early American Commercial Center 1660–1820* (Boston, 1987), 59.

16.   *Plym. Col. Recs.*, 12: 227–28, 241–42. For a discussion of the way in which Creek Indians' acquisition of livestock promoted interest in private land ownership, thereby generating internal conflict, see Claudio Saunt, *A New Order of Things: Property, Power, and the Transformation of the Creek Indians, 1733–1816* (New York, 1999), 171–75.

17.   On the Eastern Shore Indians' struggle for recognition for their towns, see Rountree and Davidson, *Eastern Shore Indians*, 106–14. For the quotation about land rights, see Robert Beverley, *The History and Present State of Virginia*, ed. Louis B. Wright (Chapel Hill, 1947), 278.

18.   Lionel Gatford, *Publick Good Without Private Interest: or, A Compendious remonstrance of the present Sad State and Condition of the English Colonie in Virginia . . .* (London, 1657), reprinted in *WMQ*, 3rd ser., 33 (1976): 141.

19.   *Va. Statutes*, 2:316–17.

20.   Chapin, ed., *Early Recs. of Warwick*, 102, 171; *R.I. Recs.*, 2:172–73; *Plym. Col. Recs.*, 11:218; *Mass. Bay Recs.*, vol. 4, pt. 2:512–13. See also Joshua Micah Marshall, "'A Melancholy People': Anglo-Indian Relations in Early Warwick, Rhode Island, 1642–1675," *NEQ*, 68 (1995): 420. Regulations about Indian

earmarks passed both in New England and the Chesapeake pertained only to swine, further evidence of the Indians' preference for those beasts.

21. *Md. Arch.,* 53:630; see also Thomas Glover, *An Account of Virginia . . . ,* reprinted in *Philosophical Transactions of the Royal Society,* 20 June 1676 (Oxford, 1904), 23.

22. For colonial population figures in New England and the Chesapeake, see John J. McCusker and Russell R. Menard, *The Economy of British America 1607– 1789* (Chapel Hill, 1985), 103, 136. While there is no way to estimate the population of livestock, animals certainly outnumbered colonists by 1670. During the winter of 1694–95, freezing weather killed over 25,000 head of cattle, 60,000 swine, and untold numbers of horses just in Maryland alone—figures that suggest something of the magnitude of the total colonial livestock population. See *Md. Arch.,* 20:191–92, 269–70.

23. James Horn, *Adapting to a New World: English Society in the Seventeenth-Century Chesapeake* (Chapel Hill, 1994), 162–63; Massachusetts and Plymouth expansion compiled from information in Paul Guzzi, ed., *Historical Data Relating to Counties, Cities and Towns in Massachusetts* (Boston, 1975).

24. Edward Bland, *The Discovery of New Brittaine* (London, 1651), in Clarence Walworth Alvord and Lee Bidgood, eds., *The First Explorations of the Trans-Allegheny Region by the Virginians 1650–1674* (Cleveland, 1912), 115; *Va. Statutes,* 1:353–54, 456–57, 467–68; 2:13–14, 34, 39, 138–39, 141, 154; Warren M. Billings, ed., "Some Acts Not in Hening's *Statutes:* The Acts of Assembly, April 1652, November 1652, and July 1653," *VMHB,* 83 (1975): 72–73.

25. *Md. Arch.,* 3:489; see also 2:196.

26. *Plym. Col. Recs.,* 3:84 (quotation), 104, 123, 142, 145, 216–17; 4:18, 20, 45, 70, 82, 97, 109, 167; 5:20, 24, 95, 96, 97–98, 98–99, 109, 126; *R. I. Recs.,* 1:418 (quotation), 424, 454 (quotation), 464, 465; Gookin, "Historical Collections," 185.

27. *Va. Statutes,* 1:456–57; 2:13–14, 34; see also 141; *Plym. Col. Recs.,* 4:21, 31, also 168–69.

28. For examples of trespass complaints from the 1650s and 1660s, see *Plym. Col. Recs.,* 3:21, 106, 119–20, 167, 192; 11:123 (quotation), 137–38; *Va. Statutes,* 2:138–40; *Md. Arch.,* 2:15 (quotation), 196–97; 3:489; 49:139.

29. Neal Salisbury, "Indians and Colonists in Southern New England after the Pequot War: An Uneasy Balance," in Laurence M. Hauptman and James D. Wherry, eds., *The Pequots in Southern New England: The Fall and Rise of an American Indian Nation* (Norman, Okla., 1990), 90–91; Neal Salisbury, "Native People and European Settlers in Eastern North America, 1600–1783," in Bruce G. Trigger and Wilcomb E. Washburn, eds., *The Cambridge History of the Native Peoples of the Americas,* 3 vols. (New York, 1996), 1:411–12.

30. Helen C. Rountree, *Pocahontas's People: The Powhatan Indians of Virginia Through Four Centuries* (Norman, Okla., 1990), 132; Rountree and Davidson, *Eastern Shore Indians,* 93; J. Frederick Fausz, "Merging and Emerging Worlds:

Anglo-Indian Interest Groups and the Development of the Seventeenth-Century Chesapeake," in Lois Green Carr, Philip D. Morgan, and Jean B. Russo, eds., *Colonial Chesapeake Society* (Chapel Hill, 1988), 87–88; Salisbury, "Native People and European Settlers," 413–15, 421.

31.   Billings, "Some Acts Not in Hening," 71; *Md. Arch.,* 3:362–64; 49:139.

32.   *Ct. Recs.,* 2:165; "Records of the Particular Court of Connecticut 1639–1663," *Collections of the Connecticut Historical Society,* 22 (1928): 208, 209; *Plym. Col. Recs.,* 4:68; 5:62; 11:143.

33.   *Plym. Col. Recs.,* 3:21, 106, 119–20, 167, 192.

34.   Salisbury, "Native People and European Settlers," 420; Rountree, *Pocahontas's People,* 105–27. For examples of land transactions, see Bangs, *Indian Deeds,* esp. 296–485.

35.   *R.I. Recs.,* 1:454; *Ct. Recs.,* 1:400.

36.   *Md. Arch.,* 2:15, 26.

37.   *Plym. Col. Recs.,* 4:66; 5:6, 22, 85.

38.   *Va. Statutes,* 2:138.

39.   William Bradford, *Of Plymouth Plantation 1620–1647,* ed. Samuel Eliot Morison (New York, 1952), 341. Thirty years later and in the wake of a catastrophic Indian war, William Hubbard felt compelled to include the Narragansetts' threat in his two histories of Anglo-Indian relations in New England; see his *A General History of New England, From the Discovery to MDCLXXX* (New York, 1972; reprinted from MHS *Colls.,* series 2, vols. 5–6 [1815]), 460; and *The History of the Indian Wars in New England From the First Settlement to the Termination of the War with King Philip, in 1677,* ed. Samuel G. Drake (New York, 1969; orig. publ. 1865), 93.

40.   Massachusetts Archives, 30:110, 150; William S. Simmons, "Narragansett," in Bruce G. Trigger, ed., *Handbook of North American Indians,* vol. 15, *Northeast* (Washington, D.C., 1978), 194; Carl Bridenbaugh, *Fat Mutton and Liberty of Conscience: Society in Rhode Island, 1636–1690* (Providence, 1974), 58; Daniel A. Romani, Jr., "The Pettaquamscut Purchase of 1657/58 and the Establishment of a Commercial Livestock Industry in Rhode Island," in Peter Benes, ed., *New England's Creatures: 1400–1900* (Boston, 1995), 45–60.

41.   For the colonists' preoccupation with Indians' pride, see James Axtell, *The Invasion Within: The Contest of Cultures in Colonial North America* (New York, 1985), ch. 7.

42.   Warren M. Billings, ed., *The Old Dominion in the Seventeenth Century: A Documentary History of Virginia, 1606–1689* (Chapel Hill, 1975), 66, see also 230; *Md. Arch.,* 1:450; 2:130; *Mass. Bay Recs.,* 4, pt. 2: 512–13; John D. Cushing, ed., *The Laws of the Pilgrims: A Facsimile Edition of the Book of the General Laws of the Inhabitants of the Jurisdiction of New-Plimouth, 1672 & 1685* (Wilmington, 1977), 44; and *Va. Statutes,* 2:316–17.

43.   Cushing, ed., *Laws of the Pilgrims,* 44; *Md. Arch.,* 1:450; 2:130; *Mass. Bay Recs.,* 4, pt. 2:512–13.

44. For ideas of justice in Indian cultures, see Daniel K. Richter, *Facing East From Indian Country: A Native History of Early America* (Cambridge, Mass., 2001), 85.

45. *Md. Arch.*, 53:629; Samuel Eliot Morison, ed., *Records of the Suffolk County Court, 1671–1680,* Publications of the Colonial Society of Massachusetts, vol. 29 (Boston, 1933), 404; see also *Plym. Col. Recs.,* 5:80; *Mass. Bay Recs.,* 4, pt. 2:361.

46. *Plym. Col. Recs.,* 9:209; *New Haven Recs.,* 2:361; *Md. Arch.,* 3:413–14, 460–61; 53:414–15.

47. The constitution of the New England Confederation is reprinted in Bradford, *Of Plymouth Plantation,* 430–37.

48. *Mass. Bay Recs.,* 4, pt. 2: 54, 361, 512–13.

49. Billings, ed., *Old Dominion in the Seventeenth Century,* 66, 230; *Md. Arch.,* 2:384–85; 3:460–61; 53:414–15.

50. *Md. Arch.,* 53:414–15. For examples of other complaints involving hogs, see "Records of the Particular Court of Connecticut," 247; *Mass. Bay Recs.,* 4, pt. 2:361, 512–13; *New Haven Recs.,* 2:361; *Plym. Col. Recs.,* 5:80; 11:218; *Va. Statutes,* 2:316–17; *Md. Arch.,*1:450; Billings, ed., *Old Dominion in the Seventeenth Century,* 66.

51. *Md. Arch.,* 2:384–85.

52. Key works on King Philip's War include James D. Drake, *King Philip's War: Civil War in New England, 1675–1676* (Amherst, 1999); and Jill Lepore, *The Name of War: King Philip's War and the Origins of American Identity* (New York, 1998). Still useful for its clear narrative of events is Douglas Edward Leach, *Flintlock and Tomahawk: New England in King Philip's War* (New York, 1958). The origins of the war are also addressed in Philip Ranlet, "Another Look at the Causes of King Philip's War," *NEQ* 61 (1988): 79–100.

53. The identity of the Doegs is somewhat confusing; their name may have been a general term for Maryland Indians. See Nancy Oestreich Lurie, "Indian Cultural Adjustment to European Civilization," in James Morton Smith, ed., *Seventeenth-Century America: Essays in Colonial History* (Chapel Hill, 1959), 42; Christian F. Feest, "Nanticoke and Neighboring Tribes," in Trigger, ed., *Handbook of North American Indians,* 15:250. The name appears only rarely in the colonial records. Virginia officials in 1663 suspected Doegs of being involved in the murder of colonists; see *Va. Statutes,* 2:193–94. The treaty with Maryland appears in *Md. Arch.,* 2:25–27.

54. Key works on the Indian war that sparked Bacon's Rebellion include Wilcomb E. Washburn, *The Governor and the Rebel: A History of Bacon's Rebellion in Virginia* (Chapel Hill, 1957); Edmund Morgan, *American Slavery, American Freedom: The Ordeal of Colonial Virginia* (New York, 1975), 250–70; Kathleen M. Brown, *Good Wives, Nasty Wenches & Anxious Patriarchs: Gender, Race, and Power in Colonial Virginia* (Chapel Hill, 1996), 159–67.

55. For succinct discussions of the general context of these wars, see Richter, *Facing East*, 99–108; Salisbury, "Native People and European Settlers," 420–22. James Drake argues that King Philip's War ought to be understood as a civil war rather than a conflict that pitted colonists against Indians; see *King Philip's War*.

56. Gookin's comments were paraphrased in a letter to him from Gov. Thomas Prince of Plymouth. Gookin had heard rumors that he had been accused of inciting Philip to attack the English; Prince's letter reassured him that that was not so; see MHS, *Colls.*, 1st ser., 6 (1799; repr. 1846): 200–1; italics in the original. It did not help matters that Christian Indians in neighboring Natick had recently acquired prime land that Dedham settlers coveted; see Drake, *King Philip's War*, 62–64; Jean M. O'Brien, *Dispossession by Degrees: Indian Land and Identity in Natick, Massachusetts, 1650–1790* (New York, 1997), 40–41.

57. Drake, *King Philip's War*, 65–68; Virginia DeJohn Anderson, "King Philip's Herds: Indians, Colonists, and the Problem of Livestock in Early New England," *WMQ*, 3rd ser., 51 (1994): 618–21; *Plym. Col. Recs.*, 5:63–64, 76–80.

58. "A Relacion of the Indyan Warre, by John Easton, 1675," in Charles H. Lincoln, ed., *Narratives of the Indian Wars, 1675–1699* (New York, 1913), 9, 11.

59. For a description of the attack on Swansea, see Leach, *Flintlock and Tomahawk*, 36–38, and the map on p. 39. For Swansea's split from Rehoboth, see Guzzi, ed., *Historical Data Relating to . . . Massachusetts*, 65, 90. Philip's dealings with Swansea and the Plymouth government can be traced in *Plym. Col. Recs.*, 5:24, 79, 106–7; Bangs, *Indian Deeds*, 406–7, 429–30. Benjamin Church, who fought in the war, described the first hostilities as "plundering and destroying cattle"; see Benjamin Church, *Diary of King Philip's War 1675–1676*, ed. Alan and Mary Simpson (Tiverton, 1975), 75.

60. The complicated story of the Narragansetts' entry into the war is concisely recounted in Drake, *King Philip's War*, 114–20. In the end, nearly all southern New England Indians except the Mohegans, Niantics, and Pequots joined in the fighting against the colonists.

61. "Capt. Thomas Wheeler's Narrative of an Expedition with Capt. Edward Hutchinson into the Nipmuck Country, and to Quaboag, now Brookfield, Mass., first published 1675," *Collections of the New-Hampshire Historical Society*, 2 (1827): 21; Douglas Edward Leach, ed., *A Rhode Islander Reports on King Philip's War: The Second William Harris Letter of August, 1676* (Providence, 1963), 44, 46, 58. See also Church, *Diary of King Philip's War*, ed., Simpson and Simpson, 172; Increase Mather, *A Brief History of the War with the Indians in New-England*, ed. Samuel G. Drake (Boston, 1862), 151; Samuel G. Drake, *The Old Indian Chronicle; Being a Collection of Exceeding Rare Tracts, Written and Published in the Time of King Philip's War . . .* (Boston, 1836), 13, 35, 58; William Hubbard, *The History of the Indian Wars in New England from the First Settlement to the Termination of the War with King Philip, in 1677*, ed. Samuel G. Drake (New York, 1969; orig. publ. 1865), 164, 192–93, 195–96, 229, 234, 242.

62. Drake, *Old Indian Chronicle,* 10.

63. *Ct. Recs.,* 2:381.

64. Hubbard, *History of the Indian Wars,* 83, 195–96, 222; see also George W. Ellis and John E. Morris, *King Philip's War, Based on the Archives and Records of Massachusetts, Plymouth, Rhode Island and Connecticut, and Contemporary Letters and Accounts* (New York, 1906), 227–28; Richard I. Melvoin, *New England Outpost: War and Society in Colonial Deerfield* (New York, 1989), 101, 107.

65. Daniel Gookin, "An Historical Account of the Doings and Sufferings of the Christian Indians in New England, in the Years 1675, 1676, 1677," American Antiquarian Society, *Archaeologia Americana,* 2 (1836): 450–51, 504, 512; O'Brien, *Dispossession by Degrees,* 60–62.

66. Mary Rowlandson, *The Sovereignty and Goodness of God,* ed. Neal Salisbury (Boston, 1997), 81.

67. For Tift's report of his experience, see LaFantasie, ed., *Corr. of Roger Williams,* 2:711. Tift, who stayed with the Narragansetts until his capture by colonial forces, was later executed for treason. There are several versions of the Medfield note, which may have been written by James Printer, a Christian Indian; the version here is from Gookin, "Historical Account . . . of the Christian Indians," 494. For discussions of both of these episodes, see Lepore, *Name of War,* 94–96, 131–36.

68. Drake, *Old Indian Chronicle,* 102; Mather, *Brief History of the War,* 132; compare with Rowlandson's descriptions of human suffering in *Sovereignty and Goodness of God,* 68–69, 78. It is impossible to know if the torture of animals had spiritual significance comparable to that associated with the treatment of human captives in mourning wars. For the latter, see Daniel K. Richter, *The Ordeal of the Longhouse: The Peoples of the Iroquois League in the Era of European Colonization* (Chapel Hill, 1992), 35–36, 66–70.

69. Church, *Diary of King Philip's War,* ed. Simpson and Simpson, 133, 136–37; Hubbard, *History of the Indian Wars,* 275–76; pt. 2, 223; see also 214–15, 229–30. For similar examples, see Mather, *Brief History of the War,* 82; "James Quanapaug's Information," MHS, *Colls.,* 1st ser., 6 (1799): 205.

70. Drake discusses casualty estimates in *King Philip's War,* 2, 4, 168–69. See also Edward Randolph's "Report to the Committee for Trade and Plantations, 12 October 1676," in Robert Noxon Toppan, ed., *Edward Randolph, Including His Letters and Official Papers . . . 1676–1703,* 7 vols. (reprinted New York, 1967), 2:246.

71. Washburn, *Governor and the Rebel,* 20–26. For a discussion of the complicated situation of the Susquehannocks, who had recently moved to the Potomac valley, see Francis Jennings, "Glory, Death, and Transfiguration: The Susquehannock Indians in the Seventeenth Century," *Proceedings of the American Philosophical Society,* 112 (1968): 33–35.

72. Washburn, *Governor and the Rebel;* Morgan, *American Slavery, American Freedom,* 250–70.

73. A provocative discussion of the way New Englanders constructed their histories of King Philip's War appears in Lepore, *Name of War,* ch. 7. Colonial Virginians' distinctive approach to their past is discussed in T. H. Breen, *Puritans and Adventurers: Change and Persistence in Early America* (New York, 1980), ch. 9. See also Beverley, *History and Present State of Virginia,* 74–86.

74. Washburn, *Governor and the Rebel,* 154–66; Horn, *Adapting to a New World,* 281, 373–79; Morgan, *American Slavery, American Freedom,* 242–46.

75. See "Bacon's Manifesto" in Billings, ed., *Old Dominion in the Seventeenth Century,* 278.

76. Thomas Mathew, "The Beginning, Progress, and Conclusion of Bacon's Rebellion, 1675–1676," in Charles M. Andrews, ed., *Narratives of the Insurrections, 1675–1690* (New York, 1915), 20; "A True Narrative of the Late Rebellion in Virginia, By the Royal Commissioners, 1677," in Andrews, ed., *Narratives,* 106; Billings, ed., *Old Dominion in the Seventeenth Century,* 233; H. R. McIlwaine, ed., *Journals of the House of Burgesses of Virginia,* 13 vols. (Richmond, 1905–15), 2:89. Rebellious colonists also attacked the livestock and other property of colonists who remained loyal to the government.

77. Beverley, *History and Present State of Virginia,* 84; McIlwaine, ed., *Journals of the House of Burgesses,* 2:69, 105, 137.

78. "William Harris to Sir Joseph Williamson, 12 August 1676," *Collections of the Rhode Island Historical Society,* 10 (1902): 165; Toppan, ed., *Edward Randolph,* 2:244–45; Karen Ordahl Kupperman, John C. Appleby, Mandy Banton, eds., *Calendar of State Papers, Colonial: North America and the West Indies* (London, 2000) (CD-ROM). On the religious interpretation of the war, see Drake, *King Philip's War,* 81–82.

79. Washburn, *Governor and the Rebel,* 118–19, 162; Alden T. Vaughan, gen. ed., *Early American Indian Documents: Treaties and Laws, 1607–1789,* 11 vols. (Washington, D.C., 1983), 4:83; *Va. Statutes,* 2:138–39.

80. Leach, *Flintlock and Tomahawk,* 246–47; Beverley, *History and Present State of Va.,* 85–86; Horn, *Adapting to a New World,* 162–63.

81. Salisbury, "Native People and European Settlers," 421; Drake, *King Philip's War,* 168–85; Richter, *Facing East,* 107–8.

82. *Ct. Recs.,* 3:42–43, 81; *Md. Arch.,* 17:348–49.

83. *Md. Arch.,* 5:482–84, 493; 8:53–54, 384–85; 17:77–78; 19:520–21; 22:329; Cotton Mather, "Decennium Luctuosum," in Lincoln, ed., *Narratives of the Indian Wars,* 186; Horatio Rogers, George Moulton Carpenter, Edward Field, eds., *The Early Records of the Town of Providence,* 21 vols. (Providence, 1892–1915), 8:129–30; *Mass. Bay Recs.,* 5:230–31. On Indian slaves in postwar New England, see Lepore, *Name of War,* 150–70.

84. *Md. Arch.,* 5:280–82, 479–81, 519, 559–60; 8:10, 317–19, 343–44, 533–35; 13:268–70; 15:175, 289–91; 17:19–21, 29–30, 311; 20:509–10; 23:189 (quota-

tion); Berthold Fernow, ed., *Documents Relating to the History and Settlements of the Towns along the Hudson and Mohawk Rivers (With the Exception of Albany) from 1630 to 1684* (Albany, 1881), 756; Massachusetts Archives, 30: 261a.

85. Carl Bridenbaugh, ed., *The Pynchon Papers,* 2 vols. (Boston, 1982–85), 1:179–81; Lawrence H. Leder, ed., *The Livingston Indian Records 1666–1723* (Gettysburg, 1956), 44, 70–71; *Md. Arch.,* 5:281 (quotation); 15:175; 17:20–21; 20:509–10. For a concise exposition of English-Iroquois relations in this period, see Salisbury, "Native People and European Settlers," 420–23.

EPILOGUE: FULL CIRCLE

1. David J. Silverman, "'We chuse to be bounded': Native American Animal Husbandry in Colonial New England," *WMQ,* 3rd ser., 60 (2003): 511–48.

2. Jared Eliot, *Essays Upon Field Husbandry in New England And Other Papers 1748–1762,* ed. Harry Carman and Rexford G. Tugwell (New York, 1934), 155; Samuel Deane, *The New-England Farmer; or, Georgical Dictionary . . . ,* (Worcester, 1790), 42, see also 166, 276; Harry J. Carman, ed., *American Husbandry,* (first publ. 1775; New York, 1939), 59, see also 55–56, 58; Percy Wells Bidwell and John I. Falconer, *History of Agriculture in the Northern United States 1620–1860* (Washington, D.C., 1925), 85, 107; Howard S. Russell, *A Long, Deep Furrow: Three Centuries of Farming in New England* (Hanover, 1976), 152, 159; Daniel Vickers, *Farmers & Fishermen: Two Centuries of Work in Essex County, Massachusetts, 1630–1850* (Chapel Hill, 1994), 296–305.

3. Lorena S. Walsh, "Plantation Management in the Chesapeake, 1620–1820," and Lois Green Carr and Russell R. Menard, "Land, Labor, and Economies of Scale in Early Maryland: Some Limits to Growth in the Chesapeake System of Husbandry," *Journal of Economic History,* 49 (1989): 393–406, 407–18; Lorena S. Walsh, "Land Use, Settlement Patterns, and the Impact of European Agriculture, 1620–1820," in Philip D. Curtin, Grace S. Brush, George W. Fisher, eds., *Discovering the Chesapeake: The History of an Ecosystem* (Baltimore, 2001), 220–44.

4. Bidwell and Falconer, *History of Agriculture,* 79; Carr and Menard, "Land, Labor, and Economies of Scale," 417–18; Lewis Cecil Gray, *History of Agriculture in the Southern United States to 1860,* 2 vols. (Washington, D.C., 1932), 1:143, 147, 150–51, 201; Carman, ed., *American Husbandry,* 190–97; William K. Boyd, ed., *William Byrd's Histories of the Dividing Line Betwixt Virginia and North Carolina* (New York, 1967), 54. See also John S. Otto, "The Origins of Cattle-Ranging in Colonial South Carolina, 1670–1715," *South Carolina Historical Magazine,* 87 (1986): 117–24; Mart A. Stewart, *"What Nature Suffers to Groe": Life, Labor, and Landscape on the Georgia Coast, 1680–1920* (Athens, 1996), 74–75.

5. The historical literature on this topic is too vast to cite in full here. For examples, see Stephen Aron, "Pigs and Hunters: 'Rights in the Woods' on the Trans-Appalachian Frontier," in Andrew R. L. Cayton and Fredrika J. Teute, eds., *Contact Points: American Frontiers from the Mohawk Valley to the Mississippi, 1750–1830* (Chapel Hill, 1998), 175–204; David J. Grettler, "Environmental Change and Conflict over Hogs in Early Nineteenth-Century Delaware," *Journal of the Early Republic,* 19 (1999): 197–220; John Mack Faragher, *Sugar Creek: Life on the Illinois Prairie* (New Haven, 1986), 34, 65, 132; Terry G. Jordan and Matti Kaups, *The American Backwoods Frontier: An Ethnic and Ecological Interpretation* (Baltimore, 1989), 119–23.

6. Andrew A. Lipscomb and Albert Ellery Bergh, eds., *The Writings of Thomas Jefferson,* 20 vols. (Washington, D.C., 1903–05), 12:270; Bernard W. Sheehan, *Seeds of Extinction: Jeffersonian Philanthropy and the American Indian* (Chapel Hill, 1973), 125; Anthony F. C. Wallace, *Jefferson and the Indians: The Tragic Fate of the First Americans* (Cambridge, Mass., 1999), 170, 223, 225.

7. Examples of works about Indians who adopted livestock as a strategy for survival include James Taylor Carson, *Searching for the Bright Path: The Mississippi Choctaws from Prehistory to Removal* (Lincoln, 1999); Claudio Saunt, *A New Order of Things: Property, Power, and the Transformation of the Creek Indians, 1733–1816* (New York, 1999); William G. McLoughlin, *Cherokee Renascence in the New Republic* (Princeton, 1986); Richard White, *The Roots of Dependency: Subsistence, Environment, and Social Change among the Choctaws, Pawnees, and Navajos* (Lincoln, 1983); Anthony F. C. Wallace, *The Death and Rebirth of the Seneca* (New York, 1969). The Redstick War offers an example of depredations against livestock as a form of resistance; see Saunt, *New Order of Things,* 256–58.

Index

Page numbers in *italics* indicate photographs or illustrations.
Page numbers in **bold** indicate entire chapters.